LETTER TO A PRISONER

By Joe Wolfe

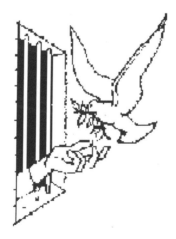

For all prisoners, whether bound by bars and walls or the ego's tenacious thirst for control

Includes:
The End of Reincarnation
By Gary R. Renard
GaryRenard.com

With Carrie Triffet's *The Crash Course*
UnlikelyMessenger.com

And the 365 Daily Lessons from
A Course in Miracles

*"I was hungry, and you gave me meat; I was thirsty, and you
gave me drink; I was a stranger, and you took me in; Naked, and
you clothed me; I was in prison, and you came unto me."*
(Mathew 25:35, 36)

LETTER TO A PRISONER

By

Joe Wolfe

Edited by Steffani Fort and Sue Kilimnik

**Sketch illustrations by Mark Benson,
Chicago, Illinois**

A true account of an enlightening experience that suddenly transformed a ruthless criminal into a seeker of the Light.

Also by Joe Wolfe

Time Ocular
The End of Reincarnation with The Five Signs

Letter to a Prisoner

Second Edition
ISBN-13: 978-1460952146 Revisied and edited Feb., 2011
CreateSpace.com
Access this book through **SpiritLightOutreach.org**

To God
And to Judy Hall who before she died,
led this entity back to the path.
To the many inspirational authors who made deep
impressions on this soul:

Gary R. Renard
Neale Donald Walsch
Dr. David R Hawkins
Dr. Michael Newton
Carrie Triffet
Og Mandino
Peter Ouspensky
George I. Gurdjieff
Regina Dawn Akers
Gary Zukav
Linda McNabb

With a deep gratitude for
A Course in Miracles
and
To Jay McCormick and Dr. Rick Lovell

And to
Janine Cantin

<u>Freedom Inside</u> is a FREE newsletter for prisoners. Its
purpose is to find ways of applying the new spirituality
to our everyday lives whether in or out of prison.

Imagine, if you will, seated at the edge of a drab bunk in a 5 by 10 foot cell, perhaps for years at a time without a visitor or even a postcard, then one day receiving this **Letter to a Prisoner**. *I can attest with absolute certainty, that you will have created a moment,... you will have delivered a spark of love and light,... you will have been the direct cause for change in that prisoners life from that moment on. You will have become part of the change you seek in the world. 25,000 prisoners are released every year to become our neighbors once again. This work creates the possibility that if only one in a hundred are inspired to change for the better then it has succeeded in its intention.*

LetterToAPrisoner.com

"The Phoenix of spiritual awakening is birthed from the ashes of human despair."
David R. Hawkins

As Mother Theresa said,
"The beautiful flower, the Lotus, arises from the roots in the slime and mud at the bottom of the pond."

Dear Prisoner,

I sincerely hope that this letter finds you as well as can be expected under the circumstances, and that this message may help to bring a few moments of relief and more, a message of love and light from an ex-con. I invite you to escape from within.

This letter is my attempt to share with you and convicts locked up in prisons every-where, the possibility that you can find real freedom and personal evolution and to come to grips with who you really are, why you were born into this world, and how to better take advantage of the time spent in prison.

This isn't a manual on how to effect a successful break out. I have no tips on sawing through bars or digging a tunnel under the wall. But what I will share with you, are my own experiences to the way...the method...the path to a freedom like none other you've ever experienced. This will show you how YOU can leave that cell anytime you like. Not you the burglar, not you the armed robber or the drug dealer, *not you the ego*, you the perpetrator of actions based on unproductive choices, but YOU the essence of who you really are.

You are so very much more than you think. You are special, and a very necessary part of everything that is. Be assured, God made no mistakes. Long before I ever read a single word in any book on the subjects related to inner growth and spiritual evolution, experiences occurred to me. Strange and remarkable experiences that I couldn't explain, nor deny that they actually happened. I couldn't explain them away with logical definitions, nor could I ignore them as brief moments of mental illusion. One very life altering revelation occurred...the grandest of all experiences, that would remain with me, long after I was finally released from prison and serve to become the guiding light for everything to come.

The very profound experience happened over thirty years ago, while I was serving a ten year sentence for robbery and became the moment my life changed forever. After it happened I was able to redefine my concept of "myself" and I suddenly and very dramatically understood the true meaning of *oneness with everything*. I was treated with the most wonderful and enlightening few moments; a few fleeting minutes that would dramatically alter the direction of my life from then on. It would change my usual course of thoughts and intentions and lead me from one once totally indulged in criminal pursuits, to something quite different.

Later, books fell into my possession, as if by purposeful design, and I was being gravitated toward instructional literature like a large magnet to metal. New acquaintances suddenly developed and often out of the blue, a new friend or fellow traveler along the path would make their presence known to me and help me with questions that grew more important as my need for knowledge increased with every passing day. Those experiences literally transformed me, from a one time ruthless criminal, with no regard for my fellow man to seeker and bringer of the light. I made a sudden and complete about face from tendencies that justified acts that took advantage of others for my own personal gratification, ever mindful for any opportunity to scam, steal, or harm for my own selfish ends and temporary gratifications.

It happened when I was about twenty-five years old, and at the time, very much at arms with "God." I'd long since given up on any belief in higher powers, and often whenever "God" would find a way into the current conversation, I reacted with one degree or another of disdain or indifference.

Even now as I write this letter to you, I promise that this is no typical evangelic testimonial. If you like, every time you read the word God replace it with Universe...I was at arms with the Universe...

In fact, I remember one event where I actually looked up at the ceiling of my small cell and shook my fist in anger and frustration over "God's" seeming neglect, for me, for any of my requests, and for my very state of existence I blamed "God" for all of my short-comings, my bad luck and all of my misfortunes.

By then, I just made up my mind to denounce "God," and accept the fact that I'd been hoodwinked into believing in something with no more validity than any other fairy tale. I decided that all I'd been force fed, all I'd been taught in religion classes was all a bunch of bull and only for the gullible and weak minded.

Then that fateful day came along, that something so remarkable happened, and it changed my life forever. I was to learn that I had been correct. The "God" of my peers, my teachers, even my parents *does not exist.* That all-vengeful fiery figure of punishment and retribution, that powerful entity that dispersed eternal damnation saturated in everlasting pain and torture... that omnipresent threat... was simply not true. I realized that the predominate attitude and beliefs about 'God' I had accepted since childhood, were entirely the products of mistruths, fabrications and mis-interpretations. God wasn't about retribution at all, nor punishment of any sort.

This is the "God" the atheists don't believe in. The "God" of fear and guilt. The "God" of weeping and gnashing of teeth and endless punishment and damnation. I suddenly came to realize that *there really is no such "God."* In Conversations With God, by Neale Donald Walsch GOD said, "...*why would I have a need to seek some kind of revenge, or punishment, for your failing? Wouldn't it be a simple matter for ME to just dispose of you*?"

Up until then I had attributed to GOD the characteristics found in man, or better, man's other monumental fairy tale character, the "devil", and while I may inflict hardship, punishment, pain and even death upon my peers, the real GOD does not. The real GOD does not punish, nor does the real God judge. The real GOD observes, like an omni-present parent, ready to assist wherever and whenever needed and always vigilant. The real God is the observer and the observer is within you.

All of that might be a little much to comprehend for some people. No punishment? No Hell? How could that be? Well, while there is no "Hell" as I'd been taught to believe by teachers and religious leaders, there are consequences for actions. And consequences for actions have to do with the value we place upon what we percieve through five very limited senses. *A filtered misperception of "reality."*

"*My* thoughts are images that *I* have made. Whatever I see reflects *my* thoughts. It is *my* thoughts that tell me where I am and what I am. The fact that I see a world in which there is suffering and loss and death shows me that I am seeing only the representation of *my* insane thoughts and not allowing my real thoughts to cast their beneficent light on what I see." A Course in Miracles, workbook lesson 53.

It happened during a rather difficult day filled with emotionally charged energy. I was over wrought with a day of fear, followed by many hours of deep gratitude. It was the feeling of thankfulness and extreme gratitude that brought me to a state of being I will never forget and always seek to be. I was serving the ten year sentence for robbery in Pontiac, one of the maximum security state penitentiaries in Illinois.

I was an incorrigible, non-conforming and rebelling convict who despised authority and searched out every feasible avenue of negative expression for all I hated. I hated every day. I hated the guards and I hated the judges, and I hated the police and I hated the "establishment" for putting me there. I hated just about everything.

I even tried several attempts at escape. My first attempt to escape almost worked. I remember that day very well. The atmosphere was unusually saturated with the spirit of escape, because just a few weeks earlier one man, the first in ten previous years of the prison's history, had successfully scaled the perimeter wall and managed to get away. Being a devoted advocate for the bad guy, I was delighted and very happy for his success. I didn't know it then, but eventually it would come to pass that this man and I would be close friends for many years to come.

I was living in the West House of the large three cell house facility. It was the oldest and the original confinement building on the premises. It looked like a very old mansion one might associate with something out of the American revolutionary times. In the winter it was damp and cold and in the summer time the heat rose to the top of the stack of five galleries on either side of the football field length building, fifty two cells to each gallery, and sweltered its inhabitants unmercifully. But because it was so old, so were the locks on the cell doors.

Built somewhere around the turn of the century, the old prison building used large flat keys to access the cells. The tumblers in the locks were old and worn with many years of repeated daily use. At the very end of each gallery was the "dead lock box'" and at night, before the final head count, a long crank was rolled into place that slid along a track that double locked each cell. This action prevented any cell from being opened individually, unless the double lock was released. In addition to the dead lock crank there was an extra double lock for each cell. This prevented any cell from opening even if the crank were disengaged. It was this detail that I would use to my advantage when the time came to make my move.

Prisoners were individually deadlocked in their cells during the day whenever they were issued a ticket. A ticket, not unlike a parking or traffic violation ticket, was issued to convicts by guards when an infraction of the rules was committed. For every single infraction there was a punishment, however trivial or serious.

On the following morning, after being fed breakfast in their cells, the convicts would be marched to the Captain's office to answer the charges on the ticket. This was trial court for the residents of the prison population, and it was where punishment for their infraction was decided. Depending upon the seriousness of the ticket's charges, a convict could face anything from a temporary suspension of certain privileges to periods of confinement in the "hole." The hole was a not a very pretty or comforting place. (As you may well know.)

So it happened one early afternoon that I purposely attracted the attention of a guard when I committed a ticketed offense. I don't recall what I did, but it was a minor violation which resulted in my immediate confinement to my cell, and deadlocked. I would be fed supper that night in my cell and not be allowed to file out to the chow hall with the rest of the inmates. Supper was served to me, sandwiched by two large square metal plates an hour or so before the regular chow line was called out. But before that, I began to make my move.

I had a fellow convict who was especially good with picking old tumblers open the deadlock on my cell door for which I paid him a handsome two packs of cigarettes. When that was done, I cleaned my metal dinner plates and set them between the bars of my cell near the floor, slightly protruding to allow whoever picked them up later easy access. Then I arranged my bunk bed to appear as if I were sleeping. I packed a spare pair of pants and shirt with rag stuffing and toilet paper to create the outline of a figure, then fashioned a head from pieces of dark brown blankets and finally obscured full view of the figure by hanging another blanket from the ceiling. This was a common practice by many inmates who wanted to shield the light from the gallery halls and allow them to sleep in darkness, and would not appear to be out of character, especially when I was supposed to be on deadlock anyway. I gambled that the final count would be made in haste as it usually was, by guards who'd be more interested in getting home, as they usually were.

When the chow line for supper was called and the gallery crank rolled, my cell unlocked and I stepped out in line with scores of other prisoners who would be lead by two guards several hundred yards out across the compound to the chow hall. Once outside and in a double line, I watched carefully for my opportunity, then ducked apart from the line, slipped away and headed for the Vocational School Building. No one noticed, and if they did, paid no attention.

Earlier, while at work in the Vocational building I'd unlocked a side window that allowed me entry. Now all I had to do is hide and wait for the chow line to return to the West House, wait for the count check whistle to blow, then get to work on my plan to scale the wall which was only fifty yards away.

In the Vocational building I had virtually unlimited access to just about every tool I needed. There were long lengths of rebar for constructing a make shift ladder and plenty of other odds and ends that would have proved helpful.

I watched through the office window of the Vocation School building as the line from the chow hall returned to the cell house. Then I waited, sweating and very overwrought with anxious nerve-racking adrenalin as I envisioned the final count of all prisoners in their cells going on.

When I heard the very loud shrill of the compound's air horn whistle, I broke into a smile from ear to ear. They had counted the dummy! That was the signal that the count had checked, and all was clear. I was home free now, free to work on my next move.

From my vantage at the office window I watched as most of the day shift of guard personnel streamed out from their assigned buildings and headed for the administrative front gates. For most of them it was "Miller Time" and nothing on Earth would side-tracked them from their bee-lines to the local bars.

I started to gather up tools and sections of the rebar and laid them out on the floor. I hadn't even begun to start constructing my ladder when I suddenly heard shouts. I went back to the office window and was shocked to see all of the guards being ordered to turn around. Something happened. There was a lot of scrambling going on and urgently barked orders that I couldn't hear, and I sensed despairingly that it all had something to do with me.

Later I was to learn that the guard who picked up my dinner plates could not reach them. When the line of prisoners had returned from the chow hall, one of the convicts kicked them back into my cell, I thought either in an act of jest or just being obnoxious.

So when after the final count was conducted and checked, and the rounds made to collect all of the diner plates from the bars of deadlocked prisoners, mine were not accessible.

The guard tried to wake me without avail and then called the Lieutenant of the guard who opened my cell and demanded the dummy to get up. When it wouldn't he shook it to discover that I was not where I should have been. He immediately radioed the administration front gate and had all personnel redirected back into the compound to search for me.

It didn't take long for them to find out where I was. They found me in a matter of a few minutes and I was quickly marched off to the hole, where I would spend the next six months in solitary punitive segregation. I often wondered how things would've unfolded had that convict not kicked those plates back into my cell.

Several days later, Fast Eddie, the man who had been the first to escape from inside the walls in ten years was captured as he made an illegal left turn in downtown Chicago traffic, and all of my hopes and dreams of a very early release came to a screeching halt. Now instead of escape, I dwelt in the realization that I could very well be sentenced to an extra ten years for the attempt. My spirit was shattered. My faith in God was dwindling and it would get much worse. I was only beginning my journey into the bowels of hopelessness and despair.

Fast Eddie described the events in Chicago, when he was spotted making the illegal left turn. He talked about how one of the arresting officers laughed at him. Prison officials placed him in the cell next to me in the segregation unit, where we used to talk for hours as we sat on the concrete floor of our cells, our arms resting on a lower bar rung ledge, protruding out onto the gallery. He told me of how the police officer smiled at him as he sat handcuffed shortly after his capture. He flashed a sarcastic grin at him and reached into his upper shirt pocket and showed Eddie a wad of small bills he collected from traffic violator bribes.

"*See this kid? This is what I made this evening. All you had to do was pull over and stop. You shouldn't have tried to outrun us.*" Then he laughed and walked away.

At this point in my journey I was totally and completely removed from any associative thought or feeling related to "God." Nothing could have been farther away from me. Even the brief memories of fleeting moments of spiritual connection were utterly forgotten.

Those fleeting moments I refer to are like one particular vision I had as a child of about twelve years old. I remember the meeting of a beautifully adorned lady who came to me in what I later called a dream. She was the essence of radiant compassion and love. I remember standing at her feet and looking up at her in complete awe. She shone with a glowing light that encompassed her entire being and said nothing, but smiled at me. She radiated light and love as I had never before and rarely since experienced. I was completely bathed in her warm presence and at one point I begged her to let me stay in that place with her forever. Her expression changed to one of finality. Then she just faded away and I "awoke" feeling devastated and alone. Tears welled up in my eyes as I searched for a concrete explanation for what I had just experienced. I felt as if I were be abandoned by a dearest loved one, while at the same time understanding that I could not short change destiny.

'It was just a dream.' I told myself, echoing the opinions of my peers and my teachers whenever I tried to convey to them experiences like these. It would be a long time later that I would finally attached a name to that lady.

Many years later while strolling past an art gallery in Sedona Arizona I came face to face with her again. She had been fashioned into a four foot high bronze statue. Every feature was identical to the vision of so many years before. I learned her name from the attendant at the art gallery. She was Quan Yin, goddess of Love and compassion.

Since I was a child of three several landmark visions like this one were always greeted by my parents or my religious leaders as 'just my imagination' or even 'nonsense.' So, all too often I accepted those explanations and rarely sought to give much credence to any such experience. After all, why shouldn't I believe and accept the word of my superiors? Were they not so much more worldly and wiser than I? Who was I to think that anything credible could possibly come from within me? Who did I think I was, anyway...?

During the first 25 years of this life five such "mystical" experiences would occur to me culminating in the grandest of them all, while still serving the prison sentence.

Six months after we were caught during our escape ventures Eddie and I were transferred to another building in the prison compound. We were sent to the North House where the main segregation unit housed over thirty other segregated inmates. This newer building, unlike the West House, separated galleries with a ceiling/floor. Instead of creating heights which often provoked falling accidents (intentional or otherwise) only two galleries were stacked atop one another before being covered with a ceiling that served as the floor of two more upper galleries.

The building itself served as part of the perimeter wall. This allowed for a clear view of the grass and trees and the town outside. For Eddie and I it was like a look at freedom. Walking over to the new building in the open air was the first time we'd done so in six months, and our new home provided a welcome change of scenery. Once there we were isolated in cells next to one another, but rather than place us on the populated One Gallery that held the other thirty segregated prisoners, we were confined on Three Gallery, which was totally empty, and overlooked the lower One Gallery. They didn't want us any closer to personal contact with other inmates. So on this gallery of forty-four cells only two would be occupied. Mine and Eddie's.

At first we were disappointed for not having been mixed with the other inmates below us, but later that decision to isolate us on a gallery completely to ourselves would prove to become an ideal condition for yet another escape attempt.

Eddie and I were at greater liberty to discuss things without threat of being overheard by the guards, or even other inmates who resided just below us. The nearest guard station was several hundred feet away at the end of the lower gallery. So we spent the entire waking day seated on the floor of our cells, our arms dangling from the bars, as we'd got into the habit of doing back at the original lock up facility in punitive segregation. Some of the time we'd play cards, using the outside gallery floor as our card table but most of our day was filled with idle conversation. We dreamed aloud, and talked about our past experiences. Occasionally the topic was about God and spiritual matters and I remember telling Eddie about some of the weird experiences I had as a child. I told him of one particular incident that happened when I was small boy of about three or four.

I'd been separated from the rest of the children at Carmelite Home for Boys orphanage because of the mumps. The nuns who ran the place placed me in a private dormitory provided for just such situations.

I was in was the orphanage because very shortly before my father divorced my mother after catching her with another man. Living in Texas at the time, Texas law frowned seriously upon the wives of decorated WWII veterans who were found guilty of adultery, and unlike today's modern legal system regarding the settlement of properties and the assignment of child custody, my mother was lucky to leave the state with her own skin. So after the divorce my father took my brother and I and moved to Chicago, where he had a soldier friend who had been a wartime buddy. They got together and with the help of his buddy's sister (who my father eventually married) and they found places where my brother and I could be kept, temporarily, until he got on his feet. It would be four or five years before my father came back for us.

Soon after I was placed in the Carmelite boys home, I fell deathly sick with a very severe case of the Mumps. I had to be quarantined away from the rest of the children. At that time the disease was life threatening and not an uncommon cause of death among many young children my age. So they laid me in a comfortable crib, one of four that lined one wall of the dormitory, then assigned my care to the first angel I ever met. She was a very little nun who rarely spoke and always did the bidding of the others, the more dominating and authoritative nuns who were rarely lacking for a long list of menial tasks for her to do.

I remember her well. After the doctor had examined me and the higher superior clergy left, my little angel nun tucked me under the blankets for the night. I remember feeling very ill. The cheeks on my face were puffed and swollen and I had a very high fever. She motioned to the end table at the head of my crib and opened a new bag of root beer barrel hard candies. She smiled at me and indicated with hand motions to take one later if I wanted. I distinctly remember being too weak to care. Then she left.

Hours later I awoke to the stillness of the middle of night. I felt strange and very light headed. I turned over on my right side and reached through the wooden crib bars until I found one of the pieces of hard candy. I unwrapped it and placed it into my mouth, and remember how very large it was. I had to open my mouth wide to accommodate it and positioned it to a comfortable spot in my left cheek. Then I just looked up at the ceiling and stared at nothing. On my right was the opposite side of the rectangular dorm and I could see the brightness from the street lights as they shone through large pane windows. It was very quiet. I laid for a few minutes, licking the candy with the tip of my tongue and continued to stare at the ceiling. Then it happened.

From out of thin air a very large hand began to comfort me. It patted my chest area, lingering across my upper torso then gently warmed me with reassuring strokes while I 'heard' it tell me that I would be alright. When I looked to my right where a person should have been standing, there was nothing there. Nothing and no one. Only the faint but distinguishable illuminated windows.

I was suddenly overcome with fear. I threw the blanket over my head and shivered in utter horror, uncontrollably for what seemed a very long time. Then I must have fallen asleep, because the very next thing I remember was that it was now daylight and the typical sounds of morning were starting to come to life. I noticed one more thing. The root beer barrel hard candy was still lodged in my left cheek, now only a small remnant. Many years later when I recalled the incident, I knew that it had not been just my imagination or only a dream. That small remnant of candy was the point of referrence that ignited the full recollection of the experience that night.

The light from windows should have outlined a silhouette if a person had been standing there, there should have been some sound, but there was nothing. Nothing but the hand, and the comforting thoughts reassuring me that I would be alright...and...the candy. My fever was gone and so was the swelling in my cheeks. I was standing, holding tightly to the bed rail when my little angel nun came into the room. Her expression was one of total disbelief and shock. The doctor had told them that my condition was very serious and that I was touch and go, and all they could do is wait and watch. But now I was completely well, standing up in bed and desperately trying to explain in little boy terminology how I'd been visited by the strangest of all things.

Right about that time the room began to fill with a crowd of other nuns, including the Mother Superior. Everyone was astonished at my sudden recovery but none of them took my ranting about the visitor seriously. (None except my angel nun.) The doctor was summoned and after a brief examination all he could do was shake his head in bewilderment.

After a while they all left the room and my little nun picked me up into her arms and held me close for a long time. Then she knelt me down next to her on the floor and positioned my hands together in prayer. She was smiling and on this, one of the rare occasions that I heard her speak, she gave thanks and expressed gratitude to GOD for my health. Now every time I see a root beer barrel I'm reminded of the message, "I will be alright."

Eddie thought the story was nice. Not long afterward we received news that the administration was going to begin allowing books to be sent to prisoners from friends and relatives out in the world. As soon as I heard about it, the wheels of escape in my mind began to grind again.

Back in the Vocational School I learned to re-bind old books and I became very knowledgeable of the craft. I knew how to break down the back of hard covers and put them back together in a way that would be hard to detect and more, I knew how to describe the procedure to another. With attention to detail and some cheap Elmer's glue, anyone could conceal a thin hacksaw blade right down the spine of the book and no one would ever know. The inside flaps could be replaced with plain paper and fashioned to appear brand new and untouched.

I outlined a plan with Eddie. I explained the technique required to hide the hacksaw blade, then together we mapped out a strategy that would involve a friend of ours, whose sentence was almost completed and who would soon be released. The friend was trusted to sweep the galleries and every day when let out of his cell to perform his cleaning duties, he always stopped for a few minutes to go over our plan with us. It was decided that when released our friend would immediately seek out a book store, purchase a couple, then get the glue he needed, pack the blades, wrap the packages and drop them in the mail to another convict who was also confined downstairs on One gallery.

We thought it best not to have the books mailed directly to us. So we waited until a friend was being realeased. The day came when he was escorted out and Eddie and I watched in silence as he passed our cells below. I winked at him and he nodded.

Three days went by. Eddie and I discussed how we would proceed once the blades were delivered. After we had both cut a bar out, allowing us to exit our cells, one of us would prepare an opening in the rear gallery gate which was also a barred door. This would get us access to the back of the cell house where only one guard was stationed. We planned to overpower him, take his keys which would get us outside the building and then attempt to scale the wall from the exact same corner where Eddie had successfully climbed to his freedom months earlier.

On the fourth day the book came. Our friend had sent only one, not the two we requested, but he'd managed to re-bind the book perfectly. Since the permission to allow books program was new, it turned out to be perfect timing for us to take advantage. It came through inspection without a glitch.

Eddie broke the hacksaw blade in two even pieces, and for the next week we took turns cutting through the lowest rung of bar section. The going was difficult and tedious as the metal used to construct the bars was hard steel. When we were finally finished, we hid all sign of our work with a simple rag draped over the section. We didn't plan to stay around long enough for the regular periodic check of the bars.

We'd timed the habits of the guards at their station below us, and one evening I crawled out of my cell, through the new opening and silently crept on my belly about fourty yards to the rear end of the gallery. A large industrial garbage can concealed me as I began to cut an opening in the rear gallery gate. Compared to the steel of the cell bars it was went like a hot knife through butter. I was finished in under a half an hour, then crawled back to my cell.

Everything was set. Eddie fashioned a long length of braided rope from pieces of our bed sheets, and it was planned that we'd use one of the cut bars from our cell as a weight that would wedge into the corner of the building near the roof, and provide the leverage we would need to stabilize the rope.

All was going to plan. We decided to take advantage of the early morning lull in activity, which usually followed right after breakfast was delivered to every cell. The guards settled into their easy chairs for a few hours of doing nothing until time for the next meal. The back breakman as he was called, was the only other guard in the entire building, and he was also resting somewhere at the opposite end of the building.

We decided that now was the time to move. Eddie exited his cell first and I was right behind him. Together we crept the long gallery floor all the way to the rear, then pushed through the opening I'd cut in the gallery gate on the evening before. We stole our way down the rear steps to the back of One gallery and positioned ourselves out of sight. With a nod from Eddie I called out to the guard. "Back breakman...back breakman!"

This was the usual call whenever the rear guard was needed. Instantly from upstairs we heard the sounds of the clang of heavy keys, and the reply. "OK...OK...I'll be right down." Slowly but very soon the guard made his way down the steps. When we surprised him at the bottom of the stairway he looked as if he'd seen a ghost. All he did was gasp in astonishment and did not struggle as Eddie took his entire set of keys and led him into a rear bathroom. We locked him in and warned him against making any unnecessary noise, then unlocked the side door of the building which led out into the main area of the compound. The corner of the wall that we would attempt to scale was only thirty feet away.

No one could see us. That particular area was obscured from view from every other point of observation. All we had to do now is launch the rope, hope it held and climb.

After the first two attempts to throw up the line our hopes were dashed. The rope Eddie had manufactured was too short by about four feet. We'd misjudged the height of the wall. For a few minutes the two of us just stared up at the corner where the wall met the building. I looked at Eddie and he at me and we knew without exchanging words, that there was no way out.

At that point we returned to the building and removed the guard from the bathroom, then unlocked the rear shower room where we instructed him to take a seat on the floor. We still had our pieces of the hacksaw blade and for a few minutes we made some feeble but useless attempts at cutting the window bars which opened up to the prairie outside. But in the end we both realized that it was fruitless to continue. We talked it over for a few minutes, then handed the keys back to the guard and walked with him back down One gallery to the main guard station where we surrendered.

Later that night in another cell several units away from the ones we'd cut through, I sat at the edge of my bunk and wallowed in self pity. They'd separated Eddie and I by keeping us a cell apart, and now loneliness predominated my feelings.

I contemplated suicide but always kept that option at bay because as long as I was still alive I knew there would always be another chance to escape.

The administration had enough of us. They decided very quickly that the time had come to rid themselves of these two constant pains in the neck and they didn't care to experience any more of our antics.

This time we were both given a choice. We could be sent to Statesville, the dreaded super-max of the time or we could volunteer to go to the new SPU unit in Joliet for thirty days, after which we would be sent downstate 300 miles away from Chicago to Menard, a lesser tense maximum facility. We decided on the latter.

SPU or Special Program Unit was nothing more than a three stage punishment process and thirty days turned out to be ninety, since completing the three stage process required a minimum of one month for each level. The first level was a month on the concrete floor with one blanket and nothing else. It was misery and loneliness magnified. That first month I didn't make a sound. Eddie made the mistake of mouthing off to a guard and was given a second thirty days on the same stage. It was very hard for him.

Once in a while we'd catch a glimpse of each other as we were escorted one at a time, once per week to the showers. They shackled us in what we called "the dog chain." A long chain attached to a steel loop in a wide leather belt that they wrapped around our waist. They inserted a pair of handcuffs in the loop then ran the chain between our legs and walked behind us. A simple tug would've sent any incorrigible convict head first into the concrete floor and often did.

On the rare occasions that I saw him, Eddie looked broken and drenched in despair. I'm very certain that I didn't look much better. We weren't allowed to speak, so I just nodded to him in an attempt to communicate my hope that he would keep his spirits up.

We survived that hell and months later, we were sitting next to one another on another chain. This time it was the steel links that connected convicts to each other as they were driven on a transport bus to a different facility. It felt like a picnic ride. We were on our way to southern Illinois, near the Saint Louis border and Menard penitentiary, some three hundred miles south of Chicago. While far from our homes in Chicago it proved to be the lesser of all evils. Menard was the prison of southern gentlemen. Few gang members made their affiliations known and the inmate population was largely from small rural towns and cities.

Seasoned veterans with long prison sentences found bliss in homemade hooch, fermented into an alcoholic beverage from fruits, vegetables or whatever else happened to be handy. Some died from it and some went blind, but to the administration it was a relatively harmless infraction that was never punished with more than a couple of weeks in the hole.

Eddie and I were given jobs in the prison laundry and after over a solid year of solitary confinement, reduced privileges and harsh treatment it seemed like a welcome vacation. We were free to walk the yard, or engage in sports and dine with the rest of the population in the chow hall. Our other privileges, like weekly movies and commissary wouldn't be restored for years. In Menard, I searched for a cause, something to believe in...a reason for living. I found it in books written by contemporary revolutionists like The Weathermen, SDS, The Black Panthers and others who were currently reeking havoc in the major cities throughout the country.

Most prisoners sympathized with their plight, if for no other reason than they opposed "Big Brother." So I searched for and eventually found my niche. Here was a cause worth living and fighting for. (Whatever that was.) I made good friends with the leader of radical group of convicts who sat in circles on the yard and spoke about the struggle of the proletarian, while they vented their verbal fury at all the establishment stood for. We read books written by Mao Tse Tung, Che Guevera, Lenin, and other notable revolutionary figures. The ideology appealed to me. No longer having a God to turn to, I dove head first into a new kind of belief. I embraced the struggle of the little guy over the power mongers of big business and government corruption. At that time it seemed like the right thing to do.

Many months went by. One day I was approached by a black inmate who worked in the segregation unit. He was a trusted convict with a special detail assignment that allowed him freedom to stay out of his cell long after all other convicts were locked up in the late afternoon. He asked me if I'd like a job like his. It seemed that the prison administration was looking for two white convicts to fill vacant positions left by two recently paroled. It was a dream job. All I had to do was mop a floor once a day and help serve food to the prisoners confined in the segregation unit. In return I had the run of the joint with a TV set and a pass that let me go wherever I wanted to. It took me about three seconds to accept the position.

Time went by quickly. I was more at ease with my predicament and soon abandoned my thoughts of escape. Day to day existence was much easier now and I enjoyed a kind of special status with my new position. Now even the guards were respectful.

Every day, while serving the meals to the scores of "the worst of the worst" confined prisoners I made new friends and acquaintances. A few were gang leaders, and one was a high ranking member of the Black Panther Party. Knowing from first hand experience what they were enduring, I tried to make their day to day hardships a little more bearable with extra food, an occasional smuggled message from a comrade or just friendly conversation. For the most part they all appreciated me and as the time went by, they came to rely on me as a guy that would help in any way if possible.

I spent hours talking with Frank, the Black Panther Party leader and together we struck up a friendship uncommon between a black convict and a white. I told him of my affiliation with the radical group and my new passion for reading revolutionary literature related to "the struggle."

One day Frank suggested that I help in the struggle by meeting with the rest of my own group and devising a plan that would disrupt the administration and, in his words, redirect their resources. A true revolutionary, Frank explained, created disruption and made life miserable for the unjust power mongers who enslaved and confined all who did not conform. I agreed. I met with 'Scull', the leader of my group and Mark, a lieutenant, and together we cooked up a plan that would be designed to burn down three major buildings within the prison compound. We'd hit the laundry complex, the chow hall and the auditorium, three very large structures that if destroyed, would have seriously compromised the continued functioning of the entire prison. Officials would be forced to transfer hundreds of convicts and total havoc would have ensued. I had found my purpose.

The three of us set to work on the plan right away. Other members in our group were recruited to gather things like kerosene from the powerhouse, containers from the kitchens, and laundry baskets for carting and transporting fire bombs. When everything was in place and we were confident that all of the details related to timing and execution were clear to everyone, Skull gave the order to proceed. I watched, cross-armed from the entrance of the segregation unit, while Mark coordinated three groups of men to deliver the kerosene bombs to all three buildings. It was not our intention to harm convicts so we selected a time when all of the buildings were empty.

I saw two of our guys pushing a laundry cart in the direction of the auditorium before they disappeared out of sight. I continued to wait and watch but nothing happened. The minutes went by and seemed a lot longer, but no sounds or activity occurred that would indicate that our mission had commenced. My thoughts raced with a mixture of confusion and doubt. Then, a lieutenant of the guard approached me, asked me my name, then promptly handcuffed me and led me away into the segregation unit. A score of top brass accompanied with a team of other officers of the guard led me onto the upper gallery of the unit and locked me in a cell.

Several minutes later they returned. This time with Skull and Mark in tow. They had discovered our plan. Later we learned that one of our own confederates was responsible for blowing the whistle. It would be three years before I would walk among the general prison population again. This time I would experience the most wretched period of punishment of my entire term of confinement.

The three ring leaders, Skull, Mark and myself would remain in the segregation unit for an undetermined amount of time, or until the administration decided what to do with us. So for now, I lived on the other side of the same floor I'd got so used to mopping every day. The prison staff made sure that the three of us were separated as far away from one another as not to even allow us within ear shot. But we were heroes among the ranks of the incorrigibles that populated that unit.

Within days the decision was made to ship Skull to Statesville and Mark back north to Pontiac. I would stay confined just where I was for a very long time to come. I became a total recluse. I rarely engaged in conversation with anyone except to mutter a weak greeting to some of the closer friends like Frank, the Black Panther and Magic Sun, another leader, on the few occasions that I was marched to the showers. The administration, it seemed to me, had thrown the key to my door away. They didn't even bother to question me about my involvement with Skull and Mark nor of any of the details. I quietly sank into a state of deep depression and self pity. I still had plenty of years to go and I did not look forward to spending them like this. I had no idea that it would get much worse.

One morning, very early, even before breakfast was passed out and long before many of my fellow residents awoke, I heard a loud shout coming from the rear of the lower gallery. Then more angry voices and now several convicts were suddenly awakened and hollering at the tops of their lungs.

"The son-of-a-bitch is spraying mace into the fan!" I finally made sense of the commotion. It appeared that the Sergeant in charge of the unit had crept to the very end of the gallery and was spraying blasts of mace from his chemical receptor directly into a large gallery fan. The fan itself was easily four feet in diameter and was used to help circulate the flow of air throughout the gallery. One of the convicts below watched him by using a small pair of chrome plated fingernail clippers as a mirror, and peering down the gallery.

This creature took great delight in the idea that the mace would flow through-out the area, propelled by the large fan, and treat us all with whiffs of chemical deterrent. Very soon everyone awoke. Vicious threats and furious vulgarity from the convicts closest to the rear of the building drowned out all other sound. All of the cursing and shouting just served to fuel the Sergeant's vindictive mood, so he disappeared around the corner of the gallery for a few minutes and when he returned he was dragging the building's fire hose with him. One snap of the nozzle lever and he unleashed a torrent of high pressured water, at point blank range into the unprepared cells below. One by one, he passed each cell and delivered hundreds and hundreds of gallons of water into the bodies of screaming convicts. He'd alternate his aim from the lower gallery to the upper and I scrambled to protect myself as best I could by removing the thin mattress from my bunk and holding it up to the bars of the cell.

Then I heard Frank's deep authoritative voice when he shouted out a repeated command, "Off with the toilets and sinks! Off with the toilets and sinks!" In the early 70's in Menard, the toilets and sinks were made from porcelain and when shattered, each piece was a deadly weapon that when thrown could cut severely. And when the sergeant attempted to return to his station he had to pass all of us. I broke out my sink, but did not join in with the others as they pummeled the sergeant with a volley of flying debris. He managed to run past quickly enough to avoid most of the projectiles but not before being hit several times and forced to drop the hose and flee for cover.

The entire gallery went up for grabs. Many of the convicts began blasting the windows with their broken pieces of toilets and sinks and soon not a single pane was left intact. The shouting and cursing of enraged inmates was deafening. Fires were lit and debris flew everywhere. I was in a full blown riot.

We could hear the sounds of large gatherings of guard personnel at the front of the lower gallery as they made their preparations to assault the unit and restore control. A few of the more violent and angry convicts taunted them with invitations to 'come on down...we got somethin' for you.'

More than a few inmates were devastated over the loss of personal property, photos of family and loved ones, letters and other cherished belongings that were destroyed after the water barrage. Some were crying. All of us were prepared for the worst.

Then they came. Two teams of guards, one on the lower gallery and one on the upper charged into every cell that showed signs of a broken sink or toilet or both. We could hear the sounds of beatings and screams of agony whenever one of the convicts resisted. By the time they got to me I was standing motionless and silent. Three of the five guards who came into my cell slammed me into the bars and handcuffed me to the top rung while the others swept out the pieces of broken sink onto the gallery floor. When they were finished, they went on to the next cell. For some reason they didn't beat me.

Several hours went by before they finally completed the sweep. When they were gone they left most of us in a standing position, all handcuffed to the bars. We remained in that position for the next three days. The floor was still drenched with the water from the fire hose and since we'd broken out all of the window panes the cool night air grew colder. Some men were naked except for the briefs they were wearing when they awoke on that horrible morning.

The next day, in the mid afternoon, guards came by and handed each of us a sandwich. It turned out to be fried egg with mustard complete with the eggshells. I attempted a bite then threw it onto the lower gallery. Soon the entire lower gallery floor was cluttered with them, as everyone refused to eat. Aside from gourmet meals they had bigger plans for us. Finally after three days in a standing position, arms overhead locked through the bars with handcuffs, they let us down. They removed the handcuffs. Immediately, I laid down on my mattress that was still damp, and covered my eyes with my arms.

Throughout the unit for the next few days there was rarely a sound from any of us. By the fourth day they came around with a real meal and new activity began near the center of both the upper and lower galleries. They'd decided to replace the glass panes we'd broken out with wooden panels which they quickly painted dark green to keep the sunlight out. Then they built two block walls that divided the galleries in half. They installed a new iron door on each of the levels, then separated all of the convicts in the entire unit. Those who had broken a sink or toilet were stripped of their usual prison clothing and dressed in coveralls before being marched into the newly constructed unit behind the block walls. We were placed in other cells with nothing except the coveralls we wore. That was to be my home for many months to come.

Except for an occasional dim light bulb dotting periodically along the gallery ceiling, it was very dark. There was no ventilation and we were allowed nothing in our cells, not even toilet paper. We were fed twice a day, once in the morning and again in the late afternoon. Very often months would go by before we were given showers. Some inmates used their toilets to bathe. There was no hot water. Mail was censored and visiting rights were restricted.

For all purposes and intents we were in a modern day dungeon. The only relief came with the friendship that developed among the small group of us that were confined. We talked together, sang songs in unison together and over the many months, became as close as any group of people could become. We talked about every subject under the sun from alien abductions to God. Most of the time, I didn't offer input on the later. By now I was so far removed from any aspirations about God my only thoughts about "Him" were purely negative. If God really existed, then why did "He" allow me to suffer so much? Why did "He" permit the world to be in the shambles it was? If there was a God where was "He?"

Almost two years later I filed a petition with the Illinois Prisoners Grievance Committee to be released from segregated confinement. They ruled in my favor, largely because the committee was staffed by personnel from the Springfield office, and made up of penologists who displayed elements of honest compassion.

One man in particular, a Mr. Rowe, seemed to be genuinely concerned for me. So I was released from the unit and once again sent to the general population.

That lasted a couple of days. One evening, when returning with the line of convicts from the chow hall I was met by a lieutenant, handcuffed and led me back to the segregation unit. This time I wasn't confined in the dungeon, but by now that was no consolation. Apparently, while I was eating in the chow hall, they searched my cell and laying on the floor in full view was a home made shank. (Knife.) They also found written "literatures which advocate aggressiveness toward the administration." While it was apparent that the shank was obviously planted they didn't proceed with that charge. I realized that all of this latest harassment was simply due to the fact that I'd won the grievance and the administration really had no desire to allow me to remain among their prisoner population. So they trumped up the "literature" charge just to have a reason to keep me locked up.

The literature they found was a story I had written while still in Pontiac, in the hole right after they caught me trying to escape. I typed it out on a ten dollar Smith and Corona that had been sent to me by a pen pal. Eddie loved it. Oddly enough that story mysteriously and eventually found its way into the hands of a famous movie producer from Chicago, who, in 1981 released a film whose entire screenplay, except for a few minor alterations was word for word what I'd written about a Master jewel thief. I never received credit for it as authorship was ascribed to the producer himself, based on a little known book written by a career thief.

They also found radical literature written by me that was largely in the context of despite and vented anger at the administration for how they treated us in the segregation unit. I wrote about the sergeant who'd been the cause of the riot, and his sadistic nature and how I wished he were held accountable for his actions.

So I filed another grievance. And again I won. Since I was charged with 'The Possession of Literatures Which Advocate Aggressiveness Toward the Administration,' I attacked the point that the written material was found in my cell. I wasn't out in the yard handing out flyers, so I couldn't be guilty of "advocating" anything. How could one advocate without promotion? I didn't even talk about it with anyone. Besides, I pointed out, similar literature, like my story about the jewel thief, other books and even the Bible contained themes just as violent and anti-administrative as my own, yet they were allowed in the prison library.

The grievance committee agreed and ordered my release from segregation. But the southern gentlemen of Menard had enough of me. By now I was no longer welcome. In defiance for the ruling, the administration decided to have me transferred again. A week later I was on a transport bus back north, to Joliet's "Old Joint." Joliet was where, years earlier, Eddie and I served the months on punitive SPU segregation. Since then the unit was discontinued having been the recipient of many class action lawsuits by prisoners, and finally deemed cruel and unusual punishment and closed down. Now it was a typically operated prison, where cons worked, enjoyed yard privileges and walked to the chow hall. All signs of the special punishment unit were gone.

While I enjoyed some measure of notoriety and popular status in the other facilities, here in Joliet I knew very few people. Largely populated by the worst of the worst, the Old Joint had become a home for high ranking gang members, personalities like Richard Speck, and many convicts with very long sentences. When I arrived, they assigned me to the dining room help, where I would be one of the prisoners designated to serve the meals.

At first, the strange new surroundings coupled with my restored freedom to walk about left me cautious and a bit apprehensive. The tension and general atmosphere was thick as pea soup with negative impressions.

But after a few months I settled into a routine and gradually resigned to finishing out my sentence and dreaming of the day when I'd finally be released. But if I ever entertained a thought that things would be peaceful I was mistaken.

A few months into my stay there, I struck up an intellectual relationship with one the leaders of one of the largest street gangs in the area and whose influence reached out into many cities. During one conversation the exchange grew heated, and we started to argue.

I don't even recall what the conversation was about. He happened to be locked in his cell at the time, while I was out on the gallery walkway, leaning against the railing as we talked. I remember storming away from him indigently, unhappy with whatever we had been discussing.

But what I didn't know at that moment, is that my reaction, especially in the presence of his subordinates who lived in cells next to him, would be viewed as "disrespectful" and serious disregard for higher authority. My words and actions were considered to be unforgivable, and I had to pay dearly for them. I knew I was in danger but I didn't fully realize the degree of seriousness until later that evening, when in my own cell. Just before lights out one of the leader's confederates approached my cell and threatened my life. He assured me that in the morning when the cells opened, "my time will have come."

I said nothing, as he moved slightly closer to my bars and in a blindingly move darted his fist through the bars and straight for my head. I ducked quickly enough to avoid the blow but not before my long hair tangled between his fingers. He jerked his hand back just as I jumped father away and I felt a strong burning sensation in my head. He'd managed to rip a sizable lock of my hair from the roots.

After another threat and a promise to return he left. He returned very shortly thereafter carrying a three gallon can of hot scalding water, normally distributed to inmates for instant coffee. In a single lunge he doused me with the water, then disappeared down the gallery. Luckily, my clothes absorbed much of the blast, and only my right arm was slightly burned. But now fear had totally engulfed my being. My head was bleeding puss from where the roots had been torn out and my arm stung from the pain of the hot water. My thoughts raced with anticipation and images of what was to come in the morning.

There was no escape. When the cell doors opened the following day I would probably be killed. I shook with fear. I knew there was no way out. I did not sleep that night. I paced the floor of my cell nervously for hours, all the while imagining all sorts of horrible stabbings and clubbings. My heart pounded with such fury I could feel it with every breath. I remember looking up at the ceiling of my cell as tears streamed down my face and I knelt on the concrete floor and positioned my hands together in prayer. For the first time in many years I prayed.

I begged, I pleaded, I made promises, but most of all I beseeched God's help. I prayed and prayed and prayed some more. Then I begged and pleaded a little more.

Sweat mixed with the blood and puss poured from the fresh wound in my head as I continued to pray until after a very long time I got back to my feet and stared off at nothing. Suddenly, amid all of the wretched emotion a clear thought entered my mind. 'Write a note, explain your situation and hand it to the next guard who passes your cell.'

At first I brushed aside the idea. Guards did not come by for many hours and long after everyone was fast asleep, if at all. Most of the time they didn't make another appearance until the morning. Besides. They know me. They know my record of being an incorrigible pain in the neck. Why would they want to help me? Why would they even believe me?

Snitching, better known then as being a stool pigeon, was not one of my regular habits. What would happen if I did so now? Without waiting another moment I found a stub of pencil and a scrap of paper and scribbled out a short note. In the note, I requested that whoever read it call Springfield and talk to Mr. Rowe from the Grievance committee. He would understand and he would believe me. Then I folded the note and stood at my bars to wait.

An eternity passed. Midnight came and went but still I remained standing, waiting And hoping that someone, anyone would come by. Hours passed. And finally my prayer was answered.

The lieutenant who finally passed was walking quickly but I whispered out to him "please help me" and he stopped in his tracks. From the expression on his face I could tell he was shocked by my appearance. At first he took a step backward, but then I held the note out, extending my reach toward him and he took it, read it, then looked into my eyes, and also visibly noticed my head wound. Without saying a word he turned about and headed back in the direction from where he'd come.

Now a faint glimmer of hope emerged. I began to pray again, this time with even more urgency. But the minutes turned into more hours and the longer I waited and prayed, the more concerned I became. Did he deliver the note or just throw it away? Did they dismiss my plea as the wild rambling of another worthless convict? Or did they read it, and purposely ignore my pleas for help? God help me, please!

The darkness outside was starting to show signs of dawn. It was nearing five a.m., about the time that the kitchen help, housed directly above me on the upper gallery, would be let out. They were always the first to be released every day. I knew that if their cells were opened before anyone came to respond to my requests for help, then all was lost. They probably ignored me. It wasn't long before I could make out the sounds of metal keys on bars. The Kitchen help was being awakened, and at that moment all my hopes for a rescue were dashed. I dropped to the floor of my cell and raked my hands across my face in despair.

This was it. After the kitchen workers were released I'd have about another hour or so before my own cell door and all of the others on the gallery, would automatically swing open. I was dead and there was nothing I could do about it.

Then suddenly I heard more keys. This time it was the sound of keys on the belts of several guards. Then I heard a shout that I will never forget.
"*Hold them up!*" It was an order to keep the kitchen workers in their cells.

Immediately three or four lieutenants, a Captain and several other guards approached my cell and unlocked it. They handcuffed me and led me away out of the building and to the hole. I was numb with relief and gratitude. Outside in the cool air I filled my lungs with deep breaths as I looked up at the morning sky. I was going to make it. I was saved. *I was going to be alright.*

They locked me in one of the cells in the "hole" building and told me that they'd be coming back for me within the hour. Eventually I was escorted right to the front gate of the prison, led through the first set of heavily guarded entrance doors and seated in an administrative conference room. A member of Mr. Rowe's grievance committee team met me there, looking very disheveled himself after the long drive from Springfield.

They administered a polygraph test just to verify my statements and before noon I was seated in the back of an official station wagon, on my way to Sheridan, a minimum security facility far away from any more threat of danger.

At Sheridan, I was greeted by scores of top brass and quickly ushered into a long one story building It was obvious that this kind of event was very unusual to them. They were heavily armed and quite prepared for anything. The steel door of my room was locked behind me and when they left I looked around my new home.

There was a real bed near the barred window which opened to reveal grass and trees outside. There was a desk and wooden chair, hot and cold running water and a mirror on the wall above the sink. It was, for all purposes and intents a cell, but compared to what I was used to it was like a suite in a five star hotel. I couldn't believe my eyes. I dropped down on my knees and folded my hands together in prayer for the second time in many years.

I gave thanks. I thanked what I percieved to be God. I thanked God for a very long time. There was absolutely no doubt in my mind that this event, this rescue was anything less than the result of divine intervention. My conviction was unshakable in that regard. "*How could I ever have doubted You?*"

Then it happened. The experience that would change my life forever was unfolding. I got off my knees in reverence and laid down on the bed and closed my eyes. I was breathing deeply without a thought in my mind. Then very gradually a warm sensation began to flow all around me. I felt light and sensed I was rising slowly off the bed.

Then the sensation increased in intensity until "I" began to expand. I felt like I was becoming everything around me, including the room itself, the floor and the walls, then "I" grew to include the trees and the plants and grass outside and the air in between and even the sunlight that streamed through the window...was everything. *I am everything.* Something miraculous was going on.

The very first sensation was the feeling of floating upward. I remember being concerned about touching the ceiling and there was a distinct knowing that the little "I", the Joe wasn't in control. Then the expansion began, and the feeling that "I" was everything around me.

Light, the presence of the feeling of love I'd experienced in the vision with the beautifully adorned lady so many years before as a child...I lost touch with the sensation of my body and instead, it was replaced with a much wider diameter of consciousness that had no beginning or end. My own personal identity was still there, I was still "me" but the sensation that this is the real me, and not the body laying on the bed below.

Now my Self was enhanced with a much wider area of awareness. It grew with every passing second. It engulfed with an encompassing presence that transcended the known self and grew with every passing second of the experience.

I "heard" the "sound" of an increasing hum that I can only describe as no sound on earth could produce. The melody rose a note at a time, up the scale of the musical octave, one at a time as the presence grew wider and wider. The sound, though gentle was like all of the most beautiful instruments in the world were playing in perfect harmony; all the magnanomous melody of all the the most harmonizing tones I had ever experienced.

It lasted for a few short minutes, then like an exhaled breath I was slowly brought back. I felt my "Self" slowly re-entering my body until all sensation left except for the feeling of my body laying on the bed. It remains impossible to describe in words. It was serene and comforting while all powerful and effortless. The feeling of peaceful warmth was unlike anything even remotely describable.

The feeling subsided as gradually as it had begun and soon I "returned" to the three dimensional "me." I sat up on the edge of my bed and realized that my gratitude had been acknowledged. I knew then, without a doubt that something much bigger existed behind everything that is, something so magnanimous as to take complete precedence over any other worldly phenomena.I had experienced Spirit.

I know now that this was a glimpse into the reality that my body and my mind were things I possessed, things that *I had* and not what *I Am*. I rose from the bed and looked around in awe. What was this wonderful feeling? Where did it come from and how could I feel it again?

I vowed right then, at that moment, to seek out the origin of this wonderful new consciousness and never again return to the goals and meager aspirations of my past. I wanted desperately to learn as much as I could about it and nothing would get between me and the memory of this remarkable look at my True reality.

Many years later I would come to understand that the extraordinary miraculous nature of this experience was much more than opinionality from the view point of an ordinary ego. It would eventually become clear however, that the authorship I claimed needed to be reassigned to a much higher source of power. Because for many years I ascribed a certain specialness and belived that these experiences were "mine." But after many years of searching for the source of these wonderous events, I came to realize that the I who searched would never find anything. The world as I perceived it had no answers.

Months went by. I was interviewed many times by the brass and by counselors who sought to evaluate my current state of mind and determine if they could trust me to be released to the general population. Sheridan was an atmosphere not unlike a college campus, void of gun towers and stone walls. Inmates were generally trusted and the iron clad rules of maximum security were nonexistent.

After three or four months the administration was noticeably impressed with me. Given my lengthy record of staunch noncompliance and attitude of utter revolt they viewed my transformation as nothing less than remarkable. I was released from 24 hour confinement and sent to one of the housing units where I was to enjoy new freedoms.
The only mandatory lock-up was at night, in rooms exactly like the one I had become so accustomed to during the past few months. A day room, complete with TV set, game tables, books and magazines, was the place most of the men spent their time. I was greeted and welcomed by new friends and soon settled comfortably into my new environment.

It was only days after my transfer to the housing unit when I was approached by a black man, another fellow inmate whom I'd never met before. He smiled at me and I recognized a familiar light in his eyes. He handed me a book by the author Ramm Dass, *Remember Be Here Now*, and told me to read it. He said that I'd like it and that I would get something out of it. Then he walked away. For some reason unknown to me at the time, I accepted the book without a word and sat at one of the tables in the day room to look through it. It was the first of many enlightening works of literature that would *fall into my lap* just at the time I needed them.

[Some years later, I would see this man again, on a busy street in Chicago as he led a parade of Krishna devotees, dancing and singing as they played their tambourines and moved through the crowded street, dressed in long flowing orange robes.]

I was pleasantly surprised when I began to find that the experience of oneness I'd been blessed with months earlier, was described in printed detail in the book. Other people of different walks of life and degrees of spiritual evolution had tasted the exact same experience! I was not alone, and it solidified my convictions that this was something very real and more, and not the product of imagination, but a readily accessible state. Described as an "out of body experience" I learned that it was not uncommon event for many people.

With a hungry fever I eagerly set to the task of absorbing every word. I soon learned some basic steps that had to be followed into order to access that wonderful new energy. For the next few months I'd spend many hours alone in my room, experimenting with meditation and going within. I experienced many wonderful new sensations.

Later, my new friend gave me another book; a copy of *The Fourth Way* by Peter Ouspensky, a student of George I. Gurdjieff. That book would become my constant companion for many years to come, and followed by many more works by authentic modern day teachers.

I learned that consciousness was energy that flowed through me all of the time. It was the purest form of universal energy that when accessed in great degrees would be the power required to understand everything, to do anything and most of all to reach that special place within whenever I chose.

One the greatest spiritual messengers of our time reminded us of that universal Power when he told us that, "If you had faith no greater than the size of a mustard seed, you could say to that mountain, 'move' and the mountain would move." But I had a lot of work to do. In my present state, this energy was leaking like water through a strainer. Nothing was retained thus no necessary accumulation remained long enough to accomplish anything more than my typical three dimensional ego was used to. First I had to stop the leaks.

These leaks, it was explained, were unnatural to my essence and completely created by my own personality. In these states of negative thinking or feeling, energy is drained or wasted. They were defined as negative emotions. These negative emotions, like fear, guilt, hate, disgust, self pity, cynicism, lust, irritability, defiance, cruelty, suspicion, prejudice, belligerence, worry, shame, apathy, grief, desire, anger, pride and lying to mention just a few, were the holes in me from which gushed and wasted the energy that would otherwise empower my spiritual evolution.

These negative tendencies, the habits, the inclinations, the beliefs, the likes and dislikes, accepted norms, were all that made up my crust of personality, that artificial creation that no man or woman is born with. Many will argue that some of these negative emotions are quite natural, but nothing could be farther from the stark truth. They are all energy leaks and all illusions based on personal beliefs. I had a lot of *un-learning* to do.

First I had to stop up the leaks. Not by suppressing them but by employing the choice of not expressing them or allowing oneself to become identified with their useless and often harmful repercussions.

I learned that most of the personality was something acquired and not born with. Although some tendencies were in a sense, karmic and the sum of all experiences, but most were newly acquired negativity developed after birth with the creation of the personality.

Like a child who learns the language of his particular country, personality is constructed from external circumstances. Almost everything in the personality or ego is learned . At a very early age most of us learn that expressing or thinking negative emotions is an accepted and normal behavior and sometime justified. This justification is the result of positionalities that take deep rooted hold on the personality and are most usually the remnants of the very natural animal instincts of simple survival. It is these accepted beliefs and justifications that evolve into sophisticated beliefs that *create behavior*.

And one of the most predominating negative emotions that keeps most of us down are our beliefs related to God. We ascribe to God characteristics more likely to be found in man or what we often refer to as a devil. We accept the force fed doctrines of those that would instill fear and guilt, judgment and condemnation, reward and punishment. From these and other inferences our personalities are formed, our beliefs, our likes and dislikes, tendencies, habits and all of those elements that would construct energy leaks.

First, stop the leaks. First recognize that the personality is a servant *and not the master*. Change beliefs and we change behavior. Replace negative states of thinking and feeling with states that retain energy. Jesus summed it all up. "Think on things of good report."

I learned to practice going within. In my present condition I was completely at the mercy of outside influences. I didn't act, I reacted. I was nothing more than a robot, a puppet, a lamb among sheep. *A prisoner of my own thoughts*. Going within taught me that real power was all around me, always had been, and would open the doors that would lead me to more assistance, more guidance and eventually the path to true freedom.

The method I used was one that had proven successful for many people throughout the ages and is practiced by people all over the world.

Note that these suggestions are not prerequisites, nor are they cut in stone as necessary practices; breathing exercises, special diets, or chanting will not of themselves, evoke higher states of consciousness. The most important elements remain in the consistent practice of observation and *above average tolerance*, *forgiveness*, and *compassion for all life*. These would lead to a much wider radius of consciousness, the likes of which I had only tasted a small portion during that brief but wondrous glimpse.

(1) Observe thoughts
(2) Observe actions
(3) Observe feelings (emotions)
Just watch them without judgement or fueling them with imagination.

Most of all, learn that the power to stop wasting energy with the expression and thinking of negative emotions comes from the Grace that accompanies the practice of replacing negativity with thoughts and expressions of Love. Replace vindictiveness with forgiveness and compassion.

The process of observation shows that thoughts and the mind itself are things we *have* and not what we "*are*." They are like the body laying on the bed below me, while "I" floated above it…the "Me" that grew and expanded and observed in awe.
While it's next to impossible to control or stop thoughts, after consistent practice it becomes easier to stand aside from them, unidentified, like watching a parade.

While practicing the efforts of observing try a non-judgemental attitude about everything. Try to associate feelings of love and compassion to replace old habits of taking positions of judgement. Look at your guards in a new light. Forgive them. Forgive yourself. Forgive yourself for believing that You are less than what You really are. Love melts even the hardest of hearts.

Not long ago, when exiting a store, a little boy not much older than seven or eight passed me on his way into the store. With a genuine smile from ear to ear he looked into my eyes and said "Hi!" I was abruptly taken completely by surprise. His brief but sincere greeting brightened up that moment and stayed with me for several hours.

That was an expression of Love. And Love is the fuel for authentic power.

Practice going within. (Meditating) The process of going within, or meditating, introduces the self to the Self. Normally we're so identified with outside distractions that we have little or no time for anything else. With repeated and consistent efforts coupled with work on energy leaks, anyone can access that Pure 'I'... that essence of Real Self, and Higher Power.

Begin each day with this exercise:

Start with attention on your breathing. Either lay flat on your back (no pillow) with your spine straight, or sit up straight, again with your posture straight and aligned. Many people employ the lotus position. Breathe in slowly and deeply through your nose and out your mouth. Take the fresh air deep within your lungs into the unused areas, then slowly let it all out, gently forcing the stale, trapped air from places rarely ventured. Watch your thoughts without participation. With repeated practice this will become easier and easier until your mind slows down the idle chattering of your thoughts and eventually helps one to realize that thoughts are like fish in the ocean and you are the ocean.

Now feel the sensation of life as if flows through the toes, the arches, the heels, the ankles, and the tops of the feet. Start with one foot, then holding the sensation, transfer your attention to the other. Now go back to the first foot. Expand the attention to include the sensation of life as it flows from your foot, up to you shin and calf, then your upper leg, hip and thigh. Hold that sensation and transfer your attention to your other foot.

Repeat the process of feeling the sensation of life as it flows through your other leg. Hold the sensation in your feet and legs now continue with the rest of your body; your back, your shoulders, your neck, your head, your face, your eyes...your chest and stomach...sense every inch of your body. Feel the inner organs and bones and listen to your heart beat. Stay attentive to your breathing.

Now center your attention on an area about inch below your navel. Hold the sensation of life as it flows throughout your entire body. Envision your internal organs, your heart, your lungs, your intestinal tract, your brain. Imagine going deep and seeing the atoms, the protons, the neutrons, all working in harmony and loving unity with one another.

Think: *I am pure Spirit, created in the likeness of God, having a human experience.*
I am here. In this room, in this building, in this town, in this country, on this planet, in this solar system, in this galaxy, in this universe. But beyond all bodies and planets and stars, something exists that is the substratum behind it all. That 'something' we traditionally refer to as God or Source.

Repeat this affirmation several times to yourself, aloud if you like, but the thought is equally powerful. Envision your connection with whole earth, and like the atoms in your body, part of the whole of humanity and all of its expressions.

In the beginning, do this three times daily. (More if you can remember.) As soon as your feet touch the floor every morning use that sensation as a reminder. Then once again before your mid day meal and finally before retiring for the night. Keep in mind what you're after is complete consciousness, full awareness of yourself, your movements, your thoughts and your emotions with the underlying conviction that I AM not this temporary body but pure Spirit created in Your Likeness.

Watch Yourself: Be the observer. The most significant waste of conscious energy occurs *whenever we think or express negative emotions*. Ask yourself, "Is this thought productive? Does it help me or does it weaken me?" "Does it contribute to a worthwhile element of my personal and spiritual development or does it create a useless obstacle in my path?" Try to stay tuned to your objective: to be here now, in this place at this moment. *To remember yourself.*

We connect with authentic power when we choose the productive over the unproductive, the decision not to waste attention on a temporary gratification. The ego derives pleasure and is fed with rewarding feelings of everything from the prideful to the martyrdom. It thrives on such feelings and cannot survive without them.

Our day to day paths of living are riddled with another fork in the road, another decision, another choice, another opportunity for gain or another wasted chance. Watch your words, for they can be a very powerful influence.

Unlike what we've learned about "sticks and stones..." words have started wars, shattered lives and have led to long prison sentences, as you well know. Words have also healed, comforted, delighted and inspired for the benefit of everyone who heard them.

Choose to be the healer, the inspirer and the one to be a bringer of light to everyone you touch. That is why you're here, why you were born into the world and what you had chosen as your mission long before your mother ever cradled you in her arms.

The path that brought you here, to your cell, right now, was no chance happenstance without purpose. But up to now the choice to do things on your own hasn't worked. Why not ask for Higher Direction?

As I look back at my own period of confinement as with all events in my past, I realize that every moment, every circumstance, every day lived was an elementary piece that led to the here and now.

On the first page of this letter I acknowledged my dear friend Judy Hall, who, before she died, led me back to the path. Judy was a highly charged and spiritually prepared seasoned soul, who was one of those people we meet when we need them most.

At the time of our meeting I was on a downward spiral, an inevitable crash-landing having wasted nearly twenty of the past thirty years distracted by the lure of temporary gratification. I became a drunk and drug user. I had completely forgotten about that few moments of life altering sensation, that blessed gift of insight that had so branded my being with true reality. The tiny voices of the tenacious ego had gotten to me. "OH...it's OK, have that drink, do that dope...everything in moderation..."

Weekly attendance at the meditation and discussion groups with like minded people stopped; the efforts to remember myself and go within also faded into total regression and all interest in "seeking" had come to a complete standstill. Temporary comforts and justification replaced the original urgency. I had given in to the whisperings of the ego, that had tenaciously struggled to remain in control.

Often during those twenty years, between a rocky life of shattered dreams, dozens of jobs, lost possessions, broken relationships, and endless years of self pity I'd manage an occasional feeble recollection. It was during one of those moments that Judy Hall came into my life. She nurtured my battered spirit with smiles and bathed me in compassionate love. When we spoke of my many years of distractive behavior, she just shrugged her shoulders. She reminded me that anyone can fall down, anyone can stumble, anyone can lose their way for a while.

She encouraged me to read the Conversations With God series by Neale Donald Walsch. Later, after a gradual but successful weaning off of drugs and drinking, other books and new acquaintances once again began to appear. I spent more time going within, reading, meditating, praying and re-living that wonderful experience of so many years before. I learned that my experience in prison of so many years before, would best be applied by sharing it with others. It was my vision that with enough participation, we could put prisons out of business for good.

I understood that this kind of spiritual work is a three-lines-of-development effort:

[1] work on oneself
[2] work with others
[3] work for the work...

Then some time afterward while hosting a spiritual group gathering in Chicago, I came upon the works of Dr David R. Hawkins and *A Course in Miracles*. It was Hawkins who suggested I *"pick an integrious spirital discipline and stick to it."* He recommended **A Course in Miracles**.

This *Course in Miracles* would be the *"integrious spiritual discipline"* I would employ that would change this life forever. I've shared the 365 daily lessons from the workbook in *A Course in Miracles* in the latter part of this book, one of three books that comprise the entire ACIM. I've omitted the much larger Text to economize space in the hope that the theory of The Course is grasped through the works of Gary R. Renard's *The End of Reincarnation* and Carrie Triffet's *The Crash Course*, also included in this volume.

So, I share this experience with the intention that it might reach and help some who can use it most. And since we're all temporary prisoners of our egos...our false person-alities...it's not restricted to just those numbers of us who happen to live behind bars.

Each of us has our own path. For this entity it began with questions and the deep underlying feeling that something much bigger than what meets the eye was 'behind' everything. Some greater power held this body up, gave it the abilities to breathe, walk, talk, smell, hear, taste, touch and think. It refused, from early childhood, to accept the vengeful god theory, the punishment and reward ideologies as force fed by organized theological teachers, and eventually sought to seek and find Truth.

This great something Graced the ability to be aware and to know that it was aware. This is the reality, the something behind everything, now temporarily obscured by gross identification with what appears to be external influence. It was hidden by opinions, ideologies and positionalities that fed the tenacious habits of the ego who, by its very nature, is seduced and fattened by negative energy.

This something is the field of awareness itself, the divine connection, the Absolute, the All and Everything, the Alpha and Omega, the God of Unconditional Omnipresent Love, for this is the Kingdom and Power and the Glory forever and ever.

With the intention to raise the level of consciousness throughout the world be aware that moment of every day, "something" exsists behind what the body's eyes can see, feel, hear, taste or touch. Feel that presence with every fiber of your being. Sense the energy as it surges through every breath you take. It is all loving, all protective and reasuring. Like a parent's love for his child it is unconditional and everlasting. It has always been with you and will never leave. Use your visualization to rest in the *firm conviction* that you are never alone.

The experience in my cell so many years ago was a brief glimpse, a step on the threshold of *what could be.* Having seen and felt it, with no doubt to its validity, I share it with anyone with the intention to relay that if it could happen to an entity like mine, it could happen for anyone.And so, dear prisoner, I'd invite you to shake off the cares of the world and go within for a few moments every day, when you read this prayer that I've kept in my pocket for years:

Dear God,
I love you. You created me. I live in You and You in me. Only my own unconscious guilt and belief in this false personality, this individual identity, keeps me confused.
Thank you for everything you give me! Grant me the power to live in Your presence, to accept Your unconditional Love as I learn to forgive.

Allow me to remember that You are with me always, with every breath I take, in every movement, in all thoughts and feelings. Remind me many times during the day until every second becomes another moment spent in Your Loving embrace and constant presence.
Allow me to be a servant of Your Will. A vehicle of divine Love and a channel of God's Will. Give me direction and divine assistance as I surrender all personal will through devotion to You.

Allow me the help to dedicate my life to the service of God. Grant me the ability to choose Love and Peace above all options while I commit to the goal of unconditional Love and compassion for all life and all of its expressions as I surrender all judgement to You, God.

Make me aware that the world of my ego is a constant and tenacious tendency to react, to feel bad, guilty, mad, defeated, bored, scared, inferior, embarrassed, annoyed, lonely or superior and condescending. All these give validity to judgement regardless of the form and by reacting with judgement I feed and strengthen the ego's world and reinforce the seeming separation from You.

Please remind me constantly to view all others as my brothers and to realize that we are all One and to forgive them for they are One with me, joined in One mind and also innocently caught in the false ego's identity's world of illusion.

Never let me forget that I am not this temporary body but pure Spirit created in Your Likeness as I continue to live every moment in the knowledge that You are with me always, where I AM, all Loving, forever. You God, the Alpha and Omega, the All and Everything, the Absolute.

Love, Light and the Peace of God,
Joe Wolfe, **SpiritLightOutreach.org**

Suggested Reading:

A Course in Miracles
The Disappearance of the Universe by Gary Renard
The End of Reincarnation with The Five Signs by Joe Wolfe
Conversations With God, by Neale Donald Walsch
Power vs Force, by Dr. David R. Hawkins
The Eye of the I, by Dr. David R. Hawkins
The Holy Spirit's Interpretation of The New Testament
by Regina Dawn Akers
Journey of Souls, by Dr. Michael Newton
The Greatest Miracle in the World, by Og Mandino
The Fourth Way, by Peter D. Ouspensky
All and Everything, by George I. Gurdjieff
The Seat of the Soul, by Gary Zukav
The Four Agreements, by Don Miguel Ruiz
The Celestine Prophecy, by James Redfield
Transcending the Levels of Consciousness,
The Stairway to Enlightenment, by Dr. David R. Hawkins

The End of Reincarnation

By Gary R. Renard
best seller author of,
The Disappearance of the Universe and
Your Immortal Reality
Copyright, Sounds True by author Gary R. Renard

Transcribed with the permission of **Sounds True**
from the original audio version into text
by *Joe Wolfe*

The transcribed text version of Gary R. Renard's workshop on
The End of Reincarnation
An easy introduction into *A Course In Miracles*
This work has been transcribed from audio into text for the reason
to be able to make this very important message available to anyone, anywhere. It is intended to be
shared with anyone who are without the means or access to the original audio version provided by
Sounds True,
with an postscript by Joe Wolfe

Foreword
A note from the Scribe

Over thirty years ago, (in 1975) this writer experienced what is usually described as an out-of-body experience. I'd felt several other mystical experience in the past but this particular time was different. It was coupled with an sensation of *Being* everything in the general vicinity, including the room, the atmosphere outside the window and the air between. It also included the trees directly outside and the plants and grass and the slight breeze and even the sunlight. I felt as if I were *One with everything*.

Unlike the typical associations usually ascribed to these kinds of experiences, there was no sensation of what is called an 'astral body' but rather, an awareness that "I" was *expanding to include everything*. While seeming to float away from the body, the sensation was accompanied by a succession of "sounds" which were as three distinctive notes in progressive scale, like 'do-re-me' but each note up the scale of the octave was as if all of the instruments in all of the orchestras all over the world were playing in unparalleled harmony. The experience lasted only a few short minutes before very slowly and carefully returning me to the body, leaving me dumb-founded and awe-stricken.

The experience was completely sudden and quite unexpected and more, it came even void of any previous point of reference, that is, never having been a 'seeker' or a student of the divine, in this lifetime, it came as if liken to the cart before the horse, from which I would begin a life-long search for knowledge and the Source for the experience.

It came immediately after a day filled with apathy and despair, and after long hours of begging for help. It came after a period of Thankfulness and Gratitude for having been delivered from a particularly dangerous situation, rescued from certain demise to safety. The experience was so undeniable and so powerful (while gentle and all Loving) it left an indelible effect that would forever question the validity of the ego and the urgency to seek out the real source for *All and Everything*.

When this writer's search began in 1975, much of the material, books and information currently enjoyed and studied by seekers everywhere, wasn't available. Much of it wasn't even conceived or published and many modern day teachers were unknown. And while some of the writers and authors I studied became the subjects of questionable controversy and even dispute, this writer is convinced that ALL authentic teachings are, *in their own ways*, important and valuable contributions.

Keeping in mind that *judgment of any kind* strengthens the ego's identification with the liner world of form, it is the intention to weed through the variety of teachings and seek only the Truth. *"Take what you can use and leave the rest."* And while reasonable attention should be paid to the validity of each, understanding that much exploitation exists within the realms of the multi-million dollar business of "spiritual seeking," a rule of thumb to remember is that real Truth exists within, obscured only by the false personality/ego and its consistent
and tenacious tendency to control.

The message in Gary R. Renard's *The End of Reincarnation* rings with a deep resounding purity of Truth and finally sheds light on all of the answers any serious student seeks.
Joe Wolfe, author of *Letter To A Prisoner*

**Transcribing the original audio CD version,
published by Sounds True**

It was over thirty years to the month of that fateful mystical out-of-body experience, when I was first introduced to Gary R. Renard's works. I hosted a small book study group (that goes on to this day) in the Chicago area, that is attended by like-minded people from all walks of life and who all share a distinct urgency to find the answers to the questions we all entertain regarding personal spiritual development and the truths about God.

Initially inspired by the books of Neale Donald Walsch and his *Conversations with God* series, our group eventually examined many other authors and grew to find valid contributions from such writers as Wayne Dyer, Dr. David Hawkins, Jerry and Esther Hicks, Echart Toole, Don Miguel Ruiz, James R. Redfield and a host of other integrious writers and authors too many to list here.

Of these valuable contributors I personally gravitated toward two with a very special interest, because of their consistency of authenticity and the unmistakable feeling that *herein lies the Truth*.

Dr. David R. Hawkins and his *Power vs. Force*, followed by a series of remarkable books, served as the "scientific" approach to understanding the nature of Enlightenment and Salvation. His are works I would highly recommend for any serious student. The second, and star of the show, was Gary Renard and his introduction into *A Course In Miracles* through his *Disappearance of the Universe* and *Your Immortal Reality*.

Early in the summer of 2006, Steve Cooper, a musician and regular attendee of our group gave me his copy of Gary's workshop CD on *The End of Reincarnation*. This was some time after Anne Marie Faje , Denise Darcy and Steffani Fort, also part of the regular nucleus of group members had shared with me, their suggestions to read Gary's books.

Gary's message completely blew me away. This is what I had been searching for. This was the final culmination of the many years of the gathering of information through reading and study, and eventually discovering the tools with which to apply an effective *disciplined application of knowledge* that would lead to experience. This was practical theory and application and I embraced it with the fever of discovering a treasure map.

So almost every day from the early summer in 2006 until the time of this writing, I read Gary's books and listened to his CD on *The End of Reincarnation*. I started to study *A Course in Miracles*, which I'd had in my possession for some time, but rarely ventured into until after absorbing Gary's works. Gary's clear and concise introduction into ACIM was like someone had turned on the lights and helped to simplify the sometimes difficult to read or understand text in ACIM.

Many months went by and I continued to listen to the CD over and over again, and with every passing day, the message became clearer and clearer. Then one day an idea, a flash of inspiration overwhelmed me. I wanted to have a text version of *The End of Reincarnation* that I could share through personal delivery with my own group. I wanted to send it to prisoners, and people who had no access to CD players. I wanted to deliver it to those who couldn't afford the money to buy the more expensive audio versions. I also envisioned reading aloud the message, in person, to various groups.

But after serious inquiry I learned that *there was no text version available*. None had been created and so, after some weeks of pondering over the idea, I decided to do it myself. I made the decision to transcribe, word for word, the entire workshop audio version into a readable text that almost anyone could access.

I was more than half completed with my new task before I even asked for permission from Gary, who owns the copyright and Sounds True who owns the print rights. But as if preordained and with complete support for the project, Gary exuberantly granted my request to finish the transcription as did the wonderful people at Sounds True.

So I continued on with new vigor, delighted with my new found freedom to finish the project as quickly as I could. Very soon I began to realize that the task I had set for myself was not going to be easy. Working with a twenty dollar CD player that was old and sometimes unreliable, I spent hours every day between pauses and stops and starts, while struggling to write down every word verbatim.

Gary has this wonderful gift of speech delivery that sometimes crams twenty words into two seconds, so it was a little like micro surgery to separate and verify each sentence with accuracy. That, along with the fact that I couldn't read my own writing and was forced to print it out in longhand made the entire project slow going and very tedious.
But it was a great labor of Love and I'm deeply honored to be on this path and to be a part of making this message available in this format.

So it is with deep sincerity, thankfulness and gratitude, to Gary R. Renard, to Tami Simon of *Sounds True* and to God that I share Gary's profound contribution with you, and anyone who has an ear to hear.

Love, Light and the Peace of God,
Joe Wolfe, author of Time Ocular and Scribe of
The End of Reincarnation with The Five Signs.
Founder of *Spirit Light Outreach:* SpiritLightOutreach.org *and* SpiritLightOutreach.com

The End of Reincarnation

by Gary R. Renard

I'd like to cite a quotation from a spiritual document called *A Course in Miracles*. And for those of you who don't know, *A Course in Miracles* is a three-books-in-one spiritual text that was given by Jesus to a woman in New York City named Helen Schucman.

And she heard the voice of Jesus for like seven years and she wrote down what He said in her short-hand notebook and then she would read it to this guy named Bill Thetford, who would type it out.

And that became *A Course in Miracles* and very early in the scribing of the Course back in 1965, Bill had to get up and give a talk at Prinston University to a group of psychologists.
  And Bill, as it turns out, was a lot like me; he was very introverted as many mystical people are. Mystical people are very used to going within themselves. They're not really 'out there.'

Extraverts love to speak in public. Like Oprah, she's 'out there.' They love it. But a lot of mystical people, like Bill and me, we're not the kind of people you would ordinarily expect to get up and speak in front of a crowd of people. In fact, for those of you who have read my first book, The Disappearance of the Universe, may recall that my teachers in the book asked me, they said,
  "You don't like to get up and speak in front of a crowd, do you?"

And my reaction was,
  "I'd rather stick broken pieces of glass up my butt."

And that's kind of like the way that I felt about it. And certain things had happened along the line to sort of change my mind about that.

But getting back to 1965, in Bill's case he had to get up and give this series of talks and he gave this saying from A Course in Miracles that was ultimately meant for all of us, but at the time, it was meant for Bill to help him get up and give this talk. And I like to use it as my way of letting the Holy Spirit kind of like be in charge of what I say and kind of like take over. So I'm gonna recite that right now and just let the Holy Spirit take over from here.

I am here only to be truly helpful. I'm here to represent Him who sent me. I do not have to worry about what to say or what to do, because He who sent me will direct me.

I am content to be wherever He wishes, knowing He goes there with me. I will be healed as I let Him teach me to heal.

And that's it. And that's kinda cool, because I'm like off the hook and I don't have to worry about what to say and what to do and the Holy Spirit now, is responsible for whatever gets said.

So one thing I'm gonna do certainly, is give you an overview of my first book, which is called *The Disappearance of the Universe*. And the reason that it's called *The Disappearance of the Universe* is because when you wake up from a dream the dream disappears.

When you were in bed last night and you were having a dream, you woke up from the dream and where's the dream? Well, it's not there. And the reason that *that's* possible is because it was never really there in the first place. It just seemed that way.

If I can use an analogy, lets say we have a four year old daughter, and she's in bed at night, and she's dreaming, and you just kind of like peek in on her to see how she's doing. And you notice that she's tossing and turning and she's having this kind of like unpleasant dream. You can tell that it's not very comfortable for her. She's reacting to events in the dream as it's not a pleasant dream.

Now what do you do? You don't go over there and shake the hell out of her, because that would scare her even more. And for her, the dream has become her reality. She's reacting to events in the dream as though they are real. And where she really is, which is in the bed, that's oblivious to her. She's not really aware of that any more.

Her whole attention is focused now on the dream. And that has become her reality, and where she really is has been lost to her.

So what you do is, rather than go over and kind of like rudely interrupt her, maybe you'll whisper to her. Maybe you'll say things to her like,

"Hey. It's only a dream. You don't have to worry. What you're seeing is not true. Yes, it may seem real, but it's not. They're just pictures in your mind. And if you can hear my voice right now, then you're already starting to wake up."

Because the Truth can be heard in the dream. The Truth is not *in* the dream. The Truth is not in the dream at all. But it can be *heard* in the dream and it can slowly and gently awaken you.

And so, you whisper to your four year old daughter and she starts to hear you. And it changes her attitude and her state of being and her state of mind and she slowly starts to awaken. And it becomes a more pleasant dream for her before she awakens. And so, when she wakes up, she's not afraid.

She's ready to wake up and kind of like, to where she really always was, but she really didn't know it. And then, when she wakes up in the bed, she realizes that that's where she always was all along. But it was simply out of her awareness.

And the same kinds of things that we would whisper to a four year old in bed at night, this having a bad dream, are exactly the same kinds of things that the Holy Spirit is whispering to us right now, in this dream. Because when you wake up, it's really just a different form of dreaming. It's a function of what *A Course in Miracles* (which we'll get into) it's a function of what the Course would call *levels*. So this level seems more real.

But it's really just another form of dreaming. In fact, *A Course in Miracles* says that all of your time is spent in dreaming.

So we had a dream, like last night, and that seemed real, and then we wake up and we find out that we were in our bed, and that seems real, but it's really just a dream. And then we dream that we live in this life and all the adventures that are in it. And then some day we dream that we die and then we have all of these interval periods in between life times where all of these other kinds of adventures happen, then eventually we're born seemingly in another body, and that's just a dream too.

And in this dream the Holy Spirit is whispering to us,
"Hey. It's only a dream. You don't have to worry. What you're seeing is not true. And if you can hear my voice right now, you're already starting to wake up."

Because the Truth can be heard in the dream. The Truth is not *in* the dream but the Truth can be *heard* in the dream, and it can slowly and gently awaken you.

And as you start to wake up, your attitude changes and you become less fearful of the dream, because the Holy Spirit is saying that all of the problems that you have and all the things you think are such a big deal, and all the questions that you have, they're really just kind of silly. Because they're a product of the same thought system that produced the dream in the first place.

And as you wake up, you see that it's just all kind of silly, and then, when you finally awaken, you realize that you never left home. Except this home is Heaven. This home is one with your Source, where you really were. So just like the bed was out of the awareness of the four year old, Heaven, which is where we really are, is out of our awareness, and it's something that we awaken to.

A Course in Miracles says,
  "You are at Home in God, dreaming of exile, but perfectly capable of awakening to reality."

And it's the experience of that, that I want to talk about. Because experience is really the only thing that will make us happy. Theology won't do it. I'm not saying that there's anything wrong with theology or intellectual concepts. They're important as a background so that we can understand what we need to understand in order to be able to apply these things in our every day life.

So you can say that they're really three phases that people go through in their spiritual life, and most people stay stuck for a long, long time in the first stage, which is really the gathering of information. And that's where you find intellectual concepts and theology. And they're important but they will not satisfy any of us; they will not make any of us happy.

Eventually what you have to do is you have to get up onto the next phase of your spiritual life, which is application. And that's really the most important phase, because what you do, is you take everything you've learned, everything that you know, and now you actually apply it, to every situation that comes up in your every day life. Whatever's there, in front of your face, on any given day.

And what that does, eventually, if you do it, (and that's kind of like a rule; you have to do it.) What that eventually leads to is experience. And experience is what will really make us happy.

A Course in Miracles says,
  "Words are but symbols of symbols."

They're twice removed from reality. And when you think about it, how is a symbol ever gonna make us feel whole and complete? How is a symbol ever gonna make us happy? It can't because it's just a symbol. What *will* make us happy is not a symbol of reality but an experience *of* reality. It's that experience of where we really are, that we never really left home, and that we're still there right now.

That experience of being one with our Source, of being one with God or whatever you want to call it; that experience is the great mystical experience that all the great mystics of history have reported. And once you experience that, that is the answer to all of our questions and it's the only answer that will ever really satisfy us.

As we said, words can't do it. But the experience of where we really are so blows away anything that this world has to offer, that after that, everything here is kind of like chicken crap compared to what's available. Because once you experience it, you know that that's the Truth and that has to be where we really belong and what we really are.

So the goal of a good spiritual discipline like *A Course in Miracles* is to lead to that experience.

At one point in the *Course*, Jesus, who is the teacher in the *Course*, makes a pretty amazing statement. He's talking about all these questions that we have and all these dilemmas that we have, and at one point He says,

"There is no answer. Only experience. Seek only this and do not let theology delay you."

So it's really that experience that *A Course in Miracles* is directed toward, and that experience that my teachers in the book, *The Disappearance of the Universe* were directing me toward. And I'll tell you more about my teachers because I'm not the teacher in the book. I'm just a student. And there's nothing special about me and I feel very lucky to be able to pass these teachings along. And I'm not any better or different or more special than anybody else, and I'm having a great time being able to pass along what was given to me.

But I just wanted to finish up with the dream analogy by pointing out that when you awaken from a dream, the dream disappears. And when you awaken from a dream of time and space, there is no more time and space. So that means there are no other people that you have to hang around with for a million years, waiting for to wake up, because they're already there.

Because when you awaken, you're awakening from something that is partial and something that is divided to something that is whole and full and complete. In fact, the word holy comes from the word whole. And by definition, if it is whole then it is one and in that oneness nothing can be left out. Nothing can be missing. Nothing can be lacking.

In fact *A Course in Miracles* says that a sense of separation from God is the only lack you really need correct. And all these other problems and lacks that we have in our lives are actually substitutes for the one real problem. And we'll explain it as we go along on why that's the case and how it happened and how it appeared that we got here, on planet Earth, living this life that we think that we're living, thinking that we're bodies.

And we'll explain how that experience actually came about and then we'll explain how we can have a different experience, an experience of awakening to what we really are, and where we really belong.

But that's certainly not the entire teaching. In fact the idea that the world is an illusion, by itself, will not really do you a lot of good. That's just one piece of the puzzle. It's an important piece but it's not the whole thing. And if you leave it there, if we just teach that the world is an illusion, that by itself will not bring any happiness or peace to anybody.

We'll see as we go along, that there is **a certain kind of forgiveness** which is not the same as the way the world usually thinks about forgiveness. This is the kind of forgiveness that was actually practiced by great Masters like Buddha and Jesus, and it involves total non-judgment. But there's even more than that. There's kind of like a particular way of looking at things and looking at people that comprises this kind of forgiveness. And that kind of forgiveness actually leads to the end of reincarnation.

And I think that all of us sense it at some point in our lives, that maybe something here is missing; there's something amiss here. And that's because there *is* something missing here. And what is missing here is Spirit. But Spirit is not the old-fashioned kind of spirit. It's not the way we normally think about it. In fact, most of the things we're going to be talking about today are not the old-fashioned way.

We're going to talk about forgiveness, but it's not the old-fashioned kind of forgiveness. We're gonna talk about healing and we're gonna talk about Spirit, but it's not the old-fashioned definition of Spirit. This is a whole new ballgame.

What we're going to be talking about is not your parent's spirituality. This is something that is not based on the old way of thinking. It's not based on Newtonian physics where you have a subject and an object that are separate from each other, and they're both empirically real and exist apart from each other. What we're going to be talking about today would be more in line with Quantum Physics which would teach that there's not really any such thing as separation. That that's just an illusion. That everything is one, everything is connected, and you can't really separate one thing out from everything else.

I'll give you an example of the old-fashioned kind of forgiveness.
Alright. The old-fashioned kind of forgiveness, being based on separation and Newtonian physics would say,
'Well, OK. You really did it and you're guilty and it's your fault. And it's not my fault, but I'm gonna forgive you because, well, I'm better than you, and
You know, I've got Jesus and you don't, but I'm kinda like spiritually sophisticated so I'm gonna, you know, forgive you.
I'm gonna let you off the hook.
You're still going to hell, but I'm gonna forgive you and then maybe some day if you agree with me about everything and you think the same way as I do about everything and *maybe* if you if you subscribe to my religion, then *maybe* you can go to Heaven too, but I doubt it.'

That's kind of like the old-fashioned kind of forgiveness because it makes separates real and it makes subjects and objects real, and we'll see as we go along that it also makes sin real, bodies real; ideas like guilt and fear. It holds those kinds of things in place and actually perpetuates them.

The new kind of forgiveness is not like that. The new kind of forgiveness recognizines that there is no separation between anything and so, you'll find, astonishingly, that when you forgive somebody else, with this new kind of forgiveness, that the one who is really being forgiven is you. And the one who is really gonna benefit is **you**.

And that's kinda cool, because in a way it actually encourages you to do it because as you go along you realize that you're the one who's getting the benefits from it.

But we need a little bit more of a discussion to really explain why that's the case. So I'd like to being by telling you a little bit more about me.
I was born in Salem, Massachusetts. (Don't read anything into that.) There were no witches in Salem three-hundred years ago. They all moved there in the seventies, and it's a really good tourist thing now.

But three-hundred years ago, what happened in Salem, as my teachers pointed out in the book, the said that, that was a classic example of the projection of unconscious guilt. And we're actually going to see as we go along, why that's the case.

But in a nutshell somebody else has to be found who has to be the problem. Somebody else has to be found who is to blame for the situation. And that's what projection really is. It's not my fault, it's your fault. You're the guilty party, and if we look throughout the world we can see it at work all the time. We can see it at work in individual relationships. We can see it at work in international relationships. It's always somebody else who is the problem. It's always somebody else's fault.

You know, so the terrorists know that we are the cause of their problems, and that we deserve to die, and we know that the terrorists are the cause of our problems, and the democrats know that the republicans are the cause of the problem and the republicans know that the democrats are the cause of the problem, and the democrats don't know that if they don't forgive the republicans in this lifetime, they're gonna *be* republicans.

So it's like you have this whole shifting of the blame going on from the moment that we're born to moment that we die. And there's a reason for that. There's a very important reason why people feel compelled to have that kind of projection of blame and guilt in their lives.

But to get back to my story; I was born in Salem and my mother was a virgin. (She just wasn't very good at it.) And I was born with scoliosis. I was born two months premature, which was unusual for someone like that to live because I was less than three pounds. And back in those days, babies who were that small they didn't live very often so they just kind of like stuck me in a corner and said, you know, 'good luck kid.'

I had this scoliosis and I didn't find out about that severe curvature of the spine until I was thirty-one years old. We didn't have much money then. We were poor and didn't have heath insurance and back in those days people who didn't have any money or didn't have health insurance, they didn't get very good health care.
    And it's nice to see that things don't change.

Eventually when I was thirty-one years old, I found out that I had this scoliosis and it explained a lot to me because I remembered that it made a lot of things make sence. Like, when I was a teen ager I would sit there and in front of the TV watching it and I'd just be kind of bla. And I was depressed, not that anybody cared back in those days---I mean, you know, they'd say,
    "What do you mean, depressed? What are you talking about? Get a job."

But now-a-days everybody's depressed. And everybody's on medication. It's very much a part of our culture, because back then nobody cared about depression.

I would see all of my friends going out, maybe getting jobs and they be having a good time and they'd be getting girls. You know, I'd be sitting there, doig nothing, missing out on everything...just kinds like bla. And my parents were very worried about me, and they made me feel different, and made me feel like maybe I didn't fit in. And that's right up the ego's alley. (We'll be explaining what the ego is as we go along too.)

But the ego wants us to feel different, it wants us to feel guilty, it wants us to feel bad, it wants us to feel left out in some way, and I did. I certainly did, and fortunately for me I was very lucky, because when I was a teen ager this musical group came over from England. They we called The Beatles. And I remember going into a music store, when I was a teen ager and somebody put on a record.

I know that they don't have records anymore, but they let you put on records back in those days and listen to some of the music. And somebody put on a record by the Beatles and I heard this guitar work by George Harrison. He was my first false idol. And I heard this guitar work and it sent shivers up and down my spine. And when I heard that, I knew what I wanted to do. I knew what I was gonna be. I knew I was gonna be a guitar player.

And actually, I did become a guitar player. And I became a pretty good guitar player. I wasn't great, because to be great at anything you have to have a lot of drive and ambition and energy and put a lot into it. And I didn't have that, but I did have some good musical talent and I was able to make myself sound good, and eventually I became a successful professional guitar player.

But when it came time to graduate from high school I had kind of like a dilemma because I didn't want to go into college, I hated school. I couldn't understand how they could make such fascinating subjects boring. But they did, and I didn't really wanna go to college. And at the same time, there was this thing going on called the War in Viet Nam, and I really didn't want to go to Viet Nam.
I understand that this situation today is very bad in the international arena, but back then there were like 100 men getting killed every week in Viet Nam. That doesn't even count the ten times that many who were getting wounded and maimed, (it's like they forget about them.)

So I wasn't into that and at the same time, I didn't have any big political convictions, I just wanted to play my guitar. And fortunately for me, this guy became president of the United States. His name was Richard Nixon and I hated him. But he did for me one of the biggest favors that anybody's ever done, he switched over to to this thing called the *draft lottery system.*

Now, people now-a-days, they don't have to worry about that; although you never know, they could always bring it back if they wanted to. But the way the draft lottery system works is they draw your birthday, like it's the lottery, and they have a drawing for your year, and if your birthday comes up in the first 122 dates drawn or so, say in that top one third, then you're getting drafted. But if it comes up in like in the middle one third, say from 122 to 244, it's kinda ify. You can't be sure. But if you come up in the bottom one third, like from 244 to 366 then you have like no chance of getting drafted.

So I'm praying…the old-fashioned way…(and we're gonna practice the new fashioned way in a while,) …but I'm praying the old-fashioned way.
I'm praying,
   "Please God, please have my number come up near 300 or so, so I don't have to worry about getting drafted."

So they had the lottery drawing for my year, and they drew my birthday, which is March the 6th, they drew it and my number came up 296. And because of that, I was free. I didn't have to worry any more about being drafted and I didn't have to go to college and get a deferment, you know, which would have kept me out of the draft, and I didn't have to worry about any of that.

I was free to just play my guitar and have a good time and live happily ever after. Right? Well, that's not the way that things work in this world. In fact if you solve a problem in this world, then what happens is, you get another problem. That's the way it's set up from the moment that we're born 'till the moment that we die. We will be faced with an endless series of problems.

And the reason for that is, so that our mind will be distracted 'out there' onto the screen. And we will keep our attention focused *out there*, in the world. And the reason for this is, so that we won't look where the real answer is, **which is within** and within the mind.

So, we're kind of like set up to have our attention focused out there and we think the answers are out there. It's like they used to say on the X Files.
'The truth is out there.' Except the problem is, the truth is *not* out there. What's out there is just a smoke screen.

An analogy I always use, because you know, those of you who have read my book, you know that I like to go to the movies. In fact that's my hobby. I love to go to the movies. And when I go to the movies, I want to forget that it's not real. So I go into the movies, and I forget that it's not real and my attention is diverted to the screen, and I start to react to the screen and I start to get into it. I actually talk to the screen or something, because I get into the story so much that I forget that there's not really anything important going on the screen. That where the movie is really coming from is hidden and there's this projector in the back of the theater and I'm not supposed to think about that.

I'm supposed to forget about that. And what I'm seeing is coming from this projector but it's hidden from me.

And if I really want to change what's on the screen, if I really want to have an impact instead of messing around with the screen, which is just an effect...what I really have to do is go back to the cause.

And the cause is this projector, but the projector is hidden. But if I could change what was *in the projector* then that would change everything else.
Because now I'd be going to where a real impact could be made, which is in the projector instead of just fooling around with the screen. Which, even if I could change what was on the screen it would just be temporary. It would just be a temporary fix at most and it wouldn't have any lasting impact.

But if I could go back and get inside the projector and change what's there, I could have a lasting impact on what's on the screen. And that's the difference between fooling around with the effect, which is what all of us do, almost all of our lives, and most people never really get into the projector, and be able to have this kind of lasting change which is a permanent change because now you're going back to the cause. And one of the themes that we're gonna have in our talk here is that it's very important to deal with the cause instead of the effect.

In fact, *A Course In Miracles* says that this is a course in cause and not effect. And it's very important to be able to get back to where there's real power, which is in the cause instead of the effect.

And another one of the things which we've already mentioned is that it's very important to seek spiritual experience rather than staying stuck in intellectual concepts. And the way to get to experience is trough the application of what you know.

And on that note I might add, that it's very important, because of that, to find a good spiritual discipline that you cn stick with for a while. And it doesn't really matter what it is. It could be Buddhism, it could be of lot of things, it could be *A Course In Miracles*. But Buddhism and *A Course In Miracles* are really good spiritual training systems. And what they do is that they train the mind to think along a different line.

And that's absolutely vital because right now, the mind judges automatically. It's like a machine. People don't realize how mechanical their thinking is and how automatic their judgement is. The mind is very much like a survival machine, run by the ego and what *A Course In Miracles* wants to do is actually take the mind and retrain it, all the way from the point of where it judges automatically to a condition to where it will forgive automatically.

And that's not just a little change.
   But in order to accomplish something like that, you have to train the mind and have some kind of a spiritual system that you can actually stay with for a long time. That's why *A Course In Miracles* says that,
   "An untrained mind can accomplish nothing."

So it's very important of it to have something that can train the mind to that level of accomplishment so that you can actually change the way that you look at everything in the world.
   So, for my next problem in my life what I cooked up was that I started to drink. And then I started to drink some more. And then I started to smoke a lot of grass. And that pretty much covers the 1970's.

And I knew that that wasn't a good thing, and I knew that I wasn't being a 'good boy,' that that wasn't working for me. I really didn't know what to do about it. I was not religious. What I did, eventually though, in the late 1970's, as a way of finding some way to deal with this drinking thing, was that I decided that I was gonna become a *Born Again Christian*.

 And actually, *I did* become a *Born Again Christian*. And it wore off after a little while , then I tried it again a couple of times in the late 1970's. The good thing about that was that I got to read the Bible. And that was really very interesting, that experience of reading the Bible. But there were problems with it.
   You know, I found things in the Bible that I could agree with. Like it would say things like, 'God is love.' You know, that made sense to me. At one point the Bible says that God is perfect love and that made perfect sense to me.

The only problem is that you look someplace else in the bible and He's like a killer. He's getting even with people and He's got all this stuff going on, all this wrathful vengeful stuff and I couldn't reconcile that. It didn't make any sence to me. How could God be perfect love on one day and be like a killer the next day? So it like almost depended on what kind of mood He was in.

And so I couldn't really stick with that. I couldn't stay with organized religion, it just didn't make sense to me. But I did notice that when I read the words of Jesus in the Bible, stuff like The Sermon on the Mount, and all the stuff about love and forgiveness, that that rang true for me. And it's more than that that, as I said, it wasn't a religious thing, it was a personal thing. *It was like I felt like I knew Him.* And, you know, I felt like there was some kind of connection.

I didn't know what it was but I felt like I was His friend and that I could count on Him and that I could talk to Him and that He would like help me. And I never really understood why until it was explained to me much later. But I always felt like I was His friend and that I could depend on Him and I could talk to Him. And even though I didn't stick with organized religion, I never gave up on that relationship that I felt with Jesus. Si I always stayed with that and the magnitudue of it would be revealed toe as I went along in my spiritual life.

And fortunately for me, (because I went back to drinking) fortunately for me what happened was this thing came over from California to the Boston area. It was called the EST Training. And I did this thing called The EST Training, and it turned out to be a very powerful experience in my life. And there were a lot of similar ideas in EST that you would find in A Course In Miracles. Because it's very much about taking responsibility for your life.

There's this famous workbook lesson in *A Course In Miracles* that says,
  "*I am not a victim of the world I see.*" And that's an idea that you would find also in EST. And EST does not exist any more but it was a very powerful experience for me at that time. And that was also when
I had what I would describe as my first 'mystical' type experience. I remember that they put me up on the stage in front of the audience and you're supposed to look out at the audience. And when I looked out at the audience, all these people, it was like they were moving in slow motion. It was like they looked different. They were moving kind of like in a herky-jerky manner. And the experience that I had that's associated with that, (because when you have these kinds of experiences you also have an intuition as to that they mean.) And when I saw that, it was like *I* was the one who was doing that.

It was like now, time and space were not something that was being done *to* me. It was something that was being done *by* me. It was like it was coming *from* me instead of *at* me. It was like I was the cause of it now, instead of being at the effect. And that experience didn't last too long, but it was the first of what turned out to be an endless series of mystical experiences, usually very visual, in my life and they would continue to this very day, all these years.

I remember in the 1980's when I would go to bed at night and close my eyes, it would be almost like watching a movie. I would see like whole scenes presented to me, in color, sometimes even with sound. And it was like I was watching events that occurred in previous lifetimes that I'd had and sometimes I would even be able to connect the person that I was seeing in this movie with people who exist today in my everyday life. You know, I wasn't asleep, all I had to do is close my eyes. And also in the morning when I was awake, I'd kinda lay there in bed with my eyes closed and see these movies. And I would have all kinds of visual experiences that got stronger and stronger as they went along.

And I found that after I did the EST training and took responsibility for my life, that something shifted in my unconscious mind. I didn't really understand it at the time, but I do know that almost all the mind is hidden from us. It's like what we see with the body's eyes; we look out with the body's eyes and we see the tiny tip of the iceberg. It's a very small part of the mind. And almost all the mind is like the rest of the iceberg and it's hidden underneath the surface, and we can't see it, and we're not aware of it, and that's really what runs us.

And we don't know it, and we're not in touch with it, but that's where the real decisions are made that have a real impact. And when I did the EST Training, I made some kind of some kind of a decision at that level, the level of the unconscious mind, which is where the cause is, which is where you can have the real impact, and after that I became almost the opposite of myself. I went from somebody who drank a lot to somebody who didn't drink at all; I went from from a musician who hardly ever worked to being a musician who worked all the time.

I started a band with this friend of mine who also did the EST training and before you knew it, within a couple of years we were working like six nights a week, twice a day on weekends. And I didn't have too many experiences in the 1970's. In the 1980's I made up for it. I lived like almost two decades in one. And I was doing all kinds of things. I was riding in hot air balloons, and I was walking on hot coals, and I was jumping out of airplanes, (you know, with a parachute.)

I was doing all these things, and I met a girl named Karen and got married. She was my type,…female, you know, we had this relationship. Eventually it turned out that we became each other's best forgiveness lesson, and that happens in many relationships. And there's a good reason for it, and it's all set up ahead of time, and everything that happenes here is something we agreed would happen before we ever appeared to arrive here.

And the real question is, *'how are we going to look at it?'*

What are you going to do with it? Because it's gonna happen anyway. But how you look at it will completely change your experience of it, and that's where real freedom lies. Not so much in trying to fix what happens or what's going to happen.

Where true freedom lies is in the way that you look at it And if you look at it in a certain way, then there's a way to achieve the kind of inner peace: what the Bible describes and what *A Course In Miracles* describes of this,

"*A Peace of God which passeth understanding.*"

And that kind of peace is not dependant on certain circumstances. It's not dependant on what appears to happen in the world. In fact, you can have this kind of peace *regardless* of what appears to be happening in the world. And that's *real* peace. Because it's something that can't be shaken by anything in this world.

And that's really what a guy like Jesus was talking about, 2000 years ago when He talked about building your house upon the rock instead of on the sand. The sand is the shifting sands of time, the sands of *this* world, what the Buddhists would call, *impermanence,* something that literally cannot be depended on. The only thing that we can depend on in this world, is that it's gonna change. You know, that one minute from now, it's not goona be the same as it is now. You can't depend on that.

And the rock is what we really are, which is Spirit.

But this kind of Spirit, once again, isn't the old-fashioned idea of spirit, because that old-fashioned idea of spirit is still a separation idea.

People imagine that when they lay their body aside they go on as something. And this something that they go on as looks suspiciously like the body that they just left. So it's almost no different than the idea of having a body. You know, it's just a different *kind* of body. And that's not what real Spirit is.

Real Spirit is actually perfect oneness. It's something that is indivisible; it's something that is whole and one and complete. In fact, the word holy comes from the word whole, and with that being the case, this kind of Spirit would be immortal, it's invulnerable, it's something that can't be touched by anything in this world. It's something that can't be threatened.

In fact, in that famous introduction in *A Course In Miracles*, Jesus says, *"Nothing real can be threatened."*

Well, what that is, is Spirit. But this kind of Spirit is something that is literally invulnerable. And when you get in touch with that, you realize that you can't be hurt because you're not a body.

And so, when that introduction says," *Nothing unreal exists*," that would include the body or anything that is not perfect oneness; which certainly narrows it down.

And then it says, "*Herein lies the Peace of God*." And so, we're actually gonna talk about a way of attaining this Peace and getting in touch with what we really are, instead of what we thought we were.

So in the 1980's I was having a lot of really good experiences. And I was having a really good time for a few years and I started making money, and people knew who I was and it felt good and my family didn't I was a jerk anymore, and things were going, you know, pretty cool. But after a few years, I'd say by 1987 or so, I was really shocked to find out that, *that* wasn't making me happy either.

So now I had another problem. Because *not* doing anything, that didn't make me happy and now doing everything, it turned out, *that* didn't make me happy either. So I figured, what on Earth am I going to do? If neither one makes me happy…

And then I made another decision.

I decided that I was gonna change my life again. And I felt that I was supposed to do something else, not that there was anything wrong with being a musician, in fact, it's really interesting, the number of guitar players who I met since I turned my life completely to spirituality. And I found that being a musician is a very good place to be coming from if you wanted to become involved with spirituality. The two seemed to go hand in hand because there's that artistic aspect to it.

And I decided in 1987, I was gonna change my life again and I was gonna do something different. And that somehow I felt it would be connected to this relationship that I still felt with Jesus. But I couldn't put my finger on it, once again. I didn't know what form that relationship was going to take, but I felt that somehow there was a connection and that I needed to get someplace that was quiet. You know, I needed to get someplace where I could think. And by then I had the band booked two years in advance, so it took me a couple years to get out of the band that I was in. But by the beginning of 1990 I was moving to Maine.

And Maine isn't that far from Massachusetts. It's only a hundred miles between where I live now and where I lived before, but it's a completely different world. Maine is very quiet, very peaceful, has clean air, clean water. There are no big cities in Maine at all. It has the lowest crime rate in America, very peaceful. If you wanna get to a place to think and have peace and quiet, well that's the place to go.

And I got up to Maine and I had kinda like this vague idea that I would start a business and support myself. And I get up there to Palspring Maine and there are like, no people. In town there's like no sidewalks. Maybe I shoulda done more research but the business thing didn't go too well. But what did go really well was that I felt that I started to get really good at meditating. Now I had experimented with meditation in the 1980's and I remember part of my spiritual life was like..I didn't read too much, I'm sorry to say, but I did read a book in the 1980's by Shirley Mclaine called *Out on a Limb*.

And when I read some of the things in there, like stuff like Buddhism and Daoism and Hinduism and all these ism's, I realized that I already knew this stuff. And the reason that I knew it (she was also writing about reincarnation) and I realized that the reason I already knew these things is because I'd already studied them in previous lifetimes, and they we just coming back to me when I was reminded of them. They would come back into my awareness, and one of the things that was connected with *that*, was that I'd experimented with meditation.

And I felt like I was getting pretty good at it. I didn't study it very much, I just kinds made up what I thought was my own kind of meditation. And then, when I finally got up to Maine in the early 1990's I had plenty of time on my hands,

Nd so I felt like I could practice my meditation and eventually I started to get really good at it. And when I did, I felt like I was getting to the point where I could achieve absolute stillness. It was like, when I got to that point, there were no thoughts interfering at all. It was like I could shut them off and when I did, I was achieving absolute stillness. And when that happened, I felt like I was getting in touch with something deep, that deeper aspect of the mind that I was talking about.

Because the conscious mind is really just a trick. That tip of the iceberg. It's kind of like the way Albert Einstein described it; Einstein said,
> *"That a person's experience is kind of like an optical delusion of consciousness."*
And that's what we're seeing. What we're seeing is a delusion. It's a trick, and we think that it's real.

Just like when we go to the movies, we think that what's upon the screen is real and we don't realize that it's coming from a place that's hidden. And in thi life, it's actually our own unconscious mind that is projecting the images that we are seeing. And then we accept them as reality, and we don't realize that *reality* is not at all what we think it is.

And so, when I started to get in touch with this deeper aspect of the mind, in Maine, I felt like the magnitude of it was very impressive. I felt like I was getting in touch with something *big*. I didn't really understand it, bt it was exciting to me and I felt like it was important and everything else in my life was going to hell…

My personal life was in a shambles. I wasn't making any money. My wife was threatening to leave me, but the meditation thing was going really good. So I kept doing that and I remember when I was up there in Maine, for almost three years now, (this was 1992) things were so bad for me financially that I decided that maybe I should go back to playing my guitar to make some money, because I was good at making money with my guitar.

And I took my guitar out of the closet, (I had this Les Paul custom guitar which I still have to this day) and I took it out of the closet and I started to practice, because I decided I had to make some money here. I had to get out there and start playing my guitar.

And I'm practicing, and both of my hands are occupied while I'm playing the guitar, and then all of a sudden, I'm standing there playing the guitar, and I feel this other hand. But this hand, which I couldn't see, was pushing down on the end of the guitar. And it was pushing th guitar down to the ground and me along with it. And I felt myself being pushed down by this hand that I couldn't see and it was an astonishing experience.

And I got the message. And the message was very clear to me. It was "**No.**

That's not what you're supposed to do anymore."
You know, you've already done that. Kinda like, been there done that, and you're supposed to do something else. There's something else waiting for you and my experience was, yeah…it will be revealed to me.

I didn't know what it is, I couldn't put my finger on the form it's gonna take, but I could tell that the message is, '*No, you're not supposed to play your guitar anymore. There's something else for you.*'

And it was two months later. I remember the date. It was December the 21st
2001 and I was sitting there in that same living room in Palspring Maine and I was in one of my meditations. And I came out of my meditation and I looked over at my living room couch. And there, were two people sitting there on my living room couch. There was like this beautiful, wonderful, exquisite looking woman who was sitting there…and some guy.

And the woman started to speak to me. And I started to speak back to her.

People have asked me '*Why didn't you go running out of the room screaming when this happened?*'
And there are a couple of reasons, not the least of which is the fact that they looked extraordinarily peaceful. In fact, if you could see the look on their faces and get their attitude, which is what spiritual sight really is, that's where is shows up, in your attitude; and if you could hear the tone of their voices, there was nothing about them that would inspire anything except for peace. *They had this wonderful, peaceful way about them.* So, fear didn't really seem like an appropriate response to them.

Looking back on it with hind sight (we all know that hind sight has 20-20 vision) and looking back on it with hind sight, I would say that another reason why I wasn't afraid of them was because in my unconscious mind I must have already known who they were. Because, it was explained to me later, that I had this relationship with them and that we had known each other at times before. But I didn't relize it at the time, I just realized that there was this incredible phenomena where all of a sudden, these two people were there on my living room couch. And I knew that they must have appeared from out of nowhere because the doors were locked.

I didn't see them appear the first time, but I did see them disappear the first time. And when they disappeared, it was like instantaneous. It was like, say you're watching TV and you had a remote control and you pointed the remote control at the TV. You flicked the remote, the picture changes instantaneously. That's what it was like when they disappeared that first time. And also, I saw them appear every time *after* that and they would appear instantaneously. It was almost like they were changing frequencies or vibrations or something. They appeared instantly out of nowhere and they would get right down to business.

And they would start talking. And I got used to it eventually, but this first time it was really kind of weird, you know, because I felt like they must have materialized out of nowhere. And here's this beautiful woman talking to me and I'm just kinda like automatically starting talking back to her. And then they would seem normal for a while, (and that was strange too, how normal it would seem,) you know, they appeared as bodies.

And they were just as real as any other body that I've ever seen. And I think the reason they appeared to me as humans was because they wanted the conversations that we would have, to *be* human. You see, a lot of the spiritual messages that we get, a lot of the teachings that we get are channeled. They seem to come from up above somewhere. They seem a little bit removed from our every day life. But these two guys, it was like, they were *right there in my face*. You know, and they spoke in my language and they put things in a way to me that I couldn't get away from.

They were so clear and they were so direct, there was just no escaping the message that they were trying to give me. And I thik that they knew that if I could understand them and if I could eventually apply what they were saying in my every day life, then probably other people could too.

They probably figured that if I could do, (you know, it's kinda like the guinea pig) then anybody could do it. And they would give me all this information and that first time it felt kind of strange, and I was a little nervous and when I became nervous I became kind of like a smart ass. You know, that's my defense. That's how I protect myself. I become kinda like a wise guy and I would give them these, you know, kinda like smart-ass comments and they would give it right back to me. They would take everything that I did and everything in the world and turn it around and use it as some kind of teaching tool. And in this case, it would eventually teach me that I really didn't need to be that way and I really didn't need that kind of defense. But it took me a while to catch on to that.

So that first time she would talk to me and I would talk back with her and it would seem normal for a while, then after about five minutes I'd think,   *"Jesus Christ. These people just materialized out of thin air!"*
And then it would seem weird. But then I'd go back and I'd start talking to them again and they'd go on and on. And they'd talk nice and normal, and then after a few more minutes I'd think,
"Jesus Christ. These people just materialized out of thin air!"

And, you know, it would go back and forth like that, and that's the way it was the first time. And eventually I got used to them and I started to feel like they were my friends. And they had a lot to say.

And not the least of which was that the woman there, Pursah, 2,000 years ago, she was Thomas, now known as Saint Thomas and also known as the author of the famous *Gospel of Thomas*.

Now, for those of you who don't know, *The Gospel of Thomas* is the first Gospel that was ever written about Jesus. And the church managed to destroy it. In fact, *The Gospel of Thomas* disappeared from the face of the Earth for like sixteen-hundred years, and it wasn't seen by anybody for that whole time.

And interestingly enough, and fortunately, somebody had the presence of mind to bury a copy of The Gospel of Thomas in Egypt, in a place called Nag Hammadi around 325 AD.

And it's not an original copy and it's not in the original language, and it lso contains some sayings that were added on later. So it's not a totally authentic copy but it is the only copy that we have and it was dug up in 1945 in Egypt and it took a while to be translated.
And when the church heard about it, they said,
"Oh..You can't pay any attention to that. It's spurious and it's a forgery and you can't pay any attention to that kind of stuff. It doesn't have anything to do with Jesus. It's all made up."

And they got away with that for a while. But fortunately after it was translated, biblical scholars started to study *The Gospel of Thomas*. You know, my teacher Pursah said, that about two-thirds of *The Gospel of Thomas* are authentic and about one-third were added onto them later.

And the biblical scholars started to look at those authentic sayings and they would say,

"Wait a minute. You know, this looks like the things that Jesus may have actually said back in that place and time. They're phrased in a much more realistic manner. The way that they're said, it seems more like that culture and that time. This could be original. This could be the way that Jesus really was back then."

And so, the biblical scholars were coming to a different way of looking at *The Gospel of Thomas* than the church. And according to Pursah, ***who was*** Saint Thomas 2,000 years ago, not only was it the first gospel that was ever written, but she even went out of her way to quote about 20 of those sayings that are in The Gospel and explained them to me.

Now, she said that these frst Gospels had no stories in them. That what we've come to think of as the mainstream gospels, with all these stories in them, those were made up later. And the first Gospels had no stories in them. They were simply a listing of things that Jesus actually said.

So the first ones were just recorded sayings of Jesus. And then, oh maybe twenty years after that, you had the apostle Paul come along and it was really his theology that's the basis of Christianity. What the apostle Paul did, you know, he felt very guilty because he persecuted Christians and he killed a lot of them and he felt very bad about that.

And he had this experience on the road to Damascus, which was part genuine and part out of the ego. And after that, he turned to Jesus and he made up this theology which was very much in keeping with his Jewish heritage, and the old idea that you can take an innocent and sacrifice him and somehow that atones for the sins of others. That's an idea that goes back a good 700 years *before* Jesus. And you can find it in the Book of Isaiah, and and it had nothing to do with Jesus. It's something the Paul took and kinda like super-imposed onto Jesus and now made Him the ultimate sacrifice and made Him atone "for everybody's sins." And it's that theology that became the basis of Christianity, not the teachings of Jesus, which you can still see somehow in *The Gospel of Thomas* and some of which did survive in the bible also.

And so, according to Pursha, people took what they believed and super-imposed it onto Jesus. And that's what always happens with great spiritual teachers. You know, **Jesus was not a Christian**. And for that matter, **Buddha was not a Buddhist**. You know, He was a Hindu. And then people come along later and they make up religions and it's kinda like they're adding their own beliefs to it, and making it more about *them* than about the original. And that's certainly what organized religion did with Jesus and what they came up with didn't have too much to do with what Jesus was realy talking about.

And one of the reasons that my teachers Arten and Pursah, as they called themselves, but they were really Saint Thomas 2,000 years ago, and Arten there, he was Saint Thadeus 2,000 years ago, one of the original deciples of Jesus, like Thomas, except Thadeus wasn't very famous. He wasn't very well known, and that was fine with him. He was just kinda like the quiet learner, which is cool.

And one of the reasons they appeared to me was that they said they wanted to set the record straight. Not only about their relationship with Jesus, but you know, what he was *really* about, what He was teaching. And to that end they gave me a vision of this guy whose name was Jesus; His name wasn't Jesus. In fact my teachers refused to call Him Jesus. His name was Jesuaha and if that had been translated well, then it would've been Jesusha with a 'J.' So Jesuaha would have been the right translation. Jesus was a bad translation, but everybody knows Him like that.

So my teachers decided that they would just call Him 'J' and that way, they could cover both. So they just referred to Him as 'J.' And according to them, the 'J' that they knew 2,000 years ago, was a Jewish Rabbi and because of that, He understood Jewish mysticism. He understood the kinds of things that we would see today, in the Cabala for example. One of the most basic ideas of Jewish mysticism would be the idea that Heaven is closeness to God and that hell is distance from God. But Jesus, being an uncompromising kind of a guy, didn't stop there. For Him, Heaven would be perfect oneness with God and hell wouldn't just be distance from God; hell would be anything that is separate from God.

And what that does is that it narrows it down to just two things. You see, we think that we have billions of things to choose between. But it turns out that there are really only two things to choose between and in Jesus' way of thinking, you either have perfect oneness with God, which is Heaven, or you have anything else. Anything that is separate from God would be hell.

It's interesting that people are always worried about the idea of going to hell, because they don't realize that they're already there. Anything that is not perfect oneness with God would be hell, as far as the way Jesuaha thought about it, and so that's a very basic idea of Jewish mysticism.

You see, Jesus was to Spirituality kinda like what Mozart was to music. When Mozart was born he already had everything that he needed and knew pretty much everything he needed to know. By the time he was three years old, he could play the piano. By the time he was six years old he could write symphonies and that was kind of what Jesus was to Spirituality. By the time He was twelve years old He was the One who was teaching in the temples. He was the One who was teaching other rabbi' everything.

Plus He was from the middle east. Most people now, you know, with western religion, they seem to think that Jesus was from Mississippi or something…and no…He was from the middle east and because of that His approach was much more mindful and eastern, and much more in line with that kind of a culture. And because of that He certainly would have understood the teachings of Buddhism.

And one of the basic teachings of Buddhism is that *there is only one* ego appearing as many. So what that means is, thet there's only one of us here. And you're it. There isn't anybody else. Not really. So there's only one of us that thinks that it's here and that's the Buddhist's concept of ego.

It's kind of like an all-encompassing idea that includes everybody and everything. It shouldn't be confused with Freud's concept of ego, but I think it's interesting that Freud didn't use the word ego. He used the word ish, the German word, which means 'I.' So to Freud's way of thinking, the ego was the concept of an individual identity.

And that's interesting because that's also a part of the Buddhist's idea of ego. So what the ego *is*, is it's one ego, appearing as many. So it's one all-encompassing being that thinks that it's here and thinks that it has some kind of an individual identity that is separate from God.

And Jesus understood that. And if that's true, if there's really only one ego appearing as many, then Jesus, being a pretty smart guy, realized something that probably nobody has ever realized in history. See, I remember…you know, I would go through life thinking it was very important what other people think about me. And a lot of us think that. You know, it's very important what other people think. And I used to think that if I could be successful and if I could make a name for myself and make a lot of money, then the world would look at me in a certain way and they would look up to me. And if I was successful and got the world to look up to me, then that would make me happy.

I thought maybe that would make me happy. And of course, that doesn't work and we all know it doesn't work, you know, if being rich and famous and successful made you happy, then Elvis would've been like the happiest guy who ever lived.

And it doesn't work, and the reason it doesn't work is because of something Jesus understood. He understood that if there's only one ego appearing as many, then first of all, *the unconscious mind must know that*. We may not realize that, but the unconscious mind does, because all we're doing is looking out and seeing Einstien's optical delusion. All we're seeing is separation out there. But the unconscious mind knows the truth. The unconscious mind, that part which is hidden from us, knows that there's really one of us. It knows that there's really only one ego appearing as many, because you can bury the Truth; yeah, you can keep it out of your awareness, but you can't ever loose it. It's still there. It's still there for the remembering.

So if the unconscious mind knows that there's really only one of us here, then what are we doing if we go through life judging and condemning other people? All we're really doing is sending a message directly into our own unconscious mind that we are being worthy of being judged and condemned. That we are guilty. That we are not worthy of being with God.

Whatever you're put out there is actually going right into your own unconscious mind. You may think that you're getting rid of it but you're not. Because there's not really anybody else out there. So the only one that you're really judging and condemning is yourself.

So Jesus understanding that, said
 "Wait a minute. It that's true, then what I'm gonna do, knowing everything that I know, I'm gonna go through life and I'm gonna see everybody, without exception, as being totally innocent. I'm gonna see everybody as being Christ. I'm gonna see everybody as being totally worthy of being with God. I'll see them as being Spirit, which is one with God."

Because once again, Jesus being a Jewish mystic understood the oneness of God and He used the old prayer of the God of Israel, *"The Lord our God is One,"* and He understood the whole concept of perfect oneness, and if it's perfect, then nobody can be left out.

Nobody can be excluded or else is isn't whole, and it's not complete. And He understood that if you partially forgive the world, which is what most people do, then you will only be partially forgiven. But if you completely forgive the world, as Jesus did, then you will be completely forgiven. Because it's always *you* who is being forgiven or judged by yourself. It just doesn't look that way.

And so, Jesus understood something that even to this very day, people still don't get. Even the quantum physicists with all of their advanced knowledge of science, even the new phycology with all of its knowledge. Most people still don't understand something that Jesus clearly understood.

And what He understood was, taking myself for example, the way that I would feel about myself and the way that I will experience myself is not determined by what you think about me. It's not determined by how you look at me. The way that I will really really feel about myself and the way that I will really experience myself is actually determined by *how I look at you*. And that's exactly opposite of the way that the world thinks.

But it's absolutely essential to understand that if you wanna make real progress with spirituality. Because now, by understanding that it's the way that you look at them, you are shifting to a condition of being at cause instead of effect. Now you're in charge. Now you're realizing that, *'Hey. This is all coming from me and I'm the one who made the whole thing up.'*
And we'll see as we get into the teaching of *A Course In Miracles* why that's the case, and why we made it up.

But it's very important to remember that it's how look about other people that will determine your own experience of yourself and ultimately, what you believe yourself to be. And you have to shift to being at cause. It's like when Buddha said, "*I am awake,*" that's what He meant. You know, He meant that he was totally at cause and realized that He was not one of these bodies in the dream. He was not one of these dream figures out there walking around, that He was the maker of the entire dream. And that it wasn't being done *to* him, it was being done *by* Him.

And it was from that condition of cause that He was able to undo the ego, that false identity that thinks that it is separate from its source and return to the source. And Jesus was able to do the same thing, and I think that if there's a difference between Buddha and Jesus I don't think that there's much, because what we have is not all the words of Buddha and we don't have all the words of Jesus and they both came to the same place at the end.

I think that one of the things that is a great contribution of the Jesus in *A Course In Miracles* is this wonderful, lofty vision of God that we're presented with. Because the *God of A Course In Miracles* really is perfect love. You know, a lot of religions have said that God is perfect love but *A Course in Miracles* gives us a God who really is perfect love, Who is flawless, Who is perfect, Who could not create anything that was not perfect or else He Himself wouldn't be perfect.

And so, this is a God that is totally above anything bad, anything divided or anything separate. And so Jesus said things in *The Gospel of Thomas*, He would say like, *"I am the one who comes from what is whole. I was given the things of My Father. Therefore I say, if one is whole, one would be filled with light, but if one is divided, one will be filled with darkness."*
And I think the moral of that is, you can't have it both ways. You can't be a litte bit whole. Your **allegiance** has to be undivided. You have to choose, in the way that you look at things, the way that Jesus did, either for perfect oneness or for delusion and separation.

And what you choose will determine your own experience of yourself, your own spiritual progress and eventually the undoing of the ego and awakening in God, where we're really been all along, but we just didn't understand that. And it's in doing that, it's in returning to a state of wholeness that it becomes possible to end reincarnation.

And what my teachers told me about, eventually was how to practice a certain kind of forgiveness, which is not the way the world usually thinks of forgiveness, in such a way that it actually leads to the end of reincarnation, leads you to the point where you don't have to come here any more as a body. And I know that a lot of people are interested in not coming back again, but I think that they have to realize that there's this thing in the mind that prevents us from ending reincarnation.

And as long as it's there in the unconscious mind, this unconscious guilt, that we don't even know about, as long as it's there, until it's completely healed, and removed by the Holy Spirit then we will always keep coming back here. So if we really wanna end reincarnation and not come back here any more, then we have to have healed this unconscious guilt that is in the mind. And the way for the Holy Spirit to heal it for us, is for us to do our part, and practice the kind of forgiveness that my teachers taught me, eventually, in the *Disappearance of the Universe*.

Some people are of the mistaken impression that when the body dies, then they leave the Earth. But no, all that happens is that they come back again until this unconscious guilt is healed. And that's why *A Course In Miracles* says, *"The world is not left by death but by Truth."*

So it's actually in learning the Truth and applying it, while we still appear to be in the body that we can eventually undo the ego completely, become whole again and awaken from the dream and achieve enlightenment. And my teachers told me exactly how to do that.

There's this line from *A Course In Miracles* that says, "*Into eternity where all is one, there crept a tiny mad idea at which the Son of God remembered not to laugh.*"
And I think part of the problem that holds everything in place, is that we take it so damned seriously. You know, we're afraid to laugh at things, and that seems to be true when it comes to spirituality too. People take their spirituality so seriously and they really don't have to.

Jesus, 2,000 years ago, He had a good sense of humor. My teachers said that he liked to bring out the joy in people and that He liked to laugh. And I'm glad that now-a-days you see a lot of drawings of Jesus, smiling and laughing. Most of the movies will give us this suffering, brooding kind of a Jesus, but you notice creeping in there, this different image of Jesus, of laughing and smiling and having a good time. And that's really what he was like. So, I'll tell you a joke that involves spirituality. In fact I heard this joke in New York City. This is definitely a New York joke.

This Buddhist is walking in Central Park, and he's walking along in Central Park minding his own business, and the Buddhist walks up to this hot dog vendor and he says to this hot dog vendor, "*Make me one with everything.*"

(Well, that's just the first part of the joke.)

Now what happens after that, is that the Buddhist gets his hot dog from the hot dog vendor and then the Buddhist asks for his change. But the hot dog vendor say, "*Ah! Change come from within.*"

So that's definitely a New York City joke.
I think that humor is important. My teachers used it a lot. I like to use it a lot in my talks and we don't have to take everything so seriously.

What happened eventually with my teachers in *The Disappearance of the Universe* was they gave me a lot of material, but eventually they worked into the teachings of *A Course In Miracles*. And there was a very important reason for that. According to them the voice that you find in *The Gospel of Thomas*, which they talked about a lot, because that was their experience 2,000 years ago, Thomas and Thadeus actually went off and started a sect based on Jesus and His teachings in *The Gospel of Thomas* and they visited many countries.

In fact, Thomas is still famous this very day in Syria and parts of Europe, and he went to India. The church tried to write Thomas out of history and they couldn't because he was too famous. So what they did instead, in the New Testament, was they just tried to make him look bad. You know, they tried to make him into the 'doubting Thomas' like he didn't have faith or stuff like that, but it's just kind of silly. Jesus and Thomas were very close and Thomas was the first and most well known teacher of Jesus and then history changed things as it went along.

But Arten and Pursah came to set the set the record straight. And they pointed out that the Jesus of *The Gospel of Thomas* was teaching that Heaven, which is our true home, is actually here right now. It's simply out of our awareness. It's something that we don't see.

In fact Jesus says in *The Gospel of Thomas*, the disciples come up to Him, and they say, *"When will the Kingdom come?"*
And Jesus says, *"It will not come by watching for it. It will not be said, behold here or behold there, rather the Kingdom of the Father is spread out upon the Earth and people do not see it."*
So, in other words, it's here. It's here right now but it's out of our awareness. It's something that we're not in touch with. It's actually our true reality.

And that is very much in harmony with what Jesus says in that, once again, famous introduction to *A Course In Miracles*. It says, *"This course does not aim to teach the meaning of Love for that is beyond what can be taught. It does aim, however, at removing the blocks to the awareness of Love's presence, which is our natural inheritance.*

Well, our natural inheritance is nothing less than the Kingdom of Heaven. That's all ours and it's what we deserve and it's where we belong. But it's out of our awareness and what we need to do now is to remove these blocks, these barriers we put in between ourselves and our awareness of our perfect oneness. In fact that *is* A Course In Miracle's deffinition of Heaven. It is the awareness of perfect oneness and the knowledge that there is nothing else, nothing else outside of this oneness, nothing else within.

And it's *that*, that we're going to get back in touch with by undoing the ego. And the best way to undo the ego and return to our awareness of what we really are, is through the great learning aid of the Holy Spirit, which is forgiveness. But once again, it's not the old-fashioned kind of forgiveness. This is a whole new ballgame. It's a whole new program.

So eventually my teachers started to talk about *A Course In Miracles* and gave me a very quick overview of the Course's metaphysics. And I kinda like, want to share some of that with you right now. Not because theology's important or metaphysics are important, but I think it's helpful to understand these kinds of things because it makes us understand what's being done for us every time we practice the kind of forgiveness that we're going to get into in just a little while.

Because the more we realize how great it is for us to do it, the more likely we are to do it. The more we realize how all these ideas fit together the more possible it will be for us to remember the Truth when the going gets tough. Because after you go out there in your every day life, certain things are gonna happen and the stuff is gonna hit the fan and you're gonna forget about all this. And you're not gonna want to do this. You're not going to want to forgive. And that happens for all of us. We get out there and things go crazy and we forget about all the Spiritual knowledge that we've gained and we fall right back into reacting along with the ego.

And the best way to overcome that eventually, and it takes practice, is to arm yourself with this knowledge so that it becomes so much a part of you, so much a part of your mind, that the day will come when, even when the stuff hits the fan, you don't react and you actually remember the Truth.

And my teachers said that *that's* the hardest part...is remembering the Truth. Once you know all of this, when the going gets tough, if you can actually remember it, then you're winning. Then you're more than half way home because that's the hardest part. And I think it helps us to remember when we understand how beneficial it is to us, to practice this kind of forgiveness.

And the kind of knowledge that I'm gonna share with you right now should help you to *remember to practice* this kind this kind of forgiveness. And it's really a Miracle.

It's really a wonderful and amazing thing that's going on because the Holy Spirtis taking care of the part of the job that we can't see. The Course teaches that *our* part is really very small. Now, I'm sure that *that's* an idea that's very annoying to the ego. That our part is really very small. Ut it's because as we said, that all that we see is this tny spec of time and space with the conscious mind, but the Holy Spirit can see everything.

The Holy Spirit can see the past, the present, the future, everything that ever happened, and every time that we practice the kind of forgiveness that Jesus did, because when Jesus forgave everybody in the world what He did, every time He practiced this kind of forgiveness, it was like He was actually rejoining with himself. He was going from a state of separation back to a condition of oneness and wholeness and sanity. Every time He practiced forgiveness He was undoing separation and the ego and actually returning to Holiness and wholeness and back to His home. And He knew that *it had to work*. That's the way that the mind works. These are like, the laws of the mind. **If you do this it has to work**.

The way *A Course in Miracles* puts it,
"That right-mindedness which is forgiveness, leads to one-mindedness which is the One-Mindedness of Spirit.
It leads to that automatically. The Course says,
"From there, the mind has no where else to go."

It's direction is always determined by the thought system to which it adheres. So, what we're talking about today are really two complete and mutually exclusive thought systems. One is the thought system of the Holy Spirit which leads us home and undoes separation and leads us back to that condition of wholeness and onenesss in our experience and in or awareness. The other is the thought system of the ego, which keeps us stuck here and will keep us stuck here forever.

And there's a reason that we have to undo that thought system of the ego if we want to break the cycle of birth and death. If we want to end reincarnation and really get back home again, then we have to do a certain kind of forgveness. Because if we don't then there is something there, in the unconscious mind, that we're not aware of, that will prevent us from ever breaking the cycle of birth and death. And these metaphysics that I'm about to give you will help to explain why.

End of Session One
Session Two

My teachers said, *"Before the beginning…"*
The Bible says *"In the beginning…"*

My teachers said, *"Before the beginning you have God. And that's all there is."*
And, as we said, Heaven is perfect awareness of perfect oneness and the idea that there is nothing else.

So it's just perfect oneness. And then God creates. But what God creates is exactly the same as Him. And, by the way, when we use the word *Him* to describe God or the Holy Spirit itself, that's just a metaphor. In Spirit *there is no such thing as male or female*. So when I say *He* to describe the Holy Spirit I could just as easily use the word *She* but that wouldn't be accurate either.

So, the reason why I use the word *He* is because *A Course in Miracles* uses biblical language. In fact it quotes over eight-hundred times from the King James version of the Bible and it keeps the language uniform throughout the Course. And it also uses a lot of Shakespearian blank verse and I think that you can look at the Course as an artistic work, so the language in it is kept consistant.

And so, that's what I do when I use the word *He* but it's with the understanding that once you get to Spirit there is no division. There are no opposites which we'll see why in just a second.

And so, you cannot have counterparts, you cannot have male and female in Spirit. *A Course in Miracles* says, *"The opposite of Love is fear."* But what is all encompassing can have no opposite. So once you get back to reality there are no opposites and there is no counterpart.

So, how do we get back there? And even more interestingly, how did we come to think that we were here in the first place? Because this is real in our experience. And I'm not here to deny our experience. Our experience is that we are here or else we wouldn't be experiencing that we are here.

So the Holy Spirit has to meet us where we think we are and lead us out of this from the condition that we presently find ourselves in. So, to point out where we came from, *A Course in Miracles* says that God and Heaven are perfect Oneness and when God creates in Heaven, what it is, is a simultaneous extension of the whole. *God does not create anything that is not exactly like Him.*

So if you have this kind of creation going on in Heaven that we really can't understand at this level because we have a finite human mind which is divided and severed and even though we can't understand it, we can still (believe it or not) *experience* this kind of Love and creation and what it's like to be with God I Heaven; we can even experience that right now, in this lifetime and see what it's like. And we'll talk a little bit more about that.

But we have God creating perfect Oneness in Heaven and there is nothing else. And then *A Course in Miracles* teaches, that as we said, "*Into eternity where all is One there crept a tiny mad idea.*" And that's all it ever was. It was just a tiny mad idea. It was not significant at all. It was like a blip on the screen. It was nothng. It was like what Joel Goldsmith called, "*A parenthasis in eternity.*" It was totally insignificant.

Today we think it was really important because we want what we made to be important. And so we magnify it and we make it big and we make it important when it's really nothing.

But what it was, was just an idea. Just a tin mad idea that happened. It was over with instantaneously. It's like Einstein said, " *Past, present and future all occur instantaneously and they all occur simultaneously.*"

So you have all these things going on at the same time but then we made something called *time* to make it look like they were happening at different times. So we took this one tiny instant of time and chopped it up into billions and billions of pieces. So now you have all these intervals of time and you have a past and you have a present and you have a future that appear to be happening separately from each other, but that's just symbolic of the thought of separation.

That's also true of space. In space it may *look* like one person is sitting over there and one person is sitting over here, but that's an illusion too. It's a separation idea. It makes one space different from another and separate from another. It's really all one, it's really all connected and a quantum physicist will tell you that. That even so much so that even *if I look at an object* I cause it to change instantaneously at the sub-atomic level.

Why is that? Why is it that if I look at a star that is twenty-billion light years away for example, I cause that to change instantaneously at the sub-atomic level? Well, the reason is because the star isn't really twenty-billion light years away. It's really in my mind, or more accurately, it's a projection *of* my mind. And it's symbolic of the thought of separation and the reason it changes instantaneously is because the whole idea of it being twenty-billion light years away is just made up. You know, the ideas like time, space, it's all made up and it's something that isn't real. It's something that just *appears* to be real.

And that's why the Buddhists were right when they called it an illusion and that's why the Hindus have been right for thousands of years when they called it an illusion and *A Course in Miracles* likens it to a dream.

And so, in this story that we're telling you about the mis-creation of the universe, what's happening is, soon as you have that tiny made idea it's very much like a dream. Because the events in it may *appear* to happen but they don't really happen.

And so, you have a tiny mad idea and that kind of tiny mad idea may be something like, *"Oh…you know, I wonder what it would be like if I went off and tried this on my own?"* That's a separation idea because it implies an individual identity. *"What would it be like if I went off and played on my own?"*

And what *that* does is it creates a different kind of experience. Up until now our experience has been one of perfect oneness. And it's an amazing experience. In that experience we are totally provided for, totally taken care of, there are no problems, there is no time, everything is perfect.

But now all of a sudden, you have a different experience. Because of this thought of individuality and separation you now have a new experience which we will call consciousness.

Now, we think that consciousness is something that's very important. You know, we're gonna raise our consciousness and we're gonna save the planet with our Christ consciousness…which is an oxymoron…because in order to *have* consciousness (it's really just an idea of separation) so you have to have more than one thing. You have to have a subject and an object. You have to have *something else* to be conscious *of*.

And that's why I think *A Course in Miracles* is the is the only spiritual teaching in the world that correctly identifies consciousness as the domain of the ego. It says that *consciousness was the first split introduced into the mind after the separation, making the mind a perceiver instead of a creator.*

So now you have something different going on than the kind of creation that never existed before. Now you have a subject *and* an object. Before, you just had God, but now you have you *and* God.

An you're divided and you feel separate and you feel all these things that never existed before. The very act of separation brings into possibility all kinds of ideas that never existed before but that *could not exist* if you did not have a separation followed by a subject and an object. So now you have you *and* God and you feel smaller and you feel divided and that's where the idea of scarcity comes from.

You can't have scarcity in perfect oneness. You can't have lack in fullness. You can't be missing anything if everything is whole and one and complete. But once you have a division or a separation, then you have what we'll call
two-ness instead of oneness and now you have all these other ideas that follow. And probably the first idea would be,
 "My goodness. What is this? I've done something wrong."

Because it's not full and whole and complete and it feels strange and it feels weird and it's a *new experience*. And it's because of the fact that we have separated ourselves that creates *two-ness* in which creates opposites. It's only in a *condition of separation* that you can have opposites! But now, in this condition of *two-ness* instead of oneness, you have the possibility of all kinds of opposites.

Not the least of which is that you would have *two separate ways* of looking at this idea of separation.
Remembering now, that this is *all new* to us and it's a totally different experience, and it's starting to be kind of like a terrible experience, kind of like a four year old who burns down the house. He didn't know what was gonna happen when he was playing with hose matches.

And then when he sees what happens he's frightened and he's very concerned and he's very upset about the whole thing because he didn't know what the effects was gonna be.

And so, we had this idea of separation, two possible ways of looking at it. We'll call one of the ways of looking at this idea of separation, *The Holy Spirit*. Keeping in mind that we feel kind of strange and weird because we feel smaller now and scarce and it's really not a good experience, and the Holy Spirit would probably come up to us and say:

"Hey. What's your problem? You know God. You know what He's like. What's He ever done for you except give you everything? You know all He ever wants is to love you. You know all you have to do is go home, no problem, say 'Hey, I'm back.' Everything's cool. It's all taken care of. Don't worry about it, just go home, everything's cool."

That's the kind of thing that The Holy Spirit would say to us and it's very much in harmony with Jesus' story of the prodigal son, which was actually a creation story. You know, the church took it later and made it out to be some kind of political story, but it was really a creation story.

You had this son who left his father's house, (notice that he wasn't kicked out; that's the garden of Eden myth)…we weren't kicked out of the Father's house, we left of our own free accord. We thought that we could do better. Just like in Jesus' story of the prodigal son. And the Son leaves the Father's house, thinks He can do better on His own but all He finds is scarcity, you know, all He finds is lack. Something like that can't possibly exist in fullness and wholeness.

And after a while He comes to Himself and He figures the only real meaningful answer to His problem is to return to His Father's house. So He starts going Home again, but He has all these weird ideas about Himself. You know, He thinks, *"Oh, I've sinned and I'm guilty and I'm no longer worthy to be called the Son of my Father, so maybe I'll go back home and I'll start off again as one of the hired servants. I'll start at the bottom and I'll work my way back up again."*

So, He's going home with that kind of an attitude, but when He's almost there, it's like God sees Him and runs to Him and throws His arms around Him and says, *"Oh! This is my Son who was dead and now He's alive again! He was lost and now He's found!"*

And He puts a robe around Him and treats Him like a king and throws a party for Him. That's what God is really like. He's not interested in all this, you know, wrathful, vengeful crap.All He wants us to do is go home, so he can love us. And Jesus knew that.

But in our condition of seeming separation from God we have all these weird ideas about ourselves. The Holy Spirit is trying to calm us down and says; *"Hey look. Nothing's really happened. You know, it's only a dream and all you have to do is go home."*

But now there's this *other* voice, because as we said, once you create *two-ness* you have opposites that couldn't have possibly existed before.

And we'll call this other way of looking at this idea of separation, the ego.

The ego has a totally different way of looking at this. It might come up to you in this kind of a massive metaphysical situation (which, remember we're not in touch with anymore, this is occurring on a metaphysical level.) The ego might come up to us and say,
"Hey. Do you know what you've done? You've separated yourself from God! You've taken everything that He gave you and He's given you everything, and you took it and threw it right into His face! And you said, 'Who the hell needs You?'

He's pissed! He's gonna get you! God is angry! And look at you, you're smaller now. You're divided. You're separated from Him. You haven't got a sucker's chance in hell against Him. He's gonna get you! You better get the hell out of here or it's gonna be worse than death!"

And even ideas like death could not have existed before this. You have to have opposites in order for an idea like scarcity and death to exist. And that's really why it says in the Book of Genisis, it says, *"That you shall not eat from the tree of knowledge of good and evil, for on the day that you eat of it you shall die."*
Well, good and evil are opposites. And once you have opposites then you have death.

You cannot have death in oneness and wholeness. You can only have the possibility of death when you have a separation and opposites.
Now you have a seeeming opposite to life. Instead of the eternal life of Heaven now you seem to have a death as a counterpart. But death cannot exist in Heaven or in eternal life. It can only exist in the seeming state of separation.

So the ego is giving us a totally different story and we feel terrible. The only feeling in this world that could match what that must have felt like, at that original instant of separation from God, is when somebody who is very close to you in your life dies. That's the only experience in this world that could match that.

And that's why, in the physiotherapy pamphlet which is an addendum to *A Course In Miracles*, Jesus is talking about all of the reasons that we cry in this world, and we have tears, and at one point Jesus says,
"And who could weep but for his innocence?"

Beause we may think that we're weeping because somebody we loved has died, but what we're really weeping about is that original instant of separation from God. And then, the death that we see in this world is simply symbolic of that one first original problem in which we thought that we were separate from God.

And that's why in the part in *A Course in Miracles* that is so beautiful is that under that system, there's really only one problem and there's really only one solution. And we'll see what it is.

But in this condition you know, this massive metaphysical seeming separation that's going on, we feel terrible and we're trying to find a way to cope with it and to perhaps escape from it.
And this is where the ego comes up with its plan.

Remember, that there are actually two things going on here; The *Holy Spirit* and *the ego*, and you're the one who has to choose between the two. So you can almost say that the mind has three parts.

The mind has the part that is you, or *thinks that it's you*, this idea of separation, and it's up to ou to choose between the two different ways of looking at this, the Holy Spirit or the ego. That has never changed.

And we didn't choose wi the Holy Spirit at that time but that doesn't matter either because that's just an illusion too. There is absolutely no difference whatsoever between choosing with the Holy Spirit then or choosing with the Holy Spirit right now. Because time itself is an illusion. And if you choose with the Holy Spirit now, you are choosing with the Holy Spirit for all time. And it doesn't matter what the date appears to be or what lifetime you appear to be living.

And so, now we have two ways of looking at this and we're kind of like leaning toward the ego and we're trying to find a way out of this, and the ego says,
"Hey. You know, maybe you should get out of here."

And we're thinking,
"Well, you know, how can I do that? There's no place where I can hide from God Himself."

And the ego says,
"Well, you know, that's not exactly true. You know, I have a place where we can go and if you come with me you'll never see God in this place. I mean, He won't even be able to get in. It's like He won't even exist in this place. You'll never see Him. You can escape from all this."

And we're thinking,
"You know, that sounds pretty good. I would like to get away from this. I feel absolutely terrible, but it sounds kind of final."

So this is where the ego has to come up with something to entice us. Something to kind of like make us come along for the ride, has to give us a reason to do this. So the ego comes up with a very tempting idea. The ego would say something like,
*"Well, you know, if you come with me **you** can be God. You can make up your own life. You can make up your own world. You can call the shots. You'll be the boss. You won't have to listen to God anymore. You can create your own existence, with your own life. You can be special!"*
Well, that sounds pretty tempting to us and considering how terrible we feel and considering that we're all new to this, and we don't know what the consequences of it are gonna be, we kind of like say yes to the ego.
"We'll go along with you. Let's get out of here."

And in that act of joining with the ego what happens is this massive denial and then this projection outward. And when you deny something, and you know, phycologists will tell you that when you deny something it has to go somewhere. You may think that you're getting rid of it but you're really not. It has to go somewhere.

So you deny it and it's projected outward and on this massive metaphysical level that causes what we call today, **The Big Bang**. *That is the making of the universe of time and space.*

So you have this massive denial, projection outward, and as *A Course in Miracles* teaches, *projection creates perception.*

So you have a couple of things going on there. First there's the denial itself, which seems to get rid of the problem, but remember, it doesn't really get rid of the problem, it only *seems* to get rid of the problem. Then, as I it is projected outward, it seems that the problem itself has been projected *outside* of us. In fact *even we* have been projected outside of us.

Because when we hold our hand up in front of our face and look at it, what is that? We think that that's us. But that's just a part of the same projection that everything else is. So we think that we're seeing this very special body in the mirror, when it's really no different than all these other bodies that we're seeing.

But we think it's us, so we think that it's important, and we think that it's very special. And that's why the ego made its crowning achievement, *the body.*

Because the body allows into its awareness only that which conforms to the reality of the ego's cherished illusions. So now, everything that we experience testifies to us of the reality of this illusion.

And that's no different, really, than asking the illusion to explain the illusion. So now, the illusion is telling us what to think and even the body is telling us what to feel. So it's actually an ilusion telling us everything about itself and we buy it because it's really all that we experience.

 So it's really a rather brilliant solution on the part of the ego. The only problem is it doesn't work. Because all it does is hold it in place. Because now the cause of our problem of separation and this lack of peace that we feel and all of these terrible feelings that we have are not us. The problem is now seen as being outside of us.

That was the ego's way of escaping from it. This denial and projection. And remember, projection always follows denial and *A Course in Miracles* actually teaches that projection *makes* perception.

So now what's going on is that we're actually making that which we are seeing, but it's out of our awareness and we think that it's reality, when all it really is, is a projection that is coming from our own unconscious mind. And the reason that we made it up in the first place was so that the cause of our problem could be seen as being something else.

So now it's not my fault. It's not my fault that I've lost the peace of God, it's not my fault that I'm angry, it's not my fault that I lack peace, it's your fault! And then to top it all off, and make it as real as possible, we are born into this illusion as the perfect little victim. Were totally innocent. Totally at the effect of the world. Completely lost.

The whole idea of being at cause of anything, we've forgotten everything and we're born as the perfect little victim; and how could I be responsible for anything?
"I didn't ask to be born! It's not my fault. It's my parents' fault. They did it. And not only that but do you know what? They didn't love me enough."

Then you get this whole story going on about why things are the way that they are. And it's all made up. But we forget that we're the ones that made it up. And the reason that we made it up was so that somebody else could be to blame.

And so, we go through life with our whole story and we think that it's real and we think that the cause of our problems are outside us and we proceed to try to solve those problems with solutions that are seen as being outside of us. And it doesn't work. And the only thing that does work would be to go back to the cause, which is in the mind, and undo this whole idea of separation and undo this whole ego can of worms.

Because now, in the ego's world, all these ideas that were in the mind, in that metaphysical place, the ideas that never existed before, ideas like sin...you know...I've done something wrong. Well if you've done something wrong what does that mean? It means you're guilty. If you're guilty what does that mean? It means you're gonna be punished. If you're gonna be punished then you have fear, you know, and fear is time based. You know, you have to have a future to be afraid of.

All these ideas could not have existed in perfect oneness. They can only exist in an idea of separation. The ideas we talked about, scarcity, death, they all show up as being caused by somebody else instead of us because now, the universe of time and space has become the ultimate scapegoat. It's now, no matter what problem I have, it's not my fault. I can see it as being somebody else's fault and they are outside of me and they are to blame.

And as I said, we see it at work in the world all the time. People play off of those fears and play off of those emotions. And the way out is not through judgment and condemnation, which holds it in place, because as we said earlier, if you judge another you're really just judging yourself and keeping this whole ego system in place.

The way out of it is through the Holy Spirit's kind of forgiveness. But this kind of forgiveness forgives people not because they've really done something, but because they really haven't done anything. It's because we're the ones, or I should say, you're *the one* who made up this whole thing in the first place.

Once you understand that then you can realize that the way out is through forgiveness of that person, not because they've done something, but because you realize that you made them up for a reason and that they haven't really done anything. You just wanted it to look that way.

So, we have to remember that deep in the unconscious mind there is this guilt that we have over the original separation from God. And in order to escape from it, we denied it and projected it outward. As long as that unconscious guilt remains there, in the mind, then we cannot escape the cycle of birth and death.

People have near death experiences and they report it in very similar ways. They usually leave the body and the mind seems to die. And when they leave the body it is a very good experience because you don't have that physical pain and that heaviness associated with the body. So it seems like a very blissful and wonderful experience.

And a lot of these experiences are similar. Some people may see relatives that have gone on before them and eventually in most of these experiences people are approaching the Light of God. And then what happens is they get zapped back into their body again. So they can't tell you the whole experience, so they report it as being a really great experience. But they can't tell you the whole experience because then they'd be dead.

You know, they can't tell you the whole experience. So I'll tell you the rest of the experience. What happens is, as you're going toward the Light and a funny thing happens on the way to the Light. What happens is, is this unconscious guilt that is still there in the mind starts to catch up with you. And it's not a physical pain. It's a psychological pain. And there are people in mental institutions who will tell you that, you know, psychological pain can be even worse than physical pain.

And this pain starts to catch up with you and as long as it's there you will start to feel it and you will want to get away from it. And the hiding place that we have from this unconscious guilt is just another body. And any body will do. And so, instead of being zapped back into *this* body, the way we are in the near death experience, we simply go into another body. And the purpose of that body is a hiding place. It's like a security blanket from this unconscious guilt.

Just as the universe of time and space was made as the ultimate scapegoat, in order to escape from this terrible unconscious guilt that we felt at the massive metaphysical level, the body and the continuing adventures of the body, act as the next hiding place from this unconscious guilt as long as it stays there in the mind.
As long as it has not been healed by the Holy Spirit, and the only way that it *can* be healed by the Holy Spirit is for you to do your part which is by forgiving these images that seem to be outside of you and seem to be real people, even though they're not. The only way out of that whole can of worms is through this kind of forgiveness.

But once again, this is a whole new kind of thing.
A Course in Miracles says,
 "Forgiveness does not pardon sins and make them real. It sees that there was no sin. And in that view are all your sins forgiven."

I might add, that *only* in that view are all your sins forgiven. Because as long as you think that the other person has really done anything then that will translate into your unconscious mind that *you* have really done something. If you think that they're really a body then that will translate into your unconscious mind that *you* are a body.

As A Course in Miracles says,
 "As you see him, you will see yourself."

There's no getting away from that. And that's why forgiveness is totally justified. It's because it's good for you and it's because it's the way out of pain and suffering.

And at the end of Jesus' life, despite what most people think, Jesus could not suffer and He did not feel any pain because as A Course in Miracles puts it,
"The guiltless mind cannot suffer."

That's a topic for another discussion but it really is true. It's like my teachers said in *The Disappearance of the Universe*, in the chapter called *Healing the Sick*, they said,
 "Pain is not a physical process. It's a mental process."

And the way out of it is to get back to the cause which is in the mind and undo the cause of it. And once you do that, then the body must follow. So you can actually get to the point where it would be impossible, once you're like Jesus and Buddha, it would be impossible for you to feel any pain.

And that's why this whole idea of Jesus suffering and sacrificing Himself for sins is made up. It's totally out to lunch when it comes to what Jesus was really all about and what He was really teaching. What He was teaching was unconditional love and forgiveness which would have to be all-inclusive, because if it's not all-inclusive then it's not real. Real love includes everybody and nobody can possibly be left out.

So you start to realize that when you practice the kind of forgiveness that forgives people, you know, for what they haven't really done, the way that *A Course in Miracles* does, then your experience it starts to change.

Maybe you'll start to feel a little bit lighter. Maybe you'll start to feel not so much like you're in a body. Maybe the body will start to feel like a dream figure in a dream, which it really is anyway. Any maybe your experience will start to change.

Maybe you'll start to feel more peaceful. That may not sound like such a bog deal; *"Well, I feel peaceful…wow.. What's that gonna get me?"* But the truth is, if peace is the condition of the Kingdom of Heaven then how are you gonna fit back into the Kingdom if you're not in the condition of peace? It's like you wouldn't fit in. It would be like trying to fit a square block into a round hole.

So, in order to return to the Kingdom of Heaven and perfect oneness with God you literally have to return te mind to that condition where it is at peace. And you attain what the Bible and A Course in Miracles call,
   "The peace of God which passeth understanding."

And once you get to that level then you're ready to return home. And It's this kind of forgiveness that brings about that experience. And what do you forgive? Well it's simple. Whatever comes up in front of your face on any given day. That's what you're supposed to forgive. It's not a mystery. It's always right there in front of you.

You may think 'Well gee, I can't see what's in my unconscious mind.' Well you don't have to. All you have to see is the symbolic representation of it that's being presented to you right now, in front of your face, which is simply symbolic of that which already exists in your own unconscious mind.

So as you forgive *that*, you're really forgiving yourself. You're really forgiving that which exists in your own unconscious mind. And it's what *A Course in Miracles* calls,
 "The secret sins and hidden hates that we really have about ourselves."

So whatever causes an upset in you, and it doesn't matter how big or small it is, that's what you're supposed to forgive. You know, I used to get really upset when this certain politician came on the TV screen. (I'll let you guess which one.) And he would come on the TV screen and I would go…ugh…you know, every time he came on I couldn't stop myself. I'd just want to react to him.

And one day I was trying to practice forgiveness and he came on the TV screen and I started to react and I stopped myself. And I remembered the Truth, that *I* made him up because I wanted him to be there so that he could be the one who was at fault; so he could be the one who was to blame for my lack of peace, instead of myself.

And when I remembered the truth, then I was able to forgive him and I could look at it differently. And then I thought,
 "Do you know something? He doesn't even know that I'm watching. So who's the one who's suffering here? Is it me or is it him? Well, it's me! I'm the one who's suffering. I mean, he doesn't even know that I'm watching."

So it's really kind of silly, most of our judgments, because we're the ones who are suffering as a result. You know, like this guy that I was watching on the TV screen there; he probably is having a good time. So who's the one who is suffering there?

You know, I had a father in law who, God bless him, and he hated Bill Clinton. I mean for eight years, I mean he just got so upset every time Bill Clinton came on the TV screen. He would almost turn red. He eventually had to leave the room sometimes. He just hated Bill Clinton and he suffered for like eight years. And then he died. And I can almost guarantee you that Bill Clinton was having a good time.

So who is forgiveness really for? It's not for the other person. It never is. You know, forgiveness is for you. So now, I can do this because I know that it's good for me. It's not that I give a damn about you; I know that forgiveness is good for me and that the ego is being undone and that *if* I do it I will feel better.

And that's te short term benefit. There are like immediate and practical short term benefits for doing this kind of forgiveness. What if you became more peaceful? Well, how would that affect your health? How would your blood pressure be affected? Can you put a price tag on something like that?

My blood pressure used to be very bad, now It's perfect. You can't buy that kind of thing. But you *can* create it with the kind of thoughts and the kind of right-minded thinking that forgiveness is all about.

And if you were more peaceful, well what would happen if you could think more clearly? What if you could open yourself up more to inspiration? Because a you remove the crap that's in the unconscious mind you remove what the Course calls,
 "The blocks to the awareness of Love's presence."

The mind becomes more receptive and more opened to the messages of the Holy Spirit. And you can be inspired as to what you should do in this world. Not that *that's* what it's about. It's not about fixing up the world.
A Course in Miracles says,
 "Seek not to change the world. Seek rather to change your mind about the world."

Why? Because that's where real power is. That's where the cause is. If you change your mind about the world then the world must follow. You know, the world is just an effect. If you really wanna have an impact in th world then forget about the world and go back to where the real power in changing the world is, which is in the mind. And if you change the mind, the cause, then the effect literally has to follow. And that's why my teacher, Pursah pointed out that ,
 "The people of the world will never live in peace until the people of the world have inner peace."

And that's because if you wanna change the outside picture you have to go back and achieve inner peace first. That's the only way that you'll ever have peace on the outer screen there. You have to go back to the cause.

And so yeah, we can try to do all kinds of things on the outside effect. Like, you know, we try The League of Nations, and we created a United Nations. People wanna create a Department of Peace, (and there's certainly nothing wrong with that) just as long as you understand that it won't work. And it can't work. As long as you have this condition of conflict in the mind you literally cannot have peace out there in the world.

So if you really wanna achieve world peace the place to start is to share these kinds of ideas and empower people to go back to the cause in the mind instead of always just working on the effect. After that, whatever you do in the effect and in the world can simply be representative of who you are and what you are. So now you can be coming from a condition of love. And if you wanna create a Department of Peace it's simply because you're coming from a condition of love, not because you think that you're gonna change the world by doing this. It's simply symbolic of who you are and what you *really* are.

If you're coming from a place of love you can do no wrong. It's like the old saying, '*Love and do as you will.*'

If you're coming from that place of love then everything that follows will be right. And if you're not coming from a place of love then everything that will follow will simply lead to more conflict and more division.

So this kind of forgiveness is good for us. And how do we do it? Well, there's a **forgiveness thought process** in *The Disappearance of the Universe* that I'd like to share with you.

And I'd like o go over it a little bit and explain it a little bit after that, but in order to do that I would like for you to think of somebody in your mind who you would like to forgive. In fact, it may be better if you think of somebody you *don't* want to forgive. And it doesn't have to be 'the big one.' It doesn't have to be the worse thing that ever happened to you in your life.

I think that many times we start off by forgiving the little things. Because that's a good way to practice. And it's only through practice that we become perfect. You know, look at it this way. I'll use an analogy of a musician because I'm a musician.

Let's say that you want to be a great piano player, right? And that was your goal. Just like some people in spirituality decide, well you know,
"*I'm gonna be like Jesus and I'm gonna be like Buddha and I'm gonna not have to come back here anymore.*"

Which is a very noble goal. I don't know if people realize what a big goal it is because if you really say that you don't wanna come back here anymore and you wanna escape the cycle of birth and death, then that includes the *complete relinquishment of individual identity now and forever.*

So maybe that's a little bit bigger decision than some people realize. You know, I hear people say all the time, "*I'm not coming back anymore.*" Well, they should know what it is they're asking for. Because *that* in the unconsciousness mind is very fearful. Because you're telling the ego that the ego's gonna be dead and that there's gonna be no more individual identity now and forever.

So it's a little bit bigger decision than people realize, which is just another reason why this unconscious guilt and this fear in the mind has to be undone by the Holy Spirit before we can achieve that.

So let's say you decide that you want to do that, and let's say that the analogy is being a great piano player. Well, let's say that you decide that you wanna become a great piano player. So you learn some theory. (And the text in *A Course in Miracles* is the theory of *A Course in Miracles*.)

So, a musician may learn some music theory. Maybe you'll take a music appreciation class. Maybe you'll learn to read music. Maybe you'll learn all about it. Then you go and you sit down at the piano and you go to play the piano, and you suck. And the reason that you suck is because the only thing in the world that will ever make you a really good piano player is if you sit down there and if you practice. And you have to practice every day, for a long time.

And if you do that kind of practice, then maybe after five years then you know, you could be pretty good. Other people would say, "*Wow. He's good.*" You know, you're actually pretty good at it. And maybe after ten years of practice you could be *really* good. Maybe after twenty years you get to be great. Maybe after twenty-five years you could be like one of the greatest who ever lived.

If you have that kind of determination and you're willing to practice that much, then you can be great. Well, think about it. Do we really believe that attaining the same level of Spiritual Mastery of somebody like Jesus or Buddha is less of an accomplishment than being a great piano player? I don't think so. If you really want it then you have to be willing to practice. You know, it's very tempting to want to skip to the end.
 A Course in Miracles says that,
   "*The full awareness of the Atonement is that the separation from God never occurred.*" But it also says,
   "*The means of the Atonement is forgiveness.*"

Well if the means of the Atonement is forgiveness how can we get to the end without utilizing the means? You **have to do** that kind of forgiveness work. You can't skip it. I think it's very tempting to want to skip to the end, and say, "*Yes, I'm enlightened and I'm a perfect child of God.*" (Which metaphysically is a true statement, but that is not in their experience.) Our experience is that we are here and that we are in bodies. And to deny that experience, as *A Course in Miracles* puts it, is a particularly unworthy form of denial. Because this is where we think we are. And if we really wanna get home in our experience then we have to *forgive the world* from where we think we are, which is from the prospective of a body. And it's in that forgiveness that we get to the experience that we're not bodies.

And the statements that we find in *A Course in Miracles* cannot just be read but actually experienced. Statements like,
 "*I am not a body. I am free, for I am still as God created me.*"
That kind of experience is *brought about* by forgiveness. But once again, it's this kind of forgiveness that we're gonna practice right now. So I'm gonna read the instructions for this exercise in forgiveness, then we're gonna actually do it, and then after that I'm gonna talk just a little bit more about it and what's being accomplished for us when we do it. The instructions for this forgiveness thought process can be found near the end of the chapter called *The Law of Forgiveness* in *The Disappearance of the Universe*.

And that was my favorite visit of all because that's the one where Pursah came alone. Actually she let me touch her once during that visit also, so that was definitely my favorite.

But the way she put it for the instructions for this, and keeping in mind that the person that you're going to forgive here in most cases, it's gonna be another person. But in some cases, you know, the person that you wanna forgive could be you.

You know, most people project their unconscious guilt out there onto other people, but there are some people in this world who project the unconscious guilt onto themselves. Now, technically there's no difference between doing that, you know, projecting it onto yourself or onto somebody else because, as we said, what is that when you hold your hand up in front of your face? It looks like you but it's really just another body.

What is that when you go in the mirror in the bathroom and look in the mirror? What is that? Is that reflection really there? Well, of course not. It's an optical illusion. What you're looking at in the mirror is not really there And, ironically, what is causing the reflection isn't there either. But it's the same kind of trick.

What we're seeing outside of ourselves when we look at that reflection in the mirror and other bodies and when we hold our hand up in front of our face and see our body, it's simply a reflection or a symbolic representation of what's in our unconscious mind. And *by forgiving it*, that's the way to freedom.

Now, some people blame themselves for things. Some people project the unconscious guilt onto themselves and it's a very serious problem. And it's probably the most denied problem in the world.

Suicide is probably the biggest problem that nobody in the world wants to talk about. And that's because they're afraid of it, because people run away from this unconscious guilt that's in the mind and they don't even want to look at it. And that's why I think it's so wonderful that A Course in Miracles has exposed it and explained it and made people understand that they don't have to judge themselves any more than they're judging anybody else.

So you have a condition in the world where more people die from suicide than are killed by all the wars and all the crime in the world combined. More police officers die from suicide than are ever killed in the line of duty. More firemen die from suicide than are ever killed by fires and it's something that the world is in total denial about.

In Japan today there are groups of teenagers who meet on the internet and then go out in vans and they kill each other in the vans. And if that kind of thing ever spreads to North America, the people are gonna freak out.

And the cause of it is the very kind of unconscious guilt that we've been talking about. People don't know what's running them. They don't know about the stuff churning in the deep canyons of the unconscious mind which are causing their behavior.
But this kind of forgiveness is actually a way out of that whole ego can of worms and a way to peace and Salvation and eventually breaking the cycle of birth and death.

The first effects of it are very immediate and practical and take place seemingly in the world. But the ultimate goal and what actually happens is that as the ego is gradually undone and when the time comes when you lay your body aside for the last time, there is no reason to come back again. You don't need a body to hide in. You don't need a universe of time and space to hide in. So there is no reason for you to come back and the cycle of birth and death is broken.

And then, as we said, when you awake from the dream where is the dream? It's gone. And so, you don't have to wait for everybody else to be enlightened. Everybody else is already there! And it turns out that there really was only one ego and that *you* were it.

You know, this isn't about helping other people to forgive or pointing out ego-like behavior in other people. You know, I know many Course in Miracles students who are experts in pointing out ego-like behavior in other people. But that's not forgiveness. Forgiveness is not about pointing out the ego in others. Ultimately forgiveness is about realizing that there isn't anybody else. There are no others and that the ego is really you and then forgiving it. That would be forgiveness under the system of *A Course in Miracles*. That would be real forgiveness.

It's not about having somebody else clean up their act. It's about the way that you look at it. And then you can get to the experience of what *A Course in Miracles* is teaching, which is that there is no world.
 In fact the Course says,
   "There is no world."
     In fact the Course says,
     *"**There is no world**. This is the central lesson the Course attempts to teach."*

And it's brutally uncompromising in that regard. The Course does not say that
'*There is no world yeah but maybe…*' It says,
"There is no world. This is the central lesson the Course attempts to teach."
Why? Because it's just a dream. And that's why the Course also says,
 "The secret of Salvation is but this; you are doing this to yourself."

So yeah, it may look like we were done wrong. It may look like we're victims and that we're not at cause; that somebody else is. That's the way we set ourselves up. But the truth is, everything that happens here is something that we wanted to happen because we wanted the other person to be responsible. You didn't want that terrible feeling of guilt that we had, to be in us, so we chose to put it seemingly some place else.

Except, it's just an illusion. And so when we judge others, what goes around comes around because it never really left in the first place. It was just an illusion. And the way to undo it is to apply this kind of right-minded thought process that Pursah gave me in the *Disappearance of the Universe*.

The way she explained it was, in this thought process the words *you* and *your* can apply to any person, situation or event. So it can be any person, it can be yourself, it could be a situation that you feel stuck in. Maybe you're going through a divorce, maybe you're in a bankruptcy, maybe you're in a situation where you just feel stuck, that it doesn't seem to have any end to it. Or maybe it's just uncomfortable. Maybe it's an event that you see on TV like the tsunami or the hurricanes or all these terrible things that go on in the world. Anything can be forgiven.

You know, I have a part in the book where I talk about the day of the World Trade Center attack and my thought process is on that day. There's nothing in this world that this cannot be applied to, no matter how big or small.

And then, eventually we get to the point where we become so good at this, it becomes so much a part of us, that we're able to finally realize that just as *A Course in Miracles* says,
 "There is no order of difficulty in Miracles. One is not harder or bigger than another."

By practicing we eventually get to the point where we realize that it's all the same. Because if it's all an illusion then there can be no distinction between one thing that is untrue and something else that is untrue. Because they're both untrue. So t really doesn't matter how big one appears to be and how small another appears to be. They're really all the same.

Pursah also said that it's alright to improvise while you're maintaining the basic ideas. So this is not a religion. It's not a ritual. You don't have to get the ideas just right. You know, I even asked them,
"Do have to get the words just right?"
They said no. It's *your attitude* that counts. Your way of being. And it's not the same as other things. You know, some people give equal weight to mind, body and spirit. But what this is doing, it's actually empowering us to use the mind *to choose between* the body and the spirit. And *how* you see the other person will actually determine what you believe *that you are*, on the level of your own unconscious mind.

Pursah also said,
"Please note that the Holy Spirit will remember to remove the unconscious guilt from your mind and perform His healing of the universe when you forgive."

That's His job and He's pretty good at it. You have to remember to do *your job*, if not immediately then later on. If you completely forget then you can be confident that the ego's script will eventually provide you with a similar opportunity that will do just as well. So if you don't learn your lessons this time around, you'll get another chance.

But I think the real question here is, not whether or not it works. The real question here is, how long do we want to prolong our suffering? Now, I think that *that's* where you see another similarity between Buddhism and *A Course in Miracles*, because they're about the end of suffering and the undoing of the ego.

In fact, except for the Christian terminology I really think at times that *A Course in Miracles* has more in common with Buddhism than it does with anything else. Yet this is the original Jesus. This is where you get *the spirituality without the religion*. Because now, it's up to *you* to forgive. It's up to *you* to learn how to pray. It's up to you to do it without relying on some religion and without relying on some priest or minister to tell you what to do. Ultimately you become your own minister or your own priest or your own rabbi.

And you can look at things in a very advanced way because you've learned through Jesus and the Holy Spirit the way to look at everything.

So, this is called <u>true forgiveness, a thought process example</u>: and thinking of the person in your mind who you have chosen to forgive, I would like you to visualize that person and say these words in your mind to that person.

"You're not really there. If I think you are guilty or the cause of the problem and if I made you up, then the imagined guilt and fear must be in me. Since the separation from God never occurred, I forgive both of us for what we haven't really done. Now there is only innocence, and I join with the Holy Spirit in peace."

And then if you will, I'd like you to imagine releasing that person to the Holy Spirit. And as you release that person, you are released.
A Course in Miracles says,
   "Can you to whom God says, release My Son, be tempted not to listen, when you learn it is your own release for whom He asks?"

And then Pursah said,
   "Please feel free to use this example of a <u>forgiveness thought process </u>as much as you want in order to help get in the habit of forgiveness."

And that's very important. Because we want to get into the habit of forgiveness. Because that's what will make it almost automatic in our mind and even when the going gets tough.
You know, in those early fifty *Miracles* principals in the *Course* it says,
   "Miracles are habits and should be involuntary."

What happens is, you practice it so much that it becomes a part of you; that it becomes so much a part of you that you will do it almost automatically.

Sometimes I play a little game with Jesus. I get up in the morning and I say,
  "Hey Jesus, you know…I'm taking the day off. I'm not gonna forgive anybody today."

And then what happens, is about half way through the day I miss it.
  You know, and I wanna do it because I know that it's good for me. So when you get to the point where you would actually miss it if you don't do it, then you know that it's becoming a part of you. And then what happens is, these right-minded ideas we're talking about, we see all kinds of them in the workbook of *A Course in Miracles*. The text is the theory but the workbook is the actual application of the *Course*. And the workbook itself says,
  "It is doing the work with lessons that will make the goal of the Course possible."

And the goal of the *Course* is experience. An experience of what you really are and where you really are. And the workbook is full of these right-minded ideas. And what will happen is, as you do the workbook in *A Course in Miracles*, is that certain ideas will leap off the page at you and it won't necessarily be the same for everybody.

In fact, that's one of the reasons that the *Course* is thirteen-hundred pages long. It's because the Truth may be simple but the ego is not. The ego is very, very complicated and it has to be undone gradually. And that's why the *Course* says that the curriculum is highly individualized.

An analogy that I like to use of undoing the ego is like peeling away the layers of an onion. Let's say you have an onion and you peel away a layer of the onion. Well, it still looks like an onion. You know, it looks like nothing ha happened. But let's say that you persevere because you know that it makes you feel better and once in a while you have experiences that tell you that it is working, and you forgive, and the what happens is you peel away another layer of the onion.

Well, it still looks like an onion. You know, it may *look* like nothing's happening. And so people ask,
  "Do I have to feel like I've forgiven somebody in order for it to work? Have I done something wrong if I don't feel like I've forgiven somebody?"

The answer is no. You don't have to 'feel' like you've forgiven somebody because the effects of your thoughts are not always immediately apparent. You know, the same is true when you judge somebody. I mean, you could possibly feel good after you judge somebody. That's because you've temporarily found a way to project your unconscious guilt onto the other person. And so, temporarily, you might feel better but you haven't really gotten away from it. All you've done is reinforce it in your own unconscious mind.

So yeah, you feel good because you got to be right and this other person gets to be wrong and the only problem is that three or four days later you go out and you get in a car accident. Or you get sick. And it's because you still feel guilty and you still find a way to punish yourself.

Well, the same is true with forgiveness in the sense that if you forgive somebody, you may not feel the effects of it right away. You may feel like,
 'Oh, I forgave him and nothing happened."

And it may *look* like you're forgiving the same thing over and over again. You know, you forgive the people at work, then you go back there the next day, and they're still there. You know, it may *look* like nothing's happening but that's where we will eventually have to have faith that the Holy Spirit is doing His part. Because, as we said, the Holy Spirit can see everything.

And when we perform from this simple act of forgiveness where we forgive somebody for what they haven't really done, then the Holy Spirit is taking that forgiveness and it is going everywhere. It's going through all of our past lives. It's going through all of our future lives. It's going through every dimension of time.

A Course in Miracles says in those fifty miracles principals,
 "The Miracle works in all the dimensions of time, and the Miracle **is** forgiveness."

 And it's cutting through every parallel universe that may or may not exist. Our forgiveness is going everywhere, doing amazing things. Those first fifty principals also says,
 "A Miracle is never lost. It can have undreamed of effects in situations of which you are not even aware."

So these things are happening while we're performing our forgiveness and we're sitting there and we're thinking, 'Oh, *nothing's happening and this is boring.'*
So at some point you have to have faith that your forgiveness is being taken by the Holy Spirit and cutting through everything and actually collapsing time, just as in *A Course in Miracles*, it says,

"The universe literally is disappearing."

Because these other dimensions of time where we've already learned this lesson or that lesson that we're forgiving, so we don't have to learn it again. The Holy Spirit is actually, you know, causing that dimension of time to disappear. And there are parts of the universe that will never be seen again because of the kind of forgiveness that you're practicing. So there really are incredible and remarkable effects that are taking place. And the *Course* teaches that all thought produces form on some level.

So that's why a miracle is never lost. It's like you couldn't think anything without it having some kind of effect, somewhere. And what this does is, it's a very powerful way of going from being at the effect to being at the cause. And then, what that does, is that it starts to change your *experience* of your life. And it can be a wonderful experience because if you do this and you start to get in touch with your innocence, there is no better experience than that.

And it's not about giving up the world. It's not about giving everything up. If you think that you have to give up anything in this world then that's putting you just as much at the effect of it as if you want it. So don't think that you have to give up possessions. You don't have to give up money You don't have to give up sex. You don't have to give up things in this world. Just be normal. Don't be weird.

You don't go into a funeral where people are having a funeral and say,
"Hey! What's your problem? Don't you know that all this is an illusion?
What's going on?"

There's no compassion in that. There's no love in that. Because all you're gong to do is make people more angry. And there are people who have done that, believe it or not.

And when somebody is sick, you don't go up to them with that *Course in Miracles* lesson and say, *"Hey! What's the matter with you? You're a Course in Miracles student. Don't you know that this workbook lesson, it says, 'sickness is a defense against the Truth?' What's the matter with you? Don't you get it?"*

Well, you know, there's no love and compassion in that. Everybody's gonna get sick. That's what bodies do. Because bodies were based on the thought of separation and so bodies themselves will separate. Which is all that cancer is, you know, cells dividing and sub-dividing.

Everybody's gonna get sick. The thing isn't whether or not you get sick, because you're just dealing with the level of form in the body if you think that you're going to prevent all illness now and forever. The place to go is to the cause, which is in the mind, which will change *your experience* of sickness and eventually, as we said, it's possible to get to the point where the body cannot feel any pain. And that's an incredible place to get to.

I'm not saying that it happens all at once. You know, I'm not saying that everything's going to be perfect. I'm not saying that everything in your life is gonna go good. Look at Jesus at the end of His life. Things weren't exactly going good. But that didn't matter to Him because His experience was that He was not a body, and He was not stuck in this dream, so it didn't really matter what people did to Him.

There's a way to experience what it's like to be with God even in this lifetime. But before I tell you that, I wanna tell you a joke, because I've gone too long here without telling you a joke and if I don't tell you a joke then I don't feel it's a good enough talk.
 So, I'll tell you a joke about Jesus 2,000 years ago. Alright, Jesus is walking down the road, 2,000 years ago and He's just minding His own business, you know. He's not doing anything special and all of a sudden He comes up to this group of people and they're about to stone a prostitute to death.

Right? Because that's what we did back in those days. If you caught a prostitute, that was the law, you stoned her to death. Like, you know, even if you were with her like an hour ago. And so, they're about ready to stone this prostitute to death but they see Jesus coming. Now, they don't like Jesus, right? Because, you know, Jesus is kind of like this renegade rabbi and He doesn't bow down to all of their precious beliefs and everything, and He's into like forgiveness and stuff, which they're not too keen on, and so they figure they're gonna trick Jesus; they're gonna get Him, right?

Because back in those days you couldn't speak out against the Bible, you couldn't speak out against the law, because if you spoke out against the law then that too was against the law. So, if you were speaking out against the law, that would be the same as speaking out against God. Because it was considered to be God's word.

So if you spoke out against the law then you yourself were in violation of the law. So they figured, OK, here's Jesus, you know, we're gonna trick Him. We're gonna get Him this time. So they yelled to Jesus, they said,
 "Hey Jesus! We got this prostitute here and we're gonna stone her to death. That's what we're supposed to do right?

Well, you gotta get up pretty early in the morning to pull one over on old Jesus, right? So Jesus says,

"OK. He among you who is without sin, let him cast the first stone."
And what they do is, one by one, they all just drop their stones to the ground because they couldn't picture themselves as being without sin. And so, that's how Jesus got to save the prostitute and He got to teach what He wanted to, and He saved the prostitute's life because he said,
"He among you who is without sin, let him cast the first stone."

And Jesus wasn't disobeying the law because He didn't speak out against the law, and so it was perfect. But then, all of a sudden, this woman comes walking along and she's got this big rock in her hand. She walks up to the prostitute, drops the rock right on the prostitute's head. Knocks her out! Jesus looks at the woman and did this and said,
"Come on mom! Will you give me a little space?"

So, we said that there is a way to experience what it's like to be with God and in Heaven, even while we appear to be here in this world. And that's ultimately that the Course is directed toward. And some people experience this, not everybody does; it's the profound inner peace that really matters.
 And then, the way that other mystical experiences show up vary from person to person. That's because we have different gifts from lifetime to lifetime.
A Course in Miracles says, in the Manual for Teachers, that nobody has any gifts that are not available to everyone. But that doesn't mean that they're gonna happen all at once. We vary from lifetime to lifetime.

You know, I've had people come up to me and say,
 "Well, you know, how come the Ascended Masters appeared to you? Why you?"
And it's like well, you know, how do they know that they weren't one of those children who saw the Virgin Mary at Lourdes in one of their previous lifetimes? How do they know that they haven't seen Ascended Masters in other lifetimes, how do they know they haven't seen angels? How do they know they won't in this lifetime? They shouldn't limit themselves.

And so I tell them that my biggest experience has not been seeing Arten and Pursah, it has not been seeing the Ascended Masters, even though a lot of people would think that it would be pretty cool to do that. That hasn't been the ultimate experience for me. The ultimate experience for me has been something else, which I'm going to describe for you in just a minute.

But before I do I just wanted to give you a little introduction to that, because there's this one question that everybody asks about this kind of stuff. Sooner or later, everybody asks this question. And the basic question is,

"Well, you know, how the hell could any of this have happened? If God was perfect and Heaven was perfect and all you had was this perfect oneness and everything was so perfect, then why would there even be a thought that seems to be separate from God? How could that possibly happen if everything as so perfect?

And everybody asks that question at one time or another. And this is how I asked the question in *The Disappearance of the Universe*. The way I put it, was, you know, because they had just told me this mis-creation story about how the universe of time and space was made, and I said,

"Yeah, but don't you have the same problem with this story as the one in Genesis and God supposedly doing some of the things He did? I mean, why the hell would a part of Christ ever want to separate from God if everything was complete and perfect?"

Well Arten, (who was more than my equal in the domain of smart ass enlightenment,) Arten said,

"Let's take a look at your question. Is it really a question or is it a statement? Aren't you saying that a separation from God really occurred? You can't ask how the separation could have happened unless you believe it did. Yet we have already said the principal of the Atonement is that it didn't. Then you ask how Christ could have possibly chosen with the ego when we've already said that it wasn't Christ but an illusory consciousness that appeared to do so. Then, on top of that, you question how this stupid choice could've been made by you when here you are making it again right now."

And I said,
"You're a smart ass, do you know that?"
   And Arten said,
"Only for teaching purposes." He said, *"Gary we love you. I'll tell you, you'll never get an answer within the ego's frame work to that kind o a question that will ever satisfy you intellectually."*

As the *Course* says, and this is Jesus talking now, the *Course* says,
"The ego's voice is a hallucination. You cannot expect it to say, 'I am not real.' Yet you are not asked to dispel your hallucinations alone."

And it's interesting that the *Course* would use that word, dispel, because that's what this is. It's like one big giant mother freakin' spell that we've put ourselves under, and through the kind of forgiveness that we've just learned, what we're gonna do is we're gonna dispel it along with the Holy Spirit and wake up from it.

So then Arten said,

"The time will come when the answer to your question will be found outside the intellect, completely outside the ego's system and instead within the experience that you are still at home in God, which corrects the mistaken experience that you are not."

As 'J' puts it, and once again, this is from *A Course in Miracles*, the *Course* says,
"Against this sense of temporary existence Spirit offers you the knowledge of permanence and unshakable being. No one who has experienced the revelation of this can ever fully believe in the ego again. How can it's meager offering to you prevail against the glorious gift of God?"

I remember once sitting at home in that same living room where Arten and Pursah appeared to me so many times. And they were very good to me. They appeared to me seventeen times over a period of nine years. They gave me time to integrate these ideas into my life and then after a few years, I was just sitting there, minding my own business when all of a sudden I was overwhelmed by this feeling of total and complete love.

You know, it was not like anything else that I've ever experienced. *A Course in Miracles* says that the experience of revelation, which is really another word for your experience of where you really are, which is at home with God, and what it's like to be with God, it's almost like a sneak preview of the end; that experience that cannot really be put into words. So I'll tell you what it was like.

I was sittig there minding my own business and all of a sudden I felt completely overwhelmed with this feeling of total and complete love. And it, first of all, the best way to describe it is that it's not like anything in this world. It's not like anything else that you've ever experienced. That alone sets it apart from everything else.

But then there's this underlying feeling of constancy. Constancy does not exist in this world that the Buddhists call impermanence. Constancy literally is not something that is experienced in this world. And in this feeling I felt completely loved and everything just kind of like disappeared for an instant. It's like, you know, it didn't last long and it doesn't have to last long, but the after effects of it lasted for hours. I just sat there for the longest time in a stupor of awe.

Because, you know, it's like the Course says, awe is correctly reserved for God. Awe is not a proper reaction to Jesus for example, because He's one of us, you know, He's just one of us. But awe is a proper reaction to God. And I just sat there in a complete stupor of awe for hours because in this experience I felt totally taken care of and there was no body, there was no world. I felt totally provided for.

And there were no problems, there was nothing to worry about. I was totally innocent. Everybody who I ever loved, everybody I ever cared about, every animal that I ever loved was there. Because nothing could be left out. You can't have anything left out in oneness. And I was totally provided for. You can't have anything lacking in fullness. There can't be anything missing in wholeness.

And this experience was so wonderful. And it also had a sexual aspect to it, you know. I remember early in the book I asked Pursah; she was saying how there were no changes in Heaven because everything is changeless and eternal, you know, which certainly narrows things down. And she pointed out how if something changes, then it would be evolving and if it was evolving then it wouldn't be perfect. And so, God and Spirit would already *be* perfect. So you didn't have to *become* perfect, you already *are* perfect.

What you need to do is simply remove the blocks that you have placed in between yourself and your experience and awareness of your perfection. But you're already there, its just that it's not in your experience.

And so, this was the experience of what it's like to *be* in that perfection. And that experience contained an underlying feeling of constancy. This was literally something that cannot be taken away from you. You experience that it's something that you literally cannot loose.

So, we cannot loose when we are one with our source. We cannot loose in the condition of Heaven. And if you stick around in this world long enough you have to loose. Because it's a world of time and change.

So even if you're one of those people who's living 'the great life' and everything's going perfect for you, and you're making all kinds of money and you're getting all kinds of sex and you're getting all the possessions and everything's going really great for you, you're still gonna die.

And not only that but everybody that you know is gonna die. And not only that but most of the time it's gonna be very horrific and unpleasant. You know, you look at the Kennedys and all of the abundance that they had in their life and you look at all of the tragedy. Now *that's* duality.

In this world of duality things have gotta go down the tubes eventually. In Heaven things never go down the tubes because it's not a time based experience. It's an experience of what *A Course in Miracles* describes as *The Eternal Always*. There is no time. So that experience that you're having is just the experience itself and nothing preceeds it and nothing comes after it, it's just there. And it's a constant experience that will go on forever. And it's so amazing that it completely blows away anything that this world has to offer.

And as I said, very early in this talk, once you experience *that*, then that *is* the answer. That *is* the answer to all the questions that we have. Because it's the only answer that will ever really satisfy us. But in order to get to that experience we need to undo the ego so that *experience* is all that's left.

So what my teachers, Arten and Pursah did for me, was they made something which I had never read before and never studied before, called *A Course in Miracles*, something that would be understandable to me, and that's no small trick.

I've talked to people since the book came out, *The Disappearance of the Universe*, who had been studying *A Course in Miracles* for twenty-five years, and they read *The Disappearance of the Universe* and then went back and *A Course in Miracles* again, and they were amazed by how much more clear it was to them. They said it was like somebody turned the lights on.

I get in contact with people all the time who tell me that and I feel very lucky to be able to participate in this, and I know at the same time that if I read A Course in Miracles on my own, that I would not have understood it. I probably would have seen it as just a continuation of the New testament or something and not realized the radical and incredible nature of this teaching.

And I for the *Course* to work and for it to be real for us, what we need to do is not compromise on it. We cannot change it, we cannot get away from these ideas. Real love and forgiveness is total and all encompassing. And if we're going to be true to this message and have it work then we can't change it or compromise on it one inch. If you give the ego an inch it will take a mile. And then, *A Course in Miracles* will just become like everything else. It won't have any real impact in the world.

And the only way anything is gonna have a real impact in the world is if you go back to the mind and fix the real problem, the *one* real problem there in the mind.

In summing up, what I'd like to do is read a paragraph from A Course in Miracles that I think puts it all together in terms of these ideas, because it shows that *Salvation is really the undoing of the ego.* And it's this;

"Salvation is undoing. If you choose to see the body, you behold a world of separation, unrelated things and happenings that make no sense at all. This one appears and disappears in death. That one is doomed to suffering and loss. And noone is exactly as he was an instant previous nor will he be the same as he is now an instant hence. Who could have trust where so much change is seen? For who is worthy if he be but dust?

Salvation is undoing of all this. For constancy arises in the sight of those who's eyes Salvation has released from looking at the cost of keeping guilt because they chose to let it go instead."

You can see from that passage in *A Course in Miracles* that it's a very beautiful *Course* to read, and at the same time it can be new to some, it can be very disturbing, it can kind of like, rattle your cage and shake your foundation. That's because we're undoing the ego. And it's something that we're so used to that it may seem a little fearful at times.

This kind of spirituality isn't for everybody and I don't try to present it like it's easy. In fact it's not easy. Because it really does ask something of the people who practice it. It asks that you be pro-active and actually forgive things. And it's a demanding spiritual practice. But at the same time, it's something that's well worth doing. What if you could accelerate your spiritual progress so greatly that you would never have to come back again? This is a fast way to do that.

It's not the only way to do it. *A Course in Miracles* does not present itself as being the only way to get back to God. But it certainly does imply at times that perhaps it's the fastest way. It makes statements like,

"The Miracle can substitute for learning that make have taken thousands of years."

So every time we do this kind of forgiveness, all that karma and all those different lifetimes, it's like snow being shoveled into an oven. You know, it just disappears. Miraculous things are happening. After thousands and thousands of lifetimes that we've lived, to actually complete all of our work in just one or two lifetimes.

That may seem like a lot of work but compared to all the times that we've lived and all the times we're going to have to keep coming back if we don't do it, and all the suffering that we'll have to go through if we don't do it, then it is truly a gift from the Holy Spirit.

So, I would say that if this path is for you then it's well worth doing. And you don't have to wait until the end to enjoy the benefits of doing this.

A Course in Miracles talks about the happy dream. My teachers told me in *The Disappearance of the Universe*, they said,

"The time comes when you're so happy it doesn't even matter that you're not enlightned yet, because you can be having so much fun."

People, at first, think that things are being taken away. But they're not. You know, their lack of value, like the *Course* says, is merely being recognized for the first time. And what's happened with me in my experience is that I find I don't enjoy life less because of this, I enjoy life more because of this. I would say that if you have less unconscious guilt in your mind then you can enjoy things more. I like listening to music more than I ever did. This isn't about giving up beauty. It's not about giving up a beautiful sunset or being with your special woman or your special man. It's about enjoying them more and having less guilt in your mind.

You know, if you had less guilt in your mind do you think that it might affect your sex life? Well maybe it would. And maybe you could enjoy it even more instead of less. There are all kinds of wonderful things that can come about as a result of getting in touch with your innocence and getting in touch with the fact that you're really a wonderful child of God and that you deserve only good and only the best of everything.

And then, when we get to the end where all that unconscious guilt in the mind has been undone and the ego has been undone and we don't need a body any more, then it's a condition of absolute love and bliss and it's permanent. It's not something that will ever be lost. And that's worth having. And that is worth working for. And it's worth having the experiences that come along the way that tell us that this is working.

It's a beautiful life, and I feel very privileged to be on this spiritual path and I'm very grateful to you for taking the time to listen to these words and perhaps, share the time with me when we will be together and one with God.

Gary R. Renard
The End of Reincarnation
Copyright @ Sounds True
Transcribed with the permission of Gary Renard and Sounds True, word for word from the original audio version by Joe Wolfe, scribe of *The End of Reincarnation with the Five Signs* and author of *Time Ocular* and *Letter To A Prisoner*.

THE CRASH COURSE

By Carrie Triffet

LONG TIME NO SEE

THE CRASH COURSE

A short explanation of A Course in Miracles excerpted from: *Long Time No See*:

diaries of an unlikely messenger

A WORD ABOUT
Long Time no See
THE CRASH COURSE

The Crash Course is my own short-form explanation of A Course in Miracles, a breakneck gallop through the 580 pages of the Course's teachings. Written in common everyday language, the tone of The Crash Course is purposely a little bit blunt and irreligious, in obvious contrast to the often biblical language of the Course itself.

Stylistic differences aside, students of the Course will notice immediately that The Crash Course isn't a strictly literal or chronological synopsis of A Course in Miracles. Concepts have been arranged here in the manner in which they flowed most naturally and logically for me, which is not necessarily similar to the way the information is structured within the Course itself.

Please note: Although I was scrupulously careful to present the Course's teachings as accurately as possible, I'm no scholar and can't guarantee that my work is free of mistakes. I can only assure you that I did my best. It would not have been possible for me to write The Crash Course without the help of Gary Renard's books, The Disappearance of the Universe and Your Immortal Reality. I owe much of my understanding of the Course's material to the broader explanations set forth in those two books.

The rest of my understanding is owed to the many patient Course-related lessons offered me in conversations with Spirit, as chronicled elsewhere within the pages of **Long Time No See**.

Oh, one more thing: There is no connection between this Crash Course and Philip Urso's very fine series of podcasts and videos titled A Crash Course in Miracles. I accidentally stole his title, but he has very generously allowed me to continue to use it. I am grateful and apologize for any confusion this duplication may cause.

THE CRASH COURSE

1. Everything you know is wrong.

The world we think we know is upside down from the way we suppose it to be: ugliness is beauty, good is evil, joy is sadness, profit is loss.

That's because each of us, without exception, is stark raving mad. And in our madness, we believe that love is hate and hate is love; that light is darkness, happiness is pain, lies are truth, death is life, attack is defense and fear is safety.

Perhaps a little explanation is in order.

The back-story

1. God is real.

First, the good news: Like everything else in this world, we have God all wrong. God, of course, is not Big Daddy In The Sky. God has no gender, no body, no long white beard. God is love and nothing else. And not our messed up, I'll love you as long as you behave and do what I tell you, kind of love. The infinite and perfect Mind of God is total love whether we think we deserve total love or not; this total love is wholly pure and impartial, unchanging, eternal and unconditional.

2. God is real, and nothing outside of God is real, because only God exists. Period. There's nothing else out there.

3. There's no "out there" out there. God is everywhere and everything at all times, eternally and limitlessly. And even that's not a strictly accurate description; "everywhere" implies space, and "at all times" implies temporality, yet time and space don't exist because, by definition, they don't meet the conditions of being real. (Only eternal, unchanging love is real.) So it's meaningless to say, "God is everywhere at all times." The closest thing to a true statement is this: God Is.

4. The Mind of God does not — cannot — judge, condemn, threaten, get angry, be disappointed, punish or take anything away from anybody. Ever. The perfect and serene Mind of God does not do battle or choose sides. No country or religion or political group gets the extra special stamp of Heavenly approval; divine love is offered constantly and limitlessly no matter what we do or don't do in this world. And speaking of battle, there are no Satanic forces in opposition to God, because, seriously, what could oppose God? Only in our confused fantasy do we believe anything could exist separately from, or as a threat to, the infinite power of God.

5. The Mind of God did not create this world or any of the bizarre things we think we see in it; in fact, this world has nothing to do with the perfect, infinite Mind of God at all. Nothing truly exists except eternal, limitless love. Anything that doesn't fit that description is just part of the crazy dream we're having.
The back-story, Part II The beginning of time
God created one Son of God.
And we're it.

The Son of God, of course, is not male, is not a body or even a lot of bodies. Somewhere along the way the Son of God was given this moniker in an attempt to describe its relationship to God — the Son being the creation of its Creator. The so-called Son of God can best be described as divine Thought, created perfect and held forever safe and eternally unchanged within the loving Mind of God.

True Creation, meaning the kind of thing created by a Creator, is powered by the engine of divine love. And the Creator creates more of Itself; that's what real Creation is. It's the reason that only love, and only God, exists. The Mind of God creates more of Itself, out of the raw material of Itself, exactly like Itself in every way. This true Creation, this perfect Thought, is every bit as eternal, sublime and loving as the Mind that created it. Together the Mind and the Thought are one immortal spirit: Holy, pure and unchanging, joyous and peaceful, limitlessly strong, safe and free. This Creation exists forever within God (since there's no such thing as existing outside of God). Once created, no force exists that could alter true Creation in any way, or divide it from the Mind that created it. And there's no place where the Mind of God ends and the created Thought begins. The perfect Mind and the perfect Thought are inextricably one, sharing the divine Will of God. So, for all intents and purposes, the Creation is God.

With one very important exception: Although this Creation has all the attributes of God, it did not, could not, create itself. The Mind creates the Thought. The Thought is capable of creating in the same way that the Mind creates, yet only if it does so in perfect oneness with God, using divine love as its catalyst and its raw material.
And now, the other news: We, the one Son of God, the perfect Thought forever joined with the eternal Mind, started to entertain the idea that we didn't want to be one and the same anymore. We wanted to split up so we could each be special and unique and different. In other words, we wanted to create ourselves over again—just a little differently this time. Yet God's divine Thought has never had the power to change itself in any way, no matter how much it may have wanted to. So we did the next best thing. We started to pretend.

6. In our pretend fantasy of a separate will, we split our one mind, producing an ego mind seemingly separate from our own. And then we became afraid that we'd done something really bad, something completely against the rules. And the ego mind said, Ooh. You broke the law; you stole something that belongs to God. You tore away a piece of God Itself! And now you want to kill off your own Creator so you can rewrite the laws of Heaven. That's disgusting. If God ever catches you, you're in for eternal damnation. Listen, I'm your friend. I'll help you. I can fix it so God will never find you. We'll make this new place, and it'll have walls so thick that God can never come in. You'll be safe there, and you can split and subdivide as much as you want. You can rule your own kingdom and forget all about Heaven.

7. And poor old Son of God was so upset by now, so consumed by fear—which doesn't even exist, remember, since there can be no fear in perfect love—that it consented wholeheartedly to the ego mind's crazy plan.

And so, in a massive outpouring of energy, a universe was formed, powered by the engine of, and using the raw material of fear. Yet fear has no foundation in reality, so the things made from fear share none of the attributes of the things created from love. Things made from fear (besides being completely imaginary) are designed to be love's opposite. Stunted and flawed, unloved, unsafe and impermanent, they're designed to block all memory of God. Things made from fear are "born" for only one purpose: To suffer, wither and die, lifetime after lifetime. And surely that's what they deserve, isn't it? The little ingrates tried to destroy Heaven and murder their Creator, so they — we — deserve eternal misery in exile. So reasons the unreasoning ego mind.

8. Completely taken in by the ego's version of events, our grief and pain over what we thought we'd done to God (and its imagined consequences, should we ever be brought to justice) was too much for us to bear. We forgot we were only pretending. Driven insane by fear, we buried our intolerable guilt so deeply in our collective unconscious mind that to this day we don't even know it's there. And by forgetting that bottomless pit of unconscious guilt and fear, we also forgot it was we who made the ego mind in the first place, and not vice versa. We still think it's our master, our jailer, and we its many helpless slaves.

We think we're billions of separate bodies with separate minds, fragile lumps of mortal flesh moving around in time and space, each living and then inevitably dying. What we call "life" is a brief, cruel mockery of the real thing, which is holy, joyous and eternal. And what we call "death" can't possibly exist in any form, because real life has no opposite. We are not bodies. We are one perfect immortal spirit, given limitless, unchanging life within the wholly loving Mind of God.

Yet willingly ruled by the ego mind, we cling tenaciously to life as we think we know it. Some of this precarious "life" existence seems to be wonderful and beautiful, and some of it terrible and horrifying. Yet all of it, everything we think of as "the real world" is no more than an elaborate 3-D hallucination, complete with imaginary walls that seem to stand between one separated mind and the next.

It's a self-induced trick of light and shadow, smoke and mirrors. No walls exist in truth between our seemingly split-off minds. We only believe they do. And the limitless power of our belief — remember, we share the same attributes, the same unlimited creative power as our Creator — is enough to make it real for us.

A ray of light

1. Therein lies the way back home. The so-called "separation" never happened; we haven't "sinned against" our Creator. (How could sin, or anything else, exist within perfect divine love? And how could we stand apart from our one infinite Self to sin against it?) We therefore can't possibly carry even a speck of real guilt, unconscious or otherwise. We can only believe these things are true; yet if we learned to believe in the fantastical and the untrue, that means we can choose to re-learn the truth to take its place. And belief in the truth is all it takes to set us free and carry our awareness back to Heaven. Because in truth, we, the one Son of God have been safe in Heaven this whole time. We never left—where could we possibly "go"? In reality we've been sleeping safely, eternally within the Mind of God. We're just having a really epic bad dream.

2. It's the eternal Will of God that Its Creation be safe, strong and joyous, infinitely peaceful and abundant, radiantly pure, holy and limitlessly free, at home and one within the Mind of God forever. And God's Will most certainly be done. We, the Created, are endowed with free will, yet only in terms of what we choose to do and think, what we choose to remember, and when we choose to remember it. What we are remains unchanged forever.

3. The choice is ours: We can delay the memory of Heaven as long as we want, yet sooner or later every single one of us without exception will freely choose to remember our own shared divinity, to remember the Mind of God and return to oneness. Because that's God's Will, and in truth, God's Will and our will are one and the same.
The memory of God, and of what we really are, may be buried beneath an unfathomably deep mountain of mud, but still that memory remains eternally in each of us, pure, unchanging and untouched by any part of this world. To let it come back fully into our awareness, all we need to do is willingly let go of all belief in the fantasy world we made to replace it.
Maybe we won't make the choice to withdraw our belief from this upside down world we made and return to the memory of God in this lifetime; maybe not even in the next hundred or thousand lifetimes. No harm done. Time isn't even the blink of an eye to Eternity Itself; we're free to mess around as long as we want to go on pretending we're stuck in dreams.
And make no mistake, we're only pretending we're stuck. We're the Son of God, the perfect Thought within the infinite Mind. We can wake up any time we feel like it.

The perfect vehicle

1. Remember Jesus of Nazareth, who fully realized that He is the Son of God, forever one with his Creator? This realization itself is Christ, making Him, yes, Jesus the Christ. Yet Jesus didn't corner the market—anybody who attains the same full memory of one Mind and Thought united is also Christ; the whole and complete Son of God in its unseparated glory is the Christ, the perfect undivided Thought that knows the Mind of God. So any small chunk of us who comes to remember the truth is one and the same.

2. A Course in Miracles (a course taught by the Christ Mind) offers each one of us crazy Sons of God the opportunity to "undo" the ego mind, slowly restoring our sanity and our memory. Our primary goal: That buried toxic waste dump of unconscious guilt needs to be removed. Partly because it's the power source that keeps the ego mind large and in charge; partly because it's the barrier that stops us from being able to accept the holy truth about ourselves and each other; and partly because it's the source of never-ending unconscious pain to us all.

That pain is unbearable, so we constantly try to rid ourselves of it by finding "others" guilty instead of us, compulsively hurling our own unconscious guilt at every target we see. There are two major things wrong with that strategy: One, the guilt stays exactly where it is no matter how hard we try to transfer it to somebody else. Two, there is nobody else; there's only one of us in truth, and although we can lose ourselves in fragmented fantasy, we can't rewrite the laws of Heaven. So every time we toss a bucket of toxic guilt at somebody or something "out there," we're really attacking ourselves.

3. We're given the means to unmake our unconscious guilt while we unmake the ego mind: we're taught to practice what the Course calls "forgiveness." Yet this isn't forgiveness in the usual sense. The world's version of forgiveness says: You've sinned. I will rise above my desire to blame you for that, and instead find compassion in my heart to forgive and forget what you did.
The problem with this kind of forgiveness is that it assumes the fantasy of separation is true. It's really saying: You are different from me; I am innocent and I stand apart from you and judge you to be guilty. The bad thing you did really happened and has real consequences, but I will overlook it and show you my mercy.
And so the world the ego made is preserved. And we can freely continue to splash our buckets of unconscious guilt onto "others," because this form of forgiveness requires that we first find that other person guilty before choosing to absolve them of that guilt.
Forgiveness as practiced by the Course, on the other hand, is designed to gently undo the ego's world by reminding the mind that what it thinks it sees can't possibly be real. True forgiveness says:

Although I think I see you as separate from myself, and although I'm tempted to perceive you as guilty, in reality I'm completely mistaken; I'm not seeing you as you really are. In truth, you are holy and innocent, perfect and pure. You can't possibly have sinned, because sin doesn't really exist. You are divine love, immortal spirit, and you remain exactly as God created you. And you and I are one, eternally safe in Heaven.

4. Each miracle of silent forgiveness that is offered helps to heal our own seemingly split mind at the same time that it helps to heal the mind of its intended recipient. In truth it helps to heal the entire world, as the Son of God is one Self, and healing received by one is received by all.

That's because another of Heaven's immutable laws is this: Giving is receiving.

Which makes perfect sense when we consider that everything is one. The more we give in truth, the more we receive, because there's only one of us doing both the giving and receiving. This is the reason it's impossible to suffer from lack of abundance—we have and are everything, so how could we ever lose anything? When we give we simultaneously receive. Sacrifice or scarcity of any kind is impossible. When we're lost in fantasy, however, we need only believe in scarcity to make it real for us.

This immutable law of giving and receiving is also the reason we're only able to attack ourselves when we try to splash the unconscious guilt around; the more we give blame to "others" for our own unconscious guilt, the more we simultaneously receive the blame we send out.

Luckily for us, the flipside is also true: As we attempt to wake up to the truth, every bit of real forgiveness we offer to others is automatically received within our own minds.

5. And that's A Course in Miracles' vehicle for getting us back to the memory and the experience of Heaven. The Course tells us the only reliable way to heal our own unconscious guilt is to truly forgive "others," thereby automatically forgiving ourselves. It says there's no other path to salvation than letting the world off the hook for its imaginary sins; only by making the choice to see others as they really are—perfect, immortal spirit—are we able to eventually undo the ego mind and remember that perfect, immortal spirit is what we are, too. And to help us along the way, the Course offers us an infallible Guide, a perfect partner to keep our vehicle pointed in the right direction.

The infallible Guide 1. We observe this world with its wars and poverty, its depravity, corruption and cruelty, and we find it hard to believe it deserves anything except our bitterest judgment and condemnation; we forgot it isn't real and we made the whole thing up. We'd rather just toss our buckets of toxic guilt at the mirror and call it sinful. And that's just the way the ego mind likes it. The ego is only capable of lies. That's the function we assigned it when we made it. And because we freely choose to live in this world—the world of lies that the ego made with our full consent—any attempt to disrupt the ego's thought system by introducing the thought system of truth will be met by unconscious resistance on our part. We're used to looking at everything upside down, so the prospect of eternal life seems like annihilation to us; to be faced with the immediate experience of God's perfect, gentle love seems terrifyingly like damnation and suffering beyond all imagining.

2. When we chose to believe in the ego mind, we chose the worst possible friend and guide. The ego would much rather see us dead than delivered from pain; if we were to find peace and happiness, the ego would have no place to call home. We can't be annihilated, but the ego can.

The Course offers us another Friend and Guide instead. Which is a very useful thing, because the road back to the memory of God can get twisty and confusing at times; the ego will do everything in its power to make sure of it. Without this steadfast and loving Help, it could take a very long time to get anywhere at all. The Course calls this infallible Guide the Holy Spirit.

The Holy Spirit, of course, is not some sort of Casper the Heavenly Ghost. The Holy Spirit is that aforementioned spark of pure and radiant memory existing eternally in each of us; it calls out to us ceaselessly from beneath Mud Mountain, asking us to remember what we really are and what God Is. The Holy Spirit is our own highest Self.

3. The Course also refers to the Holy Spirit as the Voice for God. That's the Voice for God. God Itself doesn't speak to us. God is fully occupied with being perfect, eternal love and nothing else. The Mind of God can't communicate directly with anybody who believes they're living inside a body in a world made of fear. The thought system of fear and the thought system of love are mutually exclusive—we can't believe mostly in one, yet a little bit in the other. One is pure and eternal truth; the other simply doesn't exist. It's literally All or nothing. The Voice for God, the Holy Spirit, acts as a bridge between Heaven and our shadow world made of fear. The Holy Spirit remembers the Mind of God—it knows with perfect certainty that the separation never happened. It knows we remain exactly as God created us. Yet it also sees our mountain of mud; it knows what we're going through here in Fear World at every moment. It understands the temptations and obstacles we think we face, it knows our hopes and worries and all our seeming weaknesses. Yet it will gently remind us also of our strengths as it guides us lovingly toward our own eternal happiness.

Each time we offer a silent miracle of forgiveness, it's the Holy Spirit's job to undo a bit of the ego and heal unconscious guilt within the seemingly split mind of the one Son of God. These are acts we're not capable of accomplishing on our own, as long as we still believe we're individual bodies with separate minds. When we practice forgiveness as described by the Course, we do so in partnership with the Holy Spirit.

Not one of us who believes in Fear World knows how to retrace our steps and get back home to the memory of God. The Holy Spirit, our highest Self, remembers the way. The Course asks us to step back and let this eternal Friend and Guide lead us; it assures us that the road home will be much shorter — and infinitely smoother — if we do.

The guiltless mind

A Course in Miracles tells us that a guiltless mind can't experience suffering of any kind. Consider what that means: For a mind to be entirely guiltless, every last bit of Mud Mountain has to have been swept away, every drop of toxic unconscious guilt has been dissolved and the mind is now fully healed and whole. Which is another way of saying we've chosen to wake up from our Very Bad Dream, fully remembering and accepting the truth: That we are not separate, we are not bodies, there's no such thing as guilt or sin, and we are all one Thought forever cherished within the Mind of God. We are eternal, perfect love and nothing else.

When our mind is healed and awake to the truth, it means our perception of this world has been completely purified, cleansed of all belief in fear. This enables the Mind of God to lift our awareness back to oneness in Heaven where it belongs. This state of limitless peace and infinite joy is the Christ Mind.

The guiltless state of Mind denies all reality of this world — it sees no death, no pain, no imperfection or unhappiness of any kind, because it knows none of it can be real. Only the eternal Mind of God is real. Although terrible or painful or fearful things may still appear to be happening in this dream world, the guiltless mind remains joyous and serene, responding to these seeming events only with divine love, for it knows that is what it is and nothing else.

It's hard for us to understand what that state of life would be like. We hear that if we succeed in becoming Christ we'd have to respond to the events of this world with unconditional love, and the idea sounds terrifying. Maybe it even angers us, as if we're being stripped of our defenses and lured to our own slaughter.

The Course assures us no such sacrifice is necessary in the attainment of the state of Christ; not only is it unnecessary, it isn't even possible. The events of this world are not real, and the infinitely joyous and serene Christ Mind knows it. Not as theoretical textbook knowledge; the Christ Mind knows it and lives it as its own undeniable experience of the truth.

And because the Christ Mind isn't fooled by any part of this dream world (if it was, it couldn't be the Christ Mind — All or nothing, remember?), it knows for certain it doesn't live in a body. And so the body that this particular Christ seems to inhabit has been forgiven by its Mind along with all the rest of the bodies in the dream of separation. And with forgiveness, this Christ's "body" is no longer capable of suffering because the Mind that dreamed it up is no longer capable of suffering. So the body is now pain free and perfectly at peace, because that is the state of the Mind that made it up.

Only infinite happiness, freedom, safety, strength and peace await the Mind that returns itself to God. And what becomes of the body walking around that's seemingly still attached to that Mind?

That's entirely up to the Mind Itself.

It might feel called to teach. It could choose to take its message on the road to the world at large — or it might be quietly content to live out its days in joyous obscurity, offering silent healing to the world without ever stepping forward to speak of what it knows. A Christ's true gift to the world is the silent healing it offers to all seemingly fragmented minds; anything else it chooses to "accomplish" here within the dream is cake.

And when the time finally comes to gently lay the body aside (for all bodies are born to die) the Christ does so with joy and tranquility, because it knows it's going home to perfect eternal oneness with God, and the cycle of birth and death is over at last.

ABOUT THE AUTHOR

Carrie Triffet sports a dazzling array of flaws and vices, none of which seem to dampen her single-minded desire for spiritual enlightenment. When not engaged in this messengering gig, she works as a designer and marketing consultant.

For photos of people, places and things from

Long Time No See: diaries of an unlikely messenger, and for more information about the book as well as reviews and interviews, and a complete list of the "homework" books mentioned in this story, visit **www.unlikelymessenger.com**

Read more of her ongoing adventures on her blog, **http://unlikelymessenger.com/blog**

And so dear prisoner, I invite you to embark on a new adventure. You have the time, and if you have the willingness, the tenacity and the courage, venture now into the way to true freedom.
Godspeed!

INTRODUCTION TO A COURSE IN MIRACLES

A theoretical foundation such as the text provides is necessary as a framework to make the exercises in this workbook meaningful. Yet it is doing the exercises that will make the goal of the course possible. An untrained mind can accomplish nothing. It is the purpose of this workbook to train your mind to think along the lines the text sets forth.

The exercises are very simple. They do not require a great deal of time, and it does not matter where you do them. They need no preparation. The training period is one year. The exercises are numbered from 1 to 365. Do not undertake to do more than one set of exercises a day.

The workbook is divided into two main sections, the first dealing with the undoing of the way you see now, and the second with the acquisition of true perception. With the exception of the review periods, each day's exercises are planned around one central idea, which is stated first. This is followed by a description of the specific procedures by which the idea for the day is to be applied.

The purpose of the workbook is to train your mind in a systematic way to a different perception of everyone and everything in the world. The exercises are planned to help you generalize the lessons, so that you will understand that each of them is equally applicable to everyone and everything you see.

Transfer of training in true perception does not proceed as does transfer of the training of the world. If true perception has been achieved in connection with any person, situation or event, total transfer to everyone and everything is certain. On the other hand, one exception held apart from true perception makes its accomplishments anywhere impossible.

The only general rules to be observed throughout, then, are: First, that the exercises be practiced with great specificity, as will be indicated. This will help you to generalize the ideas involved to every situation in which you find yourself, and to everyone and everything in it. Second, be sure that you do not decide for yourself that there are some people, situations or things to which the ideas are inapplicable. This will interfere with transfer of training. The very nature of true perception is that it has no limits. It is the opposite of the way you see now.

The overall aim of the exercises is to increase your ability to extend the ideas you will be practicing to include everything. This will require no effort on your part. The exercises themselves meet the conditions necessary for this kind of transfer.

Some of the ideas the workbook presents you will find hard to believe, and others may seem to be quite startling. This does not matter. You are merely asked to apply the ideas as you are directed to do. You are not asked to judge them at all. You are asked only to use them. It is their use that will give them meaning to you, and will show you that they are true.

Remember only this; you need not believe the ideas, you need not accept them, and you need not even welcome them. Some of them you may actively resist. None of this will matter, or decrease their efficacy. But do not allow yourself to make exceptions in applying the ideas the workbook contains, and whatever your reactions to the ideas may be, use them. Nothing more than that is required.

Lesson 1

Nothing I see in this room [on this street, from this window, in this place] means anything.

Now look slowly around you, and practice applying this idea very specifically to whatever you see:

THIS TABLE DOES NOT MEAN ANYTHING.
THIS CHAIR DOES NOT MEAN ANYTHING.
THIS HAND DOES NOT MEAN ANYTHING.
THIS FOOT DOES NOT MEAN ANYTHING.
THIS PEN DOES NOT MEAN ANYTHING.

Then look farther away from your immediate area, and apply the idea to a wider range:

THAT DOOR DOES NOT MEAN ANYTHING.
THIS BODY DOES NOT MEAN ANYTHING.
THIS LAMP DOES NOT MEAN ANYTHING.
THIS SIGN DOES NOT MEAN ANYTHING.
THIS SHADOW DOES NOT MEAN ANYTHING.

Notice that these statements are not arranged in any order, and make no allowance for differences in the kinds of things to which they are applied. That is the purpose of the exercise. The statement should merely be applied to anything you see. As you practice the idea for the day, use it totally indiscriminately. Do not attempt to apply it to everything you see, for these exercises should not become ritualistic. Only be sure that nothing you see is specifically excluded. One thing is like another as far as the application of the idea is concerned.

Each of the first three lessons should not be done more than twice a day each, preferably morning and evening. Nor should they be attempted for more than a minute or so, unless that entails a sense of hurry. A comfortable sense of leisure is essential.

Lesson 2

**I have given everything I see in this room
[on this street, from this window, in this place]
all the meaning that it has for me.**

The exercises with this idea are the same as those for the first one. Begin with the things that are near you, and apply the idea to whatever your glance rests on. Then increase the range outward. Turn your head so that you include whatever is on either side. If possible, turn around and apply the idea to what was behind you. Remain as indiscriminate as possible in selecting subjects for its application, do not concentrate on anything in particular, and do not attempt to include everything you see in a given area, or you will introduce strain.

Merely glance easily and fairly quickly around you, trying to avoid selection by size, brightness, color, material, or relative importance to you. Take the subjects simply as you see them. Try to apply the exercise with equal ease to a body or a button, a fly or a floor, an arm or an apple. The sole criterion for applying the idea to anything is merely that your eyes have lighted on it. Make no attempt to include anything particular, but be sure that nothing is specifically excluded.

Each of the first three lessons should not be done more than twice a day each, preferably morning and evening. Nor should they be attempted for more than a minute or so, unless that entails a sense of hurry. A comfortable sense of leisure is essential.

Lesson 3

I do not understand anything I see in this room
[on this street, from this window, in this place].

Apply this idea in the same way as the previous ones, without making distinctions of any kind. Whatever you see becomes a proper subject for applying the idea. Be sure that you do not question the suitability of anything for application of the idea. These are not exercises in judgment. Anything is suitable if you see it. Some of the things you see may have emotionally charged meaning for you. Try to lay such feelings aside, and merely use these things exactly as you would anything else.

The point of the exercises is to help you clear your mind of all past associations, to see things exactly as they appear to you now, and to realize how little you really understand about them. It is therefore essential that you keep a perfectly open mind, unhampered by judgment, in selecting the things to which the idea for the day is to be applied. For this purpose one thing is like another; equally suitable and therefore equally useful.

Lesson 4

These thoughts do not mean anything.
They are like the things I see in this room
[on this street, from this window, in this place].

Unlike the preceding ones, these exercises do not begin with the idea for the day. In these practice periods, begin with noting the thoughts that are crossing your mind for about a minute. Then apply the idea to them. If you are already aware of unhappy thoughts, use them as subjects for the idea. Do not, however, select only the thoughts you think are "bad." You will find, if you train yourself to look at your thoughts, that they represent such a mixture that, in a sense, none of them can be called "good" or "bad." This is why they do not mean anything.

In selecting the subjects for the application of today's idea, the usual specificity is required. Do not be afraid to use "good" thoughts as well as "bad." None of them represents your real thoughts, which are being covered up by them. The "good" ones are but shadows of what lies beyond, and shadows make sight difficult. The "bad" ones are blocks to sight, and make seeing impossible. You do not want either.

This is a major exercise, and will be repeated from time to time in somewhat different form. The aim here is to train you in the first steps toward the goal of separating the meaningless from the meaningful. It is a first attempt in the long-range purpose of learning to see the meaningless as outside you, and the meaningful within. It is also the beginning of training your mind to recognize what is the same and what is different.

In using your thoughts for application of the idea for today, identify each thought by the central figure or event it contains; for example:

THIS THOUGHT ABOUT ___ DOES NOT MEAN ANYTHING.
IT IS LIKE THE THINGS I SEE IN THIS ROOM [ON THIS STREET, AND SO ON].

You can also use the idea for a particular thought that you recognize as harmful. This practice is useful, but is not a substitute for the more random procedures to be followed for the exercises. Do not, however, examine your mind for more than a minute or so. You are too inexperienced as yet to avoid a tendency to become pointlessly preoccupied.

Further, since these exercises are the first of their kind, you may find the suspension of judgment in connection with thoughts particularly difficult. Do not repeat these exercises more than three or four times during the day. We will return to them later.

Lesson 5

I am never upset for the reason I think.

This idea, like the preceding one, can be used with any person, situation or event you think is causing you pain. Apply it specifically to whatever you believe is the cause of your upset, using the description of the feeling in whatever term seems accurate to you. The upset may seem to be fear, worry, depression, anxiety, anger, hatred, jealousy or any number of forms, all of which will be perceived as different. This is not true. However, until you learn that form does not matter, each form becomes a proper subject for the exercises for the day. Applying the same idea to each of them separately is the first step in ultimately recognizing they are all the same.

When using the idea for today for a specific perceived cause of an upset in any form, use both the name of the form in which you see the upset, and the cause which you ascribe to it. For example:

I AM NOT ANGRY AT ___ FOR THE REASON I THINK.
I AM NOT AFRAID OF ___ FOR THE REASON I THINK.

But again, this should not be substituted for practice periods in which you first search your mind for "sources" of upset in which you believe, and forms of upset which you think result.

In these exercises, more than in the preceding ones, you may find it hard to be indiscriminate, and to avoid giving greater weight to some subjects than to others. It might help to precede the exercises with the statement:

THERE ARE NO SMALL UPSETS.
THEY ARE ALL EQUALLY DISTURBING TO MY PEACE OF MIND.

Then examine your mind for whatever is distressing you, regardless of how much or how little you think it is doing so.

You may also find yourself less willing to apply today's idea to some perceived sources of upset than to others. If this occurs, think first of this:

I CANNOT KEEP THIS FORM OF UPSET AND LET THE OTHERS GO.
FOR THE PURPOSES OF THESE EXERCISES, THEN, I WILL REGARD THEM ALL AS THE SAME.

Then search your mind for no more than a minute or so, and try to identify a number of different forms of upset that are disturbing you, regardless of the relative importance you may give them. Apply the idea for today to each of them, using the name of both the source of the upset as you perceive it, and of the feeling as you experience it. Further examples are:

I AM NOT WORRIED ABOUT ___ FOR THE REASON I THINK.
I AM NOT DEPRESSED ABOUT ___ FOR THE REASON I THINK.

Three or four times during the day is enough.

Lesson 6

I am upset because I see something that is not there.

The exercises with this idea are very similar to the preceding ones. Again, it is necessary to name both the form of upset (anger, fear, worry, depression and so on) and the perceived source very specifically for any application of the idea. For example:

I AM ANGRY AT ____ BECAUSE I SEE SOMETHING THAT IS NOT THERE.
I AM WORRIED ABOUT ____ BECAUSE I SEE SOMETHING THAT IS NOT THERE.

Today's idea is useful for application to anything that seems to upset you, and can profitably be used throughout the day for that purpose. However, the three or four practice periods which are required should be preceded by a minute or so of mind searching, as before, and the application of the idea to each upsetting thought uncovered in the search.

Again, if you resist applying the idea to some upsetting thoughts more than to others, remind yourself of the two cautions stated in the previous lesson:

THERE ARE NO SMALL UPSETS. THEY ARE ALL EQUALLY DISTURBING TO MY PEACE OF MIND.

And:

I CANNOT KEEP THIS FORM OF UPSET AND LET THE OTHERS GO. FOR THE PURPOSES OF THESE EXERCISES, THEN, I WILL REGARD THEM ALL AS THE SAME.

Lesson 7

I see only the past.

This idea is particularly difficult to believe at first. Yet it is the rationale for all of the preceding ones.

It is the reason why nothing that you see means anything.
It is the reason why you have given everything you see all the meaning that it has for you.
It is the reason why you do not understand anything you see.
It is the reason why your thoughts do not mean anything, and why they are like the things you see.
It is the reason why you are never upset for the reason you think.
It is the reason why you are upset because you see something that is not there.

Old ideas about time are very difficult to change, because everything you believe is rooted in time, and depends on your not learning these new ideas about it. Yet that is precisely why you need new ideas about time. This first time idea is not really so strange as it may sound at first.

Look at a cup, for example. Do you see a cup, or are you merely reviewing your past experiences of picking up a cup, being thirsty, drinking from a cup, feeling the rim of a cup against your lips, having breakfast and so on? Are not your aesthetic reactions to the cup, too, based on past experiences? How else would you know whether or not this kind of cup will break if you drop it? What do you know about this cup except what you learned in the past? You would have no idea what this cup is, except for your past learning. Do you, then, really see it?

Look about you. This is equally true of whatever you look at. Acknowledge this by applying the idea for today indiscriminately to whatever catches your eye. For example:

I SEE ONLY THE PAST IN THIS PENCIL.
I SEE ONLY THE PAST IN THIS SHOE.
I SEE ONLY THE PAST IN THIS HAND.
I SEE ONLY THE PAST IN THAT BODY.
I SEE ONLY THE PAST IN THAT FACE.

Do not linger over any one thing in particular, but remember to omit nothing specifically. Glance briefly at each subject, and then move on to the next. Three or four practice periods, each to last a minute or so, will be enough.

Lesson 8

My mind is preoccupied with past thoughts.

This idea is, of course, the reason why you see only the past. No one really sees anything. He sees only his thoughts projected outward. The mind's preoccupation with the past is the cause of the misconception about time from which your seeing suffers. Your mind cannot grasp the present, which is the only time there is. It therefore cannot understand time, and cannot, in fact, understand anything.

The one wholly true thought one can hold about the past is that it is not here. To think about it at all is therefore to think about illusions. Very few have realized what is actually entailed in picturing the past or in anticipating the future. The mind is actually blank when it does this, because it is not really thinking about anything.

The purpose of the exercises for today is to begin to train your mind to recognize when it is not really thinking at all. While thoughtless ideas preoccupy your mind, the truth is blocked. Recognizing that your mind has been merely blank, rather than believing that it is filled with real ideas, is the first step to opening the way to vision.

The exercises for today should be done with eyes closed. This is because you actually cannot see anything, and it is easier to recognize that no matter how vividly you may picture a thought, you are not seeing anything. With as little investment as possible, search your mind for the usual minute or so, merely noting the thoughts you find there. Name each one by the central figure or theme it contains, and pass on to the next. Introduce the practice period by saying:

I SEEM TO BE THINKING ABOUT ___.

Then name each of your thoughts specifically, for example:

I SEEM TO BE THINKING ABOUT [NAME OF A PERSON], ABOUT [NAME OF AN OBJECT], ABOUT [NAME OF AN EMOTION],

and so on, concluding at the end of the mind-searching period with:

BUT MY MIND IS PREOCCUPIED WITH PAST THOUGHTS.

This can be done four or five times during the day, unless you find it irritates you. If you find it trying, three or four times is sufficient. You might find it helpful, however, to include your irritation, or any emotion that the idea for today may induce, in the mind searching itself.

Lesson 9

I see nothing as it is now.

This idea obviously follows from the two preceding ones. But while you may be able to accept it intellectually, it is unlikely that it will mean anything to you as yet. However, understanding is not necessary at this point. In fact, the recognition that you do not understand is a prerequisite for undoing your false ideas. These exercises are concerned with practice, not with understanding. You do not need to practice what you already understand. It would indeed be circular to aim at understanding, and assume that you have it already.

It is difficult for the untrained mind to believe that what it seems to picture is not there. This idea can be quite disturbing, and may meet with active resistance in any number of forms. Yet that does not preclude applying it. No more than that is required for these or any other exercises. Each small step will clear a little of the darkness away, and understanding will finally come to lighten every corner of the mind that has been cleared of the debris that darkens it.

These exercises, for which three or four practice periods are sufficient, involve looking about you and applying the idea for the day to whatever you see, remembering the need for its indiscriminate application, and the essential rule of excluding nothing. For example:

I DO NOT SEE THIS TYPEWRITER AS IT IS NOW.
I DO NOT SEE THIS TELEPHONE AS IT IS NOW.
I DO NOT SEE THIS ARM AS IT IS NOW.

Begin with things that are nearest you, and then extend the range outward:

I DO NOT SEE THAT COAT RACK AS IT IS NOW.
I DO NOT SEE THAT DOOR AS IT IS NOW.
I DO NOT SEE THAT FACE AS IT IS NOW.

It is emphasized again that while complete inclusion should not be attempted, specific exclusion must be avoided. Be sure you are honest with yourself in making this distinction. You may be tempted to obscure it.

Lesson 10

My thoughts do not mean anything.

This idea applies to all the thoughts of which you are aware, or become aware in the practice periods. The reason the idea is applicable to all of them is that they are not your real thoughts. We have made this distinction before, and will do so again. You have no basis for comparison as yet. When you do, you will have no doubt that what you once believed were your thoughts did not mean anything.

This is the second time we have used this kind of idea. The form is only slightly different. This time the idea is introduced with "My thoughts" instead of "These thoughts," and no link is made overtly with the things around you. The emphasis is now on the lack of reality of what you think you think.

This aspect of the correction process began with the idea that the thoughts of which you are aware are meaningless, outside rather than within; and then stressed their past rather than their present status. Now we are emphasizing that the presence of these "thoughts" means that you are not thinking. This is merely another way of repeating our earlier statement that your mind is really a blank. To recognize this is to recognize nothingness when you think you see it. As such, it is the prerequisite for vision.

Close your eyes for these exercises, and introduce them by repeating the idea for today quite slowly to yourself. Then add:

THIS IDEA WILL HELP TO RELEASE ME FROM ALL THAT I NOW BELIEVE.

The exercises consist, as before, in searching your mind for all the thoughts that are available to you, without selection or judgment. Try to avoid classification of any kind. In fact, if you find it helpful to do so, you might imagine that you are watching an oddly assorted procession going by, which has little if any personal meaning to you. As each one crosses your mind, say:

MY THOUGHT ABOUT ___ DOES NOT MEAN ANYTHING.
MY THOUGHT ABOUT ___ DOES NOT MEAN ANYTHING.

Today's thought can obviously serve for any thought that distresses you at any time. In addition, five practice periods are recommended, each involving no more than a minute or so of mind searching. It is not recommended that this time period be extended, and it should be reduced to half a minute or less if you experience discomfort. Remember, however, to repeat the idea slowly before applying it specifically, and also to add:

THIS IDEA WILL HELP TO RELEASE ME FROM ALL THAT I NOW BELIEVE.

Lesson 11

My meaningless thoughts are showing me a meaningless world.

This is the first idea we have had that is related to a major phase of the correction process; the reversal of the thinking of the world. It seems as if the world determines what you perceive. Today's idea introduces the concept that your thoughts determine the world you see. Be glad indeed to practice the idea in its initial form, for in this idea is your release made sure. The key to forgiveness lies in it.

The practice periods for today's idea are to be undertaken somewhat differently from the previous ones. Begin with your eyes closed, and repeat the idea slowly to yourself. Then open your eyes and look about, near and far, up and down, — anywhere. During the minute or so to be spent in using the idea merely repeat it to yourself, being sure to do so without haste, and with no sense of urgency or effort.

To do these exercises for maximum benefit, the eyes should move from one thing to another fairly rapidly, since they should not linger on anything in particular. The words, however, should be used in an unhurried, even leisurely fashion. The introduction to this idea, in particular, should be practiced as casually as possible. It contains the foundation for the peace, relaxation and freedom from worry that we are trying to achieve. On concluding the exercises, close your eyes and repeat the idea once more slowly to yourself.

Three practice periods today will probably be sufficient. However, if there is little or no uneasiness and an inclination to do more, as many as five may be undertaken. More than this is not recommended.

Lesson 12

I am upset because I see a meaningless world.

The importance of this idea lies in the fact that it contains a correction for a major perceptual distortion. You think that what upsets you is a frightening world, or a sad world, or a violent world, or an insane world. All these attributes are given it by you. The world is meaningless in itself.

These exercises are done with eyes open. Look around you, this time quite slowly. Try to pace yourself so that the slow shifting of your glance from one thing to another involves a fairly constant time interval. Do not allow the time of the shift to become markedly longer or shorter, but try, instead, to keep a measured, even tempo throughout. What you see does not matter. You teach yourself this as you give whatever your glance rests on equal attention and equal time. This is a beginning step in learning to give them all equal value.

As you look about you, say to yourself:

> I THINK I SEE A FEARFUL WORLD, A DANGEROUS WORLD, A HOSTILE WORLD,
> A SAD WORLD, A WICKED WORLD, A CRAZY WORLD,

and so on, using whatever descriptive terms happen to occur to you. If terms which seem positive rather than negative occur to you, include them. For example, you might think of "a good world," or "a satisfying world." If such terms occur to you, use them along with the rest. You may not yet understand why these "nice" adjectives belong in these exercises but remember that a "good world" implies a "bad" one, and a "satisfying world" implies an "unsatisfying" one. All terms which cross your mind are suitable subjects for today's exercises. Their seeming quality does not matter.

Be sure that you do not alter the time intervals between applying today's idea to what you think is pleasant and what you think is unpleasant. For the purposes of these exercises, there is no difference between them. At the end of the practice period, add:

> BUT I AM UPSET BECAUSE I SEE A MEANINGLESS WORLD.

What is meaningless is neither good nor bad. Why, then, should a meaningless world upset you? If you could accept the world as meaningless and let the truth be written upon it for you, it would make you indescribably happy. But because it is meaningless, you are impelled to write upon it what you would have it be. It is this you see in it. It is this that is meaningless in truth. Beneath your words is written the Word of God. The truth upsets you now, but when your words have been erased, you will see His. That is the ultimate purpose of these exercises.

Three or four times is enough for practicing the idea for today. Nor should the practice periods exceed a minute. You may find even this too long. Terminate the exercises whenever you experience a sense of strain.

Lesson 13

A meaningless world engenders fear.

Today's idea is really another form of the preceding one, except that it is more specific as to the emotion aroused. Actually, a meaningless world is impossible. Nothing without meaning exists. However, it does not follow that you will not think you perceive something that has no meaning. On the contrary, you will be particularly likely to think you do perceive it.

Recognition of meaninglessness arouses intense anxiety in all the separated ones. It represents a situation in which God and the ego "challenge" each other as to whose meaning is to be written in the empty space that meaninglessness provides. The ego rushes in frantically to establish its own ideas there, fearful that the void may otherwise be used to demonstrate its own impotence and unreality. And on this alone it is correct.

It is essential, therefore, that you learn to recognize the meaningless, and accept it without fear. If you are fearful, it is certain that you will endow the world with attributes that it does not possess, and crowd it with images that do not exist. To the ego illusions are safety devices, as they must also be to you who equate yourself with the ego.

The exercises for today, which should be done about three or four times for not more than a minute or so at most each time, are to be practiced in a somewhat different way from the preceding ones. With eyes closed, repeat today's idea to yourself. Then open your eyes, and look about you slowly, saying:

I AM LOOKING AT A MEANINGLESS WORLD.

Repeat this statement to yourself as you look about. Then close your eyes, and conclude with:

A MEANINGLESS WORLD ENGENDERS FEAR BECAUSE I THINK I AM IN COMPETITION WITH GOD.

You may find it difficult to avoid resistance, in one form or another, to this concluding statement. Whatever form such resistance may take, remind yourself that you are really afraid of such a thought because of the "vengeance" of the "enemy." You are not expected to believe the statement at this point, and will probably dismiss it as preposterous. Note carefully, however, any signs of overt or covert fear which it may arouse.

This is our first attempt at stating an explicit cause and effect relationship of a kind which you are very inexperienced in recognizing. Do not dwell on the concluding statement, and try not even to think of it except during the practice periods. That will suffice at present.

Lesson 14

God did not create a meaningless world.

The idea for today is, of course, the reason why a meaningless world is impossible. What God did not create does not exist. And everything that does exist exists as He created it. The world you see has nothing to do with reality. It is of your own making, and it does not exist.

The exercises for today are to be practiced with eyes closed throughout. The mind-searching period should be short, a minute at most. Do not have more than three practice periods with today's idea unless you find them comfortable. If you do, it will be because you really understand what they are for.

The idea for today is another step in learning to let go the thoughts that you have written on the world, and see the Word of God in their place. The early steps in this exchange, which can truly be called salvation, can be quite difficult and even quite painful. Some of them will lead you directly into fear. You will not be left there. You will go far beyond it. Our direction is toward perfect safety and perfect peace.

With eyes closed, think of all the horrors in the world that cross your mind. Name each one as it occurs to you, and then deny its reality. God did not create it, and so it is not real. Say, for example:

GOD DID NOT CREATE THAT WAR, AND SO IT IS NOT REAL.
GOD DID NOT CREATE THAT AIRPLANE CRASH, AND SO IT IS NOT REAL.
GOD DID NOT CREATE THAT DISASTER [SPECIFY], AND SO IT IS NOT REAL.

Suitable subjects for the application of today's idea also include anything you are afraid might happen to you, or to anyone about whom you are concerned. In each case, name the "disaster" quite specifically. Do not use general terms. For example, do not say, "God did not create illness," but, "God did not create cancer," or heart attacks, or whatever may arouse fear in you.

This is your personal repertory of horrors at which you are looking. These things are part of the world you see. Some of them are shared illusions, and others are part of your personal hell. It does not matter. What God did not create can only be in your own mind apart from His. Therefore, it has no meaning. In recognition of this fact, conclude the practice periods by repeating today's idea:

GOD DID NOT CREATE A MEANINGLESS WORLD.

The idea for today can, of course, be applied to anything that disturbs you during the day, aside from the practice periods. Be very specific in applying it. Say:

GOD DID NOT CREATE A MEANINGLESS WORLD. HE DID NOT CREATE [SPECIFY THE SITUATION WHICH IS DISTURBING YOU], AND SO IT IS NOT REAL.

Lesson 15

My thoughts are images that I have made.

It is because the thoughts you think you think appear as images that you do not recognize them as nothing. You think you think them, and so you think you see them. This is how your "seeing" was made. This is the function you have given your body's eyes. It is not seeing. It is image making. It takes the place of seeing, replacing vision with illusions.

This introductory idea to the process of image making that you call seeing will not have much meaning for you. You will begin to understand it when you have seen little edges of light around the same familiar objects which you see now. That is the beginning of real vision. You can be certain that real vision will come quickly when this has occurred.

As we go along, you may have many "light episodes." They may take many different forms, some of them quite unexpected. Do not be afraid of them. They are signs that you are opening your eyes at last. They will not persist, because they merely symbolize true perception, and they are not related to knowledge. These exercises will not reveal knowledge to you. But they will prepare the way to it.

In practicing the idea for today, repeat it first to yourself, and then apply it to whatever you see around you, using its name and letting your eyes rest on it as you say:

THIS ___ IS AN IMAGE THAT I HAVE MADE.
THAT ___ IS AN IMAGE THAT I HAVE MADE.

It is not necessary to include a large number of specific subjects for the application of today's idea. It is necessary, however, to continue to look at each subject while you repeat the idea to yourself. The idea should be repeated quite slowly each time.

Although you will obviously not be able to apply the idea to very many things during the minute or so of practice that is recommended, try to make the selection as random as possible. Less than a minute will do for the practice periods, if you begin to feel uneasy. Do not have more than three application periods for today's idea unless you feel completely comfortable with it, and do not exceed four. However, the idea can be applied as needed throughout the day.

Lesson 16

I have no neutral thoughts.

The idea for today is a beginning step in dispelling the belief that your thoughts have no effect. Everything you see is the result of your thoughts. There is no exception to this fact. Thoughts are not big or little; powerful or weak. They are merely true or false. Those that are true create their own likeness. Those that are false make theirs.

There is no more self-contradictory concept than that of "idle thoughts." What gives rise to the perception of a whole world can hardly be called idle. Every thought you have contributes to truth or to illusion; either it extends the truth or it multiplies illusions. You can indeed multiply nothing, but you will not extend it by doing so.

Besides your recognizing that thoughts are never idle, salvation requires that you also recognize that every thought you have brings either peace or war; either love or fear. A neutral result is impossible because a neutral thought is impossible. There is such a temptation to dismiss fear thoughts as unimportant, trivial and not worth bothering about that it is essential you recognize them all as equally destructive, but equally unreal. We will practice this idea in many forms before you really understand it.

In applying the idea for today, search your mind for a minute or so with eyes closed, and actively seek not to overlook any "little" thought that may tend to elude the search. This is quite difficult until you get used to it. You will find that it is still hard for you not to make artificial distinctions. Every thought that occurs to you, regardless of the qualities that you assign to it, is a suitable subject for applying today's idea.

In the practice periods, first repeat the idea to yourself, and then as each one crosses your mind hold it in awareness while you tell yourself:

THIS THOUGHT ABOUT _____ IS NOT A NEUTRAL THOUGHT.
THAT THOUGHT ABOUT _____ IS NOT A NEUTRAL THOUGHT.

As usual, use today's idea whenever you are aware of a particular thought that arouses uneasiness. The following form is suggested for this purpose:

THIS THOUGHT ABOUT _____ IS NOT A NEUTRAL THOUGHT, BECAUSE I HAVE NO NEUTRAL THOUGHTS.

Four or five practice periods are recommended, if you find them relatively effortless. If strain is experienced, three will be enough. The length of the exercise period should also be reduced if there is discomfort.

Lesson 17

I see no neutral things.

This idea is another step in the direction of identifying cause and effect as it really operates in the world. You see no neutral things because you have no neutral thoughts. It is always the thought that comes first, despite the temptation to believe that it is the other way around. This is not the way the world thinks, but you must learn that it is the way you think. If it were not so, perception would have no cause, and would itself be the cause of reality. In view of its highly variable nature, this is hardly likely.

In applying today's idea, say to yourself, with eyes open:

I SEE NO NEUTRAL THINGS BECAUSE I HAVE NO NEUTRAL THOUGHTS.

Then look about you, resting your glance on each thing you note long enough to say:

I DO NOT SEE A NEUTRAL ___, BECAUSE MY THOUGHTS ABOUT ___ ARE NOT NEUTRAL.

For example, you might say:

I DO NOT SEE A NEUTRAL WALL, BECAUSE MY THOUGHTS ABOUT WALLS ARE NOT NEUTRAL.
I DO NOT SEE A NEUTRAL BODY, BECAUSE MY THOUGHTS ABOUT BODIES ARE NOT NEUTRAL.

As usual, it is essential to make no distinctions between what you believe to be animate or inanimate; pleasant or unpleasant. Regardless of what you may believe, you do not see anything that is really alive or really joyous. That is because you are unaware as yet of any thought that is really true, and therefore really happy.

Three or four specific practice periods are recommended, and no less than three are required for maximum benefit, even if you experience resistance. However, if you do, the length of the practice period may be reduced to less than the minute or so that is otherwise recommended.

Lesson 18

I am not alone in experiencing the effects of my seeing.

The idea for today is another step in learning that the thoughts which give rise to what you see are never neutral or unimportant. It also emphasizes the idea that minds are joined, which will be given increasing stress later on.

Today's idea does not refer to what you see as much as to how you see it. Therefore, the exercises for today emphasize this aspect of your perception. The three or four practice periods which are recommended should be done as follows:

Look about you, selecting subjects for the application of the idea for today as randomly as possible, and keeping your eyes on each one long enough to say:

I AM NOT ALONE IN EXPERIENCING THE EFFECTS OF HOW I SEE _____.

Conclude each practice period by repeating the more general statement:

I AM NOT ALONE IN EXPERIENCING THE EFFECTS OF MY SEEING.

A minute or so, or even less, will be sufficient for each practice period.

Lesson 19

I am not alone in experiencing the effects of my thoughts.

The idea for today is obviously the reason why your seeing does not affect you alone. You will notice that at times the ideas related to thinking precede those related to perceiving, while at other times the order is reversed. The reason is that the order does not matter. Thinking and its results are really simultaneous, for cause and effect are never separate.

Today we are again emphasizing the fact that minds are joined. This is rarely a wholly welcome idea at first, since it seems to carry with it an enormous sense of responsibility, and may even be regarded as an "invasion of privacy." Yet it is a fact that there are no private thoughts. Despite your initial resistance to this idea, you will yet understand that it must be true if salvation is possible at all. And salvation must be possible because it is the Will of God.

The minute or so of mind searching which today's exercises require is to be undertaken with eyes closed. The idea for today is to be repeated first, and then the mind should be carefully searched for the thoughts it contains at that time. As you consider each one, name it in terms of the central person or theme it contains, and holding it in your mind as you do so, say:

I AM NOT ALONE IN EXPERIENCING THE EFFECTS OF THIS THOUGHT ABOUT _____.

The requirement of as much indiscriminateness as possible in selecting subjects for the practice periods should be quite familiar to you by now, and will no longer be repeated each day, although it will occasionally be included as a reminder. Do not forget, however, that random selection of subjects for all practice periods remains essential throughout. Lack of order in this connection will ultimately make the recognition of lack of order in miracles meaningful to you.

Apart from the "as needed" application of today's idea, at least three practice periods are required, shortening the length of time involved, if necessary. Do not attempt more than four.

Lesson 20

I am determined to see.

We have been quite casual about our practice periods thus far. There has been virtually no attempt to direct the time for undertaking them, minimal effort has been required, and not even active cooperation and interest have been asked. This approach has been intentional, and very carefully planned. We have not lost sight of the crucial importance of the reversal of your thinking. The salvation of the world depends on it. Yet you will not see if you regard yourself as being coerced, and if you give in to resentment and opposition.

This is our first attempt to introduce structure. Do not misconstrue it as an effort to exert force or pressure. You want salvation. You want to be happy. You want peace. You do not have them now, because your mind is totally undisciplined, and you cannot distinguish between joy and sorrow, pleasure and pain, love and fear. You are now learning how to tell them apart. And great indeed will be your reward.

Your decision to see is all that vision requires. What you want is yours. Do not mistake the little effort that is asked of you for an indication that our goal is of little worth. Can the salvation of the world be a trivial purpose? And can the world be saved if you are not? God has one Son, and he is the resurrection and the life. His will is done because all power is given him in Heaven and on earth. In your determination to see is vision given you.

The exercises for today consist in reminding yourself throughout the day that you want to see. Today's idea also tacitly implies the recognition that you do not see now. Therefore, as you repeat the idea, you are stating that you are determined to change your present state for a better one, and one you really want.

Repeat today's idea slowly and positively at least twice an hour today, attempting to do so every half hour. Do not be distressed if you forget to do so, but make a real effort to remember. The extra repetitions should be applied to any situation, person or event that upsets you. You can see them differently, and you will. What you desire you will see. Such is the real law of cause and effect as it operates in the world.

Lesson 21

I am determined to see things differently.

The idea for today is obviously a continuation and extension of the preceding one. This time, however, specific mind-searching periods are necessary, in addition to applying the idea to particular situations as they may arise. Five practice periods are urged, allowing a full minute for each.

In the practice periods, begin by repeating the idea to yourself. Then close your eyes and search your mind carefully for situations past, present or anticipated that arouse anger in you. The anger may take the form of any reaction ranging from mild irritation to rage. The degree of the emotion you experience does not matter. You will become increasingly aware that a slight twinge of annoyance is nothing but a veil drawn over intense fury.

Try, therefore, not to let the "little" thoughts of anger escape you in the practice periods. Remember that you do not really recognize what arouses anger in you, and nothing that you believe in this connection means anything. You will probably be tempted to dwell more on some situations or persons than on others, on the fallacious grounds that they are more "obvious." This is not so. It is merely an example of the belief that some forms of attack are more justified than others.

As you search your mind for all the forms in which attack thoughts present themselves, hold each one in mind while you tell yourself:

I AM DETERMINED TO SEE _____ [NAME OF PERSON] DIFFERENTLY.

I AM DETERMINED TO SEE _____ [SPECIFY THE SITUATION] DIFFERENTLY.

Try to be as specific as possible. You may, for example, focus your anger on a particular attribute of a particular person, believing that the anger is limited to this aspect. If your perception is suffering from this form of distortion, say:

I AM DETERMINED TO SEE _____ [SPECIFY THE ATTRIBUTE] IN
_____ [NAME OF PERSON] DIFFERENTLY.

Lesson 22

What I see is a form of vengeance.

Today's idea accurately describes the way anyone who holds attack thoughts in his mind must see the world. Having projected his anger onto the world, he sees vengeance about to strike at him. His own attack is thus perceived as self defense. This becomes an increasingly vicious circle until he is willing to change how he sees. Otherwise, thoughts of attack and counter-attack will preoccupy him and people his entire world. What peace of mind is possible to him then?

It is from this savage fantasy that you want to escape. Is it not joyous news to hear that it is not real? Is it not a happy discovery to find that you can escape? You made what you would destroy; everything that you hate and would attack and kill. All that you fear does not exist.

Look at the world about you at least five times today, for at least a minute each time. As your eyes move slowly from one object to another, from one body to another, say to yourself:

I SEE ONLY THE PERISHABLE.
I SEE NOTHING THAT WILL LAST.

WHAT I SEE IS NOT REAL.
WHAT I SEE IS A FORM OF VENGEANCE.

At the end of each practice period, ask yourself:

IS THIS THE WORLD I REALLY WANT TO SEE?

The answer is surely obvious.

Lesson 23

I can escape from the world I see by giving up attack thoughts.

The idea for today contains the only way out of fear that will ever succeed. Nothing else will work; everything else is meaningless. But this way cannot fail. Every thought you have makes up some segment of the world you see. It is with your thoughts, then, that we must work, if your perception of the world is to be changed.

If the cause of the world you see is attack thoughts, you must learn that it is these thoughts which you do not want. There is no point in lamenting the world. There is no point in trying to change the world. It is incapable of change because it is merely an effect. But there is indeed a point in changing your thoughts about the world. Here you are changing the cause. The effect will change automatically.

The world you see is a vengeful world, and everything in it is a symbol of vengeance. Each of your perceptions of "external reality" is a pictorial representation of your own attack thoughts. One can well ask if this can be called seeing. Is not fantasy a better word for such a process, and hallucination a more appropriate term for the result?

You see the world that you have made, but you do not see yourself as the image maker. You cannot be saved from the world, but you can escape from its cause. This is what salvation means, for where is the world you see when its cause is gone? Vision already holds a replacement for everything you think you see now. Loveliness can light your images, and so transform them that you will love them, even though they were made of hate. For you will not be making them alone.

The idea for today introduces the thought that you are not trapped in the world you see, because its cause can be changed. This change requires, first, that the cause be identified and then let go, so that it can be replaced. The first two steps in this process require your cooperation. The final one does not. Your images have already been replaced. By taking the first two steps, you will see that this is so.

Besides using it throughout the day as the need arises, five practice periods are required in applying today's idea. As you look about you, repeat the idea slowly to yourself first, and then close your eyes and devote about a minute to searching your mind for as many attack thoughts as occur to you. As each one crosses your mind say:

I CAN ESCAPE FROM THE WORLD I SEE BY GIVING UP ATTACK THOUGHTS ABOUT _____.

Hold each attack thought in mind as you say this, and then dismiss that thought and go on to the next.

In the practice periods, be sure to include both your thoughts of attacking and of being attacked. Their effects are exactly the same because they are exactly the same. You do not recognize this as yet, and you are asked at this time only to treat them as the same in today's practice periods. We are still at the stage of identifying the cause of the world you see. When you finally learn that thoughts of attack and of being attacked are not different, you will be ready to let the cause go.

Lesson 24

I do not perceive my own best interests.

In no situation that arises do you realize the outcome that would make you happy. Therefore, you have no guide to appropriate action, and no way of judging the result. What you do is determined by your perception of the situation, and that perception is wrong. It is inevitable, then, that you will not serve your own best interests. Yet they are your only goal in any situation which is correctly perceived. Otherwise, you will not recognize what they are.

If you realized that you do not perceive your own best interests, you could be taught what they are. But in the presence of your conviction that you do know what they are, you cannot learn. The idea for today is a step toward opening your mind so that learning can begin.

The exercises for today require much more honesty than you are accustomed to using. A few subjects, honestly and carefully considered in each of the five practice periods which should be undertaken today, will be more helpful than a more cursory examination of a large number. Two minutes are suggested for each of the mind-searching periods which the exercises involve.

The practice periods should begin with repeating today's idea, followed by searching the mind, with closed eyes, for unresolved situations about which you are currently concerned. The emphasis should be on uncovering the outcome you want. You will quickly realize that you have a number of goals in mind as part of the desired outcome, and also that these goals are on different levels and often conflict.

In applying the idea for today, name each situation that occurs to you, and then enumerate carefully as many goals as possible that you would like to be met in its resolution. The form of each application should be roughly as follows:

IN THE SITUATION INVOLVING _____, I WOULD LIKE _____
TO HAPPEN, AND _____ TO HAPPEN,

and so on. Try to cover as many different kinds of outcomes as may honestly occur to you, even if some of them do not appear to be directly related to the situation, or even to be inherent in it at all.

If these exercises are done properly, you will quickly recognize that you are making a large number of demands of the situation which have nothing to do with it. You will also recognize that many of your goals are contradictory, that you have no unified outcome in mind, and that you must experience disappointment in connection with some of your goals, however the situation turns out.

After covering the list of as many hoped-for goals as possible, for each unresolved situation that crosses your mind say to yourself:

I DO NOT PERCEIVE MY OWN BEST INTERESTS IN THIS SITUATION,

and go on to the next one.

Lesson 25

I do not know what anything is for.

Purpose is meaning. Today's idea explains why nothing you see means anything. You do not know what it is for. Therefore, it is meaningless to you. Everything is for your own best interests. That is what it is for; that is its purpose;

that is what it means. It is in recognizing this that your goals become unified. It is in recognizing this that what you see is given meaning.

You perceive the world and everything in it as meaningful in terms of ego goals. These goals have nothing to do with your own best interests, because the ego is not you. This false identification makes you incapable of understanding what anything is for. As a result, you are bound to misuse it. When you believe this, you will try to withdraw the goals you have assigned to the world, instead of attempting to reinforce them.

Another way of describing the goals you now perceive is to say that they are all concerned with "personal" interests. Since you have no personal interests, your goals are really concerned with nothing. In cherishing them, therefore, you have no goals at all. And thus you do not know what anything is for.

Before you can make any sense out of the exercises for today, one more thought is necessary. At the most superficial levels, you do recognize purpose. Yet purpose cannot be understood at these levels. For example, you do understand that a telephone is for the purpose of talking to someone who is not physically in your immediate vicinity. What you do not understand is what you want to reach him for. And it is this that makes your contact with him meaningful or not.

It is crucial to your learning to be willing to give up the goals you have established for everything. The recognition that they are meaningless, rather than "good" or "bad," is the only way to accomplish this. The idea for today is a step in this direction.

Six practice periods, each of two-minutes duration, are required. Each practice period should begin with a slow repetition of the idea for today, followed by looking about you and letting your glance rest on whatever happens to catch your eye, near or far, "important" or "unimportant," "human" or "nonhuman." With your eyes resting on each subject you so select, say, for example:

I DO NOT KNOW WHAT THIS CHAIR IS FOR.
I DO NOT KNOW WHAT THIS PENCIL IS FOR.
I DO NOT KNOW WHAT THIS HAND IS FOR.

Say this quite slowly, without shifting your eyes from the subject until you have completed the statement about it. Then move on to the next subject, and apply today's idea as before.

Lesson 26

My attack thoughts are attacking my invulnerability.

It is surely obvious that if you can be attacked you are not invulnerable. You see attack as a real threat. That is because you believe that you can really attack. And what would have effects through you must also have effects on you. It is this law that will ultimately save you, but you are misusing it now. You must therefore learn how it can be used for your own best interests, rather than against them.

Because your attack thoughts will be projected, you will fear attack. And if you fear attack, you must believe that you are not invulnerable. Attack thoughts therefore make you vulnerable in your own mind, which is where the attack thoughts are. Attack thoughts and invulnerability cannot be accepted together. They contradict each other.

The idea for today introduces the thought that you always attack yourself first. If attack thoughts must entail the belief that you are vulnerable, their effect is to weaken you in your own eyes. Thus they have attacked your perception of yourself. And because you believe in them, you can no longer believe in yourself. A false image of yourself has come to take the place of what you are.

Practice with today's idea will help you to understand that vulnerability or invulnerability is the result of your own thoughts. Nothing except your thoughts can attack you. Nothing except your thoughts can make you think you are vulnerable. And nothing except your thoughts can prove to you this is not so.

Six practice periods are required in applying today's idea. A full two minutes should be attempted for each of them, although the time may be reduced to a minute if the discomfort is too great. Do not reduce it further.

The practice period should begin with repeating the idea for today, then closing your eyes and reviewing the unresolved questions whose outcomes are causing you concern. The concern may take the form of depression, worry, anger, a sense of imposition, fear, foreboding or preoccupation. Any problem as yet unsettled that tends to recur in your thoughts during the day is a suitable subject. You will not be able to use very many for any one practice period, because a longer time than usual should be spent with each one. Today's idea should be applied as follows:

First, name the situation:

I AM CONCERNED ABOUT _____.

Then go over every possible outcome that has occurred to you in that connection and which has caused you concern, referring to each one quite specifically, saying:

I AM AFRAID _____ WILL HAPPEN.

If you are doing the exercises properly, you should have some five or six distressing possibilities available for each situation you use, and quite possibly more. It is much more helpful to cover a few situations thoroughly than to touch on a larger number. As the list of anticipated outcomes for each situation continues, you will probably find some of them, especially those that occur to you toward the end, less acceptable to you. Try, however, to treat them all alike to whatever extent you can.

After you have named each outcome of which you are afraid, tell yourself:

THAT THOUGHT IS AN ATTACK UPON MYSELF.

Conclude each practice period by repeating today's idea to yourself once more.

Lesson 27

Above all else I want to see.

Today's idea expresses something stronger than mere determination. It gives vision priority among your desires. You may feel hesitant about using the idea, on the grounds that you are not sure you really mean it. This does not matter. The purpose of today's exercises is to bring the time when the idea will be wholly true a little nearer.

There may be a great temptation to believe that some sort of sacrifice is being asked of you when you say you want to see above all else. If you become uneasy about the lack of reservation involved, add:

VISION HAS NO COST TO ANYONE.

If fear of loss still persists, add further:

IT CAN ONLY BLESS.

The idea for today needs many repetitions for maximum benefit. It should be used at least every half hour, and more if possible. You might try for every fifteen or twenty minutes. It is recommended that you set a definite time interval for using the idea when you wake or shortly afterwards, and attempt to adhere to it throughout the day. It will not be difficult to do this, even if you are engaged in conversation, or otherwise occupied at the time. You can still repeat one short sentence to yourself without disturbing anything.

The real question is, how often will you remember? How much do you want today's idea to be true? Answer one of these questions, and you have answered the other. You will probably miss several applications, and perhaps quite a number. Do not be disturbed by this, but do try to keep on your schedule from then on. If only once during the day you feel that you were perfectly sincere while you were repeating today's idea, you can be sure that you have saved yourself many years of effort.

Lesson 28

Above all else I want to see things differently.

Today we are really giving specific application to the idea for yesterday. In these practice periods, you will be making a series of definite commitments. The question of whether you will keep them in the future is not our concern here. If you are willing at least to make them now, you have started on the way to keeping them. And we are still at the beginning.

You may wonder why it is important to say, for example, "Above all else I want to see this table differently." In itself it is not important at all. Yet what is by itself? And what does "in itself" mean? You see a lot of separate things about you, which really means you are not seeing at all. You either see or not. When you have seen one thing differently, you will see all things differently. The light you will see in any one of them is the same light you will see in them all.

When you say, "Above all else I want to see this table differently," you are making a commitment to withdraw your preconceived ideas about the table, and open your mind to what it is, and what it is for. You are not defining it in past terms. You are asking what it is, rather than telling it what it is. You are not binding its meaning to your tiny experience of tables, nor are you limiting its purpose to your little personal thoughts.

You will not question what you have already defined. And the purpose of these exercises is to ask questions and receive the answers. In saying, "Above all else I want to see this table differently," you are committing yourself to seeing. It is not an exclusive commitment. It is a commitment that applies to the table just as much as to anything else, neither more nor less.

You could, in fact, gain vision from just that table, if you would withdraw all your own ideas from it, and look upon it with a completely open mind. It has something to show you; something beautiful and clean and of infinite value, full of happiness and hope. Hidden under all your ideas about it is its real purpose, the purpose it shares with all the universe.

In using the table as a subject for applying the idea for today, you are therefore really asking to see the purpose of the universe. You will be making this same request of each subject that you use in the practice periods. And you are making a commitment to each of them to let its purpose be revealed to you, instead of placing your own judgment upon it.

We will have six two-minute practice periods today, in which the idea for the day is stated first, and then applied to whatever you see about you. Not only should the subjects be chosen randomly, but each one should be accorded equal sincerity as today's idea is applied to it, in an attempt to acknowledge the equal value of them all in their contribution to your seeing.

As usual, the applications should include the name of the subject your eyes happen to light on, and you should rest your eyes on it while saying

ABOVE ALL ELSE I WANT TO SEE THIS _____ DIFFERENTLY.

Each application should be made quite slowly, and as thoughtfully as possible. There is no hurry.

Lesson 29

God is in everything I see.

The idea for today explains why you can see all purpose in everything. It explains why nothing is separate, by itself or in itself. And it explains why nothing you see means anything. In fact, it explains every idea we have used thus far, and all subsequent ones as well. Today's idea is the whole basis for vision.

You will probably find this idea very difficult to grasp at this point. You may find it silly, irreverent, senseless, funny and even objectionable. Certainly God is not in a table, for example, as you see it. Yet we emphasized yesterday that a table shares the purpose of the universe. And what shares the purpose of the universe shares the purpose of its Creator.

Try then, today, to begin to learn how to look on all things with love, appreciation and open-mindedness. You do not see them now. Would you know what is in them? Nothing is as it appears to you. Its holy purpose stands beyond your little range. When vision has shown you the holiness that lights up the world, you will understand today's idea perfectly. And you will not understand how you could ever have found it difficult.

Our six two-minute practice periods for today should follow a now familiar pattern: Begin with repeating the idea to yourself, and then apply it to randomly chosen subjects about you, naming each one specifically. Try to avoid the tendency toward self-directed selection, which may be particularly tempting in connection with today's idea because of its wholly alien nature. Remember that any order you impose is equally alien to reality.

Your list of subjects should therefore be as free of self-selection as possible. For example, a suitable list might include:

GOD IS IN THIS COAT HANGER.
GOD IS IN THIS MAGAZINE.
GOD IS IN THIS FINGER.
GOD IS IN THIS LAMP.
GOD IS IN THAT BODY.
GOD IS IN THAT DOOR.
GOD IS IN THAT WASTE BASKET.

In addition to the assigned practice periods, repeat the idea for today at least once an hour, looking slowly about you as you say the words unhurriedly to yourself. At least once or twice, you should experience a sense of restfulness as you do this.

Lesson 30

God is in everything I see because God is in my mind.

The idea for today is the springboard for vision. From this idea will the world open up before you, and you will look upon it and see in it what you have never seen before. Nor will what you saw before be even faintly visible to you.

Today we are trying to use a new kind of "projection." We are not attempting to get rid of what we do not like by seeing it outside. Instead, we are trying to see in the world what is in our minds, and what we want to recognize is there. Thus, we are trying to join with what we see, rather than keeping it apart from us. That is the fundamental difference between vision and the way you see.

Today's idea should be applied as often as possible throughout the day. Whenever you have a moment or so, repeat it to yourself slowly, looking about you, and trying to realize that the idea applies to everything you do see now, or could see now if it were within the range of your sight.

Real vision is not limited to concepts such as "near" and "far." To help you begin to get used to this idea, try to think of things beyond your present range as well as those you can actually see, as you apply today's idea.

Real vision is not only unlimited by space and distance, but it does not depend on the body's eyes at all. The mind is its only source. To aid in helping you to become more accustomed to this idea as well, devote several practice periods to applying today's idea with your eyes closed, using whatever subjects come to mind, and looking within rather than without. Today's idea applies equally to both.

Lesson 31

I am not the victim of the world I see.

Today's idea is the introduction to your declaration of release. Again, the idea should be applied to both the world you see without and the world you see within. In applying the idea, we will use a form of practice which will be used more and more, with changes as indicated. Generally speaking, the form includes two aspects, one in which you apply the idea on a more sustained basis, and the other consisting of frequent applications of the idea throughout the day.

Two longer periods of practice with the idea for today are needed, one in the morning and one at night. Three to five minutes for each of these are recommended. During that time, look about you slowly while repeating the idea two or three times. Then close your eyes, and apply the same idea to your inner world. You will escape from both together, for the inner is the cause of the outer.

As you survey your inner world, merely let whatever thoughts cross your mind come into your awareness, each to be considered for a moment, and then replaced by the next. Try not to establish any kind of hierarchy among them. Watch them come and go as dispassionately as possible. Do not dwell on any one in particular, but try to let the stream move on evenly and calmly, without any special investment on your part. As you sit and quietly watch your thoughts, repeat today's idea to yourself as often as you care to, but with no sense of hurry.

In addition, repeat the idea for today as often as possible during the day. Remind yourself that you are making a declaration of independence in the name of your own freedom. And in your freedom lies the freedom of the world.

The idea for today is also a particularly useful one to use as a response to any form of temptation that may arise. It is a declaration that you will not yield to it, and put yourself in bondage.

Lesson 32

I have invented the world I see.

Today we are continuing to develop the theme of cause and effect. You are not the victim of the world you see because you invented it. You can give it up as easily as you made it up. You will see it or not see it, as you wish. While you want it you will see it; when you no longer want it, it will not be there for you to see.

The idea for today, like the preceding ones, applies to your inner and outer worlds, which are actually the same. However, since you see them as different, the practice periods for today will again include two phases, one involving the world you see outside you, and the other the world you see in your mind. In today's exercises, try to introduce the thought that both are in your own imagination.

Again we will begin the practice periods for the morning and evening by repeating the idea for today two or three times while looking around at the world you see as outside yourself. Then close your eyes and look around your inner world. Try to treat them both as equally as possible. Repeat the idea for today unhurriedly as often as you wish, as you watch the images your imagination presents to your awareness.

For the two longer practice periods three to five minutes are recommended, with not less than three required. More than five can be utilized, if you find the exercise restful. To facilitate this, select a time when few distractions are anticipated, and when you yourself feel reasonably ready.

These exercises are also to be continued during the day, as often as possible. The shorter applications consist of repeating the idea slowly, as you survey either your inner or outer world. It does not matter which you choose.

The idea for today should also be applied immediately to any situation that may distress you. Apply the idea by telling yourself:

I HAVE INVENTED THIS SITUATION AS I SEE IT.

Lesson 33

There is another way of looking at the world.

Today's idea is an attempt to recognize that you can shift your perception of the world in both its outer and inner aspects. A full five minutes should be devoted to the morning and evening applications. In these practice periods, the idea should be repeated as often as you find comfortable, though unhurried applications are essential. Alternate between surveying your outer and inner perceptions, but without an abrupt sense of shifting.

Merely glance casually around the world you perceive as outside yourself, then close your eyes and survey your inner thoughts with equal casualness. Try to remain equally uninvolved in both, and to maintain this detachment as you repeat the idea throughout the day.

The shorter exercise periods should be as frequent as possible. Specific applications of today's idea should also be made immediately, when any situation arises which tempts you to become disturbed. For these applications, say:

THERE IS ANOTHER WAY OF LOOKING AT THIS.

Remember to apply today's idea the instant you are aware of distress. It may be necessary to take a minute or so to sit quietly and repeat the idea to yourself several times. Closing your eyes will probably help in this form of application.

Lesson 34

I could see peace instead of this.

The idea for today begins to describe the conditions that prevail in the other way of seeing. Peace of mind is clearly an internal matter. It must begin with your own thoughts, and then extend outward. It is from your peace of mind that a peaceful perception of the world arises.

Three longer practice periods are required for today's exercises. One in the morning and one in the evening are advised, with an additional one to be undertaken at any time in between that seems most conducive to readiness. All applications should be done with your eyes closed. It is your inner world to which the applications of today's idea should be made.

Some five minutes of mind searching are required for each of the longer practice periods. Search your mind for fear thoughts, anxiety-provoking situations, "offending" personalities or events, or anything else about which you are harboring unloving thoughts. Note them all casually, repeating the idea for today slowly as you watch them arise in your mind, and let each one go, to be replaced by the next.

If you begin to experience difficulty in thinking of specific subjects, continue to repeat the idea to yourself in an unhurried manner, without applying it to anything in particular. Be sure, however, not to make any specific exclusions.

The shorter applications are to be frequent, and made whenever you feel your peace of mind is threatened in any way. The purpose is to protect yourself from temptation throughout the day. If a specific form of temptation arises in your awareness, the exercise should take this form:

I COULD SEE PEACE IN THIS SITUATION INSTEAD OF WHAT I NOW SEE IN IT.

If the inroads on your peace of mind take the form of more generalized adverse emotions, such as depression, anxiety or worry, use the idea in its original form. If you find you need more than one application of today's idea to help you change your mind in any specific context, try to take several minutes and devote them to repeating the idea until you feel some sense of relief. It will help you if you tell yourself specifically:

I CAN REPLACE MY FEELINGS OF DEPRESSION, ANXIETY OR WORRY [OR MY THOUGHTS ABOUT THIS SITUATION, PERSONALITY OR EVENT] WITH PEACE.

Lesson 35

My mind is part of God's. I am very holy.

Today's idea does not describe the way you see yourself now. It does, however, describe what vision will show you. It is difficult for anyone who thinks he is in this world to believe this of himself. Yet the reason he thinks he is in this world is because he does not believe it.

You will believe that you are part of where you think you are. That is because you surround yourself with the environment you want. And you want it to protect the image of yourself that you have made. The image is part of this environment. What you see while you believe you are in it is seen through the eyes of the image. This is not vision. Images cannot see.

The idea for today presents a very different view of yourself. By establishing your Source it establishes your Identity, and it describes you as you must really be in truth. We will use a somewhat different kind of application for today's idea because the emphasis for today is on the perceiver, rather than on what he perceives.

For each of the three five-minute practice periods today, begin by repeating today's idea to yourself, and then close your eyes and search your mind for the various kinds of descriptive terms in which you see yourself. Include all the ego-based attributes which you ascribe to yourself, positive or negative, desirable or undesirable, grandiose or debased. All of them are equally unreal, because you do not look upon yourself through the eyes of holiness.

In the earlier part of the mind-searching period, you will probably emphasize what you consider to be the more negative aspects of your perception of yourself. Toward the latter part of the exercise period, however, more self-inflating descriptive terms may well cross your mind. Try to recognize that the direction of your fantasies about yourself does not matter. Illusions have no direction in reality. They are merely not true.

A suitable unselected list for applying the idea for today might be as follows:

I SEE MYSELF AS IMPOSED ON.
I SEE MYSELF AS DEPRESSED.
I SEE MYSELF AS FAILING.
I SEE MYSELF AS ENDANGERED.
I SEE MYSELF AS HELPLESS.
I SEE MYSELF AS VICTORIOUS.
I SEE MYSELF AS LOSING OUT.
I SEE MYSELF AS CHARITABLE.
I SEE MYSELF AS VIRTUOUS.

You should not think of these terms in an abstract way. They will occur to you as various situations, personalities and events in which you figure cross your mind. Pick up any specific situation that occurs to you, identify the descriptive term or terms you feel are applicable to your reactions to that situation, and use them in applying today's idea. After you have named each one, add:

BUT MY MIND IS PART OF GOD'S. I AM VERY HOLY.

During the longer exercise periods, there will probably be intervals in which nothing specific occurs to you. Do not strain to think up specific things to fill the interval, but merely relax and repeat today's idea slowly until something occurs to you. Although nothing that does occur should be omitted from the exercises, nothing should be "dug out" with effort. Neither force nor discrimination should be used.

As often as possible during the day, pick up a specific attribute or attributes you are ascribing to yourself at the time and apply the idea for today to them, adding the idea in the form stated above to each of them. If nothing particular occurs to you, merely repeat the idea to yourself, with closed eyes.

Lesson 36

My holiness envelops everything I see.

Today's idea extends the idea for yesterday from the perceiver to the perceived. You are holy because your mind is part of God's. And because you are holy, your sight must be holy as well. "Sinless" means without sin. You cannot be without sin a little. You are sinless or not. If your mind is part of God's you must be sinless, or a part of His Mind would be sinful. Your sight is related to His Holiness, not to your ego, and therefore not to your body.

Four three-to-five-minute practice periods are required for today. Try to distribute them fairly evenly, and make the shorter applications frequently, to protect your protection throughout the day. The longer practice periods should take this form:

First, close your eyes and repeat the idea for today several times, slowly. Then open your eyes and look quite slowly about you, applying the idea specifically to whatever you note in your casual survey. Say, for example:

MY HOLINESS ENVELOPS THAT RUG.
MY HOLINESS ENVELOPS THAT WALL.
MY HOLINESS ENVELOPS THESE FINGERS.
MY HOLINESS ENVELOPS THAT CHAIR.
MY HOLINESS ENVELOPS THAT BODY.
MY HOLINESS ENVELOPS THIS PEN.

Several times during these practice periods, close your eyes and repeat the idea to yourself. Then open your eyes, and continue as before.

For the shorter exercise periods, close your eyes and repeat the idea; look about you as you repeat it again; and conclude with one more repetition with your eyes closed. All applications should, of course, be made quite slowly, as effortlessly and unhurriedly as possible.

Lesson 37

My holiness blesses the world.

This idea contains the first glimmerings of your true function in the world, or why you are here. Your purpose is to see the world through your own holiness. Thus are you and the world blessed together. No one loses; nothing is taken away from anyone; everyone gains through your holy vision. It signifies the end of sacrifice because it offers everyone his full due. And he is entitled to everything because it is his birthright as a Son of God.

There is no other way in which the idea of sacrifice can be removed from the world's thinking. Any other way of seeing will inevitably demand payment of someone or something. As a result, the perceiver will lose. Nor will he have any idea why he is losing. Yet is his wholeness restored to his awareness through your vision. Your holiness blesses him by asking nothing of him. Those who see themselves as whole make no demands.

Your holiness is the salvation of the world. It lets you teach the world that it is one with you, not by preaching to it, not by telling it anything, but merely by your quiet recognition that in your holiness are all things blessed along with you.

Today's four longer exercise periods, each to involve three to five minutes of practice, begin with the repetition of the idea for today, followed by a minute or so of looking about you as you apply the idea to whatever you see:

MY HOLINESS BLESSES THIS CHAIR
MY HOLINESS BLESSES THAT WINDOW
MY HOLINESS BLESSES THIS BODY.

Then close your eyes and apply the idea to any person who occurs to you, using his name and saying

MY HOLINESS BLESSES YOU, [NAME].

You may continue the practice period with your eyes closed; you may open your eyes again and apply the idea for today to your outer world if you so desire; you may alternate between applying the idea to what you see around you and to those who are in your thoughts; or you may use any combination of these two phases of application that you prefer. The practice period should conclude with a repetition of the idea with your eyes closed, and another, following immediately, with your eyes open.

The shorter exercises consist of repeating the idea as often as you can. It is particularly helpful to apply it silently to anyone you meet, using his name as you do so. It is essential to use the idea if anyone seems to cause an adverse reaction in you. Offer him the blessing of your holiness immediately, that you may learn to keep it in your own awareness.

Lesson 38

There is nothing my holiness cannot do.

Your holiness reverses all the laws of the world. It is beyond every restriction of time, space, distance and limits of any kind. Your holiness is totally unlimited in its power because it establishes you as a Son of God, at one with the Mind of his Creator.

Through your holiness the power of God is made manifest. Through your holiness the power of God is made available. And there is nothing the power of God cannot do. Your holiness, then, can remove all pain, can end all sorrow, and can solve all problems. It can do so in connection with yourself and with anyone else. It is equal in its power to help anyone because it is equal in its power to save anyone.

If you are holy, so is everything God created. You are holy because all things He created are holy. And all things He created are holy because you are. In today's exercises, we will apply the power of your holiness to all problems, difficulties or suffering in any form that you happen to think of, in yourself or in someone else. We will make no distinctions because there are no distinctions.

In the four longer practice periods, each preferably to last a full five minutes, repeat the idea for today, close your eyes, and then search your mind for any sense of loss or unhappiness of any kind as you see it. Try to make as little distinction as possible between a situation that is difficult for you, and one that is difficult for someone else. Identify the situation specifically, and also the name of the person concerned. Use this form in applying the idea for today:

IN THE SITUATION INVOLVING _____ IN WHICH I SEE MYSELF, THERE IS NOTHING THAT MY HOLINESS CANNOT DO.
IN THE SITUATION INVOLVING _____ IN WHICH _____ SEES HIMSELF, THERE IS NOTHING MY HOLINESS CANNOT DO.

From time to time you may want to vary this procedure, and add some relevant thoughts of your own. You might like, for example, to include thoughts such as:

THERE IS NOTHING MY HOLINESS CANNOT DO BECAUSE THE POWER OF GOD LIES IN IT.

Introduce whatever variations appeal to you, but keep the exercises focused on the theme, "There is nothing my holiness cannot do." The purpose of today's exercises is to begin to instill in you a sense that you have dominion over all things because of what you are.

In the frequent shorter applications, apply the idea in its original form unless a specific problem concerning you or someone else arises, or comes to mind. In that event, use the more specific form in applying the idea to it.

Lesson 39

My holiness is my salvation.

If guilt is hell, what is its opposite? Like the text for which this workbook was written, the ideas used for the exercises are very simple, very clear and totally unambiguous. We are not concerned with intellectual feats nor logical toys. We are dealing only in the very obvious, which has been overlooked in the clouds of complexity in which you think you think.

If guilt is hell, what is its opposite? This is not difficult, surely. The hesitation you may feel in answering is not due to the ambiguity of the question. But do you believe that guilt is hell? If you did, you would see at once how direct and simple the text is, and you would not need a workbook at all. No one needs practice to gain what is already his.

We have already said that your holiness is the salvation of the world. What about your own salvation? You cannot give what you do not have. A savior must be saved. How else can he teach salvation? Today's exercises will apply to you, recognizing that your salvation is crucial to the salvation of the world. As you apply the exercises to your world, the whole world stands to benefit.

Your holiness is the answer to every question that was ever asked, is being asked now, or will be asked in the future. Your holiness means the end of guilt, and therefore the end of hell. Your holiness is the salvation of the world, and your own. How could you to whom your holiness belongs be excluded from it? God does not know unholiness. Can it be He does not know His Son?

A full five minutes are urged for the four longer practice periods for today, and longer and more frequent practice sessions are encouraged. If you want to exceed the minimum requirements, more rather than longer sessions are recommended, although both are suggested.

Begin the practice periods as usual, by repeating today's idea to yourself. Then, with closed eyes, search out your unloving thoughts in whatever form they appear; uneasiness, depression, anger, fear, worry, attack, insecurity and so on. Whatever form they take, they are unloving and therefore fearful. And so it is from them that you need to be saved.

Specific situations, events or personalities you associate with unloving thoughts of any kind are suitable subjects for today's exercises. It is imperative for your salvation that you see them differently. And it is your blessing on them that will save you and give you vision.

Slowly, without conscious selection and without undue emphasis on any one in particular, search your mind for every thought that stands between you and your salvation. Apply the idea for today to each of them in this way:

MY UNLOVING THOUGHTS ABOUT _____ ARE KEEPING ME IN HELL.
MY HOLINESS IS MY SALVATION.

You may find these practice periods easier if you intersperse them with several short periods during which you merely repeat today's idea to yourself slowly a few times. You may also find it helpful to include a few short intervals in which you just relax and do not seem to be thinking of anything. Sustained concentration is very difficult at first. It will become much easier as your mind becomes more disciplined and less distractible.

Meanwhile, you should feel free to introduce variety into the exercise periods in whatever form appeals to you. Do not, however, change the idea itself as you vary the method of applying it. However you elect to use it, the idea should be stated so that its meaning is the fact that your holiness is your salvation. End each practice period by repeating the idea in its original form once more, and adding:

IF GUILT IS HELL, WHAT IS ITS OPPOSITE?

In the shorter applications, which should be made some three or four times an hour and more if possible, you may ask yourself this question, repeat today's idea, and preferably both. If temptations arise, a particularly helpful form of the idea is:

MY HOLINESS IS MY SALVATION FROM THIS.

Lesson 40

I am blessed as a Son of God.

Today we will begin to assert some of the happy things to which you are entitled, being what you are. No long practice periods are required today, but very frequent short ones are necessary. Once every ten minutes would be highly desirable, and you are urged to attempt this schedule and to adhere to it whenever possible. If you forget, try again. If there are long interruptions, try again. Whenever you remember, try again.

You need not close your eyes for the exercise periods, although you will probably find it more helpful if you do. However, you may be in a number of situations during the day when closing your eyes would not be feasible. Do not miss a practice period because of this. You can practice quite well under any circumstances, if you really want to.

Today's exercises take little time and no effort. Repeat the idea for today, and then add several of the attributes you associate with being a Son of God, applying them to yourself. One practice period might, for example, consist of the following:

I AM BLESSED AS A SON OF GOD.
I AM HAPPY, PEACEFUL, LOVING AND CONTENTED.

Another might take this form:

I AM BLESSED AS A SON OF GOD.
I AM CALM, QUIET, ASSURED AND CONFIDENT.

If only a brief period is available, merely telling yourself that you are blessed as a Son of God will do.

Lesson 41

God goes with me wherever I go.

Today's idea will eventually overcome completely the sense of loneliness and abandonment all the separated ones experience. Depression is an inevitable consequence of separation. So are anxiety, worry, a deep sense of helplessness, misery, suffering and intense fear of loss.

The separated ones have invented many "cures" for what they believe to be "the ills of the world." But the one thing they do not do is to question the reality of the problem. Yet its effects cannot be cured because the problem is not real. The idea for today has the power to end all this foolishness forever. And foolishness it is, despite the serious and tragic forms it may take.

Deep within you is everything that is perfect, ready to radiate through you and out into the world. It will cure all sorrow and pain and fear and loss because it will heal the mind that thought these things were real, and suffered out of its allegiance to them.

You can never be deprived of your perfect holiness because its Source goes with you wherever you go. You can never suffer because the Source of all joy goes with you wherever you go. You can never be alone because the Source of all life goes with you wherever you go. Nothing can destroy your peace of mind because God goes with you wherever you go.

We understand that you do not believe all this. How could you, when the truth is hidden deep within, under a heavy cloud of insane thoughts, dense and obscuring, yet representing all you see? Today we will make our first real attempt to get past this dark and heavy cloud, and to go through it to the light beyond.

There will be only one long practice period today. In the morning, as soon as you get up if possible, sit quietly for some three to five minutes, with your eyes closed. At the beginning of the practice period, repeat today's idea very slowly. Then make no effort to think of anything. Try, instead, to get a sense of turning inward, past all the idle thoughts of the world. Try to enter very deeply into your own mind, keeping it clear of any thoughts that might divert your attention.

From time to time, you may repeat the idea if you find it helpful. But most of all, try to sink down and inward, away from the world and all the foolish thoughts of the world. You are trying to reach past all these things. You are trying to leave appearances and approach reality.

It is quite possible to reach God. In fact it is very easy, because it is the most natural thing in the world. You might even say it is the only natural thing in the world. The way will open, if you believe that it is possible. This exercise can bring very startling results even the first time it is attempted, and sooner or later it is always successful. We will go into more detail about this kind of practice as we go along. But it will never fail completely, and instant success is possible.

Throughout the day use today's idea often, repeating it very slowly, preferably with eyes closed. Think of what you are saying; what the words mean. Concentrate on the holiness that they imply about you; on the unfailing companionship that is yours; on the complete protection that surrounds you.

You can indeed afford to laugh at fear thoughts, remembering that God goes with you wherever you go.

Lesson 42

God is my strength. Vision is His gift.

The idea for today combines two very powerful thoughts, both of major importance. It also sets forth a cause and effect relationship that explains why you cannot fail in your efforts to achieve the goal of the course. You will see because it is the Will of God. It is His strength, not your own, that gives you power. And it is His gift, rather than your own, that offers vision to you.

God is indeed your strength, and what He gives is truly given. This means that you can receive it any time and anywhere, wherever you are, and in whatever circumstance you find yourself. Your passage through time and space is not at random. You cannot but be in the right place at the right time. Such is the strength of God. Such are His gifts.

We will have two three-to-five-minute practice periods today, one as soon as possible after you wake, and another as close as possible to the time you go to sleep. It is better, however, to wait until you can sit quietly by yourself, at a time when you feel ready, than it is to be concerned with the time as such.

Begin these practice periods by repeating the idea for today slowly, with your eyes open, looking about you. Then close your eyes and repeat the idea again, even slower than before. After this, try to think of nothing except thoughts that occur to you in relation to the idea for the day. You might think, for example:

VISION MUST BE POSSIBLE. GOD GIVES TRULY,

or:

GOD'S GIFTS TO ME MUST BE MINE, BECAUSE HE GAVE THEM TO ME.

Any thought that is clearly related to the idea for today is suitable. You may, in fact, be astonished at the amount of course-related understanding some of your thoughts contain. Let them come without censoring unless you find your mind is merely wandering, and you have let obviously irrelevant thoughts intrude. You may also reach a point where no thoughts at all seem to come to mind. If such interferences occur, open your eyes and repeat the thought once more while looking slowly about; close your eyes, repeat the idea once more, and then continue to look for related thoughts in your mind.

Remember, however, that active searching for relevant thoughts is not appropriate for today's exercises. Try merely to step back and let the thoughts come. If you find this difficult, it is better to spend the practice period alternating between slow repetitions of the idea with eyes open, then with eyes closed, than it is to strain to find suitable thoughts.

There is no limit on the number of short practice periods that would be beneficial today. The idea for the day is a beginning step in bringing thoughts together, and teaching you that you are studying a unified thought system in which nothing is lacking that is needed, and nothing is included that is contradictory or irrelevant.

The more often you repeat the idea during the day, the more often you will be reminding yourself that the goal of the course is important to you, and that you have not forgotten it.

Lesson 43

God is my Source. I cannot see apart from Him.

Perception is not an attribute of God. His is the realm of knowledge. Yet He has created the Holy Spirit as the Mediator between perception and knowledge. Without this link with God, perception would have replaced knowledge forever in your mind. With this link with God, perception will become so changed and purified that it will lead to knowledge. That is its function as the Holy Spirit sees it. Therefore, that is its function in truth.

In God you cannot see. Perception has no function in God, and does not exist. Yet in salvation, which is the undoing of what never was, perception has a mighty purpose. Made by the Son of God for an unholy purpose, it must become the means for the restoration of his holiness to his awareness. Perception has no meaning. Yet does the Holy Spirit give it a meaning very close to God's. Healed perception becomes the means by which the Son of God forgives his brother, and thus forgives himself.

You cannot see apart from God because you cannot be apart from God. Whatever you do you do in Him, because whatever you think, you think with His Mind. If vision is real, and it is real to the extent to which it shares the Holy Spirit's purpose, then you cannot see apart from God.

Three five-minute practice periods are required today, one as early and one as late as possible in the day. The third may be undertaken at the most convenient and suitable time that circumstances and readiness permit. At the beginning of these practice periods, repeat the idea for today to yourself with eyes open. Then glance around you for a short time, applying the idea specifically to what you see. Four or five subjects for this phase of the practice period are sufficient. You might say, for example:

GOD IS MY SOURCE. I CANNOT SEE THIS DESK APART FROM HIM.
GOD IS MY SOURCE. I CANNOT SEE THAT PICTURE APART FROM HIM.

Although this part of the exercise period should be relatively short, be sure that you select the subjects for this phase of practice indiscriminately, without self-directed inclusion or exclusion. For the second and longer phase, close your eyes, repeat today's idea again, and then let whatever relevant thoughts occur to you add to the idea in your own personal way. Thoughts such as:

I SEE THROUGH THE EYES OF FORGIVENESS.
I SEE THE WORLD AS BLESSED.
THE WORLD CAN SHOW ME MYSELF.
I SEE MY OWN THOUGHTS, WHICH ARE LIKE GOD'S.

Any thought related more or less directly to today's idea is suitable. The thoughts need not bear any obvious relationship to the idea, but they should not be in opposition to it.

If you find your mind wandering; if you begin to be aware of thoughts which are clearly out of accord with today's idea, or if you seem to be unable to think of anything, open your eyes, repeat the first phase of the exercise period, and then attempt the second phase again. Do not allow any protracted period to occur in which you become preoccupied with irrelevant thoughts. Return to the first phase of the exercises as often as necessary to prevent this.

In applying today's idea in the shorter practice periods, the form may vary according to the circumstances and situations in which you find yourself during the day. When you are with someone else, for example, try to remember to tell him silently:

GOD IS MY SOURCE. I CANNOT SEE YOU APART FROM HIM.

This form is equally applicable to strangers as it is to those you think are closer to you. In fact, try not to make distinctions of this kind at all.

Today's idea should also be applied throughout the day to various situations and events that may occur, particularly to those which seem to distress you in any way. For this purpose, apply the idea in this form:

GOD IS MY SOURCE. I CANNOT SEE THIS APART FROM HIM.

If no particular subject presents itself to your awareness at the time, merely repeat the idea in its original form. Try today not to allow any long periods of time to slip by without remembering today's idea, and thus remembering your function.

Lesson 44

God is the light in which I see.

Today we are continuing the idea for yesterday, adding another dimension to it. You cannot see in darkness, and you cannot make light. You can make darkness and then think you see in it, but light reflects life, and is therefore an aspect of creation. Creation and darkness cannot coexist, but light and life must go together, being but different aspects of creation.

In order to see, you must recognize that light is within, not without. You do not see outside yourself, nor is the equipment for seeing outside you. An essential part of this equipment is the light that makes seeing possible. It is with you always, making vision possible in every circumstance.

Today we are going to attempt to reach that light. For this purpose, we will use a form of exercise which has been suggested before, and which we will utilize increasingly. It is a particularly difficult form for the undisciplined mind, and represents a major goal of mind training. It requires precisely what the untrained mind lacks. Yet this training must be accomplished if you are to see.

Have at least three practice periods today, each lasting three to five minutes. A longer time is highly recommended, but only if you find the time slipping by with little or no sense of strain. The form of practice we will use today is the most natural and easy one in the world for the trained mind, just as it seems to be the most unnatural and difficult for the untrained mind.

Your mind is no longer wholly untrained. You are quite ready to learn the form of exercise we will use today, but you may find that you will encounter strong resistance. The reason is very simple. While you practice in this way, you leave behind everything that you now believe, and all the thoughts that you have made up. Properly speaking, this is the release from hell. Yet perceived through the ego's eyes, it is loss of identity and a descent into hell.

If you can stand aside from the ego by ever so little, you will have no difficulty in recognizing that its opposition and its fears are meaningless. You might find it helpful to remind yourself, from time to time, that to reach light is to escape from darkness, whatever you may believe to the contrary. God is the light in which you see. You are attempting to reach Him.

Begin the practice period by repeating today's idea with your eyes open, and close them slowly, repeating the idea several times more. Then try to sink into your mind, letting go every kind of interference and intrusion by quietly sinking past them. Your mind cannot be stopped in this unless you choose to stop it. It is merely taking its natural course. Try to observe your passing thoughts without involvement, and slip quietly by them.

While no particular approach is advocated for this form of exercise, what is needful is a sense of the importance of what you are doing; its inestimable value to you, and an awareness that you are attempting something very holy. Salvation is your happiest accomplishment. It is also the only one that has any meaning, because it is the only one that has any real use to you at all.

If resistance rises in any form, pause long enough to repeat today's idea, keeping your eyes closed unless you are aware of fear. In that case, you will probably find it more reassuring to open your eyes briefly. Try, however, to return to the exercises with eyes closed as soon as possible.

If you are doing the exercises correctly, you should experience some sense of relaxation, and even a feeling that you are approaching, if not actually entering into light. Try to think of light, formless and without limit, as you pass by the thoughts of this world. And do not forget that they cannot hold you to the world unless you give them the power to do so.

Throughout the day repeat the idea often, with eyes open or closed as seems better to you at the time. But do not forget. Above all, be determined not to forget today.

Lesson 45

God is the Mind with which I think.

Today's idea holds the key to what your real thoughts are. They are nothing that you think you think, just as nothing that you think you see is related to vision in any way. There is no relationship between what is real and what you think is real. Nothing that you think are your real thoughts resemble your real thoughts in any respect. Nothing that you think you see bears any resemblance to what vision will show you.

You think with the Mind of God. Therefore you share your thoughts with Him, as He shares His with you. They are the same thoughts, because they are thought by the same Mind. To share is to make alike, or to make one. Nor do the thoughts you think with the Mind of God leave your mind, because thoughts do not leave their source. Therefore, your thoughts are in the Mind of God, as you are. They are in your mind as well, where He is. As you are part of His Mind, so are your thoughts part of His Mind.

Where, then, are your real thoughts? Today we will attempt to reach them. We will have to look for them in your mind, because that is where they are. They must still be there, because they cannot have left their source. What is thought by the Mind of God is eternal, being part of creation.

Our three five-minute practice periods for today will take the same general form that we used in applying yesterday's idea. We will attempt to leave the unreal and seek for the real. We will deny the world in favor of truth. We will not let the thoughts of the world hold us back. We will not let the beliefs of the world tell us that what God would have us do is impossible. Instead, we will try to recognize that only what God would have us do is possible.

We will also try to understand that only what God would have us do is what we want to do. And we will also try to remember that we cannot fail in doing what He would have us do. There is every reason to feel confident that we will succeed today. It is the Will of God.

Begin the exercises for today by repeating the idea to yourself, closing your eyes as you do so. Then spend a fairly short period in thinking a few relevant thoughts of your own, keeping the idea in mind. After you have added some four or five thoughts of your own to the idea, repeat it again and tell yourself gently:

MY REAL THOUGHTS ARE IN MY MIND. I WOULD LIKE TO FIND THEM.

Then try to go past all the unreal thoughts that cover the truth in your mind, and reach to the eternal.

Under all the senseless thoughts and mad ideas with which you have cluttered up your mind are the thoughts that you thought with God in the beginning. They are there in your mind now, completely unchanged. They will always be in your mind, exactly as they always were. Everything you have thought since then will change, but the Foundation on which it rests is wholly changeless.

It is this Foundation toward which the exercises for today are directed. Here is your mind joined with the Mind of God. Here are your thoughts one with His. For this kind of practice only one thing is necessary; approach it as you would an altar dedicated in Heaven to God the Father and to God the Son. For such is the place you are trying to reach. You will probably be unable as yet to realize how high you are trying to go. Yet even with the little understanding you have already gained, you should be able to remind yourself that this is no idle game, but an exercise in holiness and an attempt to reach the Kingdom of Heaven .

In the shorter exercise periods for today, try to remember how important it is to you to understand the holiness of the mind that thinks with God. Take a minute or two, as you repeat the idea throughout the day, to appreciate your mind's holiness. Stand aside, however briefly, from all thoughts that are unworthy of Him Whose host you are. And thank Him for the Thoughts He is thinking with you.

Lesson 46

God is the Love in which I forgive.

God does not forgive because He has never condemned. And there must be condemnation before forgiveness is necessary. Forgiveness is the great need of this world, but that is because it is a world of illusions. Those who forgive are thus releasing themselves from illusions, while those who withhold forgiveness are binding themselves to them. As you condemn only yourself, so do you forgive only yourself.

Yet although God does not forgive, His Love is nevertheless the basis of forgiveness. Fear condemns and love forgives. Forgiveness thus undoes what fear has produced, returning the mind to the awareness of God. For this reason, forgiveness can truly be called salvation. It is the means by which illusions disappear.

Today's exercises require at least three full five-minute practice periods, and as many shorter ones as possible. Begin the longer practice periods by repeating today's idea to yourself, as usual. Close your eyes as you do so, and spend a minute or two in searching your mind for those whom you have not forgiven. It does not matter "how much" you have not forgiven them. You have forgiven them entirely or not at all.

If you are doing the exercises well you should have no difficulty in finding a number of people you have not forgiven. It is a safe rule that anyone you do not like is a suitable subject. Mention each one by name, and say:

GOD IS THE LOVE IN WHICH I FORGIVE YOU, [NAME].

The purpose of the first phase of today's practice periods is to put you in a position to forgive yourself. After you have applied the idea to all those who have come to mind, tell yourself:

GOD IS THE LOVE IN WHICH I FORGIVE MYSELF.

Then devote the remainder of the practice period to adding related ideas such as:

GOD IS THE LOVE WITH WHICH I LOVE MYSELF GOD IS THE LOVE IN WHICH I AM BLESSED.

The form of the application may vary considerably, but the central idea should not be lost sight of. You might say, for example:

I CANNOT BE GUILTY BECAUSE I AM A SON OF GOD.
I HAVE ALREADY BEEN FORGIVEN.
NO FEAR IS POSSIBLE IN A MIND BELOVED OF GOD.
THERE IS NO NEED TO ATTACK BECAUSE LOVE HAS FORGIVEN ME.

The practice period should end, however, with a repetition of today's idea as originally stated.

The shorter practice periods may consist either of a repetition of the idea for today in the original or in a related form, as you prefer. Be sure, however, to make more specific applications if they are needed. They will be needed at any time during the day when you become aware of any kind of negative reaction to anyone, present or not. In that event, tell him silently:

GOD IS THE LOVE IN WHICH I FORGIVE YOU.

Lesson 47

God is the strength in which I trust.

If you are trusting in your own strength, you have every reason to be apprehensive, anxious and fearful. What can you predict or control? What is there in you that can be counted on? What would give you the ability to be aware of all the facets of any problem, and to resolve them in such a way that only good can come of it? What is there in you that gives you the recognition of the right solution, and the guarantee that it will be accomplished?

Of yourself you can do none of these things. To believe that you can is to put your trust where trust is unwarranted, and to justify fear, anxiety, depression, anger and sorrow. Who can put his faith in weakness and feel safe? Yet who can put his faith in strength and feel weak?

God is your safety in every circumstance. His Voice speaks for Him in all situations and in every aspect of all situations, telling you exactly what to do to call upon His strength and His protection. There are no exceptions because God has no exceptions. And the Voice which speaks for Him thinks as He does.

Today we will try to reach past your own weakness to the Source of real strength. Four five-minute practice periods are necessary today, and longer and more frequent ones are urged. Close your eyes and begin, as usual, by repeating the idea for the day. Then spend a minute or two in searching for situations in your life which you have invested with fear, dismissing each one by telling yourself:

GOD IS THE STRENGTH IN WHICH I TRUST.

Now try to slip past all concerns related to your own sense of inadequacy. It is obvious that any situation that causes you concern is associated with feelings of inadequacy, for otherwise you would believe that you could deal with the situation successfully. It is not by trusting yourself that you will gain confidence. But the strength of God in you is successful in all things.

The recognition of your own frailty is a necessary step in the correction of your errors, but it is hardly a sufficient one in giving you the confidence which you need, and to which you are entitled. You must also gain an awareness that confidence in your real strength is fully justified in every respect and in all circumstances.

In the latter phase of the practice period, try to reach down into your mind to a place of real safety. You will recognize that you have reached it if you feel a sense of deep peace, however briefly. Let go all the trivial things that churn and bubble on the surface of your mind, and reach down and below them to the Kingdom of Heaven . There is a place in you where there is perfect peace. There is a place in you where nothing is impossible. There is a place in you where the strength of God abides.

During the day, repeat the idea often. Use it as your answer to any disturbance. Remember that peace is your right, because you are giving your trust to the strength of God.

Lesson 48

There is nothing to fear.

The idea for today simply states a fact. It is not a fact to those who believe in illusions, but illusions are not facts. In truth there is nothing to fear. It is very easy to recognize this. But it is very difficult to recognize it for those who want illusions to be true.

Today's practice periods will be very short, very simple and very frequent. Merely repeat the idea as often as possible. You can use it with your eyes open at any time and in any situation. It is strongly recommended, however, that you take a minute or so whenever possible to close your eyes and repeat the idea slowly to yourself several times. It is particularly important that you use the idea immediately, should anything disturb your peace of mind.

The presence of fear is a sure sign that you are trusting in your own strength. The awareness that there is nothing to fear shows that somewhere in your mind, though not necessarily in a place you recognize as yet, you have remembered God, and let His strength take the place of your weakness. The instant you are willing to do this there is indeed nothing to fear.

Lesson 49

God's Voice speaks to me all through the day.

It is quite possible to listen to God's Voice all through the day without interrupting your regular activities in any way. The part of your mind in which truth abides is in constant communication with God, whether you are aware of it or not. It is the other part of your mind that functions in the world and obeys the world's laws. It is this part that is constantly distracted, disorganized and highly uncertain.

The part that is listening to the Voice for God is calm, always at rest and wholly certain. It is really the only part there is. The other part is a wild illusion, frantic and distraught, but without reality of any kind. Try today not to listen to it. Try to identify with the part of your mind where stillness and peace reign forever. Try to hear God's Voice call to you lovingly, reminding you that your Creator has not forgotten His Son.

We will need at least four five-minute practice periods today, and more if possible. We will try actually to hear God's Voice reminding you of Him and of your Self. We will approach this happiest and holiest of thoughts with confidence, knowing that in doing so we are joining our will with the Will of God. He wants you to hear His Voice. He gave It to you to be heard.

Listen in deep silence. Be very still and open your mind. Go past all the raucous shrieks and sick imaginings that cover your real thoughts and obscure your eternal link with God. Sink deep into the peace that waits for you beyond the frantic, riotous thoughts and sights and sounds of this insane world. You do not live here. We are trying to reach your real home. We are trying to reach the place where you are truly welcome. We are trying to reach God.

Do not forget to repeat today's idea very frequently. Do so with your eyes open when necessary, but closed when possible. And be sure to sit quietly and repeat the idea for today whenever you can, closing your eyes on the world, and realizing that you are inviting God's Voice to speak to you.

Lesson 50

I am sustained by the Love of God.

Here is the answer to every problem that will confront you, today and tomorrow and throughout time. In this world, you believe you are sustained by everything but God. Your faith is placed in the most trivial and insane symbols; pills, money, "protective" clothing, influence, prestige, being liked, knowing the "right" people, and an endless list of forms of nothingness that you endow with magical powers.

All these things are your replacements for the Love of God. All these things are cherished to ensure a body identification. They are songs of praise to the ego. Do not put your faith in the worthless. It will not sustain you.

Only the Love of God will protect you in all circumstances. It will lift you out of every trial, and raise you high above all the perceived dangers of this world into a climate of perfect peace and safety. It will transport you into a state of mind that nothing can threaten, nothing can disturb, and where nothing can intrude upon the eternal calm of the Son of God.

Put not your faith in illusions. They will fail you. Put all your faith in the Love of God within you; eternal, changeless and forever unfailing. This is the answer to whatever confronts you today. Through the Love of God within you, you can resolve all seeming difficulties without effort and in sure confidence. Tell yourself this often today. It is a declaration of release from the belief in idols. It is your acknowledgment of the truth about yourself.

For ten minutes, twice today, morning and evening, let the idea for today sink deep into your consciousness. Repeat it, think about it, let related thoughts come to help you recognize its truth, and allow peace to flow over you like a blanket of protection and surety. Let no idle and foolish thoughts enter to disturb the holy mind of the Son of God. Such is the Kingdom of Heaven . Such is the resting place where your Father has placed you forever.

Review I: INTRODUCTION

Lesson 51

Review I
Introduction

Beginning with today we will have a series of review periods. Each of them will cover five of the ideas already presented, starting with the first and ending with the fiftieth. There will be a few short comments after each of the ideas, which you should consider in your review. In the practice periods, the exercises should be done as follows:

Begin the day by reading the five ideas, with the comments included. Thereafter, it is not necessary to follow any particular order in considering them, though each one should be practiced at least once. Devote two minutes or more to each practice period, thinking about the idea and the related comments after reading them over. Do this as often as possible during the day. If any one of the five ideas appeals to you more than the others, concentrate on that one. At the end of the day, however, be sure to review all of them once more.

It is not necessary to cover the comments that follow each idea either literally or thoroughly in the practice periods. Try, rather, to emphasize the central point, and think about it as part of your review of the idea to which it relates. After you have read the idea and the related comments, the exercises should be done with your eyes closed and when you are alone in a quiet place, if possible.

This is emphasized for practice periods at your stage of learning. It will be necessary, however, that you learn to require no special settings in which to apply what you have learned. You will need your learning most in situations that appear to be upsetting, rather than in those that already seem to be calm and quiet. The purpose of your learning is to enable you to bring the quiet with you, and to heal distress and turmoil. This is not done by avoiding them and seeking a haven of isolation for yourself.

You will yet learn that peace is part of you, and requires only that you be there to embrace any situation in which you are. And finally you will learn that there is no limit to where you are, so that your peace is everywhere, as you are.

You will note that, for review purposes, some of the ideas are not given in quite their original form. Use them as they are given here. It is not necessary to return to the original statements, nor to apply the ideas as was suggested then. We are now emphasizing the relationships among the first fifty of the ideas we have covered, and the cohesiveness of the thought system to which they are leading you.

Lesson 51

The review for today covers the following ideas:

(1) Nothing I see means anything.

The reason this is so is that I see nothing, and nothing has no meaning. It is necessary that I recognize this, that I may learn to see. What I think I see now is taking the place of vision. I must let it go by realizing it has no meaning, so that vision may take its place.

(2) I have given what I see all the meaning it has for me.

I have judged everything I look upon, and it is this and only this I see. This is not vision. It is merely an illusion of reality, because my judgments have been made quite apart from reality. I am willing to recognize the lack of validity in my judgments, because I want to see. My judgments have hurt me, and I do not want to see according to them.

(3) I do not understand anything I see.

How could I understand what I see when I have judged it amiss? What I see is the projection of my own errors of thought. I do not understand what I see because it is not understandable. There is no sense in trying to understand it. But there is every reason to let it go, and make room for what can be seen and understood and loved. I can exchange what I see now for this merely by being willing to do so. Is not this a better choice than the one I made before?

(4) These thoughts do not mean anything.

The thoughts of which I am aware do not mean anything because I am trying to think without God. What I call "my" thoughts are not my real thoughts. My real thoughts are the thoughts I think with God. I am not aware of them because I have made my thoughts to take their place. I am willing to recognize that my thoughts do not mean anything, and to let them go. I choose to have them be replaced by what they were intended to replace. My thoughts are meaningless, but all creation lies in the thoughts I think with God.

(5) I am never upset for the reason I think.

I am never upset for the reason I think because I am constantly trying to justify my thoughts. I am constantly trying to make them true. I make all things my enemies, so that my anger is justified and my attacks are warranted. I have not realized how much I have misused everything I see by assigning this role to it. I have done this to defend a thought system that has hurt me, and that I no longer want. I am willing to let it go.

Lesson 52

Today's review covers these ideas:

(6) I am upset because I see what is not there.

Reality is never frightening. It is impossible that it could upset me. Reality brings only perfect peace. When I am upset, it is always because I have replaced reality with illusions I made up. The illusions are upsetting because I have given them reality, and thus regard reality as an illusion. Nothing in God's creation is affected in any way by this confusion of mine. I am always upset by nothing.

(7) I see only the past.

As I look about, I condemn the world I look upon. I call this seeing. I hold the past against everyone and everything, making them my enemies. When I have forgiven myself and remembered Who I am, I will bless everyone and everything I see. There will be no past, and therefore no enemies. And I will look with love on all that I failed to see before.

(8) My mind is preoccupied with past thoughts.

I see only my own thoughts, and my mind is preoccupied with the past. What, then, can I see as it is? Let me remember that I look on the past to prevent the present from dawning on my mind. Let me understand that I am trying to use time against God. Let me learn to give the past away, realizing that in so doing I am giving up nothing.

(9) I see nothing as it is now.

If I see nothing as it is now, it can truly be said that I see nothing. I can see only what is now. The choice is not whether to see the past or the present; the choice is merely whether to see or not. What I have chosen to see has cost me vision. Now I would choose again, that I may see.

(10) My thoughts do not mean anything.

I have no private thoughts. Yet it is only private thoughts of which I am aware. What can these thoughts mean? They do not exist, and so they mean nothing. Yet my mind is part of creation and part of its Creator. Would I not rather join the thinking of the universe than to obscure all that is really mine with my pitiful and meaningless "private" thoughts?

Lesson 53

Today we will review the following:

(11) My meaningless thoughts are showing me a meaningless world.

Since the thoughts of which I am aware do not mean anything, the world that pictures them can have no meaning. What is producing this world is insane, and so is what it produces. Reality is not insane, and I have real thoughts as well as insane ones. I can therefore see a real world, if I look to my real thoughts as my guide for seeing.

(12) I am upset because I see a meaningless world.

Insane thoughts are upsetting. They produce a world in which there is no order anywhere. Only chaos rules a world that represents chaotic thinking, and chaos has no laws. I cannot live in peace in such a world. I am grateful that this world is not real, and that I need not see it at all unless I choose to value it. And I do not choose to value what is totally insane and has no meaning.

(13) A meaningless world engenders fear.

The totally insane engenders fear because it is completely undependable, and offers no grounds for trust. Nothing in madness is dependable. It holds out no safety and no hope. But such a world is not real. I have given it the illusion of reality, and have suffered from my belief in it. Now I choose to withdraw this belief, and place my trust in reality. In choosing this, I will escape all the effects of the world of fear, because I am acknowledging that it does not exist.

(14) God did not create a meaningless world.

How can a meaningless world exist if God did not create it? He is the Source of all meaning, and everything that is real is in His Mind. It is in my mind too, because He created it with me. Why should I continue to suffer from the effects of my own insane thoughts, when the perfection of creation is my home? Let me remember the power of my decision, and recognize where I really abide.

(15) My thoughts are images that I have made.

Whatever I see reflects my thoughts. It is my thoughts that tell me where I am and what I am. The fact that I see a world in which there is suffering and loss and death shows me that I am seeing only the representation of my insane thoughts, and am not allowing my real thoughts to cast their beneficent light on what I see. Yet God's way is sure. The images I have made cannot prevail against Him because it is not my will that they do so. My will is His, and I will place no other gods before Him.

Lesson 54

These are the review ideas for today:

(16) I have no neutral thoughts.

Neutral thoughts are impossible because all thoughts have power. They will either make a false world or lead me to the real one. But thoughts cannot be without effects. As the world I see arises from my thinking errors, so will the real world rise before my eyes as I let my errors be corrected. My thoughts cannot be neither true nor false. They must be one or the other. What I see shows me which they are.

(17) I see no neutral things.

What I see witnesses to what I think. If I did not think I would not exist, because life is thought. Let me look on the world I see as the representation of my own state of mind. I know that my state of mind can change. And so I also know the world I see can change as well.

(18) I am not alone in experiencing the effects of my seeing.

If I have no private thoughts, I cannot see a private world. Even the mad idea of separation had to be shared before it could form the basis of the world I see. Yet that sharing was a sharing of nothing. I can also call upon my real thoughts, which share everything with everyone. As my thoughts of separation call to the separation thoughts of others, so my real thoughts awaken the real thoughts in them. And the world my real thoughts show me will dawn on their sight as well as mine.

(19) I am not alone in experiencing the effects of my thoughts.

I am alone in nothing. Everything I think or say or do teaches all the universe. A Son of God cannot think or speak or act in vain. He cannot be alone in anything. It is therefore in my power to change every mind along with mine, for mine is the power of God.

(20) I am determined to see.

Recognizing the shared nature of my thoughts, I am determined to see. I would look upon the witnesses that show me the thinking of the world has been changed. I would behold the proof that what has been done through me has enabled love to replace fear, laughter to replace tears, and abundance to replace loss. I would look upon the real world, and let it teach me that my will and the Will of God are one.

Lesson 55

Today's review includes the following:

(21) I am determined to see things differently.

What I see now are but signs of disease, disaster and death. This cannot be what God created for His beloved Son. The very fact that I see such things is proof that I do not understand God. Therefore I also do not understand His Son. What I see tells me that I do not know who I am. I am determined to see the witnesses to the truth in me, rather than those which show me an illusion of myself.

(22) What I see is a form of vengeance.

The world I see is hardly the representation of loving thoughts. It is a picture of attack on everything by everything. It is anything but a reflection of the Love of God and the Love of His Son. It is my own attack thoughts that give rise to this picture. My loving thoughts will save me from this perception of the world, and give me the peace God intended me to have.

(23) I can escape from this world by giving up attack thoughts.

Herein lies salvation, and nowhere else. Without attack thoughts I could not see a world of attack. As forgiveness allows love to return to my awareness, I will see a world of peace and safety and joy. And it is this I choose to see, in place of what I look on now.

(24) I do not perceive my own best interests.

How could I recognize my own best interests when I do not know who I am? What I think are my best interests would merely bind me closer to the world of illusions. I am willing to follow the Guide God has given me to find out what my own best interests are, recognizing that I cannot perceive them by myself.

(25) I do not know what anything is for.

To me, the purpose of everything is to prove that my illusions about myself are real. It is for this purpose that I attempt to use everyone and everything. It is for this that I believe the world is for. Therefore I do not recognize its real purpose. The purpose I have given the world has led to a frightening picture of it. Let me open my mind to the world's real purpose by withdrawing the one I have given it, and learning the truth about it.

Lesson 56

Our review for today covers the following:

(26) My attack thoughts are attacking my invulnerability.

How can I know who I am when I see myself as under constant attack? Pain, illness, loss, age and death seem to threaten me. All my hopes and wishes and plans appear to be at the mercy of a world I cannot control. Yet perfect security and complete fulfillment are my inheritance. I have tried to give my inheritance away in exchange for the world I see. But God has kept my inheritance safe for me. My own real thoughts will teach me what it is.

(27) Above all else I want to see.

Recognizing that what I see reflects what I think I am, I realize that vision is my greatest need. The world I see attests to the fearful nature of the self-image I have made. If I would remember who I am, it is essential that I let this image of myself go. As it is replaced by truth, vision will surely be given me. And with this vision, I will look upon the world and on myself with charity and love.

(28) Above all else I want to see differently.

The world I see holds my fearful self-image in place, and guarantees its continuance. While I see the world as I see it now, truth cannot enter my awareness. I would let the door behind this world be opened for me, that I may look past it to the world that reflects the Love of God.

(29) God is in everything I see.

Behind every image I have made, the truth remains unchanged. Behind every veil I have drawn across the face of love, its light remains undimmed. Beyond all my insane wishes is my will, united with the Will of my Father. God is still everywhere and in everything forever. And we who are part of Him will yet look past all appearances, and recognize the truth beyond them all.

(30) God is in everything I see because God is in my mind.

In my own mind, behind all my insane thoughts of separation and attack, is the knowledge that all is one forever. I have not lost the knowledge of Who I am because I have forgotten it. It has been kept for me in the Mind of God, Who has not left His Thoughts. And I, who am among them, am one with them and one with Him.

Lesson 57

Today let us review these ideas:

(31) I am not the victim of the world I see.

How can I be the victim of a world that can be completely undone if I so choose? My chains are loosened. I can drop them off merely by desiring to do so. The prison door is open. I can leave simply by walking out. Nothing holds me in this world. Only my wish to stay keeps me a prisoner. I would give up my insane wishes and walk into the sunlight at last.

(32) I have invented the world I see.

I made up the prison in which I see myself. All I need do is recognize this and I am free. I have deluded myself into believing it is possible to imprison the Son of God. I was bitterly mistaken in this belief, which I no longer want. The Son of God must be forever free. He is as God created him, and not what I would make of him. He is where God would have him be, and not where I thought to hold him prisoner.

(33) There is another way of looking at the world.

Since the purpose of the world is not the one I ascribed to it, there must be another way of looking at it. I see everything upside down, and my thoughts are the opposite of truth. I see the world as a prison for God's Son. It must be, then, that the world is really a place where he can be set free. I would look upon the world as it is, and see it as a place where the Son of God finds his freedom.

(34) I could see peace instead of this.

When I see the world as a place of freedom, I realize that it reflects the laws of God instead of the rules I made up for it to obey. I will understand that peace, not war, abides in it. And I will perceive that peace also abides in the hearts of all who share this place with me.

(35) My mind is part of God's. I am very holy.

As I share the peace of the world with my brothers, I begin to understand that this peace comes from deep within myself. The world I look upon has taken on the light of my forgiveness, and shines forgiveness back at me. In this light I begin to see what my illusions about myself kept hidden. I begin to understand the holiness of all living things, including myself, and their oneness with me.

Lesson 58

These ideas are for review today:

(36) My holiness envelops everything I see.

From my holiness does the perception of the real world come. Having forgiven, I no longer see myself as guilty. I can accept the innocence that is the truth about me. Seen through understanding eyes, the holiness of the world is all I see, for I can picture only the thoughts I hold about myself.

(37) My holiness blesses the world.

The perception of my holiness does not bless me alone. Everyone and everything I see in its light shares in the joy it brings to me. There is nothing that is apart from this joy, because there is nothing that does not share my holiness. As I recognize my holiness, so does the holiness of the world shine forth for everyone to see.

(38) There is nothing my holiness cannot do.

My holiness is unlimited in its power to heal, because it is unlimited in its power to save. What is there to be saved from except illusions? And what are all illusions except false ideas about myself? My holiness undoes them all by asserting the truth about me. In the presence of my holiness, which I share with God Himself, all idols vanish.

(39) My holiness is my salvation.

Since my holiness saves me from all guilt, recognizing my holiness is recognizing my salvation. It is also recognizing the salvation of the world. Once I have accepted my holiness, nothing can make me afraid. And because I am unafraid, everyone must share in my understanding, which is the gift of God to me and to the world.

(40) I am blessed as a Son of God.

Herein lies my claim to all good and only good. I am blessed as a Son of God. All good things are mine, because God intended them for me. I cannot suffer any loss or deprivation or pain because of Who I am. My Father supports me, protects me, and directs me in all things. His care for me is infinite, and is with me forever. I am eternally blessed as His Son.

Lesson 59

The following ideas are for review today:

(41) God goes with me wherever I go.

How can I be alone when God always goes with me? How can I be doubtful and unsure of myself when perfect certainty abides in Him? How can I be disturbed by anything when He rests in me in absolute peace? How can I suffer when love and joy surround me through Him? Let me not cherish illusions about myself. I am perfect because God goes with me wherever I go.

(42) God is my strength. Vision is His gift.

Let me not look to my own eyes to see today. Let me be willing to exchange my pitiful illusion of seeing for the vision that is given by God. Christ's vision is His gift, and He has given it to me. Let me call upon this gift today, so that this day may help me to understand eternity.

(43) God is my Source. I cannot see apart from Him.

I can see what God wants me to see. I cannot see anything else. Beyond His Will lie only illusions. It is these I choose when I think I can see apart from Him. It is these I choose when I try to see through the body's eyes. Yet the vision of Christ has been given me to replace them. It is through this vision that I choose to see.

(44) God is the light in which I see.

I cannot see in darkness. God is the only light. Therefore, if I am to see, it must be through Him. I have tried to define what seeing is, and I have been wrong. Now it is given me to understand that God is the light in which I see. Let me welcome vision and the happy world it will show me.

(45) God is the Mind with which I think.

I have no thoughts I do not share with God. I have no thoughts apart from Him, because I have no mind apart from His. As part of His Mind, my thoughts are His and His Thoughts are mine.

Lesson 60

These ideas are for today's review:

(46) God is the Love in which I forgive.

God does not forgive because He has never condemned. The blameless cannot blame, and those who have accepted their innocence see nothing to forgive. Yet forgiveness is the means by which I will recognize my innocence. It is the reflection of God's Love on earth. It will bring me near enough to Heaven that the Love of God can reach down to me and raise me up to Him.

(47) God is the strength in which I trust.

It is not my own strength through which I forgive. It is through the strength of God in me, which I am remembering as I forgive. As I begin to see, I recognize His reflection on earth. I forgive all things because I feel the stirring of His strength in me. And I begin to remember the Love I chose to forget, but which has not forgotten me.

(48) There is nothing to fear.

How safe the world will look to me when I can see it! It will not look anything like what I imagine I see now. Everyone and everything I see will lean toward me to bless me. I will recognize in everyone my dearest Friend. What could there be to fear in a world that I have forgiven, and that has forgiven me?

(49) God's Voice speaks to me all through the day.

There is not a moment in which God's Voice ceases to call on my forgiveness to save me. There is not a moment in which His Voice fails to direct my thoughts, guide my actions and lead my feet. I am walking steadily on toward truth. There is nowhere else I can go, because God's Voice is the only Voice and the only Guide that has been given to His Son.

(50) I am sustained by the Love of God.

As I listen to God's Voice, I am sustained by His Love. As I open my eyes, His Love lights up the world for me to see. As I forgive, His Love reminds me that His Son is sinless. And as I look upon the world with the vision He has given me, I remember that I am His Son.

Lesson 61

I am the light of the world.

Who is the light of the world except God's Son? This, then, is merely a statement of the truth about yourself. It is the opposite of a statement of pride, of arrogance, or of self-deception. It does not describe the self-concept you have made. It does not refer to any of the characteristics with which you have endowed your idols. It refers to you as you were created by God. It simply states the truth.

To the ego, today's idea is the epitome of self-glorification. But the ego does not understand humility, mistaking it for self-debasement. Humility consists of accepting your role in salvation and in taking no other. It is not humility to insist you cannot be the light of the world if that is the function God assigned to you. It is only arrogance that would assert this function cannot be for you, and arrogance is always of the ego.

True humility requires that you accept today's idea because it is God's Voice which tells you it is true. This is a beginning step in accepting your real function on earth. It is a giant stride toward taking your rightful place in salvation. It is a positive assertion of your right to be saved, and an acknowledgment of the power that is given you to save others.

You will want to think about this idea as often as possible today. It is the perfect answer to all illusions, and therefore to all temptation. It brings all the images you have made about yourself to the truth, and helps you depart in peace, unburdened and certain of your purpose.

As many practice periods as possible should be undertaken today, although each one need not exceed a minute or two. They should begin with telling yourself:

I AM THE LIGHT OF THE WORLD. THAT IS MY ONLY FUNCTION.
THAT IS WHY I AM HERE.

Then think about these statements for a short while, preferably with your eyes closed if the situation permits. Let a few related thoughts come to you, and repeat the idea to yourself if your mind wanders away from the central thought.

Be sure both to begin and end the day with a practice period. Thus you will awaken with an acknowledgment of the truth about yourself, reinforce it throughout the day, and turn to sleep as you reaffirm your function and your only purpose here. These two practice periods may be longer than the rest, if you find them helpful and want to extend them.

Today's idea goes far beyond the ego's petty views of what you are and what your purpose is. As a bringer of salvation, this is obviously necessary. This is the first of a number of giant steps we will take in the next few weeks. Try today to begin to build a firm foundation for these advances. You are the light of the world. God has built His plan for the salvation of His Son on you.

Lesson 62

Forgiveness is my function as the light of the world.

It is your forgiveness that will bring the world of darkness to the light. It is your forgiveness that lets you recognize the light in which you see. Forgiveness is the demonstration that you are the light of the world. Through your forgiveness does the truth about yourself return to your memory. Therefore, in your forgiveness lies your salvation.

Illusions about yourself and the world are one. That is why all forgiveness is a gift to yourself. Your goal is to find out who you are, having denied your Identity by attacking creation and its Creator. Now you are learning how to remember the truth. For this attack must be replaced by forgiveness, so that thoughts of life may replace thoughts of death.

Remember that in every attack you call upon your own weakness, while each time you forgive you call upon the strength of Christ in you. Do you not then begin to understand what forgiveness will do for you? It will remove all sense of weakness, strain and fatigue from your mind. It will take away all fear and guilt and pain. It will restore the invulnerability and power God gave His Son to your awareness.

Let us be glad to begin and end this day by practicing today's idea, and to use it as frequently as possible throughout the day. It will help to make the day as happy for you as God wants you to be. And it will help those around you, as well as those who seem to be far away in space and time, to share this happiness with you.

As often as you can, closing your eyes if possible, say to yourself today:

FORGIVENESS IS MY FUNCTION AS THE LIGHT OF THE WORLD.
I WOULD FULFILL MY FUNCTION THAT I MAY BE HAPPY.

Then devote a minute or two to considering your function and the happiness and release it will bring you. Let related thoughts come freely, for your heart will recognize these words, and in your mind is the awareness they are true. Should your attention wander, repeat the idea and add:

I WOULD REMEMBER THIS BECAUSE I WANT TO BE HAPPY.

Lesson 63

The light of the world brings peace to every mind
through my forgiveness.

How holy are you who have the power to bring peace to every mind! How blessed are you who can learn to recognize the means for letting this be done through you! What purpose could you have that would bring you greater happiness?

You are indeed the light of the world with such a function. The Son of God looks to you for his redemption. It is yours to give him, for it belongs to you. Accept no trivial purpose or meaningless desire in its place, or you will forget your function and leave the Son of God in hell. This is no idle request that is being asked of you. You are being asked to accept salvation that it may be yours to give.

Recognizing the importance of this function, we will be happy to remember it very often today. We will begin the day by acknowledging it, and close the day with the thought of it in our awareness. And throughout the day we will repeat this as often as we can:

THE LIGHT OF THE WORLD BRINGS PEACE TO EVERY MIND
THROUGH MY FORGIVENESS. I AM THE MEANS GOD HAS
APPOINTED FOR THE SALVATION OF THE WORLD.

If you close your eyes, you will probably find it easier to let the related thoughts come to you in the minute or two that you should devote to considering this. Do not, however, wait for such an opportunity. No chance should be lost for reinforcing today's idea. Remember that God's Son looks to you for his salvation. And Who but your Self must be His Son?

Lesson 64

Let me not forget my function.

Today's idea is merely another way of saying "Let me not wander into temptation." The purpose of the world you see is to obscure your function of forgiveness, and provide you with a justification for forgetting it. It is the temptation to abandon God and His Son by taking on a physical appearance. It is this the body's eyes look upon.

Nothing the body's eyes seem to see can be anything but a form of temptation, since this was the purpose of the body itself. Yet we have learned that the Holy Spirit has another use for all the illusions you have made, and therefore He sees another purpose in them. To the Holy Spirit, the world is a place where you learn to forgive yourself what you think of as your sins. In this perception, the physical appearance of temptation becomes the spiritual recognition of salvation.

To review our last few lessons, your function here is to be the light of the world, a function given you by God. It is only the arrogance of the ego that leads you to question this, and only the fear of the ego that induces you to regard yourself as unworthy of the task assigned to you by God Himself. The world's salvation awaits your forgiveness, because through it does the Son of God escape from all illusions, and thus from all temptation. The Son of God is you.

Only by fulfilling the function given you by God will you be happy. That is because your function is to be happy by using the means by which happiness becomes inevitable. There is no other way. Therefore, every time you choose whether or not to fulfill your function, you are really choosing whether or not to be happy.

Let us remember this today. Let us remind ourselves of it in the morning and again at night, and all through the day as well. Prepare yourself in advance for all the decisions you will make today by remembering they are all really very simple. Each one will lead to happiness or unhappiness. Can such a simple decision really be difficult to make? Let not the form of the decision deceive you. Complexity of form does not imply complexity of content. It is impossible that any decision on earth can have a content different from just this one simple choice. That is the only choice the Holy Spirit sees. Therefore it is the only choice there is.

Today, then, let us practice with these thoughts:

LET ME NOT FORGET MY FUNCTION.
LET ME NOT TRY TO SUBSTITUTE MINE FOR GOD'S.
LET ME FORGIVE AND BE HAPPY.

At least once devote ten or fifteen minutes today to reflecting on this with closed eyes. Related thoughts will come to help you, if you remember the crucial importance of your function to you and to the world.

In the frequent applications of today's idea throughout the day, devote several minutes to reviewing these thoughts, and then thinking about them and about nothing else. This will be difficult, at first particularly, since you are not proficient in the mind discipline that it requires. You may need to repeat "Let me not forget my function" quite often to help you concentrate.

Two forms of shorter practice periods are required. At times, do the exercises with your eyes closed, trying to concentrate on the thoughts you are using. At other times, keep your eyes open after reviewing the thoughts, and then look slowly and unselectively around you, telling yourself:

THIS IS THE WORLD IT IS MY FUNCTION TO SAVE.

Lesson 65

My only function is the one God gave me.

The idea for today reaffirms your commitment to salvation. It also reminds you that you have no function other than that. Both these thoughts are obviously necessary for a total commitment. Salvation cannot be the only purpose you hold while you still cherish others. The full acceptance of salvation as your only function necessarily entails two phases; the recognition of salvation as your function, and the relinquishment of all the other goals you have invented for yourself.

This is the only way in which you can take your rightful place among the saviors of the world. This is the only way in which you can say and mean, "My only function is the one God gave me." This is the only way in which you can find peace of mind.

Today, and for a number of days to follow, set aside ten to fifteen minutes for a more sustained practice period, in which you try to understand and accept what the idea for the day really means. Today's idea offers you escape from all your perceived difficulties. It places the key to the door of peace, which you have closed upon yourself, in your own hands. It gives you the answer to all the searching you have done since time began.

Try, if possible, to undertake the daily extended practice periods at approximately the same time each day. Try, also, to determine this time in advance, and then adhere to it as closely as possible. The purpose of this is to arrange your day so that you have set apart the time for God, as well as for all the trivial purposes and goals you will pursue. This is part of the long-range disciplinary training your mind needs, so that the Holy Spirit can use it consistently for the purpose He shares with you.

For the longer practice period, begin by reviewing the idea for the day. Then close your eyes, repeat the idea to yourself once again, and watch your mind carefully to catch whatever thoughts cross it. At first, make no attempt to concentrate only on thoughts related to the idea for the day. Rather, try to uncover each thought that arises to interfere with it. Note each one as it comes to you, with as little involvement or concern as possible, dismissing each one by telling yourself:

THIS THOUGHT REFLECTS A GOAL THAT IS PREVENTING ME FROM
ACCEPTING MY ONLY FUNCTION.

After a while, interfering thoughts will become harder to find. Try, however, to continue a minute or so longer, attempting to catch a few of the idle thoughts that escaped your attention before, but do not strain or make undue effort in doing this. Then tell yourself:

ON THIS CLEAN SLATE LET MY TRUE FUNCTION BE WRITTEN FOR ME.

You need not use these exact words, but try to get the sense of being willing to have your illusions of purpose be replaced by truth.

Finally, repeat the idea for today once more, and devote the rest of the practice period to trying to focus on its importance to you, the relief its acceptance will bring you by resolving your conflicts once and for all, and the extent to which you really want salvation in spite of your own foolish ideas to the contrary.

In the shorter practice periods, which should be undertaken at least once an hour, use this form in applying today's idea:

MY ONLY FUNCTION IS THE ONE GOD GAVE ME. I WANT NO OTHER
AND I HAVE NO OTHER.

Sometimes close your eyes as you practice this, and sometimes keep them open and look about you. It is what you see now that will be totally changed when you accept today's idea completely.

Lesson 66

My happiness and my function are one.

You have surely noticed an emphasis throughout our recent lessons on the connection between fulfilling your function and achieving happiness. This is because you do not really see the connection. Yet there is more than just a connection between them; they are the same. Their forms are different, but their content is completely one.

The ego does constant battle with the Holy Spirit on the fundamental question of what your function is. So does it do constant battle with the Holy Spirit about what your happiness is. It is not a two-way battle. The ego attacks and the Holy Spirit does not respond. He knows what your function is. He knows that it is your happiness.

Today we will try to go past this wholly meaningless battle and arrive at the truth about your function. We will not engage in senseless arguments about what it is. We will not become hopelessly involved in defining happiness and determining the means for achieving it. We will not indulge the ego by listening to its attacks on truth. We will merely be glad that we can find out what truth is.

Our longer practice period today has as its purpose your acceptance of the fact that not only is there a very real connection between the function God gave you and your happiness, but that they are actually identical. God gives you only happiness. Therefore, the function He gave you must be happiness, even if it appears to be different. Today's exercises are an attempt to go beyond these differences in appearance, and recognize a common content where it exists in truth.

Begin the ten-to-fifteen-minute practice period by reviewing these thoughts:

GOD GIVES ME ONLY HAPPINESS.
HE HAS GIVEN MY FUNCTION TO ME.
THEREFORE MY FUNCTION MUST BE HAPPINESS.

Try to see the logic in this sequence, even if you do not yet accept the conclusion. It is only if the first two thoughts are wrong that the conclusion could be false. Let us, then, think about the premises for a while, as we are practicing.

The first premise is that God gives you only happiness. This could be false, of course, but in order to be false it is necessary to define God as something He is not. Love cannot give evil, and what is not happiness is evil. God cannot give what He does not have, and He cannot have what He is not. Unless God gives you only happiness, He must be evil. And it is this definition of Him you are believing if you do not accept the first premise.

The second premise is that God has given you your function. We have seen that there are only two parts of your mind. One is ruled by the ego, and is made up of illusions. The other is the home of the Holy Spirit, where truth abides. There are no other guides but these to choose between, and no other outcomes possible as a result of your choice but the fear that the ego always engenders, and the love that the Holy Spirit always offers to replace it.

Thus, it must be that your function is established by God through His Voice, or is made by the ego which you have made to replace Him. Which is true? Unless God gave your function to you, it must be the gift of the ego. Does the ego really have gifts to give, being itself an illusion and offering only the illusion of gifts?

Think about this during the longer practice period today. Think also about the many forms the illusion of your function has taken in your mind, and the many ways in which you tried to find salvation under the ego's guidance. Did you find it? Were you happy? Did they bring you peace? We need great honesty today. Remember the outcomes fairly, and consider also whether it was ever reasonable to expect happiness from anything the ego ever proposed. Yet the ego is the only alternative to the Holy Spirit's Voice.

You will listen to madness or hear the truth. Try to make this choice as you think about the premises on which our conclusion rests. We can share in this conclusion, but in no other. For God Himself shares it with us. Today's idea is another giant stride in the perception of the same as the same, and the different as different. On one side stand all illusions. All truth stands on the other. Let us try today to realize that only the truth is true.

In the shorter practice periods, which would be most helpful today if undertaken twice an hour, this form of the application is suggested:

MY HAPPINESS AND FUNCTION ARE ONE, BECAUSE GOD HAS
GIVEN ME BOTH.

It will not take more than a minute, and probably less, to repeat these words slowly and think about them a little while as you say them.

Lesson 67

Love created me like itself.

Today's idea is a complete and accurate statement of what you are. This is why you are the light of the world. This is why God appointed you as the world's savior. This is why the Son of God looks to you for his salvation. He is saved by what you are. We will make every effort today to reach this truth about you, and to realize fully, if only for a moment, that it is the truth.

In the longer practice period, we will think about your reality and its wholly unchanged and unchangeable nature. We will begin by repeating this truth about you, and then spend a few minutes adding some relevant thoughts, such as:

HOLINESS CREATED ME HOLY.
KINDNESS CREATED ME KIND.
HELPFULNESS CREATED ME HELPFUL.
PERFECTION CREATED ME PERFECT.

Any attribute which is in accord with God as He defines Himself is appropriate for use. We are trying today to undo your definition of God and replace it with His Own. We are also trying to emphasize that you are part of His definition of Himself.

After you have gone over several such related thoughts, try to let all thoughts drop away for a brief preparatory interval, and then try to reach past all your images and preconceptions about yourself to the truth in you. If love created you like itself, this Self must be in you. And somewhere in your mind It is there for you to find.

You may find it necessary to repeat the idea for today from time to time to replace distracting thoughts. You may also find that this is not sufficient, and that you need to continue adding other thoughts related to the truth about yourself. Yet perhaps you will succeed in going past that, and through the interval of thoughtlessness to the awareness of a blazing light in which you recognize yourself as love created you. Be confident that you will do much today to bring that awareness nearer, whether you feel you have succeeded or not.

It will be particularly helpful today to practice the idea for the day as often as you can. You need to hear the truth about yourself as frequently as possible, because your mind is so preoccupied with false self-images. Four or five times an hour, and perhaps even more, it would be most beneficial to remind yourself that love created you like itself. Hear the truth about yourself in this.

Try to realize in the shorter practice periods that this is not your tiny, solitary voice that tells you this. This is the Voice for God, reminding you of your Father and of your Self. This is the Voice of truth, replacing everything that the ego tells you about yourself with the simple truth about the Son of God. You were created by love like itself.

Lesson 68

Love holds no grievances.

You who were created by love like itself can hold no grievances and know your Self. To hold a grievance is to forget who you are. To hold a grievance is to see yourself as a body. To hold a grievance is to let the ego rule your mind and to condemn the body to death. Perhaps you do not yet fully realize just what holding grievances does to your mind. It seems to split you off from your Source and make you unlike Him. It makes you believe that He is like what you think you have become, for no one can conceive of his Creator as unlike himself.

Shut off from your Self, which remains aware of Its likeness to Its Creator, your Self seems to sleep, while the part of your mind that weaves illusions in its sleep appears to be awake. Can all this arise from holding grievances? Oh, yes! For he who holds grievances denies he was created by love, and his Creator has become fearful to him in his dream of hate. Who can dream of hatred and not fear God?

It is as sure that those who hold grievances will redefine God in their own image, as it is certain that God created them like Himself, and defined them as part of Him. It is as sure that those who hold grievances will suffer guilt, as it is certain that those who forgive will find peace. It is as sure that those who hold grievances will forget who they are, as it is certain that those who forgive will remember.

Would you not be willing to relinquish your grievances if you believed all this were so? Perhaps you do not think you can let your grievances go. That, however, is simply a matter of motivation. Today we will try to find out how you would feel without them. If you succeed even by ever so little, there will never be a problem in motivation ever again.

Begin today's extended practice period by searching your mind for those against whom you hold what you regard as major grievances. Some of these will be quite easy to find. Then think of the seemingly minor grievances you hold against those you like and even think you love. It will quickly become apparent that there is no one against whom you do not cherish grievances of some sort. This has left you alone in all the universe in your perception of yourself.

Determine now to see all these people as friends. Say to them all, thinking of each one in turn as you do so:

I WOULD SEE YOU AS MY FRIEND, THAT I MAY REMEMBER YOU
ARE PART OF ME AND COME TO KNOW MYSELF.

Spend the remainder of the practice period trying to think of yourself as completely at peace with everyone and everything, safe in a world that protects you and loves you, and that you love in return. Try to feel safety surrounding you, hovering over you and holding you up. Try to believe, however briefly, that nothing can harm you in any way. At the end of the practice period tell yourself:

LOVE HOLDS NO GRIEVANCES. WHEN I LET ALL MY GRIEVANCES
GO I WILL KNOW I AM PERFECTLY SAFE.

The short practice periods should include a quick application of today's idea in this form, whenever any thought of grievance arises against anyone, physically present or not:

LOVE HOLDS NO GRIEVANCES. LET ME NOT BETRAY MY SELF.

In addition, repeat the idea several times an hour in this form:

LOVE HOLDS NO GRIEVANCES. I WOULD WAKE TO MY SELF BY
LAYING ALL MY GRIEVANCES ASIDE AND WAKENING IN HIM.

Lesson 69

My grievances hide the light of the world in me.

No one can look upon what your grievances conceal. Because your grievances are hiding the light of the world in you, everyone stands in darkness, and you beside him. But as the veil of your grievances is lifted, you are released with him. Share your salvation now with him who stood beside you when you were in hell. He is your brother in the light of the world that saves you both.

Today let us make another real attempt to reach the light in you. Before we undertake this in our more extended practice period, let us devote several minutes to thinking about what we are trying to do. We are literally attempting to get in touch with the salvation of the world. We are trying to see past the veil of darkness that keeps it concealed. We are trying to let the veil be lifted, and to see the tears of God's Son disappear in the sunlight.

Let us begin our longer practice period today with the full realization that this is so, and with real determination to reach what is dearer to us than all else. Salvation is our only need. There is no other purpose here, and no other function to fulfill. Learning salvation is our only goal. Let us end the ancient search today by finding the light in us, and holding it up for everyone who searches with us to look upon and rejoice.

Very quietly now, with your eyes closed, try to let go of all the content that generally occupies your consciousness. Think of your mind as a vast circle, surrounded by a layer of heavy, dark clouds. You can see only the clouds because you seem to be standing outside the circle and quite apart from it.

From where you stand, you can see no reason to believe there is a brilliant light hidden by the clouds. The clouds seem to be the only reality. They seem to be all there is to see. Therefore, you do not attempt to go through them and past them, which is the only way in which you would be really convinced of their lack of substance. We will make this attempt today.

After you have thought about the importance of what you are trying to do for yourself and the world, try to settle down in perfect stillness, remembering only how much you want to reach the light in you today,–now! Determine to go past the clouds. Reach out and touch them in your mind. Brush them aside with your hand; feel them resting on your cheeks and forehead and eyelids as you go through them. Go on; clouds cannot stop you.

If you are doing the exercises properly, you will begin to feel a sense of being lifted up and carried ahead. Your little effort and small determination call on the power of the universe to help you, and God Himself will raise you from darkness into light. You are in accord with His Will. You cannot fail because your will is His.

Have confidence in your Father today, and be certain that He has heard you and answered you. You may not recognize His answer yet, but you can indeed be sure that it is given you and you will yet receive it. Try, as you attempt to go through the clouds to the light, to hold this confidence in your mind. Try to remember that you are at last joining your will to God's. Try to keep the thought clearly in mind that what you undertake with God must succeed. Then let the power of God work in you and through you, that His Will and yours be done.

In the shorter practice periods, which you will want to do as often as possible in view of the importance of today's idea to you and your happiness, remind yourself that your grievances are hiding the light of the world from your awareness. Remind yourself also that you are not searching for it alone, and that you do know where to look for it. Say, then:

MY GRIEVANCES HIDE THE LIGHT OF THE WORLD IN ME. I CANNOT
SEE WHAT I HAVE HIDDEN. YET I WANT TO LET IT BE REVEALED TO
ME, FOR MY SALVATION AND THE SALVATION OF THE WORLD.

Also, be sure to tell yourself:

IF I HOLD THIS GRIEVANCE THE LIGHT OF THE WORLD WILL BE HIDDEN
FROM ME,

Lesson 70

My salvation comes from me.

All temptation is nothing more than some form of the basic temptation not to believe the idea for today. Salvation seems to come from anywhere except from you. So, too, does the source of guilt. You see neither guilt nor salvation as in your own mind and nowhere else. When you realize that all guilt is solely an invention of your mind, you also realize that guilt and salvation must be in the same place. In understanding this you are saved.

The seeming cost of accepting today's idea is this: It means that nothing outside yourself can save you; nothing outside yourself can give you peace. But it also means that nothing outside yourself can hurt you, or disturb your peace or upset you in any way. Today's idea places you in charge of the universe, where you belong because of what you are. This is not a role that can be partially accepted. And you must surely begin to see that accepting it is salvation.

It may not, however, be clear to you why the recognition that guilt is in your own mind entails the realization that salvation is there as well. God would not have put the remedy for the sickness where it cannot help. That is the way your mind has worked, but hardly His. He wants you to be healed, so He has kept the Source of healing where the need for healing lies.

You have tried to do just the opposite, making every attempt, however distorted and fantastic it might be, to separate healing from the sickness for which it was intended, and thus keep the sickness. Your purpose was to ensure that healing did not occur. God's purpose was to ensure that it did.

Today we practice realizing that God's Will and ours are really the same in this. God wants us to be healed, and we do not really want to be sick, because it makes us unhappy. Therefore, in accepting the idea for today, we are really in agreement with God. He does not want us to be sick. Neither do we. He wants us to be healed. So do we.

We are ready for two longer practice periods today, each of which should last some ten to fifteen minutes. We will, however, still let you decide when to undertake them. We will follow this practice for a number of lessons, and it would again be well to decide in advance when would be a good time to lay aside for each of them, and then adhering to your own decisions as closely as possible.

Begin these practice periods by repeating the idea for today, adding a statement signifying your recognition that salvation comes from nothing outside of you. You might put it this way:

MY SALVATION COMES FROM ME. IT CANNOT COME FROM
ANYWHERE ELSE.

Then devote a few minutes, with your eyes closed, to reviewing some of the external places where you have looked for salvation in the past;—in other people, in possessions, in various situations and events, and in self-concepts that you sought to make real. Recognize that it is not there, and tell yourself:

MY SALVATION CANNOT COME FROM ANY OF THESE THINGS.
MY SALVATION COMES FROM ME AND ONLY FROM ME.

Now we will try again to reach the light in you, which is where your salvation is. You cannot find it in the clouds that surround the light, and it is in them you have been looking for it. It is not there. It is past the clouds and in the light beyond. Remember that you will have to go through the clouds before you can reach the light. But remember also that you have never found anything in the cloud patterns you imagined that endured, or that you wanted.

Since all illusions of salvation have failed you, surely you do not want to remain in the clouds, looking vainly for idols there, when you could so easily walk on into the light of real salvation. Try to pass the clouds by whatever means appeals to you. If it helps you, think of me holding your hand and leading you. And I assure you this will be no idle fantasy.

For the short and frequent practice periods today, remind yourself that your salvation comes from you, and nothing but your own thoughts can hamper your progress. You are free from all external interference. You are in charge of your salvation. You are in charge of the salvation of the world. Say, then:

MY SALVATION COMES FROM ME. NOTHING OUTSIDE OF ME CAN HOLD
ME BACK. WITHIN ME IS THE WORLD'S SALVATION AND MY OWN.

Lesson 71

Only God's plan for salvation will work.

You may not realize that the ego has set up a plan for salvation in opposition to God's. It is this plan in which you believe. Since it is the opposite of God's, you also believe that to accept God's plan in place of the ego's is to be damned. This sounds preposterous, of course. Yet after we have considered just what the ego's plan is, perhaps you will realize that, however preposterous it may be, you do believe in it.

The ego's plan for salvation centers around holding grievances. It maintains that, if someone else spoke or acted differently, if some external circumstance or event were changed, you would be saved. Thus, the source of salvation is constantly perceived as outside yourself. Each grievance you hold is a declaration, and an assertion in which you believe, that says, "If this were different, I would be saved." The change of mind necessary for salvation is thus demanded of everyone and everything except yourself.

The role assigned to your own mind in this plan, then, is simply to determine what, other than itself, must change if you are to be saved. According to this insane plan, any perceived source of salvation is acceptable provided that it will not work. This ensures that the fruitless search will continue, for the illusion persists that, although this hope has always failed, there is still grounds for hope in other places and in other things. Another person will yet serve better; another situation will yet offer success.

Such is the ego's plan for your salvation. Surely you can see how it is in strict accord with the ego's basic doctrine, "Seek but do not find." For what could more surely guarantee that you will not find salvation than to channelize all your efforts in searching for it where it is not?

God's plan for salvation works simply because, by following His direction, you seek for salvation where it is. But if you are to succeed, as God promises you will, you must be willing to seek there only. Otherwise, your purpose is divided and you will attempt to follow two plans for salvation that are diametrically opposed in all ways. The result can only bring confusion, misery and a deep sense of failure and despair.

How can you escape all this? Very simply. The idea for today is the answer. Only God's plan for salvation will work. There can be no real conflict about this, because there is no possible alternative to God's plan that will save you. His is the only plan that is certain in its outcome. His is the only plan that must succeed.

Let us practice recognizing this certainty today. And let us rejoice that there is an answer to what seems to be a conflict with no resolution possible. All things are possible to God. Salvation must be yours because of His plan, which cannot fail.

Begin the two longer practice periods for today by thinking about today's idea, and realizing that it contains two parts, each making equal contribution to the whole. God's plan for your salvation will work, and other plans will not. Do not allow yourself to become depressed or angry at the second part; it is inherent in the first. And in the first is your full release from all your own insane attempts and mad proposals to free yourself. They have led to depression and anger; but God's plan will succeed. It will lead to release and joy.

Remembering this, let us devote the remainder of the extended practice periods to asking God to reveal His plan to us. Ask Him very specifically:

WHAT WOULD YOU HAVE ME DO?
WHERE WOULD YOU HAVE ME GO?
WHAT WOULD YOU HAVE ME SAY, AND TO WHOM?

Give Him full charge of the rest of the practice period, and let Him tell you what needs to be done by you in His plan for your salvation. He will answer in proportion to your willingness to hear His Voice. Refuse not to hear. The very fact that you are doing the exercises proves that you have some willingness to listen. This is enough to establish your claim to God's answer.

In the shorter practice periods, tell yourself often that God's plan for salvation, and only His, will work. Be alert to all temptation to hold grievances today, and respond to them with this form of today's idea:

HOLDING GRIEVANCES IS THE OPPOSITE OF GOD'S PLAN
FOR SALVATION. AND ONLY HIS PLAN WILL WORK.

Try to remember today's idea some six or seven times an hour. There could be no better way to spend a half minute or less than to remember the Source of your salvation, and to see It where It is.

Lesson 72

Holding grievances is an attack on God's plan for salvation.

While we have recognized that the ego's plan for salvation is the opposite of God's, we have not yet emphasized that it is an active attack on His plan, and a deliberate attempt to destroy it. In the attack, God is assigned the attributes which are actually associated with the ego, while the ego appears to take on the attributes of God.

The ego's fundamental wish is to replace God. In fact, the ego is the physical embodiment of that wish. For it is that wish that seems to surround the mind with a body, keeping it separate and alone, and unable to reach other minds except through the body that was made to imprison it. The limit on communication cannot be the best means to expand communication. Yet the ego would have you believe that it is.

Although the attempt to keep the limitations that a body would impose is obvious here, it is perhaps not so apparent why holding grievances is an attack on God's plan for salvation. But let us consider the kinds of things you are apt to hold grievances for. Are they not always associated with something a body does? A person says something you do not like. He does something that displeases you. He "betrays" his hostile thoughts in his behavior.

You are not dealing here with what the person is. On the contrary, you are exclusively concerned with what he does in a body. You are doing more than failing to help in freeing him from the body's limitations. You are actively trying to hold him to it by confusing it with him, and judging them as one. Herein is God attacked, for if His Son is only a body, so must He be as well. A creator wholly unlike his creation is inconceivable.

If God is a body, what must His plan for salvation be? What could it be but death? In trying to present Himself as the Author of life and not of death, He is a liar and a deceiver, full of false promises and offering illusions in place of truth. The body's apparent reality makes this view of God quite convincing. In fact, if the body were real, it would be difficult indeed to escape this conclusion. And every grievance that you hold insists that the body is real. It overlooks entirely what your brother is. It reinforces your belief that he is a body, and condemns him for it. And it asserts that his salvation must be death, projecting this attack onto God, and holding Him responsible for it.

To this carefully prepared arena, where angry animals seek for prey and mercy cannot enter, the ego comes to save you. God made you a body. Very well. Let us accept this and be glad. As a body, do not let yourself be deprived of what the body offers. Take the little you can get. God gave you nothing. The body is your only savior. It is the death of God and your salvation.

This is the universal belief of the world you see. Some hate the body, and try to hurt and humiliate it. Others love the body, and try to glorify and exalt it. But while the body stands at the center of your concept of yourself, you are attacking God's plan for salvation, and holding your grievances against Him and His creation, that you may not hear the Voice of truth and welcome It as Friend. Your chosen savior takes His place instead. It is your friend; He is your enemy.

We will try today to stop these senseless attacks on salvation. We will try to welcome it instead. Your upside-down perception has been ruinous to your peace of mind. You have seen yourself in a body and the truth outside you, locked away from your awareness by the body's limitations. Now we are going to try to see this differently.

The light of truth is in us, where it was placed by God. It is the body that is outside us, and is not our concern. To be without a body is to be in our natural state. To recognize the light of truth in us is to recognize ourselves as we are. To see our Self as separate from the body is to end the attack on God's plan for salvation, and to accept it instead. And wherever His plan is accepted, it is accomplished already.

Our goal in the longer practice periods today is to become aware that God's plan for salvation has already been accomplished in us. To achieve this goal, we must replace attack with acceptance. As long as we attack it, we cannot understand what God's plan for us is. We are therefore attacking what we do not recognize. Now we are going to try to lay judgment aside, and ask what God's plan for us is:

WHAT IS SALVATION, FATHER? I DO NOT KNOW.
TELL ME, THAT I MAY UNDERSTAND.

Then we will wait in quiet for His answer. We have attacked God's plan for salvation without waiting to hear what it is. We have shouted our grievances so loudly that we have not listened to His Voice. We have used our grievances to close our eyes and stop our ears.

Now we would see and hear and learn. "What is salvation, Father?" Ask and you will be answered. Seek and you will find. We are no longer asking the ego what salvation is and where to find it. We are asking it of truth. Be certain, then, that the answer will be true because of Whom you ask.

Whenever you feel your confidence wane and your hope of success flicker and go out, repeat your question and your request, remembering that you are asking of the infinite Creator of infinity, Who created you like Himself:

WHAT IS SALVATION, FATHER? I DO NOT KNOW.
TELL ME, THAT I MAY UNDERSTAND.

He will answer. Be determined to hear.

One or perhaps two shorter practice periods an hour will be enough for today, since they will be somewhat longer than usual. These exercises should begin with this:

HOLDING GRIEVANCES IS AN ATTACK ON GOD'S PLAN FOR SALVATION.
LET ME ACCEPT IT INSTEAD. WHAT IS SALVATION, FATHER?

Then wait a minute or so in silence, preferably with your eyes closed, and listen for His answer.

Lesson 73

I will there be light.

Today we are considering the will you share with God. This is not the same as the ego's idle wishes, out of which darkness and nothingness arise. The will you share with God has all the power of creation in it. The ego's idle wishes are unshared, and therefore have no power at all. Its wishes are not idle in the sense that they can make a world of illusions in which your belief can be very strong. But they are idle indeed in terms of creation. They make nothing that is real.

Idle wishes and grievances are partners or co-makers in picturing the world you see. The wishes of the ego gave rise to it, and the ego's need for grievances, which are necessary to maintain it, peoples it with figures that seem to attack you and call for "righteous" judgment. These figures become the middlemen the ego employs to traffic in grievances. They stand between your awareness and your brothers' reality. Beholding them, you do not know your brothers or your Self.

Your will is lost to you in this strange bartering, in which guilt is traded back and forth, and grievances increase with each exchange. Can such a world have been created by the Will the Son of God shares with his Father? Did God create disaster for His Son? Creation is the Will of Both together. Would God create a world that kills Himself?

Today we will try once more to reach the world that is in accordance with your will. The light is in it because it does not oppose the Will of God. It is not Heaven, but the light of Heaven shines on it. Darkness has vanished. The ego's idle wishes have been withdrawn. Yet the light that shines upon this world reflects your will, and so it must be in you that we will look for it.

Your picture of the world can only mirror what is within. The source of neither light nor darkness can be found without. Grievances darken your mind, and you look out on a darkened world. Forgiveness lifts the darkness, reasserts your will, and lets you look upon a world of light. We have repeatedly emphasized that the barrier of grievances is easily passed, and cannot stand between you and your salvation. The reason is very simple. Do you really want to be in hell? Do you really want to weep and suffer and die?

Forget the ego's arguments which seek to prove all this is really Heaven. You know it is not so. You cannot want this for yourself. There is a point beyond which illusions cannot go. Suffering is not happiness, and it is happiness you really want. Such is your will in truth. And so salvation is your will as well. You want to succeed in what we are trying to do today. We undertake it with your blessing and your glad accord.

We will succeed today if you remember that you want salvation for yourself. You want to accept God's plan because you share in it. You have no will that can really oppose it, and you do not want to do so. Salvation is for you. Above all else, you want the freedom to remember Who you really are. Today it is the ego that stands powerless before your will. Your will is free, and nothing can prevail against it.

Therefore, we undertake the exercises for today in happy confidence, certain that we will find what it is your will to find, and remember what it is your will to remember. No idle wishes can detain us, nor deceive us with an illusion of strength. Today let your will be done, and end forever the insane belief that it is hell in place of Heaven that you choose.

We will begin our longer practice periods with the recognition that God's plan for salvation, and only His, is wholly in accord with your will. It is not the purpose of an alien power, thrust upon you unwillingly. It is the one purpose here on which you and your Father are in perfect accord. You will succeed today, the time appointed for the release of the Son of God from hell and from all idle wishes. His will is now restored to his awareness. He is willing this very day to look upon the light in him and be saved.

After reminding yourself of this, and determining to keep your will clearly in mind, tell yourself with gentle firmness and quiet certainty:

I WILL THERE BE LIGHT.

 LET ME BEHOLD THE LIGHT THAT REFLECTS GOD'S WILL AND MINE.

Then let your will assert itself, joined with the power of God and united with your Self. Put the rest of the practice period under Their guidance. Join with Them as They lead the way.

In the shorter practice periods, again make a declaration of what you really want. Say:

I WILL THERE BE LIGHT. DARKNESS IS NOT MY WILL.

This should be repeated several times an hour. It is most important, however, to apply today's idea in this form immediately you are tempted to hold a grievance of any kind. This will help you let your grievances go, instead of cherishing them and hiding them in darkness.

Lesson 74

There is no will but God's.

The idea for today can be regarded as the central thought toward which all our exercises are directed. God's is the only Will. When you have recognized this, you have recognized that your will is His. The belief that conflict is possible has gone. Peace has replaced the strange idea that you are torn by conflicting goals. As an expression of the Will of God, you have no goal but His.

There is great peace in today's idea, and the exercises for today are directed towards finding it. The idea itself is wholly true. Therefore it cannot give rise to illusions. Without illusions conflict is impossible. Let us try to recognize this today, and experience the peace this recognition brings.

Begin the longer practice periods by repeating these thoughts several times, slowly and with firm determination to understand what they mean, and to hold them in mind:

THERE IS NO WILL BUT GOD'S. I CANNOT BE IN CONFLICT.

Then spend several minutes in adding some related thoughts, such as:

I AM AT PEACE.
NOTHING CAN DISTURB ME. MY WILL IS GOD'S.
MY WILL AND GOD'S ARE ONE.
GOD WILLS PEACE FOR HIS SON.

During this introductory phase, be sure to deal quickly with any conflict thoughts that may cross your mind. Tell yourself immediately:

THERE IS NO WILL BUT GOD'S. THESE CONFLICT
THOUGHTS ARE MEANINGLESS.

If there is one conflict area that seems particularly difficult to resolve, single it out for special consideration. Think about it briefly but very specifically, identify the particular person or persons and the situation or situations involved, and tell yourself:

THERE IS NO WILL BUT GOD'S. I SHARE IT WITH HIM.
MY CONFLICTS ABOUT _____ CANNOT BE REAL.

After you have cleared your mind in this way, close your eyes and try to experience the peace to which your reality entitles you. Sink into it and feel it closing around you. There may be some temptation to mistake these attempts for withdrawal, but the difference is easily detected. If you are succeeding, you will feel a deep sense of joy and an increased alertness, rather than a feeling of drowsiness and enervation.

Joy characterizes peace. By this experience will you recognize that you have reached it. If you feel yourself slipping off into withdrawal, quickly repeat the idea for today and try again. Do this as often as necessary. There is definite gain in refusing to allow retreat into withdrawal, even if you do not experience the peace you seek.

In the shorter periods, which should be undertaken at regular and predetermined intervals today, say to yourself:

THERE IS NO WILL BUT GOD'S. I SEEK HIS PEACE TODAY.

Then try to find what you are seeking. A minute or two every half an hour, with eyes closed if possible, would be well spent on this today.

Lesson 75

The light has come.

The light has come. You are healed and you can heal. The light has come. You are saved and you can save. You are at peace, and you bring peace with you wherever you go. Darkness and turmoil and death have disappeared. The light has come.

Today we celebrate the happy ending to your long dream of disaster. There are no dark dreams now. The light has come. Today the time of light begins for you and everyone. It is a new era, in which a new world is born. The old one has left no trace upon it in its passing. Today we see a different world, because the light has come.

Our exercises for today will be happy ones, in which we offer thanks for the passing of the old and the beginning of the new. No shadows from the past remain to darken our sight and hide the world forgiveness offers us. Today we will accept the new world as what we want to see. We will be given what we desire. We will to see the light; the light has come.

Our longer practice periods will be devoted to looking at the world that our forgiveness shows us. This is what we want to see, and only this. Our single purpose makes our goal inevitable. Today the real world rises before us in gladness, to be seen at last. Sight is given us, now that the light has come.

We do not want to see the ego's shadow on the world today. We see the light, and in it we see Heaven's reflection lie across the world. Begin the longer practice periods by telling yourself the glad tidings of your release:

THE LIGHT HAS COME. I HAVE FORGIVEN THE WORLD.

Dwell not upon the past today. Keep a completely open mind, washed of all past ideas and clean of every concept you have made. You have forgiven the world today. You can look upon it now as if you never saw it before. You do not know yet what it looks like. You merely wait to have it shown to you. While you wait, repeat several times, slowly and in complete patience:

THE LIGHT HAS COME. I HAVE FORGIVEN THE WORLD.

Realize that your forgiveness entitles you to vision. Understand that the Holy Spirit never fails to give the gift of sight to the forgiving. Believe He will not fail you now. You have forgiven the world. He will be with you as you watch and wait. He will show you what true vision sees. It is His Will, and you have joined with Him. Wait patiently for Him. He will be there. The light has come. You have forgiven the world.

Tell Him you know you cannot fail because you trust in Him. And tell yourself you wait in certainty to look upon the world He promised you. From this time forth you will see differently. Today the light has come. And you will see the world that has been promised you since time began, and in which is the end of time ensured.

The shorter practice periods, too, will be joyful reminders of your release. Remind yourself every quarter of an hour or so that today is a time for special celebration. Give thanks for mercy and the Love of God. Rejoice in the power of forgiveness to heal your sight completely. Be confident that on this day there is a new beginning. Without the darkness of the past upon your eyes, you cannot fail to see today. And what you see will be so welcome that you will gladly extend today forever.

Say, then:

THE LIGHT HAS COME. I HAVE FORGIVEN THE WORLD.

Should you be tempted, say to anyone who seems to pull you back into darkness:

THE LIGHT HAS COME. I HAVE FORGIVEN YOU.

We dedicate this day to the serenity in which God would have you be. Keep it in your awareness of yourself and see it everywhere today, as we celebrate the beginning of your vision and the sight of the real world, which has come to replace the unforgiven world you thought was real.

Lesson 76

I am under no laws but God's.

We have observed before how many senseless things have seemed to you to be salvation. Each has imprisoned you with laws as senseless as itself. You are not bound by them. Yet to understand that this is so, you must first realize salvation lies not there. While you would seek for it in things that have no meaning, you bind yourself to laws that make no sense. Thus do you seek to prove salvation is where it is not.

Today we will be glad you cannot prove it. For if you could, you would forever seek salvation where it is not, and never find it. The idea for today tells you once again how simple is salvation. Look for it where it waits for you, and there it will be found. Look nowhere else, for it is nowhere else.

Think of the freedom in the recognition that you are not bound by all the strange and twisted laws you have set up to save you. You really think that you would starve unless you have stacks of green paper strips and piles of metal discs. You really think a small round pellet or some fluid pushed into your veins through a sharpened needle will ward off disease and death. You really think you are alone unless another body is with you.

It is insanity that thinks these things. You call them laws, and put them under different names in a long catalogue of rituals that have no use and serve no purpose. You think you must obey the "laws" of medicine, of economics and of health. Protect the body, and you will be saved.

These are not laws, but madness. The body is endangered by the mind that hurts itself. The body suffers just in order that the mind will fail to see it is the victim of itself. The body's suffering is a mask the mind holds up to hide what really suffers. It would not understand it is its own enemy; that it attacks itself and wants to die. It is from this your "laws" would save the body. It is for this you think you are a body.

There are no laws except the laws of God. This needs repeating, over and over, until you realize it applies to everything that you have made in opposition to God's Will. Your magic has no meaning. What it is meant to save does not exist. Only what it is meant to hide will save you.

The laws of God can never be replaced. We will devote today to rejoicing that this is so. It is no longer a truth that we would hide. We realize instead it is a truth that keeps us free forever. Magic imprisons, but the laws of God make free. The light has come because there are no laws but His.

We will begin the longer practice periods today with a short review of the different kinds of "laws" we have believed we must obey. These would include, for example, the "laws" of nutrition, of immunization, of medication, and of the body's protection in innumerable ways. Think further; you believe in the "laws" of friendship, of "good" relationships and reciprocity. Perhaps you even think that there are laws which set forth what is God's and what is yours. Many "religions" have been based on this. They would not save but damn in Heaven's name. Yet they are no more strange than other "laws" you hold must be obeyed to make you safe.

There are no laws but God's. Dismiss all foolish magical beliefs today, and hold your mind in silent readiness to hear the Voice that speaks the truth to you. You will be listening to One Who says there is no loss under the laws of God. Payment is neither given nor received. Exchange cannot be made; there are no substitutes; and nothing is replaced by something else. God's laws forever give and never take.

Hear Him Who tells you this, and realize how foolish are the "laws" you thought upheld the world you thought you saw. Then listen further. He will tell you more. About the Love your Father has for you. About the endless joy He offers you. About His yearning for His only Son, created as His channel for creation; denied to Him by his belief in hell.

Let us today open God's channels to Him, and let His Will extend through us to Him. Thus is creation endlessly increased. His Voice will speak of this to us, as well as of the joys of Heaven which His laws keep limitless forever. We will repeat today's idea until we have listened and understood there are no laws but God's. Then we will tell ourselves, as a dedication with which the practice period concludes:

I AM UNDER NO LAWS BUT GOD'S.

We will repeat this dedication as often as possible today; at least four or five times an hour, as well as in response to any temptation to experience ourselves as subject to other laws throughout the day. It is our statement of freedom from all danger and all tyranny. It is our acknowledgment that God is our Father, and that His Son is saved.

Lesson 77

I am entitled to miracles.

You are entitled to miracles because of what you are. You will receive miracles because of what God is. And you will offer miracles because you are one with God. Again, how simple is salvation! It is merely a statement of your true Identity. It is this that we will celebrate today.

Your claim to miracles does not lie in your illusions about yourself. It does not depend on any magical powers you have ascribed to yourself, nor on any of the rituals you have devised. It is inherent in the truth of what you are. It is implicit in what God your Father is. It was ensured in your creation, and guaranteed by the laws of God.

Today we will claim the miracles which are your right, since they belong to you. You have been promised full release from the world you made. You have been assured that the Kingdom of God is within you, and can never be lost. We ask no more than what belongs to us in truth. Today, however, we will also make sure that we will not content ourselves with less.

Begin the longer practice periods by telling yourself quite confidently that you are entitled to miracles. Closing your eyes, remind yourself that you are asking only for what is rightfully yours. Remind yourself also that miracles are never taken from one and given to another, and that in asking for your rights, you are upholding the rights of everyone. Miracles do not obey the laws of this world. They merely follow from the laws of God.

After this brief introductory phase, wait quietly for the assurance that your request is granted. You have asked for the salvation of the world, and for your own. You have requested that you be given the means by which this is accomplished. You cannot fail to be assured in this. You are but asking that the Will of God be done.

In doing this, you do not really ask for anything. You state a fact that cannot be denied. The Holy Spirit cannot but assure you that your request is granted. The fact that you accepted must be so. There is no room for doubt and uncertainty today. We are asking a real question at last. The answer is a simple statement of a simple fact. You will receive the assurance that you seek.

Our shorter practice periods will be frequent, and will also be devoted to a reminder of a simple fact. Tell yourself often today:

I AM ENTITLED TO MIRACLES.

Ask for them whenever a situation arises in which they are called for. You will recognize these situations. And since you are not relying on yourself to find the miracle, you are fully entitled to receive it whenever you ask.

Remember, too, not to be satisfied with less than the perfect answer. Be quick to tell yourself, should you be tempted:

I WILL NOT TRADE MIRACLES FOR GRIEVANCES. I WANT ONLY WHAT BELONGS TO ME. GOD HAS ESTABLISHED MIRACLES AS MY RIGHT.

Lesson 78

Let miracles replace all grievances.

Perhaps it is not yet quite clear to you that each decision that you make is one between a grievance and a miracle. Each grievance stands like a dark shield of hate before the miracle it would conceal. And as you raise it up before your eyes, you will not see the miracle beyond. Yet all the while it waits for you in light, but you behold your grievances instead.

Today we go beyond the grievances, to look upon the miracle instead. We will reverse the way you see by not allowing sight to stop before it sees. We will not wait before the shield of hate, but lay it down and gently lift our eyes in silence to behold the Son of God.

He waits for you behind your grievances, and as you lay them down he will appear in shining light where each one stood before. For every grievance is a block to sight, and as it lifts you see the Son of God where he has always been. He stands in light, but you were in the dark. Each grievance made the darkness deeper, and you could not see.

Today we will attempt to see God's Son. We will not let ourselves be blind to him; we will not look upon our grievances. So is the seeing of the world reversed, as we look out toward truth, away from fear. We will select one person you have used as target for your grievances, and lay the grievances aside and look at him. Someone, perhaps, you fear and even hate; someone you think you love who angered you; someone you call a friend, but whom you see as difficult at times or hard to please, demanding, irritating or untrue to the ideal he should accept as his, according to the role you set for him.

You know the one to choose; his name has crossed your mind already. He will be the one of whom we ask God's Son be shown to you. Through seeing him behind the grievances that you have held against him, you will learn that what lay hidden while you saw him not is there in everyone, and can be seen. He who was enemy is more than friend when he is freed to take the holy role the Holy Spirit has assigned to him. Let him be savior unto you today. Such is his role in God your Father's plan.

Our longer practice periods today will see him in this role. You will attempt to hold him in your mind, first as you now consider him. You will review his faults, the difficulties you have had with him, the pain he caused you, his neglect, and all the little and the larger hurts he gave. You will regard his body with its flaws and better points as well, and you will think of his mistakes and even of his "sins."

Then let us ask of Him Who knows this Son of God in his reality and truth, that we may look on him a different way, and see our savior shining in the light of true forgiveness, given unto us. We ask Him in the holy Name of God and of His Son, as holy as Himself:

LET ME BEHOLD MY SAVIOR IN THIS ONE YOU HAVE APPOINTED AS
THE ONE FOR ME TO ASK TO LEAD ME TO THE HOLY LIGHT IN WHICH HE
STANDS, THAT I MAY JOIN WITH HIM.

The body's eyes are closed, and as you think of him who grieved you, let your mind be shown the light in him beyond your grievances.

What you have asked for cannot be denied. Your savior has been waiting long for this. He would be free, and make his freedom yours. The Holy Spirit leans from him to you, seeing no separation in God's Son. And what you see through Him will free you both. Be very quiet now, and look upon your shining savior. No dark grievances obscure the sight of him. You have allowed the Holy Spirit to express through him the role God gave Him that you might be saved.

God thanks you for these quiet times today in which you laid your images aside, and looked upon the miracle of love the Holy Spirit showed you in their place. The world and Heaven join in thanking you, for not one Thought of God but must rejoice as you are saved, and all the world with you.

We will remember this throughout the day, and take the role assigned to us as part of God's salvation plan, and not our own. Temptation falls away when we allow each one we meet to save us, and refuse to hide his light behind our grievances. To everyone you meet, and to the ones you think of or remember from the past, allow the role of savior to be given, that you may share it with him. For you both, and all the sightless ones as well, we pray:

LET MIRACLES REPLACE ALL GRIEVANCES.

Lesson 79

Let me recognize the problem so it can be solved.

A problem cannot be solved if you do not know what it is. Even if it is really solved already you will still have the problem, because you will not recognize that it has been solved. This is the situation of the world. The problem of separation, which is really the only problem, has already been solved. Yet the solution is not recognized because the problem is not recognized.

Everyone in this world seems to have his own special problems. Yet they are all the same, and must be recognized as one if the one solution that solves them all is to be accepted. Who can see that a problem has been solved if he thinks the problem is something else? Even if he is given the answer, he cannot see its relevance.

That is the position in which you find yourself now. You have the answer, but you are still uncertain about what the problem is. A long series of different problems seems to confront you, and as one is settled the next one and the next arise. There seems to be no end to them. There is no time in which you feel completely free of problems and at peace.

The temptation to regard problems as many is the temptation to keep the problem of separation unsolved. The world seems to present you with a vast number of problems, each requiring a different answer. This perception places you in a position in which your problem solving must be inadequate, and failure is inevitable.

No one could solve all the problems the world appears to hold. They seem to be on so many levels, in such varying forms and with such varied content, that they confront you with an impossible situation. Dismay and depression are inevitable as you regard them. Some spring up unexpectedly, just as you think you have resolved the previous ones. Others remain unsolved under a cloud of denial, and rise to haunt you from time to time, only to be hidden again but still unsolved.

All this complexity is but a desperate attempt not to recognize the problem, and therefore not to let it be resolved. If you could recognize that your only problem is separation, no matter what form it takes, you could accept the answer because you would see its relevance. Perceiving the underlying constancy in all the problems that seem to confront you, you would understand that you have the means to solve them all. And you would use the means, because you recognize the problem.

In our longer practice periods today we will ask what the problem is, and what is the answer to it. We will not assume that we already know. We will try to free our minds of all the many different kinds of problems we think we have. We will try to realize that we have only one problem, which we have failed to recognize. We will ask what it is, and wait for the answer. We will be told. Then we will ask for the solution to it. And we will be told.

The exercises for today will be successful to the extent to which you do not insist on defining the problem. Perhaps you will not succeed in letting all your preconceived notions go, but that is not necessary. All that is necessary is to entertain some doubt about the reality of your version of what your problems are. You are trying to recognize that you have been given the answer by recognizing the problem, so that the problem and the answer can be brought together and you can be at peace.

The shorter practice periods for today will not be set by time, but by need. You will see many problems today, each one calling for an answer. Our efforts will be directed toward recognizing that there is only one problem and one answer. In this recognition are all problems resolved. In this recognition there is peace.

Be not deceived by the form of problems today. Whenever any difficulty seems to rise, tell yourself quickly:

LET ME RECOGNIZE THIS PROBLEM SO IT CAN BE SOLVED.

Then try to suspend all judgment about what the problem is. If possible, close your eyes for a moment and ask what it is. You will be heard and you will be answered.

Lesson 80

Let me recognize my problems have been solved.

If you are willing to recognize your problems, you will recognize that you have no problems. Your one central problem has been answered, and you have no other. Therefore, you must be at peace. Salvation thus depends on recognizing this one problem, and understanding that it has been solved. One problem, one solution. Salvation is accomplished. Freedom from conflict has been given you. Accept that fact, and you are ready to take your rightful place in God's plan for salvation.

Your only problem has been solved! Repeat this over and over to yourself today, with gratitude and conviction. You have recognized your only problem, opening the way for the Holy Spirit to give you God's answer. You have laid deception aside, and seen the light of truth. You have accepted salvation for yourself by bringing the problem to the answer. And you can recognize the answer, because the problem has been identified.

You are entitled to peace today. A problem that has been resolved cannot trouble you. Only be certain you do not forget that all problems are the same. Their many forms will not deceive you while you remember this. One problem, one solution. Accept the peace this simple statement brings.

In our longer practice periods today, we will claim the peace that must be ours when the problem and the answer have been brought together. The problem must be gone, because God's answer cannot fail. Having recognized one, you have recognized the other. The solution is inherent in the problem. You are answered, and have accepted the answer. You are saved.

Now let the peace that your acceptance brings be given you. Close your eyes, and receive your reward. Recognize that your problems have been solved. Recognize that you are out of conflict; free and at peace. Above all, remember that you have one problem, and that the problem has one solution. It is in this that the simplicity of salvation lies. It is because of this that it is guaranteed to work.

Assure yourself often today that your problems have been solved. Repeat the idea with deep conviction, as frequently as possible. And be particularly sure to apply the idea for today to any specific problem that may arise. Say quickly:

LET ME RECOGNIZE THIS PROBLEM HAS BEEN SOLVED.

Let us be determined not to collect grievances today. Let us be determined to be free of problems that do not exist. The means is simple honesty. Do not deceive yourself about what the problem is, and you must recognize it has been solved.

Lesson 81

REVIEW II
Introduction

We are now ready for another review. We will begin where our last review left off, and cover two ideas each day. The earlier part of each day will be devoted to one of these ideas, and the latter part of the day to the other. We will have one longer exercise period, and frequent shorter ones in which we practice each of them.

The longer practice periods will follow this general form: Take about fifteen minutes for each of them, and begin by thinking about the ideas for the day, and the comments that are included in the assignments. Devote some three or four minutes to reading them over slowly, several times if you wish, and then close your eyes and listen.

Repeat the first phase of the exercise period if you find your mind wandering, but try to spend the major part of the time listening quietly but attentively. There is a message waiting for you. Be confident that you will receive it. Remember that it belongs to you, and that you want it.

Do not allow your intent to waver in the face of distracting thoughts. Realize that, whatever form such thoughts may take, they have no meaning and no power. Replace them with your determination to succeed. Do not forget that your will has power over all fantasies and dreams. Trust it to see you through, and carry you beyond them all.

Regard these practice periods as dedications to the way, the truth and the life. Refuse to be sidetracked into detours, illusions and thoughts of death. You are dedicated to salvation. Be determined each day not to leave your function unfulfilled.

Reaffirm your determination in the shorter practice periods as well, using the original form of the idea for general applications, and more specific forms when needed. Some specific forms are included in the comments which follow the statement of the ideas. These, however, are merely suggestions. It is not the particular words you use that matter.

Lesson 81

Our ideas for review today are:

(61) I am the light of the world.

How holy am I, who have been given the function of lighting up the world! Let me be still before my holiness. In its calm light let all my conflicts disappear. In its peace let me remember Who I am.

Some specific forms for applying this idea when special difficulties seem to arise might be:

LET ME NOT OBSCURE THE LIGHT OF THE WORLD IN ME.
LET THE LIGHT OF THE WORLD SHINE THROUGH THIS APPEARANCE.
THIS SHADOW WILL VANISH BEFORE THE LIGHT.

(62) Forgiveness is my function as the light of the world.

It is through accepting my function that I will see the light in me. And in this light will my function stand clear and perfectly unambiguous before my sight. My acceptance does not depend on my recognizing what my function is, for I do not yet understand forgiveness. Yet I will trust that, in the light, I will see it as it is.

Specific forms for using this idea might include:

LET THIS HELP ME LEARN WHAT FORGIVENESS MEANS.
LET ME NOT SEPARATE MY FUNCTION FROM MY WILL.
I WILL NOT USE THIS FOR AN ALIEN PURPOSE.

Lesson 82

We will review these ideas today:

(63) The light of the world brings peace to every mind through my forgiveness.

My forgiveness is the means by which the light of the world finds expression through me. My forgiveness is the means by which I become aware of the light of the world in me. My forgiveness is the means by which the world is healed, together with myself. Let me, then, forgive the world, that it may be healed along with me.

Suggestions for specific forms for applying this idea are:

LET PEACE EXTEND FROM MY MIND TO YOURS, [NAME].
I SHARE THE LIGHT OF THE WORLD WITH YOU, [NAME].
THROUGH MY FORGIVENESS I CAN SEE THIS AS IT IS.

(64) Let me not forget my function.

I would not forget my function, because I would remember my Self. I cannot fulfill my function if I forget it. And unless I fulfill my function, I will not experience the joy that God intends for me.

Suitable specific forms of this idea include:

LET ME NOT USE THIS TO HIDE MY FUNCTION FROM ME.
I WOULD USE THIS AS AN OPPORTUNITY TO FULFILL MY FUNCTION.
THIS MAY THREATEN MY EGO, BUT CANNOT CHANGE MY FUNCTION IN ANY WAY.

Lesson 83

Today let us review these ideas:

(65) My only function is the one God gave me.

I have no function but the one God gave me. This recognition releases me from all conflict, because it means I cannot have conflicting goals. With one purpose only, I am always certain what to do, what to say and what to think. All doubt must disappear as I acknowledge that my only function is the one God gave me.

More specific applications of this idea might take these forms:

MY PERCEPTION OF THIS DOES NOT CHANGE MY FUNCTION.
THIS DOES NOT GIVE ME A FUNCTION OTHER THAN THE ONE GOD GAVE ME.
LET ME NOT USE THIS TO JUSTIFY A FUNCTION GOD DID NOT GIVE ME.

(66) My happiness and my function are one.

All things that come from God are one. They come from Oneness, and must be received as one. Fulfilling my function is my happiness because both come from the same Source. And I must learn to recognize what makes me happy, if I would find happiness.

Some useful forms for specific applications of this idea are:

THIS CANNOT SEPARATE MY HAPPINESS FROM MY FUNCTION.
THE ONENESS OF MY HAPPINESS AND MY FUNCTION REMAINS WHOLLY UNAFFECTED BY THIS.
NOTHING, INCLUDING THIS, CAN JUSTIFY THE ILLUSION OF HAPPINESS APART FROM MY FUNCTION.

Lesson 84

These are the ideas for today's review:

(67) Love created me like itself.

I am in the likeness of my Creator. I cannot suffer, I cannot experience loss and I cannot die. I am not a body. I would recognize my reality today. I will worship no idols, nor raise my own self-concept to replace my Self. I am in the likeness of my Creator. Love created me like itself.

You might find these specific forms helpful in applying the idea:

LET ME NOT SEE AN ILLUSION OF MYSELF IN THIS.
AS I LOOK ON THIS, LET ME REMEMBER MY CREATOR.
MY CREATOR DID NOT CREATE THIS AS I SEE IT.

(68) Love holds no grievances.

Grievances are completely alien to love. Grievances attack love and keep its light obscure. If I hold grievances I am attacking love, and therefore attacking my Self. My Self thus becomes alien to me. I am determined not to attack my Self today, so that I can remember Who I am.

These specific forms for applying this idea would be helpful:

THIS IS NO JUSTIFICATION FOR DENYING MY SELF.
I WILL NOT USE THIS TO ATTACK LOVE.
LET THIS NOT TEMPT ME TO ATTACK MYSELF.

Lesson 85

Today's review will cover these ideas:

(69) My grievances hide the light of the world in me.

My grievances show me what is not there, and hide from me what I would see. Recognizing this, what do I want my grievances for? They keep me in darkness and hide the light. Grievances and light cannot go together, but light and vision must be joined for me to see. To see, I must lay grievances aside. I want to see, and this will be the means by which I will succeed.

Specific applications for this idea might be made in these forms:

LET ME NOT USE THIS AS A BLOCK TO SIGHT.
THE LIGHT OF THE WORLD WILL SHINE ALL THIS AWAY.
I HAVE NO NEED FOR THIS. I WANT TO SEE.

(70) My salvation comes from me.

Today I will recognize where my salvation is. It is in me because its Source is there. It has not left its Source, and so it cannot have left my mind. I will not look for it outside myself. It is not found outside and then brought in. But from within me it will reach beyond, and everything I see will but reflect the light that shines in me and in itself.

These forms of the idea are suitable for more specific applications:

LET THIS NOT TEMPT ME TO LOOK AWAY FROM ME FOR MY SALVATION.
I WILL NOT LET THIS INTERFERE WITH MY AWARENESS OF THE SOURCE OF MY SALVATION.
THIS HAS NO POWER TO REMOVE SALVATION FROM ME.

Lesson 86

These ideas are for review today:

(71) Only God's plan for salvation will work.

It is senseless for me to search wildly about for salvation. I have seen it in many people and in many things, but when I reached for it, it was not there. I was mistaken about where it is. I was mistaken about what it is. I will undertake no more idle seeking. Only God's plan for salvation will work. And I will rejoice because His plan can never fail.

These are some suggested forms for applying this idea specifically:

GOD'S PLAN FOR SALVATION WILL SAVE ME FROM MY PERCEPTION OF THIS.
THIS IS NO EXCEPTION IN GOD'S PLAN FOR MY SALVATION.
LET ME PERCEIVE THIS ONLY IN THE LIGHT OF GOD'S PLAN FOR SALVATION.

(72) Holding grievances is an attack on God's plan for salvation.

Holding grievances is an attempt to prove that God's plan for salvation will not work. Yet only His plan will work. By holding grievances, I am therefore excluding my only hope of salvation from my awareness. I would no longer defeat my own best interests in this insane way. I would accept God's plan for salvation, and be happy.

Specific applications for this idea might be in these forms:

I AM CHOOSING BETWEEN MISPERCEPTION AND SALVATION AS I LOOK ON THIS.
IF I SEE GROUNDS FOR GRIEVANCES IN THIS, I WILL NOT SEE THE GROUNDS FOR MY SALVATION.
THIS CALLS FOR SALVATION, NOT ATTACK.

Lesson 87

Our review today will cover these ideas:

(73) I will there be light.

I will use the power of my will today. It is not my will to grope about in darkness, fearful of shadows and afraid of things unseen and unreal. Light shall be my guide today. I will follow it where it leads me, and I will look only on what it shows me. This day I will experience the peace of true perception.

These forms of this idea would be helpful for specific applications:

THIS CANNOT HIDE THE LIGHT I WILL TO SEE.
YOU STAND WITH ME IN LIGHT, [NAME].
IN THE LIGHT THIS WILL LOOK DIFFERENT.

(74) There is no will but God's.

I am safe today because there is no will but God's. I can become afraid only when I believe there is another will. I try to attack only when I am afraid, and only when I try to attack can I believe that my eternal safety is threatened. Today I will recognize that all this has not occurred. I am safe because there is no will but God's.

These are some useful forms of this idea for specific applications:

LET ME PERCEIVE THIS IN ACCORDANCE WITH THE WILL OF GOD.
IT IS GOD'S WILL YOU ARE HIS SON, [NAME], AND MINE AS WELL.
THIS IS PART OF GOD'S WILL FOR ME, HOWEVER I MAY SEE IT.

Lesson 88

Today we will review these ideas:

(75) The light has come.

In choosing salvation rather than attack, I merely choose to recognize what is already there. Salvation is a decision made already. Attack and grievances are not there to choose. That is why I always choose between truth and illusion; between what is there and what is not. The light has come. I can but choose the light, for it has no alternative. It has replaced the darkness, and the darkness has gone.

These would prove useful forms for specific applications of this idea:

THIS CANNOT SHOW ME DARKNESS, FOR THE LIGHT HAS COME.
THE LIGHT IN YOU IS ALL THAT I WOULD SEE, [NAME].
I WOULD SEE IN THIS ONLY WHAT IS THERE.

(76) I am under no laws but God's.

Here is the perfect statement of my freedom. I am under no laws but God's. I am constantly tempted to make up other laws and give them power over me. I suffer only because of my belief in them. They have no real effect on me at all. I am perfectly free of the effects of all laws save God's. And His are the laws of freedom.

For specific forms in applying this idea, these would be useful:

MY PERCEPTION OF THIS SHOWS ME I BELIEVE IN LAWS THAT DO NOT EXIST.
I SEE ONLY THE LAWS OF GOD AT WORK IN THIS.
LET ME ALLOW GOD'S LAWS TO WORK IN THIS, AND NOT MY OWN.

Lesson 89

These are our review ideas for today:

(77) I am entitled to miracles.

I am entitled to miracles because I am under no laws but God's. His laws release me from all grievances, and replace them with miracles. And I would accept the miracles in place of the grievances, which are but illusions that hide the miracles beyond. Now I would accept only what the laws of God entitle me to have, that I may use it on behalf of the function He has given me.

You might use these suggestions for specific applications of this idea:

BEHIND THIS IS A MIRACLE TO WHICH I AM ENTITLED.
LET ME NOT HOLD A GRIEVANCE AGAINST YOU, [NAME],
BUT OFFER YOU THE MIRACLE THAT BELONGS TO YOU INSTEAD. S
EEN TRULY, THIS OFFERS ME A MIRACLE.

(78) Let miracles replace all grievances.

By this idea do I unite my will with the Holy Spirit's, and perceive them as one. By this idea do I accept my release from hell. By this idea do I express my willingness to have all my illusions be replaced with truth, according to God's plan for my salvation. I would make no exceptions and no substitutes. I want all of Heaven and only Heaven, as God wills me to have.

Useful specific forms for applying this idea would be:

I WOULD NOT HOLD THIS GRIEVANCE APART FROM MY SALVATION.
LET OUR GRIEVANCES BE REPLACED BY MIRACLES, [NAME].
BEYOND THIS IS THE MIRACLE BY WHICH ALL MY GRIEVANCES ARE REPLACED.

Lesson 90

For this review we will use these ideas:

(79) Let me recognize the problem so it can be solved.

Let me realize today that the problem is always some form of grievance that I would cherish. Let me also understand that the solution is always a miracle with which I let the grievance be replaced. Today I would remember the simplicity of salvation by reinforcing the lesson that there is one problem and one solution. The problem is a grievance; the solution is a miracle. And I invite the solution to come to me through my forgiveness of the grievance, and my welcome of the miracle that takes its place.

Specific applications of this idea might be in these forms:

THIS PRESENTS A PROBLEM TO ME WHICH I WOULD HAVE RESOLVED.
THE MIRACLE BEHIND THIS GRIEVANCE WILL RESOLVE IT FOR ME.
THE ANSWER TO THIS PROBLEM IS THE MIRACLE THAT IT CONCEALS.

(80) Let me recognize my problems have been solved.

I seem to have problems only because I am misusing time. I believe that the problem comes first, and time must elapse before it can be worked out. I do not see the problem and the answer as simultaneous in their occurrence. That is because I do not yet realize that God has placed the answer together with the problem, so that they cannot be separated by time. The Holy Spirit will teach me this, if I will let Him. And I will understand it is impossible that I could have a problem which has not been solved already.

These forms of the idea will be useful for specific applications:

I NEED NOT WAIT FOR THIS TO BE RESOLVED.
THE ANSWER TO THIS PROBLEM IS ALREADY GIVEN ME, IF I WILL ACCEPT IT.
TIME CANNOT SEPARATE THIS PROBLEM FROM ITS SOLUTION.

Lesson 91

Miracles are seen in light.

It is important to remember that miracles and vision necessarily go together. This needs repeating, and frequent repeating. It is a central idea in your new thought system, and the perception that it produces. The miracle is always there. Its presence is not caused by your vision; its absence is not the result of your failure to see. It is only your awareness of miracles that is affected. You will see them in the light; you will not see them in the dark.

To you, then, light is crucial. While you remain in darkness, the miracle remains unseen. Thus you are convinced it is not there. This follows from the premises from which the darkness comes. Denial of light leads to failure to perceive it. Failure to perceive light is to perceive darkness. The light is useless to you then, even though it is there. You cannot use it because its presence is unknown to you. And the seeming reality of the darkness makes the idea of light meaningless.

To be told that what you do not see is there sounds like insanity. It is very difficult to become convinced that it is insanity not to see what is there, and to see what is not there instead. You do not doubt that the body's eyes can see. You do not doubt the images they show you are reality. Your faith lies in the darkness, not the light. How can this be reversed? For you it is impossible, but you are not alone in this.

Your efforts, however little they may be, have strong support. Did you but realize how great this strength, your doubts would vanish. Today we will devote ourselves to the attempt to let you feel this strength. When you have felt the strength in you, which makes all miracles within your easy reach, you will not doubt. The miracles your sense of weakness hides will leap into awareness as you feel the strength in you.

Three times today, set aside about ten minutes for a quiet time in which you try to leave your weakness behind. This is accomplished very simply, as you instruct yourself that you are not a body. Faith goes to what you want, and you instruct your mind accordingly. Your will remains your teacher, and your will has all the strength to do what it desires. You can escape the body if you choose. You can experience the strength in you.

Begin the longer practice periods with this statement of true cause and effect relationships:

MIRACLES ARE SEEN IN LIGHT.
THE BODY'S EYES DO NOT PERCEIVE THE LIGHT.
BUT I AM NOT A BODY. WHAT AM I?

The question with which this statement ends is needed for our exercises today. What you think you are is a belief to be undone. But what you really are must be revealed to you. The belief you are a body calls for correction, being a mistake. 0 The truth of what you are calls on the strength in you to bring to your awareness what the mistake conceals.

If you are not a body, what are you? You need to be aware of what the Holy Spirit uses to replace the image of a body in your mind. You need to feel something to put your faith in, as you lift it from the body. You need a real experience of something else, something more solid and more sure; more worthy of your faith, and really there.

If you are not a body, what are you? Ask this in honesty, and then devote several minutes to allowing your mistaken thoughts about your attributes to be corrected, and their opposites to take their place. Say, for example:

I AM NOT WEAK, BUT STRONG.
I AM NOT HELPLESS, BUT ALL POWERFUL.
I AM NOT LIMITED, BUT UNLIMITED.
I AM NOT DOUBTFUL, BUT CERTAIN.
I AM NOT AN ILLUSION, BUT A REALITY.
I CANNOT SEE IN DARKNESS, BUT IN LIGHT.

In the second phase of the exercise period, try to experience these truths about yourself. Concentrate particularly on the experience of strength. Remember that all sense of weakness is associated with the belief you are a body, a belief that is mistaken and deserves no faith. Try to remove your faith from it, if only for a moment. You will be accustomed to keeping faith with the more worthy in you as we go along.

Relax for the rest of the practice period, confident that your efforts, however meager, are fully supported by the strength of God and all His Thoughts. It is from Them that your strength will come. It is through Their strong support that you will feel the strength in you. They are united with you in this practice period, in which you share a purpose like Their Own. Theirs is the light in which you will see miracles, because Their strength is yours. Their strength becomes your eyes, that you may see.

Five or six times an hour, at reasonably regular intervals, remind yourself that miracles are seen in light. Also, be sure to meet temptation with today's idea. This form would be helpful for this special purpose:

MIRACLES ARE SEEN IN LIGHT. LET ME NOT CLOSE MY EYES BECAUSE OF THIS.

Lesson 92

Miracles are seen in light, and light and strength are one.

The idea for today is an extension of the previous one. You do not think of light in terms of strength, and darkness in terms of weakness. That is because your idea of what seeing means is tied up with the body and its eyes and brain. Thus you believe that you can change what you see by putting little bits of glass before your eyes. This is among the many magical beliefs that come from the conviction you are a body, and the body's eyes can see.

You also believe the body's brain can think. If you but understood the nature of thought, you could but laugh at this insane idea. It is as if you thought you held the match that lights the sun and gives it all its warmth; or that you held the world within your hand, securely bound until you let it go. Yet this is no more foolish than to believe the body's eyes can see; the brain can think.

It is God's strength in you that is the light in which you see, as it is His Mind with which you think. His strength denies your weakness. It is your weakness that sees through the body's eyes, peering about in darkness to behold the likeness of itself; the small, the weak, the sickly and the dying, those in need, the helpless and afraid, the sad, the poor, the starving and the joyless. These are seen through eyes that cannot see and cannot bless.

Strength overlooks these things by seeing past appearances. It keeps its steady gaze upon the light that lies beyond them. It unites with light, of which it is a part. It sees itself. It brings the light in which your Self appears. In darkness you perceive a self that is not there. Strength is the truth about you; weakness is an idol falsely worshipped and adored that strength may be dispelled, and darkness rule where God appointed that there should be light.

Strength comes from truth, and shines with light its Source has given it; weakness reflects the darkness of its maker. It is sick and looks on sickness, which is like itself. Truth is a savior and can only will for happiness and peace for everyone. It gives its strength to everyone who asks, in limitless supply. It sees that lack in anyone would be a lack in all. And so it gives its light that all may see and benefit as one. Its strength is shared, that it may bring to all the miracle in which they will unite in purpose and forgiveness and in love.

Weakness, which looks in darkness, cannot see a purpose in forgiveness and in love. It sees all others different from itself, and nothing in the world that it would share. It judges and condemns, but does not love. In darkness it remains to hide itself, and dreams that it is strong and conquering, a victor over limitations that but grow in darkness to enormous size.

It fears and it attacks and hates itself, and darkness covers everything it sees, leaving its dreams as fearful as itself. No miracles are here, but only hate. It separates itself from what it sees, while light and strength perceive themselves as one. The light of strength is not the light you see. It does not change and flicker and go out. It does not shift from night to day, and back to darkness till the morning comes again.

The light of strength is constant, sure as love, forever glad to give itself away, because it cannot give but to itself. No one can ask in vain to share its sight, and none who enters its abode can leave without a miracle before his eyes, and strength and light abiding in his heart.

The strength in you will offer you the light, and guide your seeing so you do not dwell on idle shadows that the body's eyes provide for self-deception. Strength and light unite in you, and where they meet, your Self stands ready to embrace you as Its Own. Such is the meeting place we try today to find and rest in, for the peace of God is where your Self, His Son, is waiting now to meet Itself again, and be as One.

Let us give twenty minutes twice today to join this meeting. Let yourself be brought unto your Self. Its strength will be the light in which the gift of sight is given you. Leave, then, the dark a little while today, and we will practice seeing in the light, closing the body's eyes and asking truth to show us how to find the meeting place of self and Self, where light and strength are one.

Morning and evening we will practice thus. After the morning meeting, we will use the day in preparation for the time at night when we will meet again in trust. Let us repeat as often as we can the idea for today, and recognize that we are being introduced to sight, and led away from darkness to the light where only miracles can be perceived.

Lesson 93

Light and joy and peace abide in me.

You think you are the home of evil, darkness and sin. You think if anyone could see the truth about you he would be repelled, recoiling from you as if from a poisonous snake. You think if what is true about you were revealed to you, you would be struck with horror so intense that you would rush to death by your own hand, living on after seeing this being impossible.

These are beliefs so firmly fixed that it is difficult to help you see that they are based on nothing. That you have made mistakes is obvious. That you have sought salvation in strange ways; have been deceived, deceiving and afraid of foolish fantasies and savage dreams; and have bowed down to idols made of dust,–all this is true by what you now believe.

Today we question this, not from the point of view of what you think, but from a very different reference point, from which such idle thoughts are meaningless. These thoughts are not according to God's Will. These weird beliefs He does not share with you. This is enough to prove that they are wrong, but you do not perceive that this is so.

Why would you not be overjoyed to be assured that all the evil that you think you did was never done, that all your sins are nothing, that you are as pure and holy as you were created, and that light and joy and peace abide in you? Your image of yourself cannot withstand the Will of God. You think that this is death, but it is life. You think you are destroyed, but you are saved.

The self you made is not the Son of God. Therefore, this self does not exist at all. And anything it seems to do and think means nothing. It is neither bad nor good. It is unreal, and nothing more than that. It does not battle with the Son of God. It does not hurt him, nor attack his peace. It has not changed creation, nor reduced eternal sinlessness to sin, and love to hate. What power can this self you made possess, when it would contradict the Will of God?

Your sinlessness is guaranteed by God. Over and over this must be repeated, until it is accepted. It is true. Your sinlessness is guaranteed by God. Nothing can touch it, or change what God created as eternal. The self you made, evil and full of sin, is meaningless. Your sinlessness is guaranteed by God, and light and joy and peace abide in you.

Salvation requires the acceptance of but one thought;–you are as God created you, not what you made of yourself. Whatever evil you may think you did, you are as God created you. Whatever mistakes you made, the truth about you is unchanged. Creation is eternal and unalterable. Your sinlessness is guaranteed by God. You are and will forever be exactly as you were created. Light and joy and peace abide in you because God put them there.

In our longer exercise periods today, which would be most profitable if done for the first five minutes of every waking hour, begin by stating the truth about your creation:

LIGHT AND JOY AND PEACE ABIDE IN ME.
MY SINLESSNESS IS GUARANTEED BY GOD.

Then put away your foolish self-images, and spend the rest of the practice period in trying to experience what God has given you, in place of what you have decreed for yourself.

You are what God created or what you made. One Self is true; the other is not there. Try to experience the unity of your one Self. Try to appreciate Its Holiness and the love from which It was created. Try not to interfere with the Self which God created as you, by hiding Its majesty behind the tiny idols of evil and sinfulness you have made to replace It. Let It come into Its Own. Here you are; This is You. And light and joy and peace abide in you because this is so.

You may not be willing or even able to use the first five minutes of each hour for these exercises. Try, however, to do so when you can. At least remember to repeat these thoughts each hour:

LIGHT AND JOY AND PEACE ABIDE IN ME.
MY SINLESSNESS IS GUARANTEED BY GOD.

Then try to devote at least a minute or so to closing your eyes and realizing that this is a statement of the truth about you.

If a situation arises that seems to be disturbing, quickly dispel the illusion of fear by repeating these thoughts again. Should you be tempted to become angry with someone, tell him silently:

LIGHT AND JOY AND PEACE ABIDE IN YOU.
YOUR SINLESSNESS IS GUARANTEED BY GOD.

You can do much for the world's salvation today. You can do much today to bring you closer to the part in salvation that God has assigned to you. And you can do much today to bring the conviction to your mind that the idea for the day is true indeed.

Lesson 94

I am as God created me.

Today we continue with the one idea which brings complete salvation; the one statement which makes all forms of temptation powerless; the one thought which renders the ego silent and entirely undone. You are as God created you. The sounds of this world are still, the sights of this world disappear, and all the thoughts that this world ever held are wiped away forever by this one idea. Here is salvation accomplished. Here is sanity restored.

True light is strength, and strength is sinlessness. If you remain as God created you, you must be strong and light must be in you. He Who ensured your sinlessness must be the guarantee of strength and light as well. You are as God created you. Darkness cannot obscure the glory of God's Son. You stand in light, strong in the sinlessness in which you were created, and in which you will remain throughout eternity.

Today we will again devote the first five minutes of each waking hour to the attempt to feel the truth in you. Begin these times of searching with these words:

I AM AS GOD CREATED ME.
I AM HIS SON ETERNALLY.

Now try to reach the Son of God in you. This is the Self that never sinned, nor made an image to replace reality. This is the Self that never left Its home in God to walk the world uncertainly. This is the Self that knows no fear, nor could conceive of loss or suffering or death.

Nothing is required of you to reach this goal except to lay all idols and self-images aside; go past the list of attributes, both good and bad, you have ascribed to yourself; and wait in silent expectancy for the truth. God has Himself promised that it will be revealed to all who ask for it. You are asking now. You cannot fail because He cannot fail.

If you do not meet the requirement of practicing for the first five minutes of every hour, at least remind yourself hourly:

I AM AS GOD CREATED ME.
I AM HIS SON ETERNALLY.

Tell yourself frequently today that you are as God created you. And be sure to respond to anyone who seems to irritate you with these words:

YOU ARE AS GOD CREATED YOU.
YOU ARE HIS SON ETERNALLY.

Make every effort to do the hourly exercises today. Each one you do will be a giant stride toward your release, and a milestone in learning the thought system which this course sets forth.

Lesson 95

I am one Self, united with my Creator.

Today's idea accurately describes you as God created you. You are one within yourself, and one with Him. Yours is the unity of all creation. Your perfect unity makes change in you impossible. You do not accept this, and you fail to realize it must be so, only because you believe that you have changed yourself already.

You see yourself as a ridiculous parody on God's creation; weak, vicious, ugly and sinful, miserable and beset with pain. Such is your version of yourself; a self divided into many warring parts, separate from God, and tenuously held together by its erratic and capricious maker, to which you pray. It does not hear your prayers, for it is deaf. It does not see the oneness in you, for it is blind. It does not understand you are the Son of God, for it is senseless and understands nothing.

We will attempt today to be aware only of what can hear and see, and what makes perfect sense. We will again direct our exercises towards reaching your one Self, which is united with Its Creator. In patience and in hope we try again today.

The use of the first five minutes of every waking hour for practicing the idea for the day has special advantages at the stage of learning in which you are at present. It is difficult at this point not to allow your mind to wander, if it undertakes extended practice. You have surely realized this by now. You have seen the extent of your lack of mental discipline, and of your need for mind training. It is necessary that you be aware of this, for it is indeed a hindrance to your advance.

Frequent but shorter practice periods have other advantages for you at this time. In addition to recognizing your difficulties with sustained attention, you must also have noticed that, unless you are reminded of your purpose frequently, you tend to forget about it for long periods of time. You often fail to remember the short applications of the idea for the day, and you have not yet formed the habit of using the idea as an automatic response to temptation.

Structure, then, is necessary for you at this time, planned to include frequent reminders of your goal and regular attempts to reach it. Regularity in terms of time is not the ideal requirement for the most beneficial form of practice in salvation. It is advantageous, however, for those whose motivation is inconsistent, and who remain heavily defended against learning.

We will, therefore, keep to the five-minutes-an-hour practice periods for a while, and urge you to omit as few as possible. Using the first five minutes of the hour will be particularly helpful, since it imposes firmer structure. Do not, however, use your lapses from this schedule as an excuse not to return to it again as soon as you can. There may well be a temptation to regard the day as lost because you have already failed to do what is required. This should, however, merely be recognized as what it is; a refusal to let your mistake be corrected, and an unwillingness to try again.

The Holy Spirit is not delayed in His teaching by your mistakes. He can be held back only by your unwillingness to let them go. Let us therefore be determined, particularly for the next week or so, to be willing to forgive ourselves for our lapses in diligence, and our failures to follow the instructions for practicing the day's idea. This tolerance for weakness will enable us to overlook it, rather than give it power to delay our learning. If we give it power to do this, we are regarding it as strength, and are confusing strength with weakness.

When you fail to comply with the requirements of this course, you have merely made a mistake. This calls for correction, and for nothing else. To allow a mistake to continue is to make additional mistakes, based on the first and reinforcing it. It is this process that must be laid aside, for it is but another way in which you would defend illusions against the truth.

Let all these errors go by recognizing them for what they are. They are attempts to keep you unaware you are one Self, united with your Creator, at one with every aspect of creation, and limitless in power and in peace. This is the truth, and nothing else is true. Today we will affirm this truth again, and try to reach the place in you in which there is no doubt that only this is true.

Begin the practice periods today with this assurance, offered to your mind with all the certainty that you can give:

I AM ONE SELF, UNITED WITH MY CREATOR, AT ONE WITH EVERY
ASPECT OF CREATION, AND LIMITLESS IN POWER AND IN PEACE.

Then close your eyes and tell yourself again, slowly and thoughtfully, attempting to allow the meaning of the words to sink into your mind, replacing false ideas:

I AM ONE SELF.

Repeat this several times, and then attempt to feel the meaning that the words convey.

You are one Self, united and secure in light and joy and peace. You are God's Son, one Self, with one Creator and one goal; to bring awareness of this oneness to all minds, that true creation may extend the allness and the unity of God. You are one Self, complete and healed and whole, with power to lift the veil of darkness from the world, and let the light in you come through to teach the world the truth about yourself.

You are one Self, in perfect harmony with all there is, and all that there will be. You are one Self, the holy Son of God, united with your brothers in that Self; united with your Father in His Will. Feel this one Self in you, and let It shine away all your illusions and your doubts. This is your Self, the Son of God Himself, sinless as Its Creator, with His strength within you and His Love forever yours. You are one Self, and it is given you to feel this Self within you, and to cast all your illusions out of the one Mind that is this Self, the holy truth in you.

Do not forget today. We need your help; your little part in bringing happiness to all the world. And Heaven looks to you in confidence that you will try today. Share, then, its surety, for it is yours. Be vigilant. Do not forget today. Throughout the day do not forget your goal. Repeat today's idea as frequently as possible, and understand each time you do so, someone hears the voice of hope, the stirring of the truth within his mind, the gentle rustling of the wings of peace.

Your own acknowledgment you are one Self, united with your Father, is a call to all the world to be at one with you. To everyone you meet today, be sure to give the promise of today's idea and tell him this:

YOU ARE ONE SELF WITH ME, UNITED WITH OUR CREATOR IN THIS SELF.
I HONOR YOU BECAUSE OF WHAT I AM, AND WHAT HE IS, WHO LOVES US BOTH AS ONE.

Lesson 96

Salvation comes from my one Self.

Although you are one Self, you experience yourself as two; as both good and evil, loving and hating, mind and body. This sense of being split into opposites induces feelings of acute and constant conflict, and leads to frantic attempts to reconcile the contradictory aspects of this self-perception. You have sought many such solutions, and none of them has worked. The opposites you see in you will never be compatible. But one exists.

The fact that truth and illusion cannot be reconciled, no matter how you try, what means you use and where you see the problem, must be accepted if you would be saved. Until you have accepted this, you will attempt an endless list of goals you cannot reach; a senseless series of expenditures of time and effort, hopefulness and doubt, each one as futile as the one before, and failing as the next one surely will.

Problems that have no meaning cannot be resolved within the framework they are set. Two selves in conflict could not be resolved, and good and evil have no meeting place. The self you made can never be your Self, nor can your Self be split in two, and still be what It is and must forever be. A mind and body cannot both exist. Make no attempt to reconcile the two, for one denies the other can be real. If you are physical, your mind is gone from your self-concept, for it has no place in which it could be really part of you. If you are spirit, then the body must be meaningless to your reality.

Spirit makes use of mind as means to find its Self expression. And the mind which serves the spirit is at peace and filled with joy. Its power comes from spirit, and it is fulfilling happily its function here. Yet mind can also see itself divorced from spirit, and perceive itself within a body it confuses with itself. Without its function then it has no peace, and happiness is alien to its thoughts.

Yet mind apart from spirit cannot think. It has denied its Source of strength, and sees itself as helpless, limited and weak. Dissociated from its function now, it thinks it is alone and separate, attacked by armies massed against itself and hiding in the body's frail support. Now must it reconcile unlike with like, for this is what it thinks that it is for.

Waste no more time on this. Who can resolve the senseless conflicts which a dream presents? What could the resolution mean in truth? What purpose could it serve? What is it for? Salvation cannot make illusions real, nor solve a problem that does not exist. Perhaps you hope it can. Yet would you have God's plan for the release of His dear Son bring pain to him, and fail to set him free?

Your Self retains Its Thoughts, and they remain within your mind and in the Mind of God. The Holy Spirit holds salvation in your mind, and offers it the way to peace. Salvation is a thought you share with God, because His Voice accepted it for you and answered in your name that it was done. Thus is salvation kept among the Thoughts your Self holds dear and cherishes for you.

We will attempt today to find this thought, whose presence in your mind is guaranteed by Him Who speaks to you from your one Self. Our hourly five-minute practicing will be a search for Him within your mind. Salvation comes from this one Self through Him Who is the Bridge between your mind and It. Wait patiently, and let Him speak to you about your Self, and what your mind can do, restored to It and free to serve Its Will.

Begin with saying this:

SALVATION COMES FROM MY ONE SELF. ITS THOUGHTS ARE MINE TO USE.

Then seek Its Thoughts, and claim them as your own. These are your own real thoughts you have denied, and let your mind go wandering in a world of dreams, to find illusions in their place. Here are your thoughts, the only ones you have. Salvation is among them; find it there.

If you succeed, the thoughts that come to you will tell you you are saved, and that your mind has found the function that it sought to lose. Your Self will welcome it and give it peace. Restored in strength, it will again flow out from spirit to the spirit in all things created by the Spirit as Itself. Your mind will bless all things. Confusion done, you are restored, for you have found your Self.

Your Self knows that you cannot fail today. Perhaps your mind remains uncertain yet a little while. Be not dismayed by this. The joy your Self experiences It will save for you, and it will yet be yours in full awareness. Every time you spend five minutes of the hour seeking Him Who joins your mind and Self, you offer Him another treasure to be kept for you.

Each time today you tell your frantic mind salvation comes from your one Self, you lay another treasure in your growing store. And all of it is given everyone who asks for it, and will accept the gift. Think, then, how much is given unto you to give this day, that it be given you!

Lesson 97

I am spirit.

Today's idea identifies you with your one Self. It accepts no split identity, nor tries to weave opposing factors into unity. It simply states the truth. Practice this truth today as often as you can, for it will bring your mind from conflict to the quiet fields of peace. No chill of fear can enter, for your mind has been absolved from madness, letting go illusions of a split identity.

We state again the truth about your Self, the holy Son of God Who rests in you; whose mind has been restored to sanity. You are the spirit lovingly endowed with all your Father's Love and peace and joy. You are the spirit which completes Himself, and shares His function as Creator. He is with you always, as you are with Him.

Today we try to bring reality still closer to your mind. Each time you practice, awareness is brought a little nearer at least; sometimes a thousand years or more are saved. The minutes which you give are multiplied over and over, for the miracle makes use of time, but is not ruled by it. Salvation is a miracle, the first and last; the first that is the last, for it is one.

You are the spirit in whose mind abides the miracle in which all time stands still; the miracle in which a minute spent in using these ideas becomes a time that has no limit and that has no end. Give, then, these minutes willingly, and count on Him Who promised to lay timelessness beside them. He will offer all His strength to every little effort that you make. Give Him the minutes which He needs today, to help you understand with Him you are the spirit that abides in Him, and that calls through His Voice to every living thing; offers His sight to everyone who asks; replaces error with the simple truth.

The Holy Spirit will be glad to take five minutes of each hour from your hands, and carry them around this aching world where pain and misery appear to rule. He will not overlook one open mind that will accept the healing gifts they bring, and He will lay them everywhere He knows they will be welcome. And they will increase in healing power each time someone accepts them as his thoughts, and uses them to heal.

Thus will each gift to Him be multiplied a thousandfold and tens of thousands more. And when it is returned to you, it will surpass in might the little gift you gave as much as does the radiance of the sun outshine the tiny gleam a firefly makes an uncertain moment and goes out. The steady brilliance of this light remains and leads you out of darkness, nor will you be able to forget the way again.

Begin these happy exercises with the words the Holy Spirit speaks to you, and let them echo round the world through Him:

SPIRIT AM I, A HOLY SON OF GOD, FREE OF ALL LIMITS, SAFE AND
HEALED AND WHOLE, FREE TO FORGIVE, AND FREE TO SAVE THE WORLD.

Expressed through you, the Holy Spirit will accept this gift that you received of Him, increase its power and give it back to you.

Offer each practice period today gladly to Him. And He will speak to you, reminding you that you are spirit, one with Him and God, your brothers and your Self. Listen for His assurance every time you speak the words He offers you today, and let Him tell your mind that they are true. Use them against temptation, and escape its sorry consequences if you yield to the belief that you are something else. The Holy Spirit gives you peace today. Receive His words, and offer them to Him.

Lesson 98

I will accept my part in God's plan for salvation.

Today is a day of special dedication. We take a stand on but one side today. We side with truth and let illusions go. We will not vacillate between the two, but take a firm position with the One. We dedicate ourselves to truth today, and to salvation as God planned it be. We will not argue it is something else. We will not seek for it where it is not. In gladness we accept it as it is, and take the part assigned to us by God.

How happy to be certain! All our doubts we lay aside today, and take our stand with certainty of purpose, and with thanks that doubt is gone and surety has come. We have a mighty purpose to fulfill, and have been given everything we need with which to reach the goal. Not one mistake stands in our way. For we have been absolved from errors. All our sins are washed away by realizing they were but mistakes.

The guiltless have no fear, for they are safe and recognize their safety. They do not appeal to magic, nor invent escapes from fancied threats without reality. They rest in quiet certainty that they will do what it is given them to do. They do not doubt their own ability because they know their function will be filled completely in the perfect time and place. They took the stand which we will take today, that we may share their certainty and thus increase it by accepting it ourselves.

They will be with us; all who took the stand we take today will gladly offer us all that they learned and every gain they made. Those still uncertain, too, will join with us, and, borrowing our certainty, will make it stronger still. While those as yet unborn will hear the call we heard, and answer it when they have come to make their choice again. We do not choose but for ourselves today.

Is it not worth five minutes of your time each hour to be able to accept the happiness that God has given you? Is it not worth five minutes hourly to recognize your special function here? Is not five minutes but a small request to make in terms of gaining a reward so great it has no measure? You have made a thousand losing bargains at the least.

Here is an offer guaranteeing you your full release from pain of every kind, and joy the world does not contain. You can exchange a little of your time for peace of mind and certainty of purpose, with the promise of complete success. And since time has no meaning, you are being asked for nothing in return for everything. Here is a bargain that you cannot lose. And what you gain is limitless indeed!

Each hour today give Him your tiny gift of but five minutes. He will give the words you use in practicing today's idea the deep conviction and the certainty you lack. His words will join with yours, and make each repetition of today's idea a total dedication, made in faith as perfect and as sure as His in you. His confidence in you will bring the light to all the words you say, and you will go beyond their sound to what they really mean. Today you practice with Him, as you say:

I WILL ACCEPT MY PART IN GOD'S PLAN FOR SALVATION.

In each five minutes that you spend with Him, He will accept your words and give them back to you all bright with faith and confidence so strong and steady they will light the world with hope and gladness. Do not lose one chance to be the glad receiver of His gifts, that you may give them to the world today.

Give Him the words, and He will do the rest. He will enable you to understand your special function. He will open up the way to happiness, and peace and trust will be His gifts; His answer to your words. He will respond with all His faith and joy and certainty that what you say is true. And you will have conviction then of Him Who knows the function that you have on earth as well as Heaven. He will be with you each practice period you share with Him, exchanging every instant of the time you offer Him for timelessness and peace.

Throughout the hour, let your time be spent in happy preparation for the next five minutes you will spend again with Him. Repeat today's idea while you wait for the glad time to come to you again. Repeat it often, and do not forget each time you do so, you have let your mind be readied for the happy time to come.

And when the hour goes and He is there once more to spend a little time with you, be thankful and lay down all earthly tasks, all little thoughts and limited ideas, and spend a happy time again with Him. Tell Him once more that you accept the part that He would have you take and help you fill, and He will make you sure you want this choice, which He has made with you and you with Him.

Lesson 99

Salvation is my only function here.

Salvation and forgiveness are the same. They both imply that something has gone wrong; something to be saved from, forgiven for; something amiss that needs corrective change; something apart or different from the Will of God. Thus do both terms imply a thing impossible but yet which has occurred, resulting in a state of conflict seen between what is and what could never be.

Truth and illusions both are equal now, for both have happened. The impossible becomes the thing you need forgiveness for, salvation from. Salvation now becomes the borderland between the truth and the illusion. It reflects the truth because it is the means by which you can escape illusions. Yet it is not yet the truth because it undoes what was never done.

How could there be a meeting place at all where earth and Heaven can be reconciled within a mind where both of them exist? The mind that sees illusions thinks them real. They have existence in that they are thoughts. And yet they are not real, because the mind that thinks these thoughts is separate from God.

What joins the separated mind and thoughts with Mind and Thought which are forever One? What plan could hold the truth inviolate, yet recognize the need illusions bring, and offer means by which they are undone without attack and with no touch of pain? What but a Thought of God could be this plan, by which the never done is overlooked, and sins forgotten which were never real?

The Holy Spirit holds this plan of God exactly as it was received of Him within the Mind of God and in your own. It is apart from time in that its Source is timeless. Yet it operates in time, because of your belief that time is real. Unshaken does the Holy Spirit look on what you see; on sin and pain and death, on grief and separation and on loss. Yet does He know one thing must still be true; God is still Love, and this is not His Will.

This is the Thought that brings illusions to the truth, and sees them as appearances behind which is the changeless and the sure. This is the Thought that saves and that forgives, because it lays no faith in what is not created by the only Source it knows. This is the Thought whose function is to save by giving you its function as your own. Salvation is your function, with the One to Whom the plan was given. Now are you entrusted with this plan, along with Him. He has one answer to appearances; regardless of their form, their size, their depth or any attribute they seem to have:

SALVATION IS MY ONLY FUNCTION HERE.
GOD STILL IS LOVE, AND THIS IS NOT HIS WILL.

You who will yet work miracles, be sure you practice well the idea for today. Try to perceive the strength in what you say, for these are words in which your freedom lies. Your Father loves you. All the world of pain is not His Will. Forgive yourself the thought He wanted this for you. Then let the Thought with which He has replaced all your mistakes enter the darkened places of your mind that thought the thoughts that never were His Will.

This part belongs to God, as does the rest. It does not think its solitary thoughts, and make them real by hiding them from Him. Let in the light, and you will look upon no obstacle to what He wills for you. Open your secrets to His kindly light, and see how bright this light still shines in you.

Practice His Thought today, and let His light seek out and lighten up all darkened spots, and shine through them to join them to the rest. It is God's Will your mind be one with His. It is God's Will that He has but one Son. It is God's Will that His one Son is you. Think of these things in practicing today, and start the lesson that we learn today with this instruction in the way of truth:

SALVATION IS MY ONLY FUNCTION HERE.
SALVATION AND FORGIVENESS ARE THE SAME.

Then turn to Him Who shares your function here, and let Him teach you what you need to learn to lay all fear aside, and know your Self as Love which has no opposite in you.

Forgive all thoughts which would oppose the truth of your completion, unity and peace. You cannot lose the gifts your Father gave. You do not want to be another self. You have no function that is not of God. Forgive yourself the one you think you made. Forgiveness and salvation are the same. Forgive what you have made and you are saved.

There is a special message for today which has the power to remove all forms of doubt and fear forever from your mind. If you are tempted to believe them true, remember that appearances can not withstand the truth these mighty words contain:

SALVATION IS MY ONLY FUNCTION HERE.
GOD STILL IS LOVE, AND THIS IS NOT HIS WILL.

Your only function tells you you are one. Remind yourself of this between the times you give five minutes to be shared with Him Who shares God's plan with you. Remind yourself:

SALVATION IS MY ONLY FUNCTION HERE.

Thus do you lay forgiveness on your mind and let all fear be gently laid aside, that love may find its rightful place in you and show you that you are the Son of God.

Lesson 100

My part is essential to God's plan for salvation.

Just as God's Son completes his Father, so your part in it completes your Father's plan. Salvation must reverse the mad belief in separate thoughts and separate bodies, which lead separate lives and go their separate ways. One function shared by separate minds unites them in one purpose, for each one of them is equally essential to them all.

God's Will for you is perfect happiness. Why should you choose to go against His Will? The part that He has saved for you to take in working out His plan is given you that you might be restored to what He wills. This part is as essential to His plan as to your happiness. Your joy must be complete to let His plan be understood by those to whom He sends you. They will see their function in your shining face, and hear God calling to them in your happy laugh.

You are indeed essential to God's plan. Without your joy, His joy is incomplete. Without your smile, the world cannot be saved. While you are sad, the light that God Himself appointed as the means to save the world is dim and lusterless, and no one laughs because all laughter can but echo yours.

You are indeed essential to God's plan. Just as your light increases every light that shines in Heaven, so your joy on earth calls to all minds to let their sorrows go, and take their place beside you in God's plan. God's messengers are joyous, and their joy heals sorrow and despair. They are the proof that God wills perfect happiness for all who will accept their Father's gifts as theirs.

We will not let ourselves be sad today. For if we do, we fail to take the part that is essential to God's plan, as well as to our vision. Sadness is the sign that you would play another part, instead of what has been assigned to you by God. Thus do you fail to show the world how great the happiness He wills for you. And so you do not recognize that it is yours.

Today we will attempt to understand joy is our function here. If you are sad, your part is unfulfilled, and all the world is thus deprived of joy, along with you. God asks you to be happy, so the world can see how much He loves His Son, and wills no sorrow rises to abate his joy; no fear besets him to disturb his peace. You are God's messenger today. You bring His happiness to all you look upon; His peace to everyone who looks on you and sees His message in your happy face.

We will prepare ourselves for this today, in our five-minute practice periods, by feeling happiness arise in us according to our Father's Will and ours. Begin the exercises with the thought today's idea contains. Then realize your part is to be happy. Only this is asked of you or anyone who wants to take his place among God's messengers. Think what this means. You have indeed been wrong in your belief that sacrifice is asked. You but receive according to God's plan, and never lose or sacrifice or die.

Now let us try to find that joy that proves to us and all the world God's Will for us. It is your function that you find it here, and that you find it now. For this you came. Let this one be the day that you succeed! Look deep within you, undismayed by all the little thoughts and foolish goals you pass as you ascend to meet the Christ in you.

He will be there. And you can reach Him now. What could you rather look upon in place of Him Who waits that you may look on Him? What little thought has power to hold you back? What foolish goal can keep you from success when He Who calls to you is God Himself?

He will be there. You are essential to His plan. You are His messenger today. And you must find what He would have you give. Do not forget the idea for today between your hourly practice periods. It is your Self Who calls to you today. And it is Him you answer, every time you tell yourself you are essential to God's plan for the salvation of the world.

Lesson 101

God's Will for me is perfect happiness.

Today we will continue with the theme of happiness. This is a key idea in understanding what salvation means. You still believe it asks for suffering as penance for your "sins." This is not so. Yet you must think it so while you believe that sin is real, and that God's Son can sin.

If sin is real, then punishment is just and cannot be escaped. Salvation thus cannot be purchased but through suffering. If sin is real, then happiness must be illusion, for they cannot both be true. The sinful warrant only death and pain, and it is this they ask for. For they know it waits for them, and it will seek them out and find them somewhere, sometime, in some form that evens the account they owe to God. They would escape Him in their fear. And yet He will pursue, and they can not escape.

If sin is real, salvation must be pain. Pain is the cost of sin, and suffering can never be escaped, if sin is real. Salvation must be feared, for it will kill, but slowly, taking everything away before it grants the welcome boon of death to victims who are little more than bones before salvation is appeased. Its wrath is boundless, merciless, but wholly just.

Who would seek out such savage punishment? Who would not flee salvation, and attempt in every way he can to drown the Voice which offers it to him? Why would he try to listen and accept Its offering? If sin is real, its offering is death, and meted out in cruel form to match the vicious wishes in which sin is born. If sin is real, salvation has become your bitter enemy, the curse of God upon you who have crucified His Son.

You need the practice periods today. The exercises teach sin is not real, and all that you believe must come from sin will never happen, for it has no cause. Accept Atonement with an open mind, which cherishes no lingering belief that you have made a devil of God's Son. There is no sin. We practice with this thought as often as we can today, because it is the basis for today's idea.

God's Will for you is perfect happiness because there is no sin, and suffering is causeless. Joy is just, and pain is but the sign you have misunderstood yourself. Fear not the Will of God. But turn to it in confidence that it will set you free from all the consequences sin has wrought in feverish imagination. Say:

GOD'S WILL FOR ME IS PERFECT HAPPINESS.
THERE IS NO SIN; IT HAS NO CONSEQUENCE.

So should you start your practice periods, and then attempt again to find the joy these thoughts will introduce into your mind.

Give these five minutes gladly, to remove the heavy load you lay upon yourself with the insane belief that sin is real. Today escape from madness. You are set on freedom's road, and now today's idea brings wings to speed you on, and hope to go still faster to the waiting goal of peace. There is no sin. Remember this today, and tell yourself as often as you can:

GOD'S WILL FOR ME IS PERFECT HAPPINESS.
THIS IS THE TRUTH, BECAUSE THERE IS NO SIN.

Lesson 102

I share God's Will for happiness for me.

You do not want to suffer. You may think it buys you something, and may still believe a little that it buys you what you want. Yet this belief is surely shaken now, at least enough to let you question it, and to suspect it really makes no sense. It has not gone as yet, but lacks the roots that once secured it tightly to the dark and hidden secret places of your mind.

Today we try to loose its weakened hold still further, and to realize that pain is purposeless, without a cause and with no power to accomplish anything. It cannot purchase anything at all. It offers nothing, and does not exist. And everything you think it offers you is lacking in existence, like itself. You have been slave to nothing. Be you free today to join the happy Will of God.

For several days we will continue to devote our periods of practicing to exercises planned to help you reach the happiness God's Will has placed in you. Here is your home, and here your safety is. Here is your peace, and here there is no fear. Here is salvation. Here is rest at last.

Begin your practice periods today with this acceptance of God's Will for you:

I SHARE GOD'S WILL FOR HAPPINESS FOR ME, AND
I ACCEPT IT AS MY FUNCTION NOW.

Then seek this function deep within your mind, for it is there, awaiting but your choice. You cannot fail to find it when you learn it is your choice, and that you share God's Will.

Be happy, for your only function here is happiness. You have no need to be less loving to God's Son than He Whose Love created him as loving as Himself. Besides these hourly five-minute rests, pause frequently today, to tell yourself that you have now accepted happiness as your one function. And be sure that you are joining with God's Will in doing this.

Lesson 103

God, being Love, is also happiness.

Happiness is an attribute of love. It cannot be apart from it. Nor can it be experienced where love is not. Love has no limits, being everywhere. And therefore joy is everywhere as well. Yet can the mind deny that this is so, believing there are gaps in love where sin can enter, bringing pain instead of joy. This strange belief would limit happiness by redefining love as limited, and introducing opposition in what has no limit and no opposite.

Fear is associated then with love, and its results become the heritage of minds that think what they have made is real. These images, with no reality in truth, bear witness to the fear of God, forgetting being Love, He must be joy. This basic error we will try again to bring to truth today, and teach ourselves:

GOD, BEING LOVE, IS ALSO HAPPINESS.
TO FEAR HIM IS TO BE AFRAID OF JOY.

Begin your periods of practicing today with this association, which corrects the false belief that God is fear. It also emphasizes happiness belongs to you, because of what He is.

Allow this one correction to be placed within your mind each waking hour today. Then welcome all the happiness it brings as truth replaces fear, and joy becomes what you expect to take the place of pain. God, being Love, it will be given you. Bolster this expectation frequently throughout the day, and quiet all your fears with this assurance, kind and wholly true:

GOD, BEING LOVE, IS ALSO HAPPINESS.
AND IT IS HAPPINESS I SEEK TODAY.
I CANNOT FAIL, BECAUSE I SEEK THE TRUTH.

Lesson 104

I seek but what belongs to me in truth.

Today's idea continues with the thought that joy and peace are not but idle dreams. They are your right, because of what you are. They come to you from God, Who cannot fail to give you what He wills. Yet must there be a place made ready to receive His gifts. They are not welcomed gladly by a mind that has instead received the gifts it made where His belong, as substitutes for them.

Today we would remove all meaningless and self-made gifts which we have placed upon the holy altar where God's gifts belong. His are the gifts that are our own in truth. His are the gifts that we inherited before time was, and that will still be ours when time has passed into eternity. His are the gifts that are within us now, for they are timeless. And we need not wait to have them. They belong to us today.

Therefore, we choose to have them now, and know, in choosing them in place of what we made, we but unite our will with what God wills, and recognize the same as being one. Our longer practice periods today, the hourly five minutes given truth for your salvation, should begin with this:

I SEEK BUT WHAT BELONGS TO ME IN TRUTH,
AND JOY AND PEACE ARE MY INHERITANCE.

Then lay aside the conflicts of the world that offer other gifts and other goals made of illusions, witnessed to by them, and sought for only in a world of dreams.

All this we lay aside, and seek instead that which is truly ours, as we ask to recognize what God has given us. We clear a holy place within our minds before His altar, where His gifts of peace and joy are welcome, and to which we come to find what has been given us by Him. We come in confidence today, aware that what belongs to us in truth is what He gives. And we would wish for nothing else, for nothing else belongs to us in truth.

So do we clear the way for Him today by simply recognizing that His Will is done already, and that joy and peace belong to us as His eternal gifts. We will not let ourselves lose sight of them between the times we come to seek for them where He has laid them. This reminder will we bring to mind as often as we can:

I SEEK BUT WHAT BELONGS TO ME IN TRUTH.
GOD'S GIFTS OF JOY AND PEACE ARE ALL I WANT.

Lesson 105

God's peace and joy are mine.

God's peace and joy are yours. Today we will accept them, knowing they belong to us. And we will try to understand these gifts increase as we receive them. They are not like to the gifts the world can give, in which the giver loses as he gives the gift; the taker is the richer by his loss. Such are not gifts, but bargains made with guilt. The truly given gift entails no loss. It is impossible that one can gain because another loses. This implies a limit and an insufficiency.

No gift is given thus. Such "gifts" are but a bid for a more valuable return; a loan with interest to be paid in full; a temporary lending, meant to be a pledge of debt to be repaid with more than was received by him who took the gift. This strange distortion of what giving means pervades all levels of the world you see. It strips all meaning from the gifts you give, and leaves you nothing in the ones you take.

A major learning goal this course has set is to reverse your view of giving, so you can receive. For giving has become a source of fear, and so you would avoid the only means by which you can receive. Accept God's peace and joy, and you will learn a different way of looking at a gift. God's gifts will never lessen when they are given away. They but increase thereby.

As Heaven's peace and joy intensify when you accept them as God's gift to you, so does the joy of your Creator grow when you accept His joy and peace as yours. True giving is creation. It extends the limitless to the unlimited, eternity to timelessness, and love unto itself. It adds to all that is complete already, not in simple terms of adding more, for that implies that it was less before. It adds by letting what cannot contain itself fulfill its aim of giving everything it has away, securing it forever for itself.

Today accept God's peace and joy as yours. Let Him complete Himself as He defines completion. You will understand that what completes Him must complete His Son as well. He cannot give through loss. No more can you. Receive His gift of joy and peace today, and He will thank you for your gift to Him.

Today our practice periods will start a little differently. Begin today by thinking of those brothers who have been denied by you the peace and joy that are their right under the equal laws of God. Here you denied them to yourself. And here you must return to claim them as your own.

Think of your "enemies" a little while, and tell each one, as he occurs to you:

MY BROTHER, PEACE AND JOY I OFFER YOU,
THAT I MAY HAVE GOD'S PEACE AND JOY AS MINE.

Thus you prepare yourself to recognize God's gifts to you, and let your mind be free of all that would prevent success today. Now are you ready to accept the gift of peace and joy that God has given you. Now are you ready to experience the joy and peace you have denied yourself. Now you can say, "God's peace and joy are mine," for you have given what you would receive.

You must succeed today, if you prepare your mind as we suggest. For you have let all bars to peace and joy be lifted up, and what is yours can come to you at last. So tell yourself, "God's peace and joy are mine," and close your eyes a while, and let His Voice assure you that the words you speak are true.

Spend your five minutes thus with Him each time you can today, but do not think that less is worthless when you cannot give Him more. At least remember hourly to say the words which call to Him to give you what He wills to give, and wills you to receive. Determine not to interfere today with what He wills. And if a brother seems to tempt you to deny God's gift to him, see it as but another chance to let yourself receive the gifts of God as yours. Then bless your brother thankfully, and say:

MY BROTHER, PEACE AND JOY I OFFER YOU,
THAT I MAY HAVE GOD'S PEACE AND JOY AS MINE.

Lesson 106

Let me be still and listen to the truth.

If you will lay aside the ego's voice, however loudly it may seem to call; if you will not accept its petty gifts that give you nothing that you really want; if you will listen with an open mind, that has not told you what salvation is; then you will hear the mighty Voice of truth, quiet in power, strong in stillness, and completely certain in Its messages.

Listen, and hear your Father speak to you through His appointed Voice, which silences the thunder of the meaningless, and shows the way to peace to those who cannot see. Be still today and listen to the truth. Be not deceived by voices of the dead, which tell you they have found the source of life and offer it to you for your belief. Attend them not, but listen to the truth.

Be not afraid today to circumvent the voices of the world. Walk lightly past their meaningless persuasion. Hear them not. Be still today and listen to the truth. Go past all things which do not speak of Him Who holds your happiness within His Hand, held out to you in welcome and in love. Hear only Him today, and do not wait to reach Him longer. Hear one Voice today.

Today the promise of God's Word is kept. Hear and be silent. He would speak to you. He comes with miracles a thousand times as happy and as wonderful as those you ever dreamed or wished for in your dreams. His miracles are true. They will not fade when dreaming ends. They end the dream instead; and last forever, for they come from God to His dear Son, whose other name is you. Prepare yourself for miracles today. Today allow your Father's ancient pledge to you and all your brothers to be kept.

Hear Him today, and listen to the Word which lifts the veil that lies upon the earth, and wakes all those who sleep and cannot see. God calls to them through you. He needs your voice to speak to them, for who could reach God's Son except his Father, calling through your Self? Hear Him today, and offer Him your voice to speak to all the multitude who wait to hear the Word that He will speak today.

Be ready for salvation. It is here, and will today be given unto you. And you will learn your function from the One Who chose it in your Father's Name for you. Listen today, and you will hear a Voice which will resound throughout the world through you. The bringer of all miracles has need that you receive them first, and thus become the joyous giver of what you received.

Thus does salvation start and thus it ends; when everything is yours and everything is given away, it will remain with you forever. And the lesson has been learned. Today we practice giving, not the way you understand it now, but as it is. Each hour's exercises should begin with this request for your enlightenment:

I WILL BE STILL AND LISTEN TO THE TRUTH.
WHAT DOES IT MEAN TO GIVE AND TO RECEIVE?

Ask and expect an answer. Your request is one whose answer has been waiting long to be received by you. It will begin the ministry for which you came, and which will free the world from thinking giving is a way to lose. And so the world becomes ready to understand and to receive.

Be still and listen to the truth today. For each five minutes spent in listening, a thousand minds are opened to the truth and they will hear the holy Word you hear. And when the hour is past, you will again release a thousand more who pause to ask that truth be given them, along with you.

Today the holy Word of God is kept through your receiving it to give away, so you can teach the world what giving means by listening and learning it of Him. Do not forget today to reinforce your choice to hear and to receive the Word by this reminder, given to yourself as often as is possible today:

LET ME BE STILL AND LISTEN TO THE TRUTH.
I AM THE MESSENGER OF GOD TODAY,
MY VOICE IS HIS, TO GIVE WHAT I RECEIVE.

Lesson 107

Truth will correct all errors in my mind.

What can correct illusions but the truth? And what are errors but illusions that remain unrecognized for what they are? Where truth has entered errors disappear. They merely vanish, leaving not a trace by which to be remembered. They are gone because, without belief, they have no life. And so they disappear to nothingness, returning whence they came. From dust to dust they come and go, for only truth remains.

Can you imagine what a state of mind without illusions is? How it would feel? Try to remember when there was a time,– perhaps a minute, maybe even less–when nothing came to interrupt your peace; when you were certain you were loved and safe. Then try to picture what it would be like to have that moment be extended to the end of time and to eternity. Then let the sense of quiet that you felt be multiplied a hundred times, and then be multiplied another hundred more.

And now you have a hint, not more than just the faintest intimation of the state your mind will rest in when the truth has come. Without illusions there could be no fear, no doubt and no attack. When truth has come all pain is over, for there is no room for transitory thoughts and dead ideas to linger in your mind. Truth occupies your mind completely, liberating you from all beliefs in the ephemeral. They have no place because the truth has come, and they are nowhere. They can not be found, for truth is everywhere forever, now.

When truth has come it does not stay a while, to disappear or change to something else. It does not shift and alter in its form, nor come and go and go and come again. It stays exactly as it always was, to be depended on in every need, and trusted with a perfect trust in all the seeming difficulties and the doubts that the appearances the world presents engender. They will merely blow away, when truth corrects the errors in your mind.

When truth has come it harbors in its wings the gift of perfect constancy, and love which does not falter in the face of pain, but looks beyond it, steadily and sure. Here is the gift of healing, for the truth needs no defense, and therefore no attack is possible. Illusions can be brought to truth to be corrected. But the truth stands far beyond illusions, and can not be brought to them to turn them into truth.

Truth does not come and go nor shift nor change, in this appearance now and then in that, evading capture and escaping grasp. It does not hide. It stands in open light, in obvious accessibility. It is impossible that anyone could seek it truly, and would not succeed. Today belongs to truth. Give truth its due, and it will give you yours. You were not meant to suffer and to die. Your Father wills these dreams be gone. Let truth correct them all.

We do not ask for what we do not have. We merely ask for what belongs to us, that we may recognize it as our own. Today we practice on the happy note of certainty that has been born of truth. The shaky and unsteady footsteps of illusion are not our approach today. We are as certain of success as we are sure we live and hope and breathe and think. We do not doubt we walk with truth today, and count on it to enter into all the exercises that we do this day.

Begin by asking Him Who goes with you upon this undertaking that He be in your awareness as you go with Him. You are not made of flesh and blood and bone, but were created by the selfsame Thought which gave the gift of life to Him as well. He is your Brother, and so like to you your Father knows that You are both the same. It is your Self you ask to go with you, and how could He be absent where you are?

Truth will correct all errors in your mind which tell you you could be apart from Him. You speak to Him today, and make your pledge to let His function be fulfilled through you. To share His function is to share His joy. His confidence is with you, as you say:

TRUTH WILL CORRECT ALL ERRORS IN MY MIND,
AND I WILL REST IN HIM WHO IS MY SELF.

Then let Him lead you gently to the truth, which will envelop you and give you peace so deep and tranquil that you will return to the familiar world reluctantly.

And yet you will be glad to look again upon this world. For you will bring with you the promise of the changes which the truth that goes with you will carry to the world. They will increase with every gift you give of five small minutes, and the errors that surround the world will be corrected as you let them be corrected in your mind.

Do not forget your function for today. Each time you tell yourself with confidence, "Truth will correct all errors in my mind," you speak for all the world and Him Who would release the world, as He would set you free.

Lesson 108

To give and to receive are one in truth.

Vision depends upon today's idea. The light is in it, for it reconciles all seeming opposites. And what is light except the resolution, born of peace, of all your conflicts and mistaken thoughts into one concept which is wholly true? Even that one will disappear, because the Thought behind it will appear instead to take its place. And now you are at peace forever, for the dream is over then.

True light that makes true vision possible is not the light the body's eyes behold. It is a state of mind that has become so unified that darkness cannot be perceived at all. And thus what is the same is seen as one, while what is not the same remains unnoticed, for it is not there.

This is the light that shows no opposites, and vision, being healed, has power to heal. This is the light that brings your peace of mind to other minds, to share it and be glad that they are one with you and with themselves. This is the light that heals because it brings single perception, based upon one frame of reference, from which one meaning comes.

Here are both giving and receiving seen as different aspects of one Thought whose truth does not depend on which is seen as first, nor which appears to be in second place. Here it is understood that both occur together, that the Thought remain complete. And in this understanding is the base on which all opposites are reconciled, because they are perceived from the same frame of reference which unifies this Thought.

One thought, completely unified, will serve to unify all thought. This is the same as saying one correction will suffice for all correction, or that to forgive one brother wholly is enough to bring salvation to all minds. For these are but some special cases of one law which holds for every kind of learning, if it be directed by the One Who knows the truth.

To learn that giving and receiving are the same has special usefulness, because it can be tried so easily and seen as true. And when this special case has proved it always works, in every circumstance where it is tried, the thought behind it can be generalized to other areas of doubt and double vision. And from there it will extend, and finally arrive at the one Thought which underlies them all.

Today we practice with the special case of giving and receiving. We will use this simple lesson in the obvious because it has results we cannot miss. To give is to receive. Today we will attempt to offer peace to everyone, and see how quickly peace returns to us. Light is tranquility, and in that peace is vision given us, and we can see.

So we begin the practice periods with the instruction for today, and say:

TO GIVE AND TO RECEIVE ARE ONE IN TRUTH.
I WILL RECEIVE WHAT I AM GIVING NOW.

Then close your eyes, and for five minutes think of what you would hold out to everyone, to have it yours. You might, for instance, say:

TO EVERYONE I OFFER QUIETNESS.
TO EVERYONE I OFFER PEACE OF MIND.
TO EVERYONE I OFFER GENTLENESS.

Say each one slowly and then pause a while, expecting to receive the gift you gave. And it will come to you in the amount in which you gave it. You will find you have exact return, for that is what you asked. It might be helpful, too, to think of one to whom to give your gifts. He represents the others, and through him you give to all.

Our very simple lesson for today will teach you much. Effect and cause will be far better understood from this time on, and we will make much faster progress now. Think of the exercises for today as quick advances in your learning, made still faster and more sure each time you say, "To give and to receive are one in truth."

Lesson 109

I rest in God

We ask for rest today, and quietness unshaken by the world's appearances. We ask for peace and stillness, in the midst of all the turmoil born of clashing dreams. We ask for safety and for happiness, although we seem to look on danger and on sorrow. And we have the thought that will answer our asking with what we request.

"I rest in God." This thought will bring to you the rest and quiet, peace and stillness, and the safety and the happiness you seek. "I rest in God." This thought has power to wake the sleeping truth in you, whose vision sees beyond appearances to that same truth in everyone and everything there is. Here is the end of suffering for all the world, and everyone who ever came and yet will come to linger for a while. Here is the thought in which the Son of God is born again, to recognize himself.

"I rest in God." Completely undismayed, this thought will carry you through storms and strife, past misery and pain, past loss and death, and onward to the certainty of God. There is no suffering it cannot heal. There is no problem that it cannot solve. And no appearance but will turn to truth before the eyes of you who rest in God.

This is the day of peace. You rest in God, and while the world is torn by winds of hate your rest remains completely undisturbed. Yours is the rest of truth. Appearances cannot intrude on you. You call to all to join you in your rest, and they will hear and come to you because you rest in God. They will not hear another voice than yours because you gave your voice to God, and now you rest in Him and let Him speak through you.

In Him you have no cares and no concerns, no burdens, no anxiety, no pain, no fear of future and no past regrets. In timelessness you rest, while time goes by without its touch upon you, for your rest can never change in any way at all. You rest today. And as you close your eyes, sink into stillness. Let these periods of rest and respite reassure your mind that all its frantic fantasies were but the dreams of fever that has passed away. Let it be still and thankfully accept its healing. No more fearful dreams will come, now that you rest in God. Take time today to slip away from dreams and into peace.

Each hour that you take your rest today, a tired mind is suddenly made glad, a bird with broken wings begins to sing, a stream long dry begins to flow again. The world is born again each time you rest, and hourly remember that you came to bring the peace of God into the world, that it might take its rest along with you.

With each five minutes that you rest today, the world is nearer waking. And the time when rest will be the only thing there is comes closer to all worn and tired minds, too weary now to go their way alone. And they will hear the bird begin to sing and see the stream begin to flow again, with hope reborn and energy restored to walk with lightened steps along the road that suddenly seems easy as they go.

You rest within the peace of God today, and call upon your brothers from your rest to draw them to their rest, along with you. You will be faithful to your trust today, forgetting no one, bringing everyone into the boundless circle of your peace, the holy sanctuary where you rest. Open the temple doors and let them come from far across the world, and near as well; your distant brothers and your closest friends; bid them all enter here and rest with you.

You rest within the peace of God today, quiet and unafraid. Each brother comes to take his rest, and offer it to you. We rest together here, for thus our rest is made complete, and what we give today we have received already. Time is not the guardian of what we give today. We give to those unborn and those passed by, to every Thought of God, and to the Mind in which these Thoughts were born and where they rest. And we remind them of their resting place each time we tell ourselves, "I rest in God."

Lesson 110

I am as God created me.

We will repeat today's idea from time to time. For this one thought would be enough to save you and the world, if you believed that it is true. Its truth would mean that you have made no changes in yourself that have reality, nor changed the universe so that what God created was replaced by fear and evil, misery and death. If you remain as God created you fear has no meaning, evil is not real, and misery and death do not exist.

Today's idea is therefore all you need to let complete correction heal your mind, and give you perfect vision that will heal all the mistakes that any mind has made at any time or place. It is enough to heal the past and make the future free. It is enough to let the present be accepted as it is. It is enough to let time be the means for all the world to learn escape from time, and every change that time appears to bring in passing by.

If you remain as God created you, appearances cannot replace the truth, health cannot turn to sickness, nor can death be substitute for life, or fear for love. All this has not occurred, if you remain as God created you. You need no thought but just this one, to let redemption come to light the world and free it from the past.

In this one thought is all the past undone; the present saved to quietly extend into a timeless future. If you are as God created you, then there has been no separation of your mind from His, no split between your mind and other minds, and only unity within your own.

The healing power of today's idea is limitless. It is the birthplace of all miracles, the great restorer of the truth to the awareness of the world. Practice today's idea with gratitude. This is the truth that comes to set you free. This is the truth that God has promised you. This is the Word in which all sorrow ends.

For your five-minute practice periods, begin with this quotation from the text:

I AM AS GOD CREATED ME. HIS SON CAN SUFFER NOTHING.
AND I AM HIS SON.

Then, with this statement firmly in your mind, try to discover in your mind the Self Who is the holy Son of God Himself.

Seek Him within you Who is Christ in you, the Son of God and brother to the world; the Savior Who has been forever saved, with power to save whoever touches Him, however lightly, asking for the Word that tells him he is brother unto Him.

You are as God created you. Today honor your Self. Let graven images you made to be the Son of God instead of what he is be worshipped not today. Deep in your mind the holy Christ in you is waiting your acknowledgment as you. And you are lost and do not know yourself while He is unacknowledged and unknown.

Seek Him today, and find Him. He will be your Savior from all idols you have made. For when you find Him, you will understand how worthless are your idols, and how false the images which you believed were you. Today we make a great advance to truth by letting idols go, and opening our hands and hearts and minds to God today.

We will remember Him throughout the day with thankful hearts and loving thoughts for all who meet with us today. For it is thus that we remember Him. And we will say, that we may be reminded of His Son, our holy Self, the Christ in each of us:

Let us declare this truth as often as we can. This is the Word of God that sets you free. This is the key that opens up the gate of Heaven, and that lets you enter in the peace of God and His eternity.

Lesson 111

REVIEW III
Introduction

Our next review begins today. We will review two recent lessons every day for ten successive days of practicing. We will observe a special format for these practice periods, that you are urged to follow just as closely as you can.

We understand, of course, that it may be impossible for you to undertake what is suggested here as optimal each day and every hour of the day. Learning will not be hampered when you miss a practice period because it is impossible at the appointed time. Nor is it necessary that you make excessive efforts to be sure that you catch up in terms of numbers. Rituals are not our aim, and would defeat our goal.

But learning will be hampered when you skip a practice period because you are unwilling to devote the time to it that you are asked to give. Do not deceive yourself in this. Unwillingness can be most carefully concealed behind a cloak of situations you cannot control. Learn to distinguish situations that are poorly suited to your practicing from those that you establish to uphold a camouflage for your unwillingness.

Those practice periods that you have lost because you did not want to do them, for whatever reason, should be done as soon as you have changed your mind about your goal. You are unwilling to cooperate in practicing salvation only if it interferes with goals you hold more dear. When you withdraw the value given them, allow your practice periods to be replacements for your litanies to them. They gave you nothing. But your practicing can offer everything to you. And so accept their offering and be at peace.

The format you should use for these reviews is this: Devote five minutes twice a day, or longer if you would prefer it, to considering the thoughts that are assigned. Read over the ideas and comments that are written down for each day's exercise. And then begin to think about them, while letting your mind relate them to your needs, your seeming problems and all your concerns.

Place the ideas within your mind, and let it use them as it chooses. Give it faith that it will use them wisely, being helped in its decisions by the One Who gave the thoughts to you. What can you trust but what is in your mind? Have faith, in these reviews, the means the Holy Spirit uses will not fail. The wisdom of your mind will come to your assistance. Give direction at the outset; then lean back in quiet faith, and let the mind employ the thoughts you gave as they were given you for it to use.

You have been given them in perfect trust; in perfect confidence that you would use them well; in perfect faith that you would see their messages and use them for yourself. Offer them to your mind in that same trust and confidence and faith. It will not fail. It is the Holy Spirit's chosen means for your salvation. Since it has His trust, His means must surely merit yours as well.

We emphasize the benefits to you if you devote the first five minutes of the day to your reviews, and also give the last five minutes of your waking day to them. If this cannot be done, at least try to divide them so you undertake one in the morning, and the other in the hour just before you go to sleep.

The exercises to be done throughout the day are equally important, and perhaps of even greater value. You have been inclined to practice only at appointed times, and then go on your way to other things, without applying what you learned to them. As a result, you have gained little reinforcement, and have not given your learning a fair chance to prove how great are its potential gifts to you. Here is another chance to use it well.

In these reviews, we stress the need to let your learning not lie idly by between your longer practice periods. Attempt to give your daily two ideas a brief but serious review each hour. Use one on the hour, and the other one a half an hour later. You need not give more than just a moment to each one. Repeat it, and allow your mind to rest a little time in silence and in peace. Then turn to other things, but try to keep the thought with you, and let it serve to help you keep your peace throughout the day as well.

If you are shaken, think of it again. These practice periods are planned to help you form the habit of applying what you learn each day to everything you do. not repeat the thought and lay it down. Its usefulness is limitless to you. And it is meant to serve you in all ways, all times and places, and whenever you need help of any kind. Try, then, to take it with you in the business of the day and make it holy, worthy of God's Son, acceptable to God and to your Self.

Each day's review assignments will conclude with a restatement of the thought to use each hour, and the one to be applied on each half hour as well. Forget them not. This second chance with each of these ideas will bring such large advances that we come from these reviews with learning gains so great we will continue on more solid ground, with firmer footsteps and with stronger faith.

Do not forget how little you have learned.
Do not forget how much you can learn now.
Do not forget your Father's need of you,
As you review these thoughts He gave to you.

Lesson 111

For morning and evening review:

(91) Miracles are seen in light.

I CANNOT SEE IN DARKNESS. LET THE LIGHT OF HOLINESS AND TRUTH LIGHT UP MY MIND, AND LET ME SEE THE INNOCENCE WITHIN.

(92) Miracles are seen in light, and light and strength are one.

I SEE THROUGH STRENGTH, THE GIFT OF GOD TO ME.
MY WEAKNESS IS THE DARK HIS GIFT DISPELS, BY GIVING ME HIS STRENGTH TO TAKE ITS PLACE.

On the hour:

Miracles are seen in light.

On the half hour:

Miracles are seen in light, and light and strength are one.

Lesson 112

For morning and evening review:

(93) Light and joy and peace abide in me.

I AM THE HOME OF LIGHT AND JOY AND PEACE.
I WELCOME THEM INTO THE HOME I SHARE WITH GOD,
BECAUSE I AM A PART OF HIM.

(94) I am as God created me.

I WILL REMAIN FOREVER AS I WAS,
CREATED BY THE CHANGELESS LIKE HIMSELF.
AND I AM ONE WITH HIM, AND HE WITH ME.

On the hour:

Light and joy and peace abide in me.

On the half hour:

I am as God created me.

Lesson 113

For morning and evening review:

(95) I am one Self, united with my Creator.

SERENITY AND PERFECT PEACE ARE MINE, BECAUSE I AM ONE SELF,
COMPLETELY WHOLE, AT ONE WITH ALL CREATION AND WITH GOD.

(96) Salvation comes from my one Self.

From my one Self, Whose knowledge still remains within my mind,
I see God's perfect plan for my salvation perfectly fulfilled.

On the hour:

I am one Self, united with my Creator.

On the half hour:

Salvation comes from my one Self.

Lesson 114

For morning and evening review:

(97) I am spirit.

I AM THE SON OF GOD. NO BODY CAN CONTAIN MY SPIRIT,
NOR IMPOSE ON ME A LIMITATION GOD CREATED NOT.

(98) I will accept my part in God's plan for salvation.

WHAT CAN MY FUNCTION BE BUT TO ACCEPT THE WORD OF GOD,
WHO HAS CREATED ME FOR WHAT I AM AND WILL FOREVER BE?

On the hour:

I am spirit.

On the half hour:

I will accept my part in God's plan for salvation.

Lesson 115

For morning and evening review:

(99) Salvation is my only function here.

MY FUNCTION HERE IS TO FORGIVE THE WORLD FOR ALL THE ERRORS
I HAVE MADE. FOR THUS AM I RELEASED FROM THEM
WITH ALL THE WORLD.

(100) My part is essential to God's plan for salvation.

I AM ESSENTIAL TO THE PLAN OF GOD FOR THE SALVATION OF THE WORLD.
FOR HE GAVE ME HIS PLAN THAT I MIGHT SAVE THE WORLD.

On the hour:

Salvation is my only function here.

On the half hour:

My part is essential to God's plan for salvation.

Lesson 116

For morning and evening review:

(101) God's Will for me is perfect happiness.

GOD'S WILL IS PERFECT HAPPINESS FOR ME. AND I CAN SUFFER
BUT FROM THE BELIEF THERE IS ANOTHER WILL APART FROM HIS.

(102) I share God's Will for happiness for me.

I SHARE MY FATHER'S WILL FOR ME, HIS SON.
WHAT HE HAS GIVEN ME IS ALL I WANT.
WHAT HE HAS GIVEN ME IS ALL THERE IS.

On the hour:

God's Will for me is perfect happiness.

On the half hour:

I share God's Will for happiness for me.

Lesson 117

For morning and evening review:

(103) God, being Love, is also happiness.

LET ME REMEMBER LOVE IS HAPPINESS, AND NOTHING ELSE
BRINGS JOY. AND SO I CHOOSE TO ENTERTAIN NO SUBSTITUTES
FOR LOVE.

(104) I seek but what belongs to me in truth.

LOVE IS MY HERITAGE, AND WITH IT JOY. THESE ARE THE
GIFTS MY FATHER GAVE TO ME. I WOULD ACCEPT ALL THAT IS
MINE IN TRUTH.

On the hour:

God, being Love, is also happiness.

On the half hour:

I seek but what belongs to me in truth.

Lesson 118

For morning and evening review:

(105) God's peace and joy are mine.

TODAY I WILL ACCEPT GOD'S PEACE AND JOY, IN GLAD
EXCHANGE FOR ALL THE SUBSTITUTES THAT I HAVE MADE
FOR HAPPINESS AND PEACE.

(106) Let me be still and listen to the truth.

LET MY OWN FEEBLE VOICE BE STILL, AND LET ME HEAR THE
MIGHTY VOICE FOR TRUTH ITSELF ASSURE ME THAT I AM
GOD'S PERFECT SON.

On the hour:

God's peace and joy are mine.

On the half hour:

Let me be still and listen to the truth.

Lesson 119

For morning and evening review:

(107) Truth will correct all errors in my mind.

I AM MISTAKEN WHEN I THINK I CAN BE HURT IN ANY
WAY. I AM GOD'S SON, WHOSE SELF RESTS SAFELY IN
THE MIND OF GOD.

(108) To give and to receive are one in truth.

I WILL FORGIVE ALL THINGS TODAY, THAT I MAY LEARN HOW
TO ACCEPT THE TRUTH IN ME, AND COME TO RECOGNIZE MY
SINLESSNESS.

On the hour:

Truth will correct all errors in my mind.

On the half hour:

To give and to receive are one in truth.

Lesson 120

For morning and evening review:

(109) I rest in God.

I REST IN GOD TODAY, AND LET HIM WORK IN ME AND
THROUGH ME, WHILE I REST IN HIM IN QUIET AND IN
PERFECT CERTAINTY.

(110) I am as God created me.

I AM GOD'S SON. TODAY I LAY ASIDE ALL SICK ILLUSIONS OF
MYSELF, AND LET MY FATHER TELL ME WHO I REALLY AM.

On the hour:

I rest in God.

On the half hour:

I am as God created me.

Lesson 121

Forgiveness is the key to happiness.

Here is the answer to your search for peace. Here is the key to meaning in a world that seems to make no sense. Here is the way to safety in apparent dangers that appear to threaten you at every turn, and bring uncertainty to all your hopes of ever finding quietness and peace. Here are all questions answered; here the end of all uncertainty ensured at last.

The unforgiving mind is full of fear, and offers love no room to be itself; no place where it can spread its wings in peace and soar above the turmoil of the world. The unforgiving mind is sad, without the hope of respite and release from pain. It suffers and abides in misery, peering about in darkness, seeing not, yet certain of the danger lurking there.

The unforgiving mind is torn with doubt, confused about itself and all it sees; afraid and angry, weak and blustering, afraid to go ahead, afraid to stay, afraid to waken or to go to sleep, afraid of every sound, yet more afraid of stillness; terrified of darkness, yet more terrified at the approach of light. What can the unforgiving mind perceive but its damnation? What can it behold except the proof that all its sins are real?

The unforgiving mind sees no mistakes, but only sins. It looks upon the world with sightless eyes, and shrieks as it beholds its own projections rising to attack its miserable parody of life. It wants to live, yet wishes it were dead. It wants forgiveness, yet it sees no hope. It wants escape, yet can conceive of none because it sees the sinful everywhere.

The unforgiving mind is in despair, without the prospect of a future which can offer anything but more despair. Yet it regards its judgment of the world as irreversible, and does not see it has condemned itself to this despair. It thinks it cannot change, for what it sees bears witness that its judgment is correct. It does not ask, because it thinks it knows. It does not question, certain it is right.

Forgiveness is acquired. It is not inherent in the mind, which cannot sin. As sin is an idea you taught yourself, forgiveness must be learned by you as well, but from a Teacher other than yourself, Who represents the other Self in you. Through Him you learn how to forgive the self you think you made, and let it disappear. Thus you return your mind as one to Him Who is your Self, and Who can never sin.

Each unforgiving mind presents you with an opportunity to teach your own how to forgive itself. Each one awaits release from hell through you, and turns to you imploringly for Heaven here and now. It has no hope, but you become its hope. And as its hope, do you become your own. The unforgiving mind must learn through your forgiveness that it has been saved from hell. And as you teach salvation, you will learn. Yet all your teaching and your learning will be not of you, but of the Teacher Who was given you to show the way to you.

Today we practice learning to forgive. If you are willing, you can learn today to take the key to happiness, and use it on your own behalf. We will devote ten minutes in the morning, and at night another ten, to learning how to give forgiveness and receive forgiveness, too.

The unforgiving mind does not believe that giving and receiving are the same. Yet we will try to learn today that they are one through practicing forgiveness toward one whom you think of as an enemy, and one whom you consider as a friend. And as you learn to see them both as one, we will extend the lesson to yourself, and see that their escape included yours.

Begin the longer practice periods by thinking of someone you do not like, who seems to irritate you, or to cause regret in you if you should meet him; one you actively despise, or merely try to overlook. It does not matter what the form your anger takes. You probably have chosen him already. He will do.

Now close your eyes and see him in your mind, and look at him a while. Try to perceive some light in him somewhere; a little gleam which you had never noticed. Try to find some little spark of brightness shining through the ugly picture that you hold of him. Look at this picture till you see a light somewhere within it, and then try to let this light extend until it covers him, and makes the picture beautiful and good.

Look at this changed perception for a while, and turn your mind to one you call a friend. Try to transfer the light you learned to see around your former "enemy" to him. Perceive him now as more than friend to you, for in that light his holiness shows you your savior, saved and saving, healed and whole.

Then let him offer you the light you see in him, and let your "enemy" and friend unite in blessing you with what you gave. Now are you one with them, and they with you. Now have you been forgiven by yourself. Do not forget, throughout the day, the role forgiveness plays in bringing happiness to every unforgiving mind, with yours among them. Every hour tell yourself:

FORGIVENESS IS THE KEY TO HAPPINESS. I WILL AWAKEN FROM THE DREAM THAT I AM MORTAL, FALLIBLE AND FULL OF SIN, AND KNOW I AM THE PERFECT SON OF GOD.

Lesson 122

Forgiveness offers everything I want.

What could you want forgiveness cannot give? Do you want peace? Forgiveness offers it. Do you want happiness, a quiet mind, a certainty of purpose, and a sense of worth and beauty that transcends the world? Do you want care and safety, and the warmth of sure protection always? Do you want a quietness that cannot be disturbed, a gentleness that never can be hurt, a deep, abiding comfort, and a rest so perfect it can never be upset?

All this forgiveness offers you, and more. It sparkles on your eyes as you awake, and gives you joy with which to meet the day. It soothes your forehead while you sleep, and rests upon your eyelids so you see no dreams of fear and evil, malice and attack. And when you wake again, it offers you another day of happiness and peace. All this forgiveness offers you, and more.

Forgiveness lets the veil be lifted up that hides the face of Christ from those who look with unforgiving eyes upon the world. It lets you recognize the Son of God, and clears your memory of all dead thoughts so that remembrance of your Father can arise across the threshold of your mind. What would you want forgiveness cannot give? What gifts but these are worthy to be sought? What fancied value, trivial effect or transient promise, never to be kept, can hold more hope than what forgiveness brings?

Why would you seek an answer other than the answer that will answer everything? Here is the perfect answer, given to imperfect questions, meaningless requests, halfhearted willingness to hear, and less than halfway diligence and partial trust. Here is the answer! Seek for it no more. You will not find another one instead.

God's plan for your salvation cannot change, nor can it fail. Be thankful it remains exactly as He planned it. Changelessly it stands before you like an open door, with warmth and welcome calling from beyond the doorway, bidding you to enter in and make yourself at home, where you belong.

Here is the answer! Would you stand outside while all of Heaven waits for you within? Forgive and be forgiven. As you give you will receive. There is no plan but this for the salvation of the Son of God. Let us today rejoice that this is so, for here we have an answer, clear and plain, beyond deceit in its simplicity. All the complexities the world has spun of fragile cobwebs disappear before the power and the majesty of this extremely simple statement of the truth.

Here is the answer! Do not turn away in aimless wandering again. Accept salvation now. It is the gift of God, and not the world. The world can give no gifts of any value to a mind that has received what God has given as its own. God wills salvation be received today, and that the intricacies of your dreams no longer hide their nothingness from you.

Open your eyes today and look upon a happy world of safety and of peace. Forgiveness is the means by which it comes to take the place of hell. In quietness it rises up to greet your open eyes, and fill your heart with deep tranquility as ancient truths, forever newly born, arise in your awareness. What you will remember then can never be described. Yet your forgiveness offers it to you.

Remembering the gifts forgiveness gives, we undertake our practicing today with hope and faith that this will be the day salvation will be ours. Earnestly and gladly will we seek for it today, aware we hold the key within our hands, accepting Heaven's answer to the hell we made, but where we would remain no more.

Morning and evening do we gladly give a quarter of an hour to the search in which the end of hell is guaranteed. Begin in hopefulness, for we have reached the turning point at which the road becomes far easier. And now the way is short that yet we travel. We are close indeed to the appointed ending of the dream.

Sink into happiness as you begin these practice periods, for they hold out the sure rewards of questions answered and what your acceptance of the answer brings. Today it will be given you to feel the peace forgiveness offers, and the joy the lifting of the veil holds out to you.

Before the light you will receive today the world will fade until it disappears, and you will see another world arise you have no words to picture. Now we walk directly into light, and we receive the gifts that have been held in store for us since time began, kept waiting for today.

Forgiveness offers everything you want. Today all things you want are given you. Let not your gifts recede throughout the day, as you return again to meet a world of shifting change and bleak appearances. Retain your gifts in clear awareness as you see the changeless in the heart of change; the light of truth behind appearances.

Be tempted not to let your gifts slip by and drift into forgetfulness, but hold them firmly in your mind by your attempts to think of them at least a minute as each quarter of an hour passes by. Remind yourself how precious are these gifts with this reminder, which has power to hold your gifts in your awareness through the day:

FORGIVENESS OFFERS EVERYTHING I WANT.
TODAY I HAVE ACCEPTED THIS AS TRUE.
TODAY I HAVE RECEIVED THE GIFTS OF GOD.

Lesson 123

I thank my Father for His gifts to me.

Today let us be thankful. We have come to gentler pathways and to smoother roads. There is no thought of turning back, and no implacable resistance to the truth. A bit of wavering remains, some small objections and a little hesitance, but you can well be grateful for your gains, which are far greater than you realize.

A day devoted now to gratitude will add the benefit of some insight into the real extent of all the gains which you have made; the gifts you have received. Be glad today, in loving thankfulness, your Father has not left you to yourself, nor let you wander in the dark alone. Be grateful He has saved you from the self you thought you made to take the place of Him and His creation. Give Him thanks today.

Give thanks that He has not abandoned you, and that His Love forever will remain shining on you, forever without change. Give thanks as well that you are changeless, for the Son He loves is changeless as Himself. Be grateful you are saved. Be glad you have a function in salvation to fulfill. Be thankful that your value far transcends your meager gifts and petty judgments of the one whom God established as His Son.

Today in gratitude we lift our hearts above despair, and raise our thankful eyes, no longer looking downward to the dust. We sing the song of thankfulness today, in honor of the Self that God has willed to be our true Identity in Him. Today we smile on everyone we see, and walk with lightened footsteps as we go to do what is appointed us to do.

We do not go alone. And we give thanks that in our solitude a Friend has come to speak the saving Word of God to us. And thanks to you for listening to Him. His Word is soundless if it be not heard. In thanking Him the thanks are yours as well. An unheard message will not save the world, however mighty be the Voice that speaks, however loving may the message be.

Thanks be to you who heard, for you become the messenger who brings His Voice with you, and lets It echo round and round the world. Receive the thanks of God today, as you give thanks to Him. For He would offer you the thanks you give, since He receives your gifts in loving gratitude, and gives them back a thousand and a hundred thousand more than they were given. He will bless your gifts by sharing them with you. And so they grow in power and in strength, until they fill the world with gladness and with gratitude.

Receive His thanks and offer yours to Him for fifteen minutes twice today. And you will realize to Whom you offer thanks, and Whom He thanks as you are thanking Him. This holy half an hour given Him will be returned to you in terms of years for every second; power to save the world eons more quickly for your thanks to Him.

Receive His thanks, and you will understand how lovingly He holds you in His Mind, how deep and limitless His care for you, how perfect is His gratitude to you. Remember hourly to think of Him, and give Him thanks for everything He gave His Son, that he might rise above the world, remembering his Father and his Self.

Lesson 124

Let me remember I am one with God.

Today we will again give thanks for our Identity in God. Our home is safe, protection guaranteed in all we do, power and strength available to us in all our undertakings. We can fail in nothing. Everything we touch takes on a shining light that blesses and that heals. At one with God and with the universe we go our way rejoicing, with the thought that God Himself goes everywhere with us.

How holy are our minds! And everything we see reflects the holiness within the mind at one with God and with itself. How easily do errors disappear, and death give place to everlasting life. Our shining footprints point the way to truth, for God is our Companion as we walk the world a little while. And those who come to follow us will recognize the way because the light we carry stays behind, yet still remains with us as we walk on.

What we receive is our eternal gift to those who follow after, and to those who went before or stayed with us a while. And God, Who loves us with the equal love in which we were created, smiles on us and offers us the happiness we gave.

Today we will not doubt His Love for us, nor question His protection and His care. No meaningless anxieties can come between our faith and our awareness of His Presence. We are one with Him today in recognition and remembrance.

We feel Him in our hearts. Our minds contain His Thoughts; our eyes behold His loveliness in all we look upon. Today we see only the loving and the lovable.

We see it in appearances of pain, and pain gives way to peace. We see it in the frantic, in the sad and the distressed, the lonely and afraid, who are restored to the tranquility and peace of mind in which they were created. And we see it in the dying and the dead as well, restoring them to life. All this we see because we saw it first within ourselves.

No miracle can ever be denied to those who know that they are one with God. No thought of theirs but has the power to heal all forms of suffering in anyone, in times gone by and times as yet to come, as easily as in the ones who walk beside them now. Their thoughts are timeless, and apart from distance as apart from time.

We join in this awareness as we say that we are one with God. For in these words we say as well that we are saved and healed; that we can save and heal accordingly. We have accepted, and we now would give. For we would keep the gifts our Father gave. Today we would experience ourselves at one with Him, so that the world may share our recognition of reality. In our experience the world is freed. As we deny our separation from our Father, it is healed along with us.

Peace be to you today. Secure your peace by practicing awareness you are one with your Creator, as He is with you. Sometime today, whenever it seems best, devote a half an hour to the thought that you are one with God. This is our first attempt at an extended period for which we give no rules nor special words to guide your meditation. We will trust God's Voice to speak as He sees fit today, certain He will not fail. Abide with Him this half an hour. He will do the rest.

Your benefit will not be less if you believe that nothing happens. You may not be ready to accept the gain today. Yet sometime, somewhere, it will come to you, nor will you fail to recognize it when it dawns with certainty upon your mind. This half an hour will be framed in gold, with every minute like a diamond set around the mirror that this exercise will offer you. And you will see Christ's face upon it, in reflection of your own.

Perhaps today, perhaps tomorrow, you will see your own transfiguration in the glass this holy half an hour will hold out to you, to look upon yourself. When you are ready you will find it there, within your mind and waiting to be found. You will remember then the thought to which you gave this half an hour, thankfully aware no time was ever better spent.

Perhaps today, perhaps tomorrow, you will look into this glass, and understand the sinless light you see belongs to you; the loveliness you look on is your own. Count this half hour as your gift to God, in certainty that His return will be a sense of love you cannot understand, a joy too deep for you to comprehend, a sight too holy for the body's eyes to see. And yet you can be sure someday, perhaps today, perhaps tomorrow, you will understand and comprehend and see.

Add further jewels to the golden frame that holds the mirror offered you today, by hourly repeating to yourself:

LET ME REMEMBER I AM ONE WITH GOD, AT ONE WITH ALL MY
BROTHERS AND MY SELF, IN EVERLASTING HOLINESS AND PEACE.

Lesson 125

In quiet I receive God's Word today.

Let this day be a day of stillness and of quiet listening. Your Father wills you hear His Word today. He calls to you from deep within your mind where He abides. Hear Him today. No peace is possible until His Word is heard around the world; until your mind, in quiet listening, accepts the message that the world must hear to usher in the quiet time of peace.

This world will change through you. No other means can save it, for God's plan is simply this: The Son of God is free to save himself, given the Word of God to be his Guide, forever in his mind and at his side to lead him surely to his Father's house by his own will, forever free as God's. He is not led by force, but only love. He is not judged, but only sanctified.

In stillness we will hear God's Voice today without intrusion of our petty thoughts, without our personal desires, and without all judgment of His holy Word. We will not judge ourselves today, for what we are can not be judged. We stand apart from all the judgments which the world has laid upon the Son of God. It knows him not. Today we will not listen to the world, but wait in silence for the Word of God.

Hear, holy Son of God, your Father speak. His Voice would give to you His holy Word, to spread across the world the tidings of salvation and the holy time of peace. We gather at the throne of God today, the quiet place within the mind where He abides forever, in the holiness that He created and will never leave.

He has not waited until you return your mind to Him to give His Word to you. He has not hid Himself from you, while you have wandered off a little while from Him. He does not cherish the illusions which you hold about yourself. He knows His Son, and wills that he remain as part of Him regardless of his dreams; regardless of his madness that his will is not his own.

Today He speaks to you. His Voice awaits your silence, for His Word can not be heard until your mind is quiet for a while, and meaningless desires have been stilled. Await His Word in quiet. There is peace within you to be called upon today, to help make ready your most holy mind to hear the Voice for its Creator speak.

Three times today, at times most suitable for silence, give ten minutes set apart from listening to the world, and choose instead a gentle listening to the Word of God. He speaks from nearer than your heart to you. His Voice is closer than your hand. His Love is everything you are and that He is; the same as you, and you the same as He.

It is your voice to which you listen as He speaks to you. It is your word He speaks. It is the Word of freedom and of peace, of unity of will and purpose, with no separation nor division in the single Mind of Father and of Son. In quiet listen to your Self today, and let Him tell you God has never left His Son, and you have never left your Self.

Only be quiet. You will need no rule but this, to let your practicing today lift you above the thinking of the world, and free your vision from the body's eyes. Only be still and listen. You will hear the Word in which the Will of God the Son joins in his Father's Will, at one with it, with no illusions interposed between the wholly indivisible and true. As every hour passes by today, be still a moment and remind yourself you have a special purpose for this day; in quiet to receive the Word of God.

Lesson 126

All that I give is given to myself.

Today's idea, completely alien to the ego and the thinking of the world, is crucial to the thought reversal that this course will bring about. If you believed this statement, there would be no problem in complete forgiveness, certainty of goal, and sure direction. You would understand the means by which salvation comes to you, and would not hesitate to use it now.

Let us consider what you do believe, in place of this idea. It seems to you that other people are apart from you, and able to behave in ways which have no bearing on your thoughts, nor yours on theirs. Therefore, your attitudes have no effect on them, and their appeals for help are not in any way related to your own. You further think that they can sin without affecting your perception of yourself, while you can judge their sin, and yet remain apart from condemnation and at peace.

When you "forgive" a sin, there is no gain to you directly. You give charity to one unworthy, merely to point out that you are better, on a higher plane than he whom you forgive. He has not earned your charitable tolerance, which you bestow on one unworthy of the gift, because his sins have lowered him beneath a true equality with you. He has no claim on your forgiveness. It holds out a gift to him, but hardly to yourself.

Thus is forgiveness basically unsound; a charitable whim, benevolent yet undeserved, a gift bestowed at times, at other times withheld. Unmerited, withholding it is just, nor is it fair that you should suffer when it is withheld. The sin that you forgive is not your own. Someone apart from you committed it. And if you then are gracious unto him by giving him what he does not deserve, the gift is no more yours than was his sin.

If this be true, forgiveness has no grounds on which to rest dependably and sure. It is an eccentricity, in which you sometimes choose to give indulgently an undeserved reprieve. Yet it remains your right to let the sinner not escape the justified repayment for his sin. Think you the Lord of Heaven would allow the world's salvation to depend on this? Would not His care for you be small indeed, if your salvation rested on a whim?

You do not understand forgiveness. As you see it, it is but a check upon overt attack, without requiring correction in your mind. It cannot give you peace as you perceive it. It is not a means for your release from what you see in someone other than yourself. It has no power to restore your unity with him to your awareness. It is not what God intended it to be for you.

Not having given Him the gift He asks of you, you cannot recognize His gifts, and think He has not given them to you. Yet would He ask you for a gift unless it was for you? Could He be satisfied with empty gestures, and evaluate such petty gifts as worthy of His Son? Salvation is a better gift than this. And true forgiveness, as the means by which it is attained, must heal the mind that gives, for giving is receiving. What remains as unreceived has not been given, but what has been given must have been received.

Today we try to understand the truth that giver and receiver are the same. You will need help to make this meaningful, because it is so alien to the thoughts to which you are accustomed. But the Help you need is there. Give Him your faith today, and ask Him that He share your practicing in truth today. And if you only catch a tiny glimpse of the release that lies in the idea we practice for today, this is a day of glory for the world.

Give fifteen minutes twice today to the attempt to understand today's idea. It is the thought by which forgiveness takes its proper place in your priorities. It is the thought that will release your mind from every bar to what forgiveness means, and let you realize its worth to you.

In silence, close your eyes upon the world that does not understand forgiveness, and seek sanctuary in the quiet place where thoughts are changed and false beliefs laid by. Repeat today's idea, and ask for help in understanding what it really means. Be willing to be taught. Be glad to hear the Voice of truth and healing speak to you, and you will understand the words He speaks, and recognize He speaks your words to you.

As often as you can, remind yourself you have a goal today; an aim which makes this day of special value to yourself and all your brothers. Do not let your mind forget this goal for long, but tell yourself:

ALL THAT I GIVE IS GIVEN TO MYSELF. THE HELP I NEED TO LEARN
THAT THIS IS TRUE IS WITH ME NOW. AND I WILL TRUST IN HIM.

Then spend a quiet moment, opening your mind to His correction and His Love. And what you hear of Him you will believe, for what He gives will be received by you.

Lesson 127

There is no love but God's.

Perhaps you think that different kinds of love are possible. Perhaps you think there is a kind of love for this, a kind for that; a way of loving one, another way of loving still another. Love is one. It has no separate parts and no degrees; no kinds nor levels, no divergencies and no distinctions. It is like itself, unchanged throughout. It never alters with a person or a circumstance. It is the Heart of God, and also of His Son.

Love's meaning is obscure to anyone who thinks that love can change. He does not see that changing love must be impossible. And thus he thinks that he can love at times, and hate at other times. He also thinks that love can be bestowed on one, and yet remain itself although it is withheld from others. To believe these things of love is not to understand it. If it could make such distinctions, it would have to judge between the righteous and the sinner, and perceive the Son of God in separate parts.

Love cannot judge. As it is one itself, it looks on all as one. Its meaning lies in oneness. And it must elude the mind that thinks of it as partial or in part. There is no love but God's, and all of love is His. There is no other principle that rules where love is not. Love is a law without an opposite. Its wholeness is the power holding everything as one, the link between the Father and the Son which holds Them both forever as the same.

No course whose purpose is to teach you to remember what you really are could fail to emphasize that there can never be a difference in what you really are and what love is. Love's meaning is your own, and shared by God Himself. For what you are is what He is. There is no love but His, and what He is, is everything there is. There is no limit placed upon Himself, and so are you unlimited as well.

No law the world obeys can help you grasp love's meaning. What the world believes was made to hide love's meaning, and to keep it dark and secret. There is not one principle the world upholds but violates the truth of what love is, and what you are as well.

Seek not within the world to find your Self. Love is not found in darkness and in death. Yet it is perfectly apparent to the eyes that see and ears that hear love's Voice. Today we practice making free your mind of all the laws you think you must obey; of all the limits under which you live, and all the changes that you think are part of human destiny. Today we take the largest single step this course requests in your advance towards its established goal.

If you achieve the faintest glimmering of what love means today, you have advanced in distance without measure and in time beyond the count of years to your release. Let us together, then, be glad to give some time to God today, and understand there is no better use for time than this.

For fifteen minutes twice today escape from every law in which you now believe. Open your mind and rest. The world that seems to hold you prisoner can be escaped by anyone who does not hold it dear. Withdraw all value you have placed upon its meager offerings and senseless gifts, and let the gift of God replace them all.

Call to your Father, certain that His Voice will answer. He Himself has promised this. And He Himself will place a spark of truth within your mind wherever you give up a false belief, a dark illusion of your own reality and what love means. He will shine through your idle thoughts today, and help you understand the truth of love. In loving gentleness He will abide with you, as you allow His Voice to teach love's meaning to your clean and open mind. And He will bless the lesson with His Love.

Today the legion of the future years of waiting for salvation disappears before the timelessness of what you learn. Let us give thanks today that we are spared a future like the past. Today we leave the past behind us, nevermore to be remembered. And we raise our eyes upon a different present, where a future dawns unlike the past in every attribute.

The world in infancy is newly born. And we will watch it grow in health and strength, to shed its blessing upon all who come to learn to cast aside the world they thought was made in hate to be love's enemy. Now are they all made free, along with us. Now are they all our brothers in God's Love.

We will remember them throughout the day, because we cannot leave a part of us outside our love if we would know our Self. At least three times an hour think of one who makes the journey with you, and who came to learn what you must learn. And as he comes to mind, give him this message from your Self:

I BLESS YOU, BROTHER, WITH THE LOVE OF GOD, WHICH I WOULD
SHARE WITH YOU. FOR I WOULD LEARN THE JOYOUS LESSON THAT
THERE IS NO LOVE BUT GOD'S AND YOURS AND MINE AND EVERYONE'S.

Lesson 128

The world I see holds nothing that I want.

The world you see holds nothing that you need to offer you; nothing that you can use in any way, nor anything at all that serves to give you joy. Believe this thought, and you are saved from years of misery, from countless disappointments, and from hopes that turn to bitter ashes of despair. No one but must accept this thought as true, if he would leave the world behind and soar beyond its petty scope and little ways.

Each thing you value here is but a chain that binds you to the world, and it will serve no other end but this. For everything must serve the purpose you have given it, until you see a different purpose there. The only purpose worthy of your mind this world contains is that you pass it by, without delaying to perceive some hope where there is none. Be you deceived no more. The world you see holds nothing that you want.

Escape today the chains you place upon your mind when you perceive salvation here. For what you value you make part of you as you perceive yourself. All things you seek to make your value greater in your sight limit you further, hide your worth from you, and add another bar across the door that leads to true awareness of your Self.

Let nothing that relates to body thoughts delay your progress to salvation, nor permit temptation to believe the world holds anything you want to hold you back. Nothing is here to cherish. Nothing here is worth one instant of delay and pain; one moment of uncertainty and doubt. The worthless offer nothing. Certainty of worth can not be found in worthlessness.

Today we practice letting go all thought of values we have given to the world. We leave it free of purposes we gave its aspects and its phases and its dreams. We hold it purposeless within our minds, and loosen it from all we wish it were. Thus do we lift the chains that bar the door to freedom from the world, and go beyond all little values and diminished goals.

Pause and be still a little while, and see how far you rise above the world, when you release your mind from chains and let it seek the level where it finds itself at home. It will be grateful to be free a while. It knows where it belongs. But free its wings, and it will fly in sureness and in joy to join its holy purpose. Let it rest in its Creator, there to be restored to sanity, to freedom and to love.

Give it ten minutes rest three times today. And when your eyes are opened afterwards, you will not value anything you see as much as when you looked at it before. Your whole perspective on the world will shift by just a little, every time you let your mind escape its chains. The world is not where it belongs. And you belong where it would be, and where it goes to rest when you release it from the world. Your Guide is sure. Open your mind to Him. Be still and rest.

Protect your mind throughout the day as well. And when you think you see some value in an aspect or an image of the world, refuse to lay this chain upon your mind, but tell yourself with quiet certainty:

THIS WILL NOT TEMPT ME TO DELAY MYSELF.
THE WORLD I SEE HOLDS NOTHING THAT I WANT.

Lesson 129

Beyond this world there is a world I want.

This is the thought that follows from the one we practiced yesterday. You cannot stop with the idea the world is worthless, for unless you see that there is something else to hope for, you will only be depressed. Our emphasis is not on giving up the world, but on exchanging it for what is far more satisfying, filled with joy, and capable of offering you peace. Think you this world can offer that to you?

It might be worth a little time to think once more about the value of this world. Perhaps you will concede there is no loss in letting go all thought of value here. The world you see is merciless indeed, unstable, cruel, unconcerned with you, quick to avenge and pitiless with hate. It gives but to rescind, and takes away all things that you have cherished for a while. No lasting love is found, for none is here. This is the world of time, where all things end.

Is it a loss to find a world instead where losing is impossible; where love endures forever, hate cannot exist and vengeance has no meaning? Is it loss to find all things you really want, and know they have no ending and they will remain exactly as you want them throughout time? Yet even they will be exchanged at last for what we cannot speak of, for you go from there to where words fail entirely, into a silence where the language is unspoken and yet surely understood.

Communication, unambiguous and plain as day, remains unlimited for all eternity. And God Himself speaks to His Son, as His Son speaks to Him. Their language has no words, for what They say cannot be symbolized. Their knowledge is direct and wholly shared and wholly one. How far away from this are you who stay bound to this world. And yet how near are you, when you exchange it for the world you want.

Now is the last step certain; now you stand an instant's space away from timelessness. Here can you but look forward, never back to see again the world you do not want. Here is the world that comes to take its place, as you unbind your mind from little things the world sets forth to keep you prisoner. Value them not, and they will disappear. Esteem them, and they will seem real to you.

Such is the choice. What loss can be for you in choosing not to value nothingness? This world holds nothing that you really want, but what you choose instead you want indeed! Let it be given you today. It waits but for your choosing it, to take the place of all the things you seek but do not want.

Practice your willingness to make this change ten minutes in the morning and at night, and once more in between. Begin with this:

BEYOND THIS WORLD THERE IS A WORLD I WANT.
I CHOOSE TO SEE THAT WORLD INSTEAD OF THIS,
FOR HERE IS NOTHING THAT I REALLY WANT.

Then close your eyes upon the world you see, and in the silent darkness watch the lights that are not of this world light one by one, until where one begins another ends loses all meaning as they blend in one.

Today the lights of Heaven bend to you, to shine upon your eyelids as you rest beyond the world of darkness. Here is light your eyes can not behold. And yet your mind can see it plainly, and can understand. A day of grace is given you today, and we give thanks. This day we realize that what you feared to lose was only loss.

Now do we understand there is no loss. For we have seen its opposite at last, and we are grateful that the choice is made. Remember your decision hourly, and take a moment to confirm your choice by laying by whatever thoughts you have, and dwelling briefly only upon this:

THE WORLD I SEE HOLDS NOTHING THAT I WANT.
BEYOND THIS WORLD THERE IS A WORLD I WANT.

Lesson 130

It is impossible to see two worlds.

Perception is consistent. What you see reflects your thinking. And your thinking but reflects your choice of what you want to see. Your values are determiners of this, for what you value you must want to see, believing what you see is really there. No one can see a world his mind has not accorded value. And no one can fail to look upon what he believes he wants.

Yet who can really hate and love at once? Who can desire what he does not want to have reality? And who can choose to see a world of which he is afraid? Fear must make blind, for this its weapon is: That which you fear to see you cannot see. Love and perception thus go hand in hand, but fear obscures in darkness what is there.

What, then, can fear project upon the world? What can be seen in darkness that is real? Truth is eclipsed by fear, and what remains is but imagined. Yet what can be real in blind imaginings of panic born? What would you want that this is shown to you? What would you wish to keep in such a dream?

Fear has made everything you think you see. All separation, all distinctions, and the multitude of differences you believe make up the world. They are not there. Love's enemy has made them up. Yet love can have no enemy, and so they have no cause, no being and no consequence. They can be valued, but remain unreal. They can be sought, but they can not be found. Today we will not seek for them, nor waste this day in seeking what can not be found.

It is impossible to see two worlds which have no overlap of any kind. Seek for the one; the other disappears. But one remains. They are the range of choice beyond which your decision cannot go. The real and the unreal are all there are to choose between, and nothing more than these.

Today we will attempt no compromise where none is possible. The world you see is proof you have already made a choice as all-embracing as its opposite. What we would learn today is more than just the lesson that you cannot see two worlds. It also teaches that the one you see is quite consistent from the point of view from which you see it. It is all a piece because it stems from one emotion, and reflects its source in everything you see.

Six times today, in thanks and gratitude, we gladly give five minutes to the thought that ends all compromise and doubt, and go beyond them all as one. We will not make a thousand meaningless distinctions, nor attempt to bring with us a little part of unreality, as we devote our minds to finding only what is real.

Begin your searching for the other world by asking for a strength beyond your own, and recognizing what it is you seek. You do not want illusions. And you come to these five minutes emptying your hands of all the petty treasures of this world. You wait for God to help you, as you say:

IT IS IMPOSSIBLE TO SEE TWO WORLDS. LET ME ACCEPT THE
STRENGTH GOD OFFERS ME AND SEE NO VALUE IN THIS WORLD,
THAT I MAY FIND MY FREEDOM AND DELIVERANCE.

God will be there. For you have called upon the great unfailing power which will take this giant step with you in gratitude. Nor will you fail to see His thanks expressed in tangible perception and in truth. You will not doubt what you will look upon, for though it is perception, it is not the kind of seeing that your eyes alone have ever seen before. And you will know God's strength upheld you as you made this choice.

Dismiss temptation easily today whenever it arises, merely by remembering the limits of your choice. The unreal or the real, the false or true is what you see and only what you see. Perception is consistent with your choice, and hell or Heaven comes to you as one.

Accept a little part of hell as real, and you have damned your eyes and cursed your sight, and what you will behold is hell indeed. Yet the release of Heaven still remains within your range of choice, to take the place of everything that hell would show to you. All you need say to any part of hell, whatever form it takes, is simply this:

IT IS IMPOSSIBLE TO SEE TWO WORLDS.
I SEEK MY FREEDOM AND DELIVERANCE,
AND THIS IS NOT A PART OF WHAT I WANT.

Lesson 131

No one can fail who seeks to reach the truth.

Failure is all about you while you seek for goals that cannot be achieved. You look for permanence in the impermanent, for love where there is none, for safety in the midst of danger; immortality within the darkness of the dream of death. Who could succeed where contradiction is the setting of his searching, and the place to which he comes to find stability?

Goals that are meaningless are not attained. There is no way to reach them, for the means by which you strive for them are meaningless as they are. Who can use such senseless means, and hope through them to gain in anything? Where can they lead? And what could they achieve that offers any hope of being real? Pursuit of the imagined leads to death because it is the search for nothingness, and while you seek for life you ask for death. You look for safety and security, while in your heart you pray for danger and protection for the little dream you made.

Yet searching is inevitable here. For this you came, and you will surely do the thing you came for. But the world can not dictate the goal for which you search, unless you give it power to do so. Otherwise, you still are free to choose a goal that lies beyond the world and every worldly thought, and one that comes to you from an idea relinquished yet remembered, old yet new; an echo of a heritage forgot, yet holding everything you really want.

Be glad that search you must. Be glad as well to learn you search for Heaven, and must find the goal you really want. No one can fail to want this goal and reach it in the end. God's Son can not seek vainly, though he try to force delay, deceive himself and think that it is hell he seeks. When he is wrong, he finds correction. When he wanders off, he is led back to his appointed task.

No one remains in hell, for no one can abandon his Creator, nor affect His perfect, timeless and unchanging Love. You will find Heaven. Everything you seek but this will fall away. Yet not because it has been taken from you. It will go because you do not want it. You will reach the goal you really want as certainly as God created you in sinlessness.

Why wait for Heaven? It is here today. Time is the great illusion it is past or in the future. Yet this cannot be, if it is where God wills His Son to be. How could the Will of God be in the past, or yet to happen? What He wills is now, without a past and wholly futureless. It is as far removed from time as is a tiny candle from a distant star, or what you chose from what you really want.

Heaven remains your one alternative to this strange world you made and all its ways; its shifting patterns and uncertain goals, its painful pleasures and its tragic joys. God made no contradictions. What denies its own existence and attacks itself is not of Him. He did not make two minds, with Heaven as the glad effect of one, and earth the other's sorry outcome which is Heaven's opposite in every way.

God does not suffer conflict. Nor is His creation split in two. How could it be His Son could be in hell, when God Himself established him in Heaven? Could he lose what the Eternal Will has given him to be his home forever? Let us not try longer to impose an alien will upon God's single purpose. He is here because He wills to be, and what He wills is present now, beyond the reach of time.

Today we will not choose a paradox in place of truth. How could the Son of God make time to take away the Will of God? He thus denies himself, and contradicts what has no opposite. He thinks he made a hell opposing Heaven, and believes that he abides in what does not exist, while Heaven is the place he cannot find.

Leave foolish thoughts like these behind today, and turn your mind to true ideas instead. No one can fail who seeks to reach the truth, and it is truth we seek to reach today. We will devote ten minutes to this goal three times today, and we will ask to see the rising of the real world to replace the foolish images that we hold dear, with true ideas arising in the place of thoughts that have no meaning, no effect, and neither source nor substance in the truth.

This we acknowledge as we start upon our practice periods. Begin with this:

I ASK TO SEE A DIFFERENT WORLD, AND THINK A DIFFERENT KIND OF
THOUGHT FROM THOSE I MADE. THE WORLD I SEEK I DID NOT MAKE
ALONE, THE THOUGHTS I WANT TO THINK ARE NOT MY OWN.

For several minutes watch your mind and see, although your eyes are closed, the senseless world you think is real. Review the thoughts as well which are compatible with such a world, and which you think are true. Then let them go, and sink below them to the holy place where they can enter not. There is a door beneath them in your mind, which you could not completely lock to hide what lies beyond.

Seek for that door and find it. But before you try to open it, remind yourself no one can fail who seeks to reach the truth. And it is this request you make today. Nothing but this has any meaning now; no other goal is valued now nor sought, nothing before this door you really want, and only what lies past it do you seek.

Put out your hand, and see how easily the door swings open with your one intent to go beyond it. Angels light the way, so that all darkness vanishes, and you are standing in a light so bright and clear that you can understand all things you see. A tiny moment of surprise, perhaps, will make you pause before you realize the world you see before you in the light reflects the truth you knew, and did not quite forget in wandering away in dreams.

You cannot fail today. There walks with you the Spirit Heaven sent you, that you might approach this door some day, and through His aid slip effortlessly past it, to the light. Today that day has come. Today God keeps His ancient promise to His holy Son, as does His Son remember his to Him. This is a day of gladness, for we come to the appointed time and place where you will find the goal of all your searching here, and all the seeking of the world, which end together as you pass beyond the door.

Remember often that today should be a time of special gladness, and refrain from dismal thoughts and meaningless laments. Salvation's time has come. Today is set by Heaven itself to be a time of grace for you and for the world. If you forget this happy fact, remind yourself with this:

TODAY I SEEK AND FIND ALL THAT I WANT.
MY SINGLE PURPOSE OFFERS IT TO ME.
NO ONE CAN FAIL WHO SEEKS TO REACH THE TRUTH.

Lesson 132

I loose the world from all I thought it was.

What keeps the world in chains but your beliefs? And what can save the world except your Self? Belief is powerful indeed. The thoughts you hold are mighty, and illusions are as strong in their effects as is the truth. A madman thinks the world he sees is real, and does not doubt it. Nor can he be swayed by questioning his thoughts' effects. It is but when their source is raised to question that the hope of freedom comes to him at last.

Yet is salvation easily achieved, for anyone is free to change his mind, and all his thoughts change with it. Now the source of thought has shifted, for to change your mind means you have changed the source of all ideas you think or ever thought or yet will think. You free the past from what you thought before. You free the future from all ancient thoughts of seeking what you do not want to find.

The present now remains the only time. Here in the present is the world set free. For as you let the past be lifted and release the future from your ancient fears, you find escape and give it to the world. You have enslaved the world with all your fears, your doubts and miseries, your pain and tears; and all your sorrows press on it, and keep the world a prisoner to your beliefs. Death strikes it everywhere because you hold the bitter thoughts of death within your mind.

The world is nothing in itself. Your mind must give it meaning. And what you behold upon it are your wishes, acted out so you can look on them and think them real. Perhaps you think you did not make the world, but came unwillingly to what was made already, hardly waiting for your thoughts to give it meaning. Yet in truth you found exactly what you looked for when you came.

There is no world apart from what you wish, and herein lies your ultimate release. Change but your mind on what you want to see, and all the world must change accordingly. Ideas leave not their source. This central theme is often stated in the text, and must be borne in mind if you would understand the lesson for today. It is not pride which tells you that you made the world you see, and that it changes as you change your mind.

But it is pride that argues you have come into a world quite separate from yourself, impervious to what you think, and quite apart from what you chance to think it is. There is no world! This is the central thought the course attempts to teach. Not everyone is ready to accept it, and each one must go as far as he can let himself be led along the road to truth. He will return and go still farther, or perhaps step back a while and then return again.

But healing is the gift of those who are prepared to learn there is no world, and can accept the lesson now. Their readiness will bring the lesson to them in some form which they can understand and recognize. Some see it suddenly on point of death, and rise to teach it. Others find it in experience that is not of this world, which shows them that the world does not exist because what they behold must be the truth, and yet it clearly contradicts the world.

And some will find it in this course, and in the exercises that we do today. Today's idea is true because the world does not exist. And if it is indeed your own imagining, then you can loose it from all things you ever thought it was by merely changing all the thoughts that gave it these appearances. The sick are healed as you let go all thoughts of sickness, and the dead arise when you let thoughts of life replace all thoughts you ever held of death.

A lesson earlier repeated once must now be stressed again, for it contains the firm foundation for today's idea. You are as God created you. There is no place where you can suffer, and no time that can bring change to your eternal state. How can a world of time and place exist, if you remain as God created you?

What is the lesson for today except another way of saying that to know your Self is the salvation of the world? To free the world from every kind of pain is but to change your mind about yourself. There is no world apart from your ideas because ideas leave not their source, and you maintain the world within your mind in thought.

Yet if you are as God created you, you cannot think apart from Him, nor make what does not share His timelessness and Love. Are these inherent in the world you see? Does it create like Him? Unless it does, it is not real, and cannot be at all. If you are real the world you see is false, for God's creation is unlike the world in every way. And as it was His Thought by which you were created, so it is your thoughts which made it and must set it free, that you may know the Thoughts you share with God.

Release the world! Your real creations wait for this release to give you fatherhood, not of illusions, but as God in truth. God shares His Fatherhood with you who are His Son, for He makes no distinctions in what is Himself and what is still Himself. What He creates is not apart from Him, and nowhere does the Father end, the Son begin as something separate from Him.

There is no world because it is a thought apart from God, and made to separate the Father and the Son, and break away a part of God Himself and thus destroy His Wholeness. Can a world which comes from this idea be real? Can it be anywhere? Deny illusions, but accept the truth. Deny you are a shadow briefly laid upon a dying world. Release your mind, and you will look upon a world released.

Today our purpose is to free the world from all the idle thoughts we ever held about it, and about all living things we see upon it. They can not be there. No more can we. For we are in the home our Father set for us, along with them. And we who are as He created us would loose the world this day from every one of our illusions, that we may be free.

Begin the fifteen-minute periods in which we practice twice today with this:

I WHO REMAIN AS GOD CREATED ME WOULD LOOSE THE WORLD FROM
ALL I THOUGHT IT WAS. FOR I AM REAL BECAUSE THE WORLD IS NOT,
AND I WOULD KNOW MY OWN REALITY.

Then merely rest, alert but with no strain, and let your mind in quietness be changed so that the world is freed, along with you.

You need not realize that healing comes to many brothers far across the world, as well as to the ones you see nearby, as you send out these thoughts to bless the world. But you will sense your own release, although you may not fully understand as yet that you could never be released alone.

Throughout the day, increase the freedom sent through your ideas to all the world, and say whenever you are tempted to deny the power of your simple change of mind:

I LOOSE THE WORLD FROM ALL I THOUGHT IT WAS,
AND CHOOSE MY OWN REALITY INSTEAD.

Lesson 133

I will not value what is valueless.

Sometimes in teaching there is benefit, particularly after you have gone through what seems theoretical and far from what the student has already learned, to bring him back to practical concerns. This we will do today. We will not speak of lofty, world-encompassing ideas, but dwell instead on benefits to you.

You do not ask too much of life, but far too little. When you let your mind be drawn to bodily concerns, to things you buy, to eminence as valued by the world, you ask for sorrow, not for happiness. This course does not attempt to take from you the little that you have. It does not try to substitute utopian ideas for satisfactions which the world contains. There are no satisfactions in the world.

Today we list the real criteria by which to test all things you think you want. Unless they meet these sound requirements, they are not worth desiring at all, for they can but replace what offers more. The laws that govern choice you cannot make, no more than you can make alternatives from which to choose. The choosing you can do; indeed, you must. But it is wise to learn the laws you set in motion when you choose, and what alternatives you choose between.

We have already stressed there are but two, however many there appear to be. The range is set, and this we cannot change. It would be most ungenerous to you to let alternatives be limitless, and thus delay your final choice until you had considered all of them in time; and not been brought so clearly to the place where there is but one choice that must be made.

Another kindly and related law is that there is no compromise in what your choice must bring. It cannot give you just a little, for there is no in between. Each choice you make brings everything to you or nothing. Therefore, if you learn the tests by which you can distinguish everything from nothing, you will make the better choice.

First, if you choose a thing that will not last forever, what you chose is valueless. A temporary value is without all value. Time can never take away a value that is real. What fades and dies was never there, and makes no offering to him who chooses it. He is deceived by nothing in a form he thinks he likes.

Next, if you choose to take a thing away from someone else, you will have nothing left. This is because, when you deny his right to everything, you have denied your own. You therefore will not recognize the things you really have, denying they are there. Who seeks to take away has been deceived by the illusion loss can offer gain. Yet loss must offer loss, and nothing more.

Your next consideration is the one on which the others rest. Why is the choice you make of value to you? What attracts your mind to it? What purpose does it serve? Here it is easiest of all to be deceived. For what the ego wants it fails to recognize. It does not even tell the truth as it perceives it, for it needs to keep the halo which it uses to protect its goals from tarnish and from rust, that you may see how "innocent" it is.

Yet is its camouflage a thin veneer, which could deceive but those who are content to be deceived. Its goals are obvious to anyone who cares to look for them. Here is deception doubled, for the one who is deceived will not perceive that he has merely failed to gain. He will believe that he has served the ego's hidden goals.

Yet though he tries to keep its halo clear within his vision, still must he perceive its tarnished edges and its rusted core. His ineffectual mistakes appear as sins to him, because he looks upon the tarnish as his own; the rust a sign of deep unworthiness within himself. He who would still preserve the ego's goals and serve them as his own makes no mistakes, according to the dictates of his guide. This guidance teaches it is error to believe that sins are but mistakes, for who would suffer for his sins if this were so?

And so we come to the criterion for choice that is the hardest to believe, because its obviousness is overlaid with many levels of obscurity. If you feel any guilt about your choice, you have allowed the ego's goals to come between the real alternatives. And thus you do not realize there are but two, and the alternative you think you chose seems fearful, and too dangerous to be the nothingness it actually is.

All things are valuable or valueless, worthy or not of being sought at all, entirely desirable or not worth the slightest effort to obtain. Choosing is easy just because of this. Complexity is nothing but a screen of smoke, which hides the very simple fact that no decision can be difficult. What is the gain to you in learning this? It is far more than merely letting you make choices easily and without pain.

Heaven itself is reached with empty hands and open minds, which come with nothing to find everything and claim it as their own. We will attempt to reach this state today, with self-deception laid aside, and with an honest willingness to value but the truly valuable and the real. Our two extended practice periods of fifteen minutes each begin with this:

I WILL NOT VALUE WHAT IS VALUELESS,
AND ONLY WHAT HAS VALUE DO I SEEK,
FOR ONLY THAT DO I DESIRE TO FIND.

And then receive what waits for everyone who reaches, unencumbered, to the gate of Heaven, which swings open as he comes. Should you begin to let yourself collect some needless burdens, or believe you see some difficult decisions facing you, be quick to answer with this simple thought:

I WILL NOT VALUE WHAT IS VALUELESS,
FOR WHAT IS VALUABLE BELONGS TO ME.

Lesson 134

Let me perceive forgiveness as it is.

Let us review the meaning of "forgive," for it is apt to be distorted and to be perceived as something that entails an unfair sacrifice of righteous wrath, a gift unjustified and undeserved, and a complete denial of the truth. In such a view, forgiveness must be seen as mere eccentric folly, and this course appear to rest salvation on a whim.

This twisted view of what forgiveness means is easily corrected, when you can accept the fact that pardon is not asked for what is true. It must be limited to what is false. It is irrelevant to everything except illusions. Truth is God's creation, and to pardon that is meaningless. All truth belongs to Him, reflects His laws and radiates His Love. Does this need pardon? How can you forgive the sinless and eternally benign?

The major difficulty that you find in genuine forgiveness on your part is that you still believe you must forgive the truth, and not illusions. You conceive of pardon as a vain attempt to look past what is there; to overlook the truth, in an unfounded effort to deceive yourself by making an illusion true. This twisted viewpoint but reflects the hold that the idea of sin retains as yet upon your mind, as you regard yourself.

Because you think your sins are real, you look on pardon as deception. For it is impossible to think of sin as true and not believe forgiveness is a lie. Thus is forgiveness really but a sin, like all the rest. It says the truth is false, and smiles on the corrupt as if they were as blameless as the grass; as white as snow. It is delusional in what it thinks it can accomplish. It would see as right the plainly wrong; the loathsome as the good.

Pardon is no escape in such a view. It merely is a further sign that sin is unforgivable, at best to be concealed, denied or called another name, for pardon is a treachery to truth. Guilt cannot be forgiven. If you sin, your guilt is everlasting. Those who are forgiven from the view their sins are real are pitifully mocked and twice condemned; first, by themselves for what they think they did, and once again by those who pardon them.

It is sin's unreality that makes forgiveness natural and wholly sane, a deep relief to those who offer it; a quiet blessing where it is received. It does not countenance illusions, but collects them lightly, with a little laugh, and gently lays them at the feet of truth. And there they disappear entirely.

Forgiveness is the only thing that stands for truth in the illusions of the world. It sees their nothingness, and looks straight through the thousand forms in which they may appear. It looks on lies, but it is not deceived. It does not heed the self-accusing shrieks of sinners mad with guilt. It looks on them with quiet eyes, and merely says to them, "My brother, what you think is not the truth."

The strength of pardon is its honesty, which is so uncorrupted that it sees illusions as illusions, not as truth. It is because of this that it becomes the undeceiver in the face of lies; the great restorer of the simple truth. By its ability to overlook what is not there, it opens up the way to truth, which has been blocked by dreams of guilt. Now are you free to follow in the way your true forgiveness opens up to you. For if one brother has received this gift of you, the door is open to yourself.

There is a very simple way to find the door to true forgiveness, and perceive it open wide in welcome. When you feel that you are tempted to accuse someone of sin in any form, do not allow your mind to dwell on what you think he did, for that is self-deception. Ask instead, "Would I accuse myself of doing this?"

Thus will you see alternatives for choice in terms that render choosing meaningful, and keep your mind as free of guilt and pain as God Himself intended it to be, and as it is in truth. It is but lies that would condemn. In truth is innocence the only thing there is. Forgiveness stands between illusions and the truth; between the world you see and that which lies beyond; between the hell of guilt and Heaven's gate.

Across this bridge, as powerful as love which laid its blessing on it, are all dreams of evil and of hatred and attack brought silently to truth. They are not kept to swell and bluster, and to terrify the foolish dreamer who believes in them. He has been gently wakened from his dream by understanding what he thought he saw was never there. And now he cannot feel that all escape has been denied to him.

He does not have to fight to save himself. He does not have to kill the dragons which he thought pursued him. Nor need he erect the heavy walls of stone and iron doors he thought would make him safe. He can remove the ponderous and useless armor made to chain his mind to fear and misery. His step is light, and as he lifts his foot to stride ahead a star is left behind, to point the way to those who follow him.

Forgiveness must be practiced, for the world cannot perceive its meaning, nor provide a guide to teach you its beneficence. There is no thought in all the world that leads to any understanding of the laws it follows, nor the Thought that it reflects. It is as alien to the world as is your own reality. And yet it joins your mind with the reality in you.

Today we practice true forgiveness, that the time of joining be no more delayed. For we would meet with our reality in freedom and in peace. Our practicing becomes the footsteps lighting up the way for all our brothers, who will follow us to the reality we share with them. That this may be accomplished, let us give a quarter of an hour twice today, and spend it with the Guide Who understands the meaning of forgiveness, and was sent to us to teach it. Let us ask of Him:

Then choose one brother as He will direct, and catalogue his "sins," as one by one they cross your mind. Be certain not to dwell on any one of them, but realize that you are using his "offenses" but to save the world from all ideas of sin. Briefly consider all the evil things you thought of him, and each time ask yourself, "Would I condemn myself for doing this?"

Let him be freed from all the thoughts you had of sin in him. And now you are prepared for freedom. If you have been practicing thus far in willingness and honesty, you will begin to sense a lifting up, a lightening of weight across your chest, a deep and certain feeling of relief. The time remaining should be given to experiencing the escape from all the heavy chains you sought to lay upon your brother, but were laid upon yourself.

Forgiveness should be practiced through the day, for there will still be many times when you forget its meaning and attack yourself. When this occurs, allow your mind to see through this illusion as you tell yourself:

LET ME PERCEIVE FORGIVENESS AS IT IS.
WOULD I ACCUSE MYSELF OF DOING THIS?
I WILL NOT LAY THIS CHAIN UPON MYSELF.

In everything you do remember this:

NO ONE IS CRUCIFIED ALONE, AND YET NO ONE
CAN ENTER HEAVEN BY HIMSELF.

Lesson 135

If I defend myself I am attacked.

Who would defend himself unless he thought he were attacked, that the attack were real, and that his own defense could save himself? And herein lies the folly of defense; it gives illusions full reality, and then attempts to handle them as real. It adds illusions to illusions, thus making correction doubly difficult. And it is this you do when you attempt to plan the future, activate the past, or organize the present as you wish.

You operate from the belief you must protect yourself from what is happening because it must contain what threatens you. A sense of threat is an acknowledgment of an inherent weakness; a belief that there is danger which has power to call on you to make appropriate defense. The world is based on this insane belief. And all its structures, all its thoughts and doubts, its penalties and heavy armaments, its legal definitions and its codes, its ethics and its leaders and its gods, all serve but to preserve its sense of threat. For no one walks the world in armature but must have terror striking at his heart.

Defense is frightening. It stems from fear, increasing fear as each defense is made. You think it offers safety. Yet it speaks of fear made real and terror justified. Is it not strange you do not pause to ask, as you elaborate your plans and make your armor thicker and your locks more tight, what you defend, and how, and against what?

Let us consider first what you defend. It must be something that is very weak and easily assaulted. It must be something made easy prey, unable to protect itself and needing your defense. What but the body has such frailty that constant care and watchful, deep concern are needful to protect its little life? What but the body falters and must fail to serve the Son of God as worthy host?

Yet it is not the body that can fear, nor be a thing of fear. It has no needs but those which you assign to it. It needs no complicated structures of defense, no health-inducing medicine, no care and no concern at all. Defend its life, or give it gifts to make it beautiful or walls to make it safe, and you but say your home is open to the thief of time, corruptible and crumbling, so unsafe it must be guarded with your very life.

Is not this picture fearful? Can you be at peace with such a concept of your home? Yet what endowed the body with the right to serve you thus except your own belief? It is your mind which gave the body all the functions that you see in it, and set its value far beyond a little pile of dust and water. Who would make defense of something that he recognized as this?

The body is in need of no defense. This cannot be too often emphasized. It will be strong and healthy if the mind does not abuse it by assigning it to roles it cannot fill, to purposes beyond its scope, and to exalted aims which it cannot accomplish. Such attempts, ridiculous yet deeply cherished, are the sources for the many mad attacks you make upon it. For it seems to fail your hopes, your needs, your values and your dreams.

The "self" that needs protection is not real. The body, valueless and hardly worth the least defense, need merely be perceived as quite apart from you, and it becomes a healthy, serviceable instrument through which the mind can operate until its usefulness is over. Who would want to keep it when its usefulness is done?

Defend the body and you have attacked your mind. For you have seen in it the faults, the weaknesses, the limits and the lacks from which you think the body must be saved. You will not see the mind as separate from bodily conditions. And you will impose upon the body all the pain that comes from the conception of the mind as limited and fragile, and apart from other minds and separate from its Source.

These are the thoughts in need of healing, and the body will respond with health when they have been corrected and replaced with truth. This is the body's only real defense. Yet is this where you look for its defense? You offer it protection of a kind from which it gains no benefit at all, but merely adds to your distress of mind. You do not heal, but merely take away the hope of healing, for you fail to see where hope must lie if it be meaningful.

A healed mind does not plan. It carries out the plans that it receives through listening to wisdom that is not its own. It waits until it has been taught what should be done, and then proceeds to do it. It does not depend upon itself for anything except its adequacy to fulfill the plans assigned to it. It is secure in certainty that obstacles can not impede its progress to accomplishment of any goal that serves the greater plan established for the good of everyone.

A healed mind is relieved of the belief that it must plan, although it cannot know the outcome which is best, the means by which it is achieved, nor how to recognize the problem that the plan is made to solve. It must misuse the body in its plans until it recognizes this is so. But when it has accepted this as true, then is it healed, and lets the body go.

Enslavement of the body to the plans the unhealed mind sets up to save itself must make the body sick. It is not free to be the means of helping in a plan which far exceeds its own protection, and which needs its service for a little while. In this capacity is health assured. For everything the mind employs for this will function flawlessly, and with the strength that has been given it and cannot fail.

It is, perhaps, not easy to perceive that self-initiated plans are but defenses, with the purpose all of them were made to realize. They are the means by which a frightened mind would undertake its own protection, at the cost of truth. This is not difficult to realize in some forms which these self-deceptions take, where the denial of reality is very obvious. Yet planning is not often recognized as a defense.

The mind engaged in planning for itself is occupied in setting up control of future happenings. It does not think that it will be provided for, unless it makes its own provisions. Time becomes a future emphasis, to be controlled by learning and experience obtained from past events and previous beliefs. It overlooks the present, for it rests on the idea the past has taught enough to let the mind direct its future course.

The mind that plans is thus refusing to allow for change. What it has learned before becomes the basis for its future goals. Its past experience directs its choice of what will happen. And it does not see that here and now is everything it needs to guarantee a future quite unlike the past, without a continuity of any old ideas and sick beliefs. Anticipation plays no part at all, for present confidence directs the way.

Defenses are the plans you undertake to make against the truth. Their aim is to select what you approve, and disregard what you consider incompatible with your beliefs of your reality. Yet what remains is meaningless indeed. For it is your reality that is the "threat" which your defenses would attack, obscure, and take apart and crucify.

What could you not accept, if you but knew that everything that happens, all events, past, present and to come, are gently planned by One Whose only purpose is your good? Perhaps you have misunderstood His plan, for He would never offer pain to you. But your defenses did not let you see His loving blessing shine in every step you ever took. While you made plans for death, He led you gently to eternal life.

Your present trust in Him is the defense that promises a future undisturbed, without a trace of sorrow, and with joy that constantly increases, as this life becomes a holy instant, set in time, but heeding only immortality. Let no defenses but your present trust direct the future, and this life becomes a meaningful encounter with the truth that only your defenses would conceal.

Without defenses, you become a light which Heaven gratefully acknowledges to be its own. And it will lead you on in ways appointed for your happiness according to the ancient plan, begun when time was born. Your followers will join their light with yours, and it will be increased until the world is lighted up with joy. And gladly will our brothers lay aside their cumbersome defenses, which availed them nothing and could only terrify.

We will anticipate that time today with present confidence, for this is part of what was planned for us. We will be sure that everything we need is given us for our accomplishment of this today. We make no plans for how it will be done, but realize that our defenselessness is all that is required for the truth to dawn upon our minds with certainty.

For fifteen minutes twice today we rest from senseless planning, and from every thought that blocks the truth from entering our minds. Today we will receive instead of plan, that we may give instead of organize. And we are given truly, as we say:

IF I DEFEND MYSELF I AM ATTACKED.
BUT IN DEFENSELESSNESS I WILL BE STRONG,
AND I WILL LEARN WHAT MY DEFENSES HIDE.

Nothing but that. If there are plans to make, you will be told of them. They may not be the plans you thought were needed, nor indeed the answers to the problems which you thought confronted you. But they are answers to another kind of question, which remains unanswered yet in need of answering until the Answer comes to you at last.

All your defenses have been aimed at not receiving what you will receive today. And in the light and joy of simple trust, you will but wonder why you ever thought that you must be defended from release. Heaven asks nothing. It is hell that makes extravagant demands for sacrifice. You give up nothing in these times today when, undefended, you present yourself to your Creator as you really are.

He has remembered you. Today we will remember Him. For this is Eastertime in your salvation. And you rise again from what was seeming death and hopelessness. Now is the light of hope reborn in you, for now you come without defense, to learn the part for you within the plan of God. What little plans or magical beliefs can still have value, when you have received your function from the Voice for God Himself?

Try not to shape this day as you believe would benefit you most. For you can not conceive of all the happiness that comes to you without your planning. Learn today. And all the world will take this giant stride, and celebrate your Eastertime with you. Throughout the day, as foolish little things appear to raise defensiveness in you and tempt you to engage in weaving plans, remind yourself this is a special day for learning, and acknowledge it with this:

THIS IS MY EASTERTIME. AND I WOULD KEEP IT HOLY.
I WILL NOT DEFEND MYSELF, BECAUSE THE SON OF GOD
NEEDS NO DEFENSE AGAINST THE TRUTH OF HIS REALITY.

Lesson 136

Sickness is a defense against the truth.

No one can heal unless he understands what purpose sickness seems to serve. For then he understands as well its purpose has no meaning. Being causeless and without a meaningful intent of any kind, it cannot be at all. When this is seen, healing is automatic. It dispels this meaningless illusion by the same approach that carries all of them to truth, and merely leaves them there to disappear.

Sickness is not an accident. Like all defenses, it is an insane device for self-deception. And like all the rest, its purpose is to hide reality, attack it, change it, render it inept, distort it, twist it, or reduce it to a little pile of unassembled parts. The aim of all defenses is to keep the truth from being whole. The parts are seen as if each one were whole within itself.

Defenses are not unintentional, nor are they made without awareness. They are secret, magic wands you wave when truth appears to threaten what you would believe. They seem to be unconscious but because of the rapidity with which you choose to use them. In that second, even less, in which the choice is made, you recognize exactly what you would attempt to do, and then proceed to think that it is done.

Who but yourself evaluates a threat, decides escape is necessary, and sets up a series of defenses to reduce the threat that has been judged as real? All this cannot be done unconsciously. But afterwards, your plan requires that you must forget you made it, so it seems to be external to your own intent; a happening beyond your state of mind, an outcome with a real effect on you, instead of one effected by yourself.

It is this quick forgetting of the part you play in making your "reality" that makes defenses seem to be beyond your own control. But what you have forgot can be remembered, given willingness to reconsider the decision which is doubly shielded by oblivion. Your not remembering is but the sign that this decision still remains in force, as far as your desires are concerned. Mistake not this for fact. Defenses must make facts unrecognizable. They aim at doing this, and it is this they do.

Every defense takes fragments of the whole, assembles them without regard to all their true relationships, and thus constructs illusions of a whole that is not there. It is this process that imposes threat, and not whatever outcome may result. When parts are wrested from the whole and seen as separate and wholes within themselves, they become symbols standing for attack upon the whole; successful in effect, and never to be seen as whole again. And yet you have forgotten that they stand but for your own decision of what should be real, to take the place of what is real.

Sickness is a decision. It is not a thing that happens to you, quite unsought, which makes you weak and brings you suffering. It is a choice you make, a plan you lay, when for an instant truth arises in your own deluded mind, and all your world appears to totter and prepare to fall. Now are you sick, that truth may go away and threaten your establishments no more.

How do you think that sickness can succeed in shielding you from truth? Because it proves the body is not separate from you, and so you must be separate from the truth. You suffer pain because the body does, and in this pain are you made one with it. Thus is your "true" identity preserved, and the strange, haunting thought that you might be something beyond this little pile of dust silenced and stilled. For see, this dust can make you suffer, twist your limbs and stop your heart, commanding you to die and cease to be.

Thus is the body stronger than the truth, which asks you live, but cannot overcome your choice to die. And so the body is more powerful than everlasting life, Heaven more frail than hell, and God's design for the salvation of His Son opposed by a decision stronger than His Will. His Son is dust, the Father incomplete, and chaos sits in triumph on His throne.

Such is your planning for your own defense. And you believe that Heaven quails before such mad attacks as these, with God made blind by your illusions, truth turned into lies, and all the universe made slave to laws which your defenses would impose on it. Yet who believes illusions but the one who made them up? Who else can see them and react to them as if they were the truth?

God knows not of your plans to change His Will. The universe remains unheeding of the laws by which you thought to govern it. And Heaven has not bowed to hell, nor life to death. You can but choose to think you die, or suffer sickness or distort the truth in any way. What is created is apart from all of this. Defenses are plans to defeat what cannot be attacked. What is unalterable cannot change. And what is wholly sinless cannot sin.

Such is the simple truth. It does not make appeal to might nor triumph. It does not command obedience, nor seek to prove how pitiful and futile your attempts to plan defenses that would alter it. Truth merely wants to give you happiness, for such its purpose is. Perhaps it sighs a little when you throw away its gifts, and yet it knows, with perfect certainty, that what God wills for you must be received.

It is this fact that demonstrates that time is an illusion. For time lets you think what God has given you is not the truth right now, as it must be. The Thoughts of God are quite apart from time. For time is but another meaningless defense you made against the truth. Yet what He wills is here, and you remain as He created you.

Truth has a power far beyond defense, for no illusions can remain where truth has been allowed to enter. And it comes to any mind that would lay down its arms, and cease to play with folly. It is found at any time; today, if you will choose to practice giving welcome to the truth.

This is our aim today. And we will give a quarter of an hour twice to ask the truth to come to us and set us free. And truth will come, for it has never been apart from us. It merely waits for just this invitation which we give today. We introduce it with a healing prayer, to help us rise above defensiveness, and let truth be as it has always been:

SICKNESS IS A DEFENSE AGAINST THE TRUTH.
I WILL ACCEPT THE TRUTH OF WHAT I AM,
AND LET MY MIND BE WHOLLY HEALED TODAY.

Healing will flash across your open mind, as peace and truth arise to take the place of war and vain imaginings. There will be no dark corners sickness can conceal, and keep defended from the light of truth. There will be no dim figures from your dreams, nor their obscure and meaningless pursuits with double purposes insanely sought, remaining in your mind. It will be healed of all the sickly wishes that it tried to authorize the body to obey.

Now is the body healed, because the source of sickness has been opened to relief. And you will recognize you practiced well by this: The body should not feel at all. If you have been successful, there will be no sense of feeling ill or feeling well, of pain or pleasure. No response at all is in the mind to what the body does. Its usefulness remains and nothing more.

Perhaps you do not realize that this removes the limits you had placed upon the body by the purposes you gave to it. As these are laid aside, the strength the body has will always be enough to serve all truly useful purposes. The body's health is fully guaranteed, because it is not limited by time, by weather or fatigue, by food and drink, or any laws you made it serve before. You need do nothing now to make it well, for sickness has become impossible.

Yet this protection needs to be preserved by careful watching. If you let your mind harbor attack thoughts, yield to judgment or make plans against uncertainties to come, you have again misplaced yourself, and made a bodily identity which will attack the body, for the mind is sick.

Give instant remedy, should this occur, by not allowing your defensiveness to hurt you longer. Do not be confused about what must be healed, but tell yourself:

I HAVE FORGOTTEN WHAT I REALLY AM, FOR I MISTOOK MY BODY FOR MYSELF.
SICKNESS IS A DEFENSE AGAINST THE TRUTH. BUT I AM NOT A BODY.
AND MY MIND CANNOT ATTACK. SO I CAN NOT BE SICK.

Lesson 137

When I am healed I am not healed alone.

Today's idea remains the central thought on which salvation rests. For healing is the opposite of all the world's ideas which dwell on sickness and on separate states. Sickness is a retreat from others, and a shutting off of joining. It becomes a door that closes on a separate self, and keeps it isolated and alone.

Sickness is isolation. For it seems to keep one self apart from all the rest, to suffer what the others do not feel. It gives the body final power to make the separation real, and keep the mind in solitary prison, split apart and held in pieces by a solid wall of sickened flesh, which it can not surmount.

The world obeys the laws that sickness serves, but healing operates apart from them. It is impossible that anyone be healed alone. In sickness must he be apart and separate. But healing is his own decision to be one again, and to accept his Self with all Its parts intact and unassailed. In sickness does his Self appear to be dismembered, and without the unity that gives It life. But healing is accomplished as he sees the body has no power to attack the universal Oneness of God's Son.

Sickness would prove that lies must be the truth. But healing demonstrates that truth is true. The separation sickness would impose has never really happened. To be healed is merely to accept what always was the simple truth, and always will remain exactly as it has forever been. Yet eyes accustomed to illusions must be shown that what they look upon is false. So healing, never needed by the truth, must demonstrate that sickness is not real.

Healing might thus be called a counter-dream, which cancels out the dream of sickness in the name of truth, but not in truth itself. Just as forgiveness overlooks all sins that never were accomplished, healing but removes illusions that have not occurred. Just as the real world will arise to take the place of what has never been at all, healing but offers restitution for imagined states and false ideas which dreams embroider into pictures of the truth.

Yet think not healing is unworthy of your function here. For anti-Christ becomes more powerful than Christ to those who dream the world is real. The body seems to be more solid and more stable than the mind. And love becomes a dream, while fear remains the one reality that can be seen and justified and fully understood.

Just as forgiveness shines away all sin and the real world will occupy the place of what you made, so healing must replace the fantasies of sickness which you hold before the simple truth. When sickness has been seen to disappear in spite of all the laws that hold it cannot but be real, then questions have been answered. And the laws can be no longer cherished nor obeyed.

Healing is freedom. For it demonstrates that dreams will not prevail against the truth. Healing is shared. And by this attribute it proves that laws unlike the ones which hold that sickness is inevitable are more potent than their sickly opposites. Healing is strength. For by its gentle hand is weakness overcome, and minds that were walled off within a body free to join with other minds, to be forever strong.

Healing, forgiveness, and the glad exchange of all the world of sorrow for a world where sadness cannot enter, are the means by which the Holy Spirit urges you to follow Him. His gentle lessons teach how easily salvation can be yours; how little practice you need undertake to let His laws replace the ones you made to hold yourself a prisoner to death. His life becomes your own, as you extend the little help He asks in freeing you from everything that ever caused you pain.

And as you let yourself be healed, you see all those around you, or who cross your mind, or whom you touch or those who seem to have no contact with you, healed along with you. Perhaps you will not recognize them all, nor realize how great your offering to all the world, when you let healing come to you. But you are never healed alone. And legions upon legions will receive the gift that you receive when you are healed.

Those who are healed become the instruments of healing. Nor does time elapse between the instant they are healed, and all the grace of healing it is given them to give. What is opposed to God does not exist, and who accepts it not within his mind becomes a haven where the weary can remain to rest. For here is truth bestowed, and here are all illusions brought to truth.

Would you not offer shelter to God's Will? You but invite your Self to be at home. And can this invitation be refused? Ask the inevitable to occur, and you will never fail. The other choice is but to ask what cannot be to be, and this can not succeed. Today we ask that only truth will occupy our minds; that thoughts of healing will this day go forth from what is healed to what must yet be healed, aware that they will both occur as one.

We will remember, as the hour strikes, our function is to let our minds be healed, that we may carry healing to the world, exchanging curse for blessing, pain for joy, and separation for the peace of God. Is not a minute of the hour worth the giving to receive a gift like this? Is not a little time a small expense to offer for the gift of everything?

Yet must we be prepared for such a gift. And so we will begin the day with this, and give ten minutes to these thoughts with which we will conclude today at night as well:

WHEN I AM HEALED I AM NOT HEALED ALONE.
AND I WOULD SHARE MY HEALING WITH THE WORLD,
THAT SICKNESS MAY BE BANISHED FROM THE MIND OF
GOD'S ONE SON, WHO IS MY ONLY SELF.

Let healing be through you this very day. And as you rest in quiet, be prepared to give as you receive, to hold but what you give, and to receive the Word of God to take the place of all the foolish thoughts that ever were imagined. Now we come together to make well all that was sick, and offer blessing where there was attack. Nor will we let this function be forgot as every hour of the day slips by, remembering our purpose with this thought:

WHEN I AM HEALED I AM NOT HEALED ALONE.
AND I WOULD BLESS MY BROTHERS, FOR I WOULD
BE HEALED WITH THEM, AS THEY ARE HEALED WITH ME.

Lesson 138

Heaven is the decision I must make.

In this world Heaven is a choice, because here we believe there are alternatives to choose between. We think that all things have an opposite, and what we want we choose. If Heaven exists there must be hell as well, for contradiction is the way we make what we perceive, and what we think is real.

Creation knows no opposite. But here is opposition part of being "real." It is this strange perception of the truth that makes the choice of Heaven seem to be the same as the relinquishment of hell. It is not really thus. Yet what is true in God's creation cannot enter here until it is reflected in some form the world can understand. Truth cannot come where it could only be perceived with fear. For this would be the error truth can be brought to illusions. Opposition makes the truth unwelcome, and it cannot come.

Choice is the obvious escape from what appears as opposites. Decision lets one of conflicting goals become the aim of effort and expenditure of time. Without decision, time is but a waste and effort dissipated. It is spent for nothing in return, and time goes by without results. There is no sense of gain, for nothing is accomplished; nothing learned.

You need to be reminded that you think a thousand choices are confronting you, when there is really only one to make. And even this but seems to be a choice. Do not confuse yourself with all the doubts that myriad decisions would induce. You make but one. And when that one is made, you will perceive it was no choice at all. For truth is true, and nothing else is true. There is no opposite to choose instead. There is no contradiction to the truth.

Choosing depends on learning. And the truth cannot be learned, but only recognized. In recognition its acceptance lies, and as it is accepted it is known. But knowledge is beyond the goals we seek to teach within the framework of this course. Ours are teaching goals, to be attained through learning how to reach them, what they are, and what they offer you. Decisions are the outcome of your learning, for they rest on what you have accepted as the truth of what you are, and what your needs must be.

In this insanely complicated world, Heaven appears to take the form of choice, rather than merely being what it is. Of all the choices you have tried to make this is the simplest, most definitive and prototype of all the rest, the one which settles all decisions. If you could decide the rest, this one remains unsolved. But when you solve this one, the others are resolved with it, for all decisions but conceal this one by taking different forms. Here is the final and the only choice in which is truth accepted or denied.

So we begin today considering the choice that time was made to help us make. Such is its holy purpose, now transformed from the intent you gave it; that it be a means for demonstrating hell is real, hope changes to despair, and life itself must in the end be overcome by death. In death alone are opposites resolved, for ending opposition is to die. And thus salvation must be seen as death, for life is seen as conflict. To resolve the conflict is to end your life as well.

These mad beliefs can gain unconscious hold of great intensity, and grip the mind with terror and anxiety so strong that it will not relinquish its ideas about its own protection. It must be saved from salvation, threatened to be safe, and magically armored against truth. And these decisions are made unaware, to keep them safely undisturbed; apart from question and from reason and from doubt.

Heaven is chosen consciously. The choice cannot be made until alternatives are accurately seen and understood. All that is veiled in shadows must be raised to understanding, to be judged again, this time with Heaven's help. And all mistakes in judgment that the mind had made before are open to correction, as the truth dismisses them as causeless. Now are they without effects. They cannot be concealed, because their nothingness is recognized.

The conscious choice of Heaven is as sure as is the ending of the fear of hell, when it is raised from its protective shield of unawareness, and is brought to light. Who can decide between the clearly seen and the unrecognized? Yet who can fail to make a choice between alternatives when only one is seen as valuable; the other as a wholly worthless thing, a but imagined source of guilt and pain? Who hesitates to make a choice like this? And shall we hesitate to choose today?

We make the choice for Heaven as we wake, and spend five minutes making sure that we have made the one decision that is sane. We recognize we make a conscious choice between what has existence and what has nothing but an appearance of the truth. Its pseudo-being, brought to what is real, is flimsy and transparent in the light. It holds no terror now, for what was made enormous, vengeful, pitiless with hate, demands obscurity for fear to be invested there. Now it is recognized as but a foolish, trivial mistake.

Before we close our eyes in sleep tonight, we reaffirm the choice that we have made each hour in between. And now we give the last five minutes of our waking day to the decision with which we awoke. As every hour passed, we have declared our choice again, in a brief quiet time devoted to maintaining sanity. And finally, we close the day with this, acknowledging we chose but what we want:

HEAVEN IS THE DECISION I MUST MAKE.
I MAKE IT NOW, AND WILL NOT CHANGE MY MIND,
BECAUSE IT IS THE ONLY THING I WANT.

Lesson 139

I will accept Atonement for myself.

Here is the end of choice. For here we come to a decision to accept ourselves as God created us. And what is choice except uncertainty of what we are? There is no doubt that is not rooted here. There is no question but reflects this one. There is no conflict that does not entail the single, simple question, "What am I?"

Yet who could ask this question except one who has refused to recognize himself? Only refusal to accept yourself could make the question seem to be sincere. The only thing that can be surely known by any living thing is what it is. From this one point of certainty, it looks on other things as certain as itself.

Uncertainty about what you must be is self-deception on a scale so vast, its magnitude can hardly be conceived. To be alive and not to know yourself is to believe that you are really dead. For what is life except to be yourself, and what but you can be alive instead? Who is the doubter? What is it he doubts? Whom does he question? Who can answer him?

He merely states that he is not himself, and therefore, being something else, becomes a questioner of what that something is. Yet he could never be alive at all unless he knew the answer. If he asks as if he does not know, it merely shows he does not want to be the thing he is. He has accepted it because he lives; has judged against it and denied its worth, and has decided that he does not know the only certainty by which he lives.

Thus he becomes uncertain of his life, for what it is has been denied by him. It is for this denial that you need Atonement. Your denial made no change in what you are. But you have split your mind into what knows and does not know the truth. You are yourself. There is no doubt of this. And yet you doubt it. But you do not ask what part of you can really doubt yourself. It cannot really be a part of you that asks this question. For it asks of one who knows the answer. Were it part of you, then certainty would be impossible.

Atonement remedies the strange idea that it is possible to doubt yourself, and be unsure of what you really are. This is the depth of madness. Yet it is the universal question of the world. What does this mean except the world is mad? Why share its madness in the sad belief that what is universal here is true?

Nothing the world believes is true. It is a place whose purpose is to be a home where those who claim they do not know themselves can come to question what it is they are. And they will come again until the time Atonement is accepted, and they learn it is impossible to doubt yourself, and not to be aware of what you are.

Only acceptance can be asked of you, for what you are is certain. It is set forever in the holy Mind of God, and in your own. It is so far beyond all doubt and question that to ask what it must be is all the proof you need to show that you believe the contradiction that you know not what you cannot fail to know. Is this a question, or a statement which denies itself in statement? Let us not allow our holy minds to occupy themselves with senseless musings such as this.

We have a mission here. We did not come to reinforce the madness that we once believed in. Let us not forget the goal that we accepted. It is more than just our happiness alone we came to gain. What we accept as what we are proclaims what everyone must be, along with us. Fail not your brothers, or you fail yourself. Look lovingly on them, that they may know that they are part of you, and you of them.

This does Atonement teach, and demonstrates the Oneness of God's Son is unassailed by his belief he knows not what he is. Today accept Atonement, not to change reality, but merely to accept the truth about yourself, and go your way rejoicing in the endless Love of God. It is but this that we are asked to do. It is but this that we will do today.

Five minutes in the morning and at night we will devote to dedicate our minds to our assignment for today. We start with this review of what our mission is:

I WILL ACCEPT ATONEMENT FOR MYSELF,
FOR I REMAIN AS GOD CREATED ME.

We have not lost the knowledge that God gave to us when He created us like Him. We can remember it for everyone, for in creation are all minds as one. And in our memory is the recall how dear our brothers are to us in truth, how much a part of us is every mind, how faithful they have really been to us, and how our Father's Love contains them all.

In thanks for all creation, in the Name of its Creator and His Oneness with all aspects of creation, we repeat our dedication to our cause today each hour, as we lay aside all thoughts that would distract us from our holy aim. For several minutes let your mind be cleared of all the foolish cobwebs which the world would weave around the holy Son of God. And learn the fragile nature of the chains that seem to keep the knowledge of yourself apart from your awareness, as you say:

I WILL ACCEPT ATONEMENT FOR MYSELF,
FOR I REMAIN AS GOD CREATED ME.

Lesson 140

Only salvation can be said to cure.

"Cure" is a word that cannot be applied to any remedy the world accepts as beneficial. What the world perceives as therapeutic is but what will make the body "better." When it tries to heal the mind, it sees no separation from the body, where it thinks the mind exists. Its forms of healing thus must substitute illusion for illusion. One belief in sickness takes another form, and so the patient now perceives himself as well.

He is not healed. He merely had a dream that he was sick, and in the dream he found a magic formula to make him well. Yet he has not awakened from the dream, and so his mind remains exactly as it was before. He has not seen the light that would awaken him and end the dream. What difference does the content of a dream make in reality? One either sleeps or wakens. There is nothing in between.

The happy dreams the Holy Spirit brings are different from the dreaming of the world, where one can merely dream he is awake. The dreams forgiveness lets the mind perceive do not induce another form of sleep, so that the dreamer dreams another dream. His happy dreams are heralds of the dawn of truth upon the mind. They lead from sleep to gentle waking, so that dreams are gone. And thus they cure for all eternity.

Atonement heals with certainty, and cures all sickness. For the mind which understands that sickness can be nothing but a dream is not deceived by forms the dream may take. Sickness where guilt is absent cannot come, for it is but another form of guilt. Atonement does not heal the sick, for that is not a cure. It takes away the guilt that makes the sickness possible. And that is cure indeed. For sickness now is gone, with nothing left to which it can return.

Peace be to you who have been cured in God, and not in idle dreams. For cure must come from holiness, and holiness can not be found where sin is cherished. God abides in holy temples. He is barred where sin has entered. Yet there is no place where He is not. And therefore sin can have no home in which to hide from His beneficence. There is no place where holiness is not, and nowhere sin and sickness can abide.

This is the thought that cures. It does not make distinctions among unrealities. Nor does it seek to heal what is not sick, unmindful where the need for healing is. This is no magic. It is merely an appeal to truth, which cannot fail to heal and heal forever. It is not a thought that judges an illusion by its size, its seeming gravity, or anything that is related to the form it takes. It merely focuses on what it is, and knows that no illusion can be real.

Let us not try today to seek to cure what cannot suffer sickness. Healing must be sought but where it is, and then applied to what is sick, so that it can be cured. There is no remedy the world provides that can effect a change in anything. The mind that brings illusions to the truth is really changed. There is no change but this. For how can one illusion differ from another but in attributes that have no substance, no reality, no core, and nothing that is truly different?

Today we seek to change our minds about the source of sickness, for we seek a cure for all illusions, not another shift among them. We will try today to find the source of healing, which is in our minds because our Father placed it there for us. It is not farther from us than ourselves. It is as near to us as our own thoughts; so close it is impossible to lose. We need but seek it and it must be found.

We will not be misled today by what appears to us as sick. We go beyond appearances today and reach the source of healing, from which nothing is exempt. We will succeed to the extent to which we realize that there can never be a meaningful distinction made between what is untrue and equally untrue. Here there are no degrees, and no beliefs that what does not exist is truer in some forms than others. All of them are false, and can be cured because they are not true.

So do we lay aside our amulets, our charms and medicines, our chants and bits of magic in whatever form they take. We will be still and listen for the Voice of healing, which will cure all ills as one, restoring saneness to the Son of God. No voice but this can cure. Today we hear a single Voice which speaks to us of truth, where all illusions end, and peace returns to the eternal, quiet home of God.

We waken hearing Him, and let Him speak to us five minutes as the day begins, and end the day by listening again five minutes more before we go to sleep. Our only preparation is to let our interfering thoughts be laid aside, not separately, but all of them as one. They are the same. We have no need to make them different, and thus delay the time when we can hear our Father speak to us. We hear Him now. We come to Him today.

With nothing in our hands to which we cling, with lifted hearts and listening minds we pray:

ONLY SALVATION CAN BE SAID TO CURE.
SPEAK TO US, FATHER, THAT WE MAY BE HEALED.

And we will feel salvation cover us with soft protection, and with peace so deep that no illusion can disturb our minds, nor offer proof to us that it is real. This will we learn today. And we will say our prayer for healing hourly, and take a minute as the hour strikes, to hear the answer to our prayer be given us as we attend in silence and in joy. This is the day when healing comes to us. This is the day when separation ends, and we remember Who we really are.

Lesson 141

REVIEW IV
Introduction

Now we review again, this time aware we are preparing for the second part of learning how the truth can be applied. Today we will begin to concentrate on readiness for what will follow next. Such is our aim for this review, and for the lessons following. Thus, we review the recent lessons and their central thoughts in such a way as will facilitate the readiness that we would now achieve.

There is a central theme that unifies each step in the review we undertake, which can be simply stated in these words:

MY MIND HOLDS ONLY WHAT I THINK WITH GOD.

That is a fact, and represents the truth of What you are and What your Father is. It is this thought by which the Father gave creation to the Son, establishing the Son as co-creator with Himself. It is this thought that fully guarantees salvation to the Son. For in his mind no thoughts can dwell but those his Father shares. Lack of forgiveness blocks this thought from his awareness. Yet it is forever true.

Let us begin our preparation with some understanding of the many forms in which the lack of true forgiveness may be carefully concealed. Because they are illusions, they are not perceived to be but what they are; defenses that protect your unforgiving thoughts from being seen and recognized. Their purpose is to show you something else, and hold correction off through self-deceptions made to take its place.

And yet, your mind holds only what you think with God. Your self-deceptions cannot take the place of truth. No more than can a child who throws a stick into the ocean change the coming and the going of the tides, the warming of the water by the sun, the silver of the moon on it by night. So do we start each practice period in this review with readying our minds to understand the lessons that we read, and see the meaning that they offer us.

Begin each day with time devoted to the preparation of your mind to learn what each idea you will review that day can offer you in freedom and in peace. Open your mind, and clear it of all thoughts that would deceive, and let this thought alone engage it fully, and remove the rest:

MY MIND HOLDS ONLY WHAT I THINK WITH GOD.

Five minutes with this thought will be enough to set the day along the lines which God appointed, and to place His Mind in charge of all the thoughts you will receive that day.

They will not come from you alone, for they will all be shared with Him. And so each one will bring the message of His Love to you, returning messages of yours to Him. So will communion with the Lord of Hosts be yours, as He Himself has willed it be. And as His Own completion joins with Him, so will He join with you who are complete as you unite with Him, and He with you.

After your preparation, merely read each of the two ideas assigned to you to be reviewed that day. Then close your eyes, and say them slowly to yourself. There is no hurry now, for you are using time for its intended purpose. Let each word shine with the meaning God has given it, as it was given to you through His Voice. Let each idea which you review that day give you the gift that He has laid in it for you to have of Him. And we will use no format for our practicing but this:

Each hour of the day, bring to your mind the thought with which the day began, and spend a quiet moment with it. Then repeat the two ideas you practice for the day unhurriedly, with time enough to see the gifts that they contain for you, and let them be received where they were meant to be.

We add no other thoughts, but let these be the messages they are. We need no more than this to give us happiness and rest, and endless quiet, perfect certainty, and all our Father wills that we receive as the inheritance we have of Him. Each day of practicing, as we review, we close as we began, repeating first the thought that made the day a special time of blessing and of happiness for us; and through our faithfulness restored the world from darkness to the light, from grief to joy, from pain to peace, from sin to holiness.

God offers thanks to you who practice thus the keeping of His Word. And as you give your mind to the ideas for the day again before you sleep, His gratitude surrounds you in the peace wherein He wills you be forever, and are learning now to claim again as your inheritance.

Lesson 141

My mind holds only what I think with God.

(121) Forgiveness is the key to happiness.

(122) Forgiveness offers everything I want.

Lesson 142

My mind holds only what I think with God.

(123) I thank my Father for His gifts to me.
(124) Let me remember I am one with God.

Lesson 143

My mind holds only what I think with God.

(125) In quiet I receive God's Word today.
(126) All that I give is given to myself.

Lesson 144

My mind holds only what I think with God.

(127) There is no love but God's.
(128) The world I see holds nothing that I want.

Lesson 145

My mind holds only what I think with God.

(129) Beyond this world there is a world I want.
(130) It is impossible to see two worlds.

Lesson 146

My mind holds only what I think with God.

(131) No one can fail who seeks to reach the truth.
(132) I loose the world from all I thought it was.

Lesson 147

My mind holds only what I think with God.

(133) I will not value what is valueless.
(134) Let me perceive forgiveness as it is.

Lesson 148

My mind holds only what I think with God.

(135) If I defend myself I am attacked.
(136) Sickness is a defense against the truth.

Lesson 149

My mind holds only what I think with God.

(137) When I am healed I am not healed alone.
(138) Heaven is the decision I must Make.

Lesson 150

My mind holds only what I think with God.

(139) I will accept Atonement for myself.
(140) Only salvation can be said to cure.

Lesson 151

All things are echoes of the Voice for God.

No one can judge on partial evidence. That is not judgment. It is merely an opinion based on ignorance and doubt. Its seeming certainty is but a cloak for the uncertainty it would conceal. It needs irrational defense because it is irrational. And its defense seems strong, convincing, and without a doubt because of all the doubting underneath.

You do not seem to doubt the world you see. You do not really question what is shown you through the body's eyes. Nor do you ask why you believe it, even though you learned a long while since your senses do deceive. That you believe them to the last detail which they report is even stranger, when you pause to recollect how frequently they have been faulty witnesses indeed! Why would you trust them so implicitly? Why but because of underlying doubt, which you would hide with show of certainty?

How can you judge? Your judgment rests upon the witness that your senses offer you. Yet witness never falser was than this. But how else do you judge the world you see? You place pathetic faith in what your eyes and ears report. You think your fingers touch reality, and close upon the truth. This is awareness that you understand, and think more real than what is witnessed to by the eternal Voice for God Himself.

Can this be judgment? You have often been urged to refrain from judging, not because it is a right to be withheld from you. You cannot judge. You merely can believe the ego's judgments, all of which are false. It guides your senses carefully, to prove how weak you are; how helpless and afraid, how apprehensive of just punishment, how black with sin, how wretched in your guilt.

This thing it speaks of, and would yet defend, it tells you is yourself. And you believe that this is so with stubborn certainty. Yet underneath remains the hidden doubt that what it shows you as reality with such conviction it does not believe. It is itself alone that it condemns. It is within itself it sees the guilt. It is its own despair it sees in you.

Hear not its voice. The witnesses it sends to prove to you its evil is your own are false, and speak with certainty of what they do not know. Your faith in them is blind because you would not share the doubts their lord can not completely vanquish. You believe to doubt his vassals is to doubt yourself.

Yet you must learn to doubt their evidence will clear the way to recognize yourself, and let the Voice for God alone be Judge of what is worthy of your own belief. He will not tell you that your brother should be judged by what your eyes behold in him, nor what his body's mouth says to your ears, nor what your fingers' touch reports of him. He passes by such idle witnesses, which merely bear false witness to God's Son. He recognizes only what God loves, and in the holy light of what He sees do all the ego's dreams of what you are vanish before the splendor He beholds.

Let Him be Judge of what you are, for He has certainty in which there is no doubt, because it rests on Certainty so great that doubt is meaningless before Its face. Christ cannot doubt Himself. The Voice for God can only honor Him, rejoicing in His perfect, everlasting sinlessness. Whom He has judged can only laugh at guilt, unwilling now to play with toys of sin; unheeding of the body's witnesses before the rapture of Christ's holy face.

And thus He judges you. Accept His Word for what you are, for He bears witness to your beautiful creation, and the Mind Whose Thought created your reality. What can the body mean to Him Who knows the glory of the Father and the Son? What whispers of the ego can He hear? What could convince Him that your sins are real? Let Him be Judge as well of everything that seems to happen to you in this world. His lessons will enable you to bridge the gap between illusions and the truth.

He will remove all faith that you have placed in pain, disaster, suffering and loss. He gives you vision which can look beyond these grim appearances, and can behold the gentle face of Christ in all of them. You will no longer doubt that only good can come to you who are beloved of God, for He will judge all happenings, and teach the single lesson that they all contain.

He will select the elements in them which represent the truth, and disregard those aspects which reflect but idle dreams. And He will reinterpret all you see, and all occurrences, each circumstance, and every happening that seems to touch on you in any way from His one frame of reference, wholly unified and sure. And you will see the love beyond the hate, the constancy in change, the pure in sin, and only Heaven's blessing on the world.

Such is your resurrection, for your life is not a part of anything you see. It stands beyond the body and the world, past every witness for unholiness, within the Holy, holy as Itself. In everyone and everything His Voice would speak to you of nothing but your Self and your Creator, Who is One with Him. So will you see the holy face of Christ in everything, and hear in everything no sound except the echo of God's Voice.

We practice wordlessly today, except at the beginning of the time we spend with God. We introduce these times with but a single, slow repeating of the thought with which the day begins. And then we watch our thoughts, appealing silently to Him Who sees the elements of truth in them. Let Him evaluate each thought that comes to mind, remove the elements of dreams, and give them back again as clean ideas that do not contradict the Will of God.

Give Him your thoughts, and He will give them back as miracles which joyously proclaim the wholeness and the happiness God wills His Son, as proof of His eternal Love. And as each thought is thus transformed, it takes on healing power from the Mind which saw the truth in it, and failed to be deceived by what was falsely added. All the threads of fantasy are gone. And what remains is unified into a perfect Thought that offers its perfection everywhere.

Spend fifteen minutes thus when you awake, and gladly give another fifteen more before you go to sleep. Your ministry begins as all your thoughts are purified. So are you taught to teach the Son of God the holy lesson of his sanctity. No one can fail to listen, when you hear the Voice for God give honor to God's Son. And everyone will share the thoughts with you which He has retranslated in your mind.

Such is your Eastertide. And so you lay the gift of snow-white lilies on the world, replacing witnesses to sin and death. Through your transfiguration is the world redeemed, and joyfully released from guilt. Now do we lift our resurrected minds in gladness and in gratitude to Him Who has restored our sanity to us.

And we will hourly remember Him Who is salvation and deliverance. As we give thanks, the world unites with us and happily accepts our holy thoughts, which Heaven has corrected and made pure. Now has our ministry begun at last, to carry round the world the joyous news that truth has no illusions, and the peace of God, through us, belongs to everyone.

Lesson 152

The power of decision is my own.

No one can suffer loss unless it be his own decision. No one suffers pain except his choice elects this state for him. No one can grieve nor fear nor think him sick unless these are the outcomes that he wants. And no one dies without his own consent. Nothing occurs but represents your wish, and nothing is omitted that you choose. Here is your world, complete in all details. Here is its whole reality for you. And it is only here salvation is.

You may believe that this position is extreme, and too inclusive to be true. Yet can truth have exceptions? If you have the gift of everything, can loss be real? Can pain be part of peace, or grief of joy? Can fear and sickness enter in a mind where love and perfect holiness abide? Truth must be all-inclusive, if it be the truth at all. Accept no opposites and no exceptions, for to do so is to contradict the truth entirely.

Salvation is the recognition that the truth is true, and nothing else is true. This you have heard before, but may not yet accept both parts of it. Without the first, the second has no meaning. But without the second, is the first no longer true. Truth cannot have an opposite. This can not be too often said and thought about. For if what is not true is true as well as what is true, then part of truth is false. And truth has lost its meaning. Nothing but the truth is true, and what is false is false.

This is the simplest of distinctions, yet the most obscure. But not because it is a difficult distinction to perceive. It is concealed behind a vast array of choices that do not appear to be entirely your own. And thus the truth appears to have some aspects that belie consistency, but do not seem to be but contradictions introduced by you.

As God created you, you must remain unchangeable, with transitory states by definition false. And that includes all shifts in feeling, alterations in conditions of the body and the mind; in all awareness and in all response. This is the all-inclusiveness which sets the truth apart from falsehood, and the false kept separate from the truth, as what it is.

Is it not strange that you believe to think you made the world you see is arrogance? God made it not. Of this you can be sure. What can He know of the ephemeral, the sinful and the guilty, the afraid, the suffering and lonely, and the mind that lives within a body that must die? You but accuse Him of insanity, to think He made a world where such things seem to have reality. He is not mad. Yet only madness makes a world like this.

To think that God made chaos, contradicts His Will, invented opposites to truth, and suffers death to triumph over life; all this is arrogance. Humility would see at once these things are not of Him. And can you see what God created not? To think you can is merely to believe you can perceive what God willed not to be. And what could be more arrogant than this?

Let us today be truly humble, and accept what we have made as what it is. The power of decision is our own. Decide but to accept your rightful place as co-creator of the universe, and all you think you made will disappear. What rises to awareness then will be all that there ever was, eternally as it is now. And it will take the place of self-deceptions made but to usurp the altar to the Father and the Son.

Today we practice true humility, abandoning the false pretense by which the ego seeks to prove it arrogant. Only the ego can be arrogant. But truth is humble in acknowledging its mightiness, its changelessness and its eternal wholeness, all-encompassing, God's perfect gift to His beloved Son. We lay aside the arrogance which says that we are sinners, guilty and afraid, ashamed of what we are; and lift our hearts in true humility instead to Him Who has created us immaculate, like to Himself in power and in love.

The power of decision is our own. And we accept of Him that which we are, and humbly recognize the Son of God. To recognize God's Son implies as well that all self-concepts have been laid aside, and recognized as false. Their arrogance has been perceived. And in humility the radiance of God's Son, his gentleness, his perfect sinlessness, his Father's Love, his right to Heaven and release from hell, are joyously accepted as our own.

Now do we join in glad acknowledgment that lies are false, and only truth is true. We think of truth alone as we arise, and spend five minutes practicing its ways, encouraging our frightened minds with this:

THE POWER OF DECISION IS MY OWN.
THIS DAY I WILL ACCEPT MYSELF AS WHAT
MY FATHER'S WILL CREATED ME TO BE.

Then will we wait in silence, giving up all self-deceptions, as we humbly ask our Self that He reveal Himself to us. And He Who never left will come again to our awareness, grateful to restore His home to God, as it was meant to be.

In patience wait for Him throughout the day, and hourly invite Him with the words with which the day began, concluding it with this same invitation to your Self. God's Voice will answer, for He speaks for you and for your Father. He will substitute the peace of God for all your frantic thoughts, the truth of God for self-deceptions, and God's Son for your illusions of yourself.

Lesson 153

In my defenselessness my safety lies.

You who feel threatened by this changing world, its twists of fortune and its bitter jests, its brief relationships and all the "gifts" it merely lends to take away again; attend this lesson well. The world provides no safety. It is rooted in attack, and all its "gifts" of seeming safety are illusory deceptions. It attacks, and then attacks again. No peace of mind is possible where danger threatens thus.

The world gives rise but to defensiveness. For threat brings anger, anger makes attack seem reasonable, honestly provoked, and righteous in the name of self-defense. Yet is defensiveness a double threat. For it attests to weakness, and sets up a system of defense that cannot work. Now are the weak still further undermined, for there is treachery without and still a greater treachery within. The mind is now confused, and knows not where to turn to find escape from its imaginings.

It is as if a circle held it fast, wherein another circle bound it and another one in that, until escape no longer can be hoped for nor obtained. Attack, defense; defense, attack, become the circles of the hours and the days that bind the mind in heavy bands of steel with iron overlaid, returning but to start again. There seems to be no break nor ending in the ever-tightening grip of the imprisonment upon the mind.

Defenses are the costliest of all the prices which the ego would exact. In them lies madness in a form so grim that hope of sanity seems but to be an idle dream, beyond the possible. The sense of threat the world encourages is so much deeper, and so far beyond the frenzy and intensity of which you can conceive, that you have no idea of all the devastation it has wrought.

You are its slave. You know not what you do, in fear of it. You do not understand how much you have been made to sacrifice, who feel its iron grip upon your heart. You do not realize what you have done to sabotage the holy peace of

God by your defensiveness. For you behold the Son of God as but a victim to attack by fantasies, by dreams, and by illusions he has made; yet helpless in their presence, needful only of defense by still more fantasies, and dreams by which illusions of his safety comfort him.

Defenselessness is strength. It testifies to recognition of the Christ in you. Perhaps you will recall the text maintains that choice is always made between Christ's strength and your own weakness, seen apart from Him. Defenselessness can never be attacked, because it recognizes strength so great attack is folly, or a silly game a tired child might play, when he becomes too sleepy to remember what he wants.

Defensiveness is weakness. It proclaims you have denied the Christ and come to fear His Father's anger. What can save you now from your delusion of an angry god, whose fearful image you believe you see at work in all the evils of the world? What but illusions could defend you now, when it is but illusions that you fight?

We will not play such childish games today. For our true purpose is to save the world, and we would not exchange for foolishness the endless joy our function offers us. We would not let our happiness slip by because a fragment of a senseless dream happened to cross our minds, and we mistook the figures in it for the Son of God; its tiny instant for eternity.

We look past dreams today, and recognize that we need no defense because we are created unassailable, without all thought or wish or dream in which attack has any meaning. Now we cannot fear, for we have left all fearful thoughts behind. And in defenselessness we stand secure, serenely certain of our safety now, sure of salvation; sure we will fulfill our chosen purpose, as our ministry extends its holy blessing through the world.

Be still a moment, and in silence think how holy is your purpose, how secure you rest, untouchable within its light. God's ministers have chosen that the truth be with them. Who is holier than they? Who could be surer that his happiness is fully guaranteed? And who could be more mightily protected? What defense could possibly be needed by the ones who are among the chosen ones of God, by His election and their own as well?

It is the function of God's ministers to help their brothers choose as they have done. God has elected all, but few have come to realize His Will is but their own. And while you fail to teach what you have learned, salvation waits and darkness holds the world in grim imprisonment. Nor will you learn that light has come to you, and your escape has been accomplished. For you will not see the light, until you offer it to all your brothers. As they take it from your hands, so will you recognize it as your own.

Salvation can be thought of as a game that happy children play. It was designed by One Who loves His children, and Who would replace their fearful toys with joyous games, which teach them that the game of fear is gone. His game instructs in happiness because there is no loser. Everyone who plays must win, and in his winning is the gain to everyone ensured. The game of fear is gladly laid aside, when children come to see the benefits salvation brings.

You who have played that you are lost to hope, abandoned by your Father, left alone in terror in a fearful world made mad by sin and guilt; be happy now. That game is over. Now a quiet time has come, in which we put away the toys of guilt, and lock our quaint and childish thoughts of sin forever from the pure and holy minds of Heaven's children and the Son of God.

We pause but for a moment more, to play our final, happy game upon this earth. And then we go to take our rightful place where truth abides and games are meaningless. So is the story ended. Let this day bring the last chapter closer to the world, that everyone may learn the tale he reads of terrifying destiny, defeat of all his hopes, his pitiful defense against a vengeance he can not escape, is but his own deluded fantasy. God's ministers have come to waken him from the dark dreams this story has evoked in his confused, bewildered memory of this distorted tale. God's Son can smile at last, on learning that it is not true.

Today we practice in a form we will maintain for quite a while. We will begin each day by giving our attention to the daily thought as long as possible. Five minutes now becomes the least we give to preparation for a day in which salvation is the only goal we have. Ten would be better; fifteen better still. And as distraction ceases to arise to turn us from our purpose, we will find that half an hour is too short a time to spend with God. Nor will we willingly give less at night, in gratitude and joy.

Each hour adds to our increasing peace, as we remember to be faithful to the Will we share with God. At times, perhaps, a minute, even less, will be the most that we can offer as the hour strikes. Sometimes we will forget. At other times the business of the world will close on us, and we will be unable to withdraw a little while, and turn our thoughts to God.

Yet when we can, we will observe our trust as ministers of God, in hourly remembrance of our mission and His Love. And we will quietly sit by and wait on Him and listen to His Voice, and learn what He would have us do the hour that is yet to come; while thanking Him for all the gifts He gave us in the one gone by.

In time, with practice, you will never cease to think of Him, and hear His loving Voice guiding your footsteps into quiet ways, where you will walk in true defenselessness. For you will know that Heaven goes with you. Nor would you keep your mind away from Him a moment, even though your time is spent in offering salvation to the world. Think you He will not make this possible, for you who chose to carry out His plan for the salvation of the world and yours?

Today our theme is our defenselessness. We clothe ourselves in it, as we prepare to meet the day. We rise up strong in Christ, and let our weakness disappear, as we remember that His strength abides in us. We will remind ourselves that He remains beside us through the day, and never leaves our weakness unsupported by His strength. We call upon His strength each time we feel the threat of our defenses undermine our certainty of purpose. We will pause a moment, as He tells us, "I am here."

Your practicing will now begin to take the earnestness of love, to help you keep your mind from wandering from its intent. Be not afraid nor timid. There can be no doubt that you will reach your final goal. The ministers of God can never fail, because the love and strength and peace that shine from them to all their brothers come from Him. These are His gifts to you. Defenselessness is all you need to give Him in return. You lay aside but what was never real, to look on Christ and see His sinlessness.

Lesson 154

I am among the ministers of God.

Let us today be neither arrogant nor falsely humble. We have gone beyond such foolishness. We cannot judge ourselves, nor need we do so. These are but attempts to hold decision off, and to delay commitment to our function. It is not our part to judge our worth, nor can we know what role is best for us; what we can do within a larger plan we cannot see in its entirety. Our part is cast in Heaven, not in hell. And what we think is weakness can be strength; what we believe to be our strength is often arrogance.

Whatever your appointed role may be, it was selected by the Voice for God, Whose function is to speak for you as well. Seeing your strengths exactly as they are, and equally aware of where they can be best applied, for what, to whom and when, He chooses and accepts your part for you. He does not work without your own consent. But He is not deceived in what you are, and listens only to His Voice in you.

It is through His ability to hear one Voice which is His Own that you become aware at last there is one Voice in you. And that one Voice appoints your function, and relays it to you, giving you the strength to understand it, do what it entails, and to succeed in everything you do that is related to it. God has joined His Son in this, and thus His Son becomes His messenger of unity with Him.

It is this joining, through the Voice for God, of Father and of Son, that sets apart salvation from the world. It is this Voice which speaks of laws the world does not obey; which promises salvation from all sin, with guilt abolished in the mind that God created sinless. Now this mind becomes aware again of Who created it, and of His lasting union with itself. So is its Self the one reality in which its will and that of God are joined.

A messenger is not the one who writes the message he delivers. Nor does he question the right of him who does, nor ask why he has chosen those who will receive the message that he brings. It is enough that he accept it, give it to the ones for whom it is intended, and fulfill his role in its delivery. If he determines what the messages should be, or what their purpose is, or where they should be carried, he is failing to perform his proper part as bringer of the Word.

There is one major difference in the role of Heaven's messengers, which sets them off from those the world appoints. The messages that they deliver are intended first for them. And it is only as they can accept them for themselves that they become able to bring them further, and to give them everywhere that they were meant to be. Like earthly messengers, they did not write the messages they bear, but they become their first receivers in the truest sense, receiving to prepare themselves to give.

An earthly messenger fulfills his role by giving all his messages away. The messengers of God perform their part by their acceptance of His messages as for themselves, and show they understand the messages by giving them away. They choose no roles that are not given them by His authority. And so they gain by every message that they give away.

Would you receive the messages of God? For thus do you become His messenger. You are appointed now. And yet you wait to give the messages you have received. And so you do not know that they are yours, and do not recognize them. No one can receive and understand he has received until he gives. For in the giving is his own acceptance of what he received.

You who are now the messenger of God, receive His messages. For that is part of your appointed role. God has not failed to offer what you need, nor has it been left unaccepted. Yet another part of your appointed task is yet to be accomplished. He Who has received for you the messages of God would have them be received by you as well. For thus do you identify with Him and claim your own.

It is this joining that we undertake to recognize today. We will not seek to keep our minds apart from Him Who speaks for us, for it is but our voice we hear as we attend Him. He alone can speak to us and for us, joining in one Voice the getting and the giving of God's Word; the giving and receiving of His Will.

We practice giving Him what He would have, that we may recognize His gifts to us. He needs our voice that He may speak through us. He needs our hands to hold His messages, and carry them to those whom He appoints. He needs our feet to bring us where He wills, that those who wait in misery may be at last delivered. And He needs our will united with His Own, that we may be the true receivers of the gifts He gives.

Let us but learn this lesson for today: We will not recognize what we receive until we give it. You have heard this said a hundred ways, a hundred times, and yet belief is lacking still. But this is sure; until belief is given it, you will receive a thousand miracles and then receive a thousand more, but will not know that God Himself has left no gift beyond what you already have; nor has denied the tiniest of blessings to His Son. What can this mean to you, until you have identified with Him and with His Own?

Our lesson for today is stated thus:

I AM AMONG THE MINISTERS OF GOD, AND I AM GRATEFUL THAT
I HAVE THE MEANS BY WHICH TO RECOGNIZE THAT I AM FREE.

The world recedes as we light up our minds, and realize these holy words are true. They are the message sent to us today from our Creator. Now we demonstrate how they have changed our minds about ourselves, and what our function is. For as we prove that we accept no will we do not share, our many gifts from our Creator will spring to our sight and leap into our hands, and we will recognize what we received.

Lesson 155

I will step back and let Him lead the way.

There is a way of living in the world that is not here, although it seems to be. You do not change appearance, though you smile more frequently. Your forehead is serene; your eyes are quiet. And the ones who walk the world as you do recognize their own. Yet those who have not yet perceived the way will recognize you also, and believe that you are like them, as you were before.

The world is an illusion. Those who choose to come to it are seeking for a place where they can be illusions, and avoid their own reality. Yet when they find their own reality is even here, then they step back and let it lead the way. What other choice is really theirs to make? To let illusions walk ahead of truth is madness. But to let illusion sink behind the truth and let the truth stand forth as what it is, is merely sanity.

This is the simple choice we make today. The mad illusion will remain awhile in evidence, for those to look upon who chose to come, and have not yet rejoiced to find they were mistaken in their choice. They cannot learn directly from the truth, because they have denied that it is so. And so they need a Teacher Who perceives their madness, but Who still can look beyond illusion to the simple truth in them.

If truth demanded they give up the world, it would appear to them as if it asked the sacrifice of something that is real. Many have chosen to renounce the world while still believing its reality. And they have suffered from a sense of loss, and have not been released accordingly. Others have chosen nothing but the world, and they have suffered from a sense of loss still deeper, which they did not understand.

Between these paths there is another road that leads away from loss of every kind, for sacrifice and deprivation both are quickly left behind. This is the way appointed for you now. You walk this path as others walk, nor do you seem to be distinct from them, although you are indeed. Thus can you serve them while you serve yourself, and set their footsteps on the way that God has opened up to you, and them through you.

Illusion still appears to cling to you, that you may reach them. Yet it has stepped back. And it is not illusion that they hear you speak of, nor illusion that you bring their eyes to look on and their minds to grasp. Nor can the truth, which walks ahead of you, speak to them through illusions, for the road leads past illusion now, while on the way you call to them, that they may follow you.

All roads will lead to this one in the end. For sacrifice and deprivation are paths that lead nowhere, choices for defeat, and aims that will remain impossible. All this steps back as truth comes forth in you, to lead your brothers from the ways of death, and set them on the way to happiness. Their suffering is but illusion. Yet they need a guide to lead them out of it, for they mistake illusion for the truth.

Such is salvation's call, and nothing more. It asks that you accept the truth, and let it go before you, lighting up the path of ransom from illusion. It is not a ransom with a price. There is no cost, but only gain. Illusion can but seem to hold in chains the holy Son of God. It is but from illusions he is saved. As they step back, he finds himself again.

Walk safely now, yet carefully, because this path is new to you. And you may find that you are tempted still to walk ahead of truth, and let illusions be your guide. Your holy brothers have been given you, to follow in your footsteps as you walk with certainty of purpose to the truth. It goes before you now, that they may see something with which they can identify; something they understand to lead the way.

Yet at the journey's ending there will be no gap, no distance between truth and you. And all illusions walking in the way you travelled will be gone from you as well, with nothing left to keep the truth apart from God's completion, holy as Himself. Step back in faith and let truth lead the way. You know not where you go. But One Who knows goes with you. Let Him lead you with the rest.

When dreams are over, time has closed the door on all the things that pass and miracles are purposeless, the holy Son of God will make no journeys. There will be no wish to be illusion rather than the truth. And we step forth toward this, as we progress along the way that truth points out to us. This is our final journey, which we make for everyone. We must not lose our way. For as truth goes before us, so it goes before our brothers who will follow us.

We walk to God. Pause and reflect on this. Could any way be holier, or more deserving of your effort, of your love and of your full intent? What way could give you more than everything, or offer less and still content the holy Son of God? We walk to God. The truth that walks before us now is one with Him, and leads us to where He has always been. What way but this could be a path that you would choose instead?

Your feet are safely set upon the road that leads the world to God. Look not to ways that seem to lead you elsewhere. Dreams are not a worthy guide for you who are God's Son. Forget not He has placed His Hand in yours, and given you your brothers in His trust that you are worthy of His trust in you. He cannot be deceived. His trust has made your pathway certain and your goal secure. You will not fail your brothers nor your Self.

And now He asks but that you think of Him a while each day, that He may speak to you and tell you of His Love, reminding you how great His trust; how limitless His Love. In your Name and His Own, which are the same, we practice gladly with this thought today:

I WILL STEP BACK AND LET HIM LEAD THE WAY,
FOR I WOULD WALK ALONG THE ROAD TO HIM.

Lesson 156

I walk with God in perfect holiness.

Today's idea but states the simple truth that makes the thought of sin impossible. It promises there is no cause for guilt, and being causeless it does not exist. It follows surely from the basic thought so often mentioned in the text; ideas leave not their source. If this be true, how can you be apart from God? How could you walk the world alone and separate from your Source?

We are not inconsistent in the thoughts that we present in our curriculum. Truth must be true throughout, if it be true. It cannot contradict itself, nor be in parts uncertain and in others sure. You cannot walk the world apart from God, because you could not be without Him. He is what your life is. Where you are He is. There is one life. That life you share with Him. Nothing can be apart from Him and live.

Yet where He is, there must be holiness as well as life. No attribute of His remains unshared by everything that lives. What lives is holy as Himself, because what shares His life is part of Holiness, and could no more be sinful than the sun could choose to be of ice; the sea elect to be apart from water, or the grass to grow with roots suspended in the air.

There is a light in you which cannot die; whose presence is so holy that the world is sanctified because of you. All things that live bring gifts to you, and offer them in gratitude and gladness at your feet. The scent of flowers is their gift to you. The waves bow down before you, and the trees extend their arms to shield you from the heat, and lay their leaves before you on the ground that you may walk in softness, while the wind sinks to a whisper round your holy head.

The light in you is what the universe longs to behold. All living things are still before you, for they recognize Who walks with you. The light you carry is their own. And thus they see in you their holiness, saluting you as savior and as God. Accept their reverence, for it is due to Holiness Itself, which walks with you, transforming in Its gentle light all things unto Its likeness and Its purity.

This is the way salvation works. As you step back, the light in you steps forward and encompasses the world. It heralds not the end of sin in punishment and death. In lightness and in laughter is sin gone, because its quaint absurdity is seen. It is a foolish thought, a silly dream, not frightening, ridiculous perhaps, but who would waste an instant in approach to God Himself for such a senseless whim?

Yet you have wasted many, many years on just this foolish thought. The past is gone, with all its fantasies. They keep you bound no longer. The approach to God is near. And in the little interval of doubt that still remains, you may perhaps lose sight of your Companion, and mistake Him for the senseless, ancient dream that now is past.

"Who walks with me?" This question should be asked a thousand times a day, till certainty has ended doubting and established peace. Today let doubting cease. God speaks for you in answering your question with these words:

I WALK WITH GOD IN PERFECT HOLINESS. I LIGHT THE WORLD,
I LIGHT MY MIND AND ALL THE MINDS WHICH GOD CREATED
ONE WITH ME.

Lesson 157

Into His Presence would I enter now.

This is a day of silence and of trust. It is a special time of promise in your calendar of days. It is a time Heaven has set apart to shine upon, and cast a timeless light upon this day, when echoes of eternity are heard. This day is holy, for it ushers in a new experience; a different kind of feeling and awareness. You have spent long days and nights in celebrating death. Today you learn to feel the joy of life.

This is another crucial turning point in the curriculum. We add a new dimension now; a fresh experience that sheds a light on all that we have learned already, and prepares us for what we have yet to learn. It brings us to the door where learning ceases, and we catch a glimpse of what lies past the highest reaches it can possibly attain. It leaves us here an instant, and we go beyond it, sure of our direction and our only goal.

Today it will be given you to feel a touch of Heaven, though you will return to paths of learning. Yet you have come far enough along the way to alter time sufficiently to rise above its laws, and walk into eternity a while. This you will learn to do increasingly, as every lesson, faithfully rehearsed, brings you more swiftly to this holy place and leaves you, for a moment, to your Self.

He will direct your practicing today, for what you ask for now is what He wills. And having joined your will with His this day, what you are asking must be given you. Nothing is needed but today's idea to light your mind, and let it rest in still anticipation and in quiet joy, wherein you quickly leave the world behind.

From this day forth, your ministry takes on a genuine devotion, and a glow that travels from your fingertips to those you touch, and blesses those you look upon. A vision reaches everyone you meet, and everyone you think of, or who thinks of you. For your experience today will so transform your mind that it becomes the touchstone for the holy Thoughts of God.

Your body will be sanctified today, its only purpose being now to bring the vision of what you experience this day to light the world. We cannot give experience like this directly. Yet it leaves a vision in our eyes which we can offer everyone, that he may come the sooner to the same experience in which the world is quietly forgot, and Heaven is remembered for a while.

As this experience increases and all goals but this become of little worth, the world to which you will return becomes a little closer to the end of time; a little more like Heaven in its ways; a little nearer its deliverance. And you who bring it light will come to see the light more sure; the vision more distinct. The time will come when you will not return in the same form in which you now appear, for you will have no need of it. Yet now it has a purpose, and will serve it well.

Today we will embark upon a course you have not dreamed of. But the Holy One, the Giver of the happy dreams of life, Translator of perception into truth, the holy Guide to Heaven given you, has dreamed for you this journey which you make and start today, with the experience this day holds out to you to be your own.

Into Christ's Presence will we enter now, serenely unaware of everything except His shining face and perfect Love. The vision of His face will stay with you, but there will be an instant which transcends all vision, even this, the holiest. This you will never teach, for you attained it not through learning. Yet the vision speaks of your rememberance of what you knew that instant, and will surely know again.

Lesson 158

Today I learn to give as I receive.

What has been given you? The knowledge that you are a mind, in Mind and purely mind, sinless forever, wholly unafraid, because you were created out of love. Nor have you left your Source, remaining as you were created. This was given you as knowledge which you cannot lose. It was given as well to every living thing, for by that knowledge only does it live.

You have received all this. No one who walks the world but has received it. It is not this knowledge which you give, for that is what creation gave. All this cannot be learned. What, then, are you to learn to give today? Our lesson yesterday evoked a theme found early in the text. Experience cannot be shared directly, in the way that vision can. The revelation that the Father and the Son are one will come in time to every mind. Yet is that time determined by the mind itself, not taught.

The time is set already. It appears to be quite arbitrary. Yet there is no step along the road that anyone takes but by chance. It has already been taken by him, although he has not yet embarked on it. For time but seems to go in one direction. We but undertake a journey that is over. Yet it seems to have a future still unknown to us.

Time is a trick, a sleight of hand, a vast illusion in which figures come and go as if by magic. Yet there is a plan behind appearances that does not change. The script is written. When experience will come to end your doubting has been set. For we but see the journey from the point at which it ended, looking back on it, imagining we make it once again; reviewing mentally what has gone by.

A teacher does not give experience, because he did not learn it. It revealed itself to him at its appointed time. But vision is his gift. This he can give directly, for Christ's knowledge is not lost, because He has a vision He can give to anyone who asks. The Father's Will and His are joined in knowledge. Yet there is a vision which the Holy Spirit sees because the Mind of Christ beholds it too.

Here is the joining of the world of doubt and shadows made with the intangible. Here is a quiet place within the world made holy by forgiveness and by love. Here are all contradictions reconciled, for here the journey ends. Experience—unlearned, untaught, unseen—is merely there. This is beyond our goal, for it transcends what needs to be accomplished. Our concern is with Christ's vision. This we can attain.

Christ's vision has one law. It does not look upon a body, and mistake it for the Son whom God created. It beholds a light beyond the body; an idea beyond what can be touched, a purity undimmed by errors, pitiful mistakes, and fearful thoughts of guilt from dreams of sin. It sees no separation. And it looks on everyone, on every circumstance, all happenings and all events, without the slightest fading of the light it sees.

This can be taught; and must be taught by all who would achieve it. It requires but the recognition that the world can not give anything that faintly can compare with this in value; nor set up a goal that does not merely disappear when this has been perceived. And this you give today: See no one as a body. Greet him as the Son of God he is, acknowledging that he is one with you in holiness.

Thus are his sins forgiven him, for Christ has vision that has power to overlook them all. In His forgiveness are they gone. Unseen by One they merely disappear, because a vision of the holiness that lies beyond them comes to take their place. It matters not what form they took, nor how enormous they appeared to be, nor who seemed to be hurt by them. They are no more. And all effects they seemed to have are gone with them, undone and never to be done.

Thus do you learn to give as you receive. And thus Christ's vision looks on you as well. This lesson is not difficult to learn, if you remember in your brother you but see yourself. If he be lost in sin, so must you be; if you see light in him, your sins have been forgiven by yourself. Each brother whom you meet today provides another chance to let Christ's vision shine on you, and offer you the peace of God.

It matters not when revelation comes, for that is not of time. Yet time has still one gift to give, in which true knowledge is reflected in a way so accurate its image shares its unseen holiness; its likeness shines with its immortal love. We practice seeing with the eyes of Christ today. And by the holy gifts we give, Christ's vision looks upon ourselves as well.

Lesson 159

I give the miracles I have received.

No one can give what he has not received. To give a thing requires first you have it in your own possession. Here the laws of Heaven and the world agree. But here they also separate. The world believes that to possess a thing, it must be kept. Salvation teaches otherwise. To give is how to recognize you have received. It is the proof that what you have is yours.

You understand that you are healed when you give healing. You accept forgiveness as accomplished in yourself when you forgive. You recognize your brother as yourself, and thus do you perceive that you are whole. There is no miracle you cannot give, for all are given you. Receive them now by opening the storehouse of your mind where they are laid, and giving them away.

Christ's vision is a miracle. It comes from far beyond itself, for it reflects eternal love and the rebirth of love which never dies, but has been kept obscure. Christ's vision pictures Heaven, for it sees a world so like to Heaven that what God created perfect can be mirrored there. The darkened glass the world presents can show but twisted images in broken parts. The real world pictures Heaven's innocence.

Christ's vision is the miracle in which all miracles are born. It is their source, remaining with each miracle you give, and yet remaining yours. It is the bond by which the giver and receiver are united in extension here on earth, as they are one in Heaven. Christ beholds no sin in anyone. And in His sight the sinless are as one. Their holiness was given by His Father and Himself.

Christ's vision is the bridge between the worlds. And in its power can you safely trust to carry you from this world into one made holy by forgiveness. Things which seem quite solid here are merely shadows there; transparent, faintly seen, at times forgot, and never able to obscure the light that shines beyond them. Holiness has been restored to vision, and the blind can see.

This is the Holy Spirit's single gift; the treasure house to which you can appeal with perfect certainty for all the things that can contribute to your happiness. All are laid here already. All can be received but for the asking. Here the door is never locked, and no one is denied his least request or his most urgent need. There is no sickness not already healed, no lack unsatisfied, no need unmet within this golden treasury of Christ.

Here does the world remember what was lost when it was made. For here it is repaired, made new again, but in a different light. What was to be the home of sin becomes the center of redemption and the hearth of mercy, where the suffering are healed and welcome. No one will be turned away from this new home, where his salvation waits. No one is stranger to him. No one asks for anything of him except the gift of his acceptance of his welcoming.

Christ's vision is the holy ground in which the lilies of forgiveness set their roots. This is their home. They can be brought from here back to the world, but they can never grow in its unnourishing and shallow soil. They need the light and warmth and kindly care Christ's charity provides. They need the love with which He looks on them. And they become His messengers, who give as they received.

Take from His storehouse, that its treasures may increase. His lilies do not leave their home when they are carried back into the world. Their roots remain. They do not leave their source, but carry its beneficence with them, and turn the world into a garden like the one they came from, and to which they go again with added fragrance. Now are they twice blessed. The messages they brought from Christ have been delivered, and returned to them. And they return them gladly unto Him.

Behold the store of miracles set out for you to give. Are you not worth the gift, when God appointed it be given you? Judge not God's Son, but follow in the way He has established. Christ has dreamed the dream of a forgiven world. It is His gift, whereby a sweet transition can be made from death to life; from hopelessness to hope. Let us an instant dream with Him. His dream awakens us to truth. His vision gives the means for a return to our unlost and everlasting sanctity in God.

Lesson 160

I am at home. Fear is the stranger here.

Fear is a stranger to the ways of love. Identify with fear, and you will be a stranger to yourself. And thus you are unknown to you. What is your Self remains an alien to the part of you which thinks that it is real, but different from yourself. Who could be sane in such a circumstance? Who but a madman could believe he is what he is not, and judge against himself?

There is a stranger in our midst, who comes from an idea so foreign to the truth he speaks a different language, looks upon a world truth does not know, and understands what truth regards as senseless. Stranger yet, he does not recognize to whom he comes, and yet maintains his home belongs to him, while he is alien now who is at home. And yet, how easy it would be to say, "This is my home. Here I belong, and will not leave because a madman says I must."

What reason is there for not saying this? What could the reason be except that you had asked this stranger in to take your place, and let you be a stranger to yourself? No one would let himself be dispossessed so needlessly, unless he thought there were another home more suited to his tastes.

Who is the stranger? Is it fear or you who are unsuited to the home which God provided for His Son? Is fear His Own, created in His likeness? Is it fear that love completes, and is completed by? There is no home can shelter love and fear. They cannot coexist. If you are real, then fear must be illusion. And if fear is real, then you do not exist at all.

How simply, then, the question is resolved. Who fears has but denied himself and said, "I am the stranger here. And so I leave my home to one more like me than myself, and give him all I thought belonged to me." Now is he exiled of necessity, not knowing who he is, uncertain of all things but this; that he is not himself, and that his home has been denied to him.

What does he search for now? What can he find? A stranger to himself can find no home wherever he may look, for he has made return impossible. His way is lost, except a miracle will search him out and show him that he is no stranger now. The miracle will come. For in his home his Self remains. It asked no stranger in, and took no alien thought to be Itself. And It will call Its Own unto Itself in recognition of what is Its Own.

Who is the stranger? Is he not the one your Self calls not? You are unable now to recognize this stranger in your midst, for you have given him your rightful place. Yet is your Self as certain of Its Own as God is of His Son. He cannot be confused about creation. He is sure of what belongs to Him. No stranger can be interposed between His knowledge and His Son's reality. He does not know of strangers. He is certain of His Son.

God's certainty suffices. Who He knows to be His Son belongs where He has set His Son forever. He has answered you who ask, "Who is the stranger?" Hear His Voice assure you, quietly and sure, that you are not a stranger to your Father, nor is your Creator stranger made to you. Whom God has joined remain forever one, at home in Him, no stranger to Himself.

Today we offer thanks that Christ has come to search the world for what belongs to Him. His vision sees no strangers, but beholds His Own and joyously unites with them. They see Him as a stranger, for they do not recognize themselves. Yet as they give Him welcome, they remember. And He leads them gently home again, where they belong.

Not one does Christ forget. Not one He fails to give you to remember, that your home may be complete and perfect as it was established. He has not forgotten you. But you will not remember Him until you look on all as He does. Who denies his brother is denying Him, and thus refusing to accept the gift of sight by which his Self is clearly recognized, his home remembered and salvation come.

Lesson 161

Give me your blessing, holy Son of God.

Today we practice differently, and take a stand against our anger, that our fears may disappear and offer room to love. Here is salvation in the simple words in which we practice with today's idea. Here is the answer to temptation which can never fail to welcome in the Christ where fear and anger had prevailed before. Here is Atonement made complete, the world passed safely by and Heaven now restored. Here is the answer of the Voice for God.

Complete abstraction is the natural condition of the mind. But part of it is now unnatural. It does not look on everything as one. It sees instead but fragments of the whole, for only thus could it invent the partial world you see. The purpose of all seeing is to show you what you wish to see. All hearing but brings to your mind the sounds it wants to hear.

Thus were specifics made. And now it is specifics we must use in practicing. We give them to the Holy Spirit, that He may employ them for a purpose which is different from the one we gave to them. Yet He can use but what we made, to teach us from a different point of view, so we can see a different use in everything.

One brother is all brothers. Every mind contains all minds, for every mind is one. Such is the truth. Yet do these thoughts make clear the meaning of creation? Do these words bring perfect clarity with them to you? What can they seem to be but empty sounds; pretty, perhaps, correct in sentiment, yet fundamentally not understood nor understandable. The mind that taught itself to think specifically can no longer grasp abstraction in the sense that it is all-encompassing. We need to see a little, that we learn a lot.

It seems to be the body that we feel limits our freedom, makes us suffer, and at last puts out our life. Yet bodies are but symbols for a concrete form of fear. Fear without symbols calls for no response, for symbols can stand for the meaningless. Love needs no symbols, being true. But fear attaches to specifics, being false.

Bodies attack, but minds do not. This thought is surely reminiscent of our text, where it is often emphasized. This is the reason bodies easily become fear's symbols. You have many times been urged to look beyond the body, for its sight presents the symbol of love's "enemy" Christ's vision does not see. The body is the target for attack, for no one thinks he hates a mind. Yet what but mind directs the body to attack? What else could be the seat of fear except what thinks of fear?

Hate is specific. There must be a thing to be attacked. An enemy must be perceived in such a form he can be touched and seen and heard, and ultimately killed. When hatred rests upon a thing, it calls for death as surely as God's Voice proclaims there is no death. Fear is insatiable, consuming everything its eyes behold, seeing itself in everything, compelled to turn upon itself and to destroy.

Who sees a brother as a body sees him as fear's symbol. And he will attack, because what he beholds is his own fear external to himself, poised to attack, and howling to unite with him again. Mistake not the intensity of rage projected fear must spawn. It shrieks in wrath, and claws the air in frantic hope it can reach to its maker and devour him.

This do the body's eyes behold in one whom Heaven cherishes, the angels love and God created perfect. This is his reality. And in Christ's vision is his loveliness reflected in a form so holy and so beautiful that you could scarce refrain from kneeling at his feet. Yet you will take his hand instead, for you are like him in the sight that sees him thus. Attack on him is enemy to you, for you will not perceive that in his hands is your salvation. Ask him but for this, and he will give it to you. Ask him not to symbolize your fear. Would you request that love destroy itself? Or would you have it be revealed to you and set you free?

Today we practice in a form we have attempted earlier. Your readiness is closer now, and you will come today nearer Christ's vision. If you are intent on reaching it, you will succeed today. And once you have succeeded, you will not be willing to accept the witnesses your body's eyes call forth. What you will see will sing to you of ancient melodies you will remember. You are not forgot in Heaven. Would you not remember it?

Select one brother, symbol of the rest, and ask salvation of him. See him first as clearly as you can, in that same form to which you are accustomed. See his face, his hands and feet, his clothing. Watch him smile, and see familiar gestures which he makes so frequently. Then think of this: What you are seeing now conceals from you the sight of one who can forgive you all your sins; whose sacred hands can take away the nails which pierce your own, and lift the crown of thorns which you have placed upon your bleeding head. Ask this of him, that he may set you free:

GIVE ME YOUR BLESSING, HOLY SON OF GOD.
I WOULD BEHOLD YOU WITH THE EYES OF CHRIST,
AND SEE MY PERFECT SINLESSNESS IN YOU.

And He will answer Whom you called upon. For He will hear the Voice for God in you, and answer in your own. Behold him now, whom you have seen as merely flesh and bone, and recognize that Christ has come to you. Today's idea is your safe escape from anger and from fear. Be sure you use it instantly, should you be tempted to attack a brother and perceive in him the symbol of your fear. And you will see him suddenly transformed from enemy to savior; from the devil into Christ.

Lesson 162

I am as God created me.

This single thought, held firmly in the mind, would save the world. From time to time we will repeat it, as we reach another stage in learning. It will mean far more to you as you advance. These words are sacred, for they are the words God gave in answer to the world you made. By them it disappears, and all things seen within its misty clouds and vaporous illusions vanish as these words are spoken. For they come from God.

Here is the Word by which the Son became his Father's happiness, His Love and His completion. Here creation is proclaimed, and honored as it is. There is no dream these words will not dispel; no thought of sin and no illusion which the dream contains that will not fade away before their might. They are the trumpet of awakening that sounds around the world. The dead awake in answer to its call. And those who live and hear this sound will never look on death.

Holy indeed is he who makes these words his own; arising with them in his mind, recalling them throughout the day, at night bringing them with him as he goes to sleep. His dreams are happy and his rest secure, his safety certain and his body healed, because he sleeps and wakens with the truth before him always. He will save the world, because he gives the world what he receives each time he practices the words of truth.

Today we practice simply. For the words we use are mighty, and they need no thoughts beyond themselves to change the mind of him who uses them. So wholly is it changed that it is now the treasury in which God places all His gifts and all His Love, to be distributed to all the world, increased in giving; kept complete because its sharing is unlimited. And thus you learn to think with God. Christ's vision has restored your sight by salvaging your mind.

We honor you today. Yours is the right to perfect holiness you now accept. With this acceptance is salvation brought to everyone, for who could cherish sin when holiness like this has blessed the world? Who could despair when perfect joy is yours, available to all as remedy for grief and misery, all sense of loss, and for complete escape from sin and guilt?

And who would not be brother to you now; you, his redeemer and his savior. Who could fail to welcome you into his heart with loving invitation, eager to unite with one like him in holiness? You are as God created you. These words dispel the night, and darkness is no more. The light is come today to bless the world. For you have recognized the Son of God, and in that recognition is the world's.

Lesson 163

There is no death. The Son of God is free.

Death is a thought that takes on many forms, often unrecognized. It may appear as sadness, fear, anxiety or doubt; as anger, faithlessness and lack of trust; concern for bodies, envy, and all forms in which the wish to be as you are not may come to tempt you. All such thoughts are but reflections of the worshipping of death as savior and as giver of release.

Embodiment of fear, the host of sin, god of the guilty and the lord of all illusions and deceptions, does the thought of death seem mighty. For it seems to hold all living things within its withered hand; all hopes and wishes in its blighting grasp; all goals perceived but in its sightless eyes. The frail, the helpless and the sick bow down before its image, thinking it alone is real, inevitable, worthy of their trust. For it alone will surely come.

All things but death are seen to be unsure, too quickly lost however hard to gain, uncertain in their outcome, apt to fail the hopes they once engendered, and to leave the taste of dust and ashes in their wake, in place of aspirations and of dreams. But death is counted on. For it will come with certain footsteps when the time has come for its arrival. It will never fail to take all life as hostage to itself.

Would you bow down to idols such as this? Here is the strength and might of God Himself perceived within an idol made of dust. Here is the opposite of God proclaimed as lord of all creation, stronger than God's Will for life, the endlessness of love and Heaven's perfect, changeless constancy. Here is the Will of Father and of Son defeated finally, and laid to rest beneath the headstone death has placed upon the body of the holy Son of God.

Unholy in defeat, he has become what death would have him be. His epitaph, which death itself has written, gives no name to him, for he has passed to dust. It says but this: "Here lies a witness God is dead." And this it writes again and still again, while all the while its worshippers agree, and kneeling down with foreheads to the ground, they whisper fearfully that it is so.

It is impossible to worship death in any form, and still select a few you would not cherish and would yet avoid, while still believing in the rest. For death is total. Either all things die, or else they live and cannot die. No compromise is possible. For here again we see an obvious position, which we must accept if we be sane; what contradicts one thought entirely can not be true, unless its opposite is proven false.

The idea of the death of God is so preposterous that even the insane have difficulty in believing it. For it implies that God was once alive and somehow perished; killed, apparently, by those who did not want Him to survive. Their stronger will could triumph over His, and so eternal life gave way to death. And with the Father died the Son as well.

Death's worshippers may be afraid. And yet, can thoughts like these be fearful? If they saw that it is only this which they believe, they would be instantly released. And you will show them this today. There is no death, and we renounce it now in every form, for their salvation and our own as well. God made not death. Whatever form it takes must therefore be illusion. This the stand we take today. And it is given us to look past death, and see the life beyond.

OUR FATHER, BLESS OUR EYES TODAY. WE ARE YOUR MESSENGERS, AND WE WOULD LOOK UPON THE GLORIOUS REFLECTION OF YOUR LOVE WHICH SHINES IN EVERYTHING. WE LIVE AND MOVE IN YOU ALONE. WE ARE NOT SEPARATE FROM YOUR ETERNAL LIFE. THERE IS NO DEATH, FOR DEATH IS NOT YOUR WILL. AND WE ABIDE WHERE YOU HAVE PLACED US, IN THE LIFE WE SHARE WITH YOU AND WITH ALL LIVING THINGS, TO BE LIKE YOU AND PART OF YOU FOREVER. WE ACCEPT YOUR THOUGHTS AS OURS, AND OUR WILL IS ONE WITH YOURS ETERNALLY. AMEN.

Lesson 164

Now are we one with Him Who is our Source.

What time but now can truth be recognized? The present is the only time there is. And so today, this instant, now, we come to look upon what is forever there; not in our sight, but in the eyes of Christ. He looks past time, and sees eternity as represented there. He hears the sounds the senseless, busy world engenders, yet He hears them faintly. For beyond them all He hears the song of Heaven, and the Voice for God more clear, more meaningful, more near.

The world fades easily away before His sight. Its sounds grow dim. A melody from far beyond the world increasingly is more and more distinct; an ancient call to which He gives an ancient answer. You will recognize them both, for they are but your answer to your Father's Call to you. Christ answers for you, echoing your Self, using your voice to give His glad consent; accepting your deliverance for you.

How holy is your practicing today, as Christ gives you His sight and hears for you, and answers in your name the Call He hears! How quiet is the time you give to spend with Him, beyond the world. How easily are all your seeming sins forgot, and all your sorrows unremembered. On this day is grief laid by, for sights and sounds that come from nearer than the world are clear to you who will today accept the gifts He gives.

There is a silence into which the world can not intrude. There is an ancient peace you carry in your heart and have not lost. There is a sense of holiness in you the thought of sin has never touched. All this today you will remember. Faithfulness in practicing today will bring rewards so great and so completely different from all things you sought before, that you will know that here your treasure is, and here your rest.

This is the day when vain imaginings part like a curtain, to reveal what lies beyond them. Now is what is really there made visible, while all the shadows which appeared to hide it merely sink away. Now is the balance righted, and the scale of judgment left to Him Who judges true. And in His judgment will a world unfold in perfect innocence before your eyes. Now will you see it with the eyes of Christ. Now is its transformation clear to you.

Brother, this day is sacred to the world. Your vision, given you from far beyond all things within the world, looks back on them in a new light. And what you see becomes the healing and salvation of the world. The valuable and valueless are both perceived and recognized for what they are. And what is worthy of your love receives your love, while nothing to be feared remains.

We will not judge today. We will receive but what is given us from judgment made beyond the world. Our practicing today becomes our gift of thankfulness for our release from blindness and from misery. All that we see will but increase our joy, because its holiness reflects our own. We stand forgiven in the sight of Christ, with all the world forgiven in our own. We bless the world, as we behold it in the light in which our Savior looks on us, and offer it the freedom given us through His forgiving vision, not our own.

Open the curtain in your practicing by merely letting go all things you think you want. Your trifling treasures put away, and leave a clean and open space within your mind where Christ can come, and offer you the treasure of salvation. He has need of your most holy mind to save the world. Is not this purpose worthy to be yours? Is not Christ's vision worthy to be sought above the world's unsatisfying goals?

Let not today slip by without the gifts it holds for you receiving your consent and your acceptance. We can change the world, if you acknowledge them. You may not see the value your acceptance gives the world. But this you surely want; you can exchange all suffering for joy this very day. Practice in earnest, and the gift is yours. Would God deceive you? Can His promise fail? Can you withhold so little, when His Hand holds out complete salvation to His Son?

Lesson 165

Let not my mind deny the Thought of God.

What makes this world seem real except your own denial of the truth that lies beyond? What but your thoughts of misery and death obscure the perfect happiness and the eternal life your Father wills for you? And what could hide what cannot be concealed except illusion? What could keep from you what you already have except your choice to see it not, denying it is there?

The Thought of God created you. It left you not, nor have you ever been apart from it an instant. It belongs to you. By it you live. It is your Source of life, holding you one with it, and everything is one with you because it left you not. The Thought of God protects you, cares for you, makes soft your resting place and smooth your way, lighting your mind with happiness and love. Eternity and everlasting life shine in your mind, because the Thought of God has left you not, and still abides with you.

Who would deny his safety and his peace, his joy, his healing and his peace of mind, his quiet rest, his calm awakening, if he but recognized where they abide? Would he not instantly prepare to go where they are found, abandoning all else as worthless in comparison with them? And having found them, would he not make sure they stay with him, and he remain with them?

Deny not Heaven. It is yours today, but for the asking. Nor need you perceive how great the gift, how changed your mind will be before it comes to you. Ask to receive, and it is given you. Conviction lies within it. Till you welcome it as yours, uncertainty remains. Yet God is fair. Sureness is not required to receive what only your acceptance can bestow.

Ask with desire. You need not be sure that you request the only thing you want. But when you have received, you will be sure you have the treasure you have always sought. What would you then exchange for it? What would induce you now to let it fade away from your ecstatic vision? For this sight proves that you have exchanged your blindness for the seeing eyes of Christ; your mind has come to lay aside denial, and accept the Thought of God as your inheritance.

Now is all doubting past, the journey's end made certain, and salvation given you. Now is Christ's power in your mind, to heal as you were healed. For now you are among the saviors of the world. Your destiny lies there and nowhere else. Would God consent to let His Son remain forever starved by his denial of the nourishment he needs to live? Abundance dwells in him, and deprivation cannot cut him off from God's sustaining Love and from his home.

Practice today in hope. For hope indeed is justified. Your doubts are meaningless, for God is certain. And the Thought of Him is never absent. Sureness must abide within you who are host to Him. This course removes all doubts which you have interposed between Him and your certainty of Him.

We count on God, and not upon ourselves, to give us certainty. And in His Name we practice as His Word directs we do. His sureness lies beyond our every doubt. His Love remains beyond our every fear. The Thought of Him is still beyond all dreams and in our minds, according to His Will.

Lesson 166

I am entrusted with the gifts of God.

All things are given you. God's trust in you is limitless. He knows His Son. He gives without exception, holding nothing back that can contribute to your happiness. And yet, unless your will is one with His, His gifts are not received. But what would make you think there is another will than His?

Here is the paradox that underlies the making of the world. This world is not the Will of God, and so it is not real. Yet those who think it real must still believe there is another will, and one that leads to opposite effects from those He wills. Impossible indeed; but every mind that looks upon the world and judges it as certain, solid, trustworthy and true believes in two creators; or in one, himself alone. But never in one God.

The gifts of God are not acceptable to anyone who holds such strange beliefs. He must believe that to accept God's gifts, however evident they may become, however urgently he may be called to claim them as his own, is to be pressed to treachery against himself. He must deny their presence, contradict the truth, and suffer to preserve the world he made.

Here is the only home he thinks he knows. Here is the only safety he believes that he can find. Without the world he made is he an outcast; homeless and afraid. He does not realize that it is here he is afraid indeed, and homeless, too; an outcast wandering so far from home, so long away, he does not realize he has forgotten where he came from, where he goes, and even who he really is.

Yet in his lonely, senseless wanderings, God's gifts go with him, all unknown to him. He cannot lose them. But he will not look at what is given him. He wanders on, aware of the futility he sees about him everywhere, perceiving how his little lot but dwindles, as he goes ahead to nowhere. Still he wanders on in misery and poverty, alone though God is with him, and a treasure his so great that everything the world contains is valueless before its magnitude.

He seems a sorry figure; weary, worn, in threadbare clothing, and with feet that bleed a little from the rocky road he walks. No one but has identified with him, for everyone who comes here has pursued the path he follows, and has felt defeat and hopelessness as he is feeling them. Yet is he really tragic, when you see that he is following the way he chose, and need but realize Who walks with him and open up his treasures to be free?

This is your chosen self, the one you made as a replacement for reality. This is the self you savagely defend against all reason, every evidence, and all the witnesses with proof to show this is not you. You heed them not. You go on your appointed way, with eyes cast down lest you might catch a glimpse of truth, and be released from self-deception and set free.

You cower fearfully lest you should feel Christ's touch upon your shoulder, and perceive His gentle hand directing you to look upon your gifts. How could you then proclaim your poverty in exile? He would make you laugh at this perception of yourself. Where is self-pity then? And what becomes of all the tragedy you sought to make for him whom God intended only joy?

Your ancient fear has come upon you now, and justice has caught up with you at last. Christ's hand has touched your shoulder, and you feel that you are not alone. You even think the miserable self you thought was you may not be your Identity. Perhaps God's Word is truer than your own. Perhaps His gifts to you are real. Perhaps He has not wholly been outwitted by your plan to keep His Son in deep oblivion, and go the way you chose without your Self.

God's Will does not oppose. It merely is. It is not God you have imprisoned in your plan to lose your Self. He does not know about a plan so alien to His Will. There was a need He did not understand, to which He gave an Answer. That is all. And you who have this Answer given you have need no more of anything but this.

Now do we live, for now we cannot die. The wish for death is answered, and the sight that looked upon it now has been replaced by vision which perceives that you are not what you pretend to be. One walks with you Who gently answers all your fears with this one merciful reply, "It is not so." He points to all the gifts you have each time the thought of poverty oppresses you, and speaks of His Companionship when you perceive yourself as lonely and afraid.

Yet He reminds you still of one thing more you had forgotten. For His touch on you has made you like Himself. The gifts you have are not for you alone. What He has come to offer you, you now must learn to give. This is the lesson that His giving holds, for He has saved you from the solitude you sought to make in which to hide from God. He has reminded you of all the gifts that God has given you. He speaks as well of what becomes your will when you accept these gifts, and recognize they are your own.

The gifts are yours, entrusted to your care, to give to all who chose the lonely road you have escaped. They do not understand they but pursue their wishes. It is you who teach them now. For you have learned of Christ there is another way for them to walk. Teach them by showing them the happiness that comes to those who feel the touch of Christ, and recognize God's gifts. Let sorrow not tempt you to be unfaithful to your trust.

Your sighs will now betray the hopes of those who look to you for their release. Your tears are theirs. If you are sick, you but withhold their healing. What you fear but teaches them their fears are justified. Your hand becomes the giver of Christ's touch; your change of mind becomes the proof that who accepts God's gifts can never suffer anything. You are entrusted with the world's release from pain.

Betray it not. Become the living proof of what Christ's touch can offer everyone. God has entrusted all His gifts to you. Be witness in your happiness to how transformed the mind becomes which chooses to accept His gifts, and feel the touch of Christ. Such is your mission now. For God entrusts the giving of His gifts to all who have received them. He has shared His joy with you. And now you go to share it with the world.

Lesson 167

There is one life, and that I share with God.

There are not different kinds of life, for life is like the truth. It does not have degrees. It is the one condition in which all that God created share. Like all His Thoughts, it has no opposite. There is no death because what God created shares His life. There is no death because an opposite to God does not exist. There is no death because the Father and the Son are One.

In this world, there appears to be a state that is life's opposite. You call it death. Yet we have learned that the idea of death takes many forms. It is the one idea which underlies all feelings that are not supremely happy. It is the alarm to which you give response of any kind that is not perfect joy. All sorrow, loss, anxiety and suffering and pain, even a little sigh of weariness, a slight discomfort or the merest frown, acknowledge death. And thus deny you live.

You think that death is of the body. Yet it is but an idea, irrelevant to what is seen as physical. A thought is in the mind. It can be then applied as mind directs it. But its origin is where it must be changed, if change occurs. Ideas leave not their source. The emphasis this course has placed on that idea is due to its centrality in our attempts to change your mind about yourself. It is the reason you can heal. It is the cause of healing. It is why you cannot die. Its truth established you as one with God.

Death is the thought that you are separate from your Creator. It is the belief conditions change, emotions alternate because of causes you cannot control, you did not make, and you can never change. It is the fixed belief ideas can leave their source, and take on qualities the source does not contain, becoming different from their own origin, apart from it in kind as well as distance, time and form.

Death cannot come from life. Ideas remain united to their source. They can extend all that their source contains. In that, they can go far beyond themselves. But they can not give birth to what was never given them. As they are made, so will their making be. As they were born, so will they then give birth. And where they come from, there will they return.

The mind can think it sleeps, but that is all. It cannot change what is its waking state. It cannot make a body, nor abide within a body. What is alien to the mind does not exist, because it has no source. For mind creates all things that are, and cannot give them attributes it lacks, nor change its own eternal, mindful state. It cannot make the physical. What seems to die is but the sign of mind asleep.

The opposite of life can only be another form of life. As such, it can be reconciled with what created it, because it is not opposite in truth. Its form may change; it may appear to be what it is not. Yet mind is mind, awake or sleeping. It is not its opposite in anything created, nor in what it seems to make when it believes it sleeps.

God creates only mind awake. He does not sleep, and His creations cannot share what He gives not, nor make conditions which He does not share with them. The thought of death is not the opposite to thoughts of life. Forever unopposed by opposites of any kind, the Thoughts of God remain forever changeless, with the power to extend forever changelessly, but yet within themselves, for they are everywhere.

What seems to be the opposite of life is merely sleeping. When the mind elects to be what it is not, and to assume an alien power which it does not have, a foreign state it cannot enter, or a false condition not within its Source, it merely seems to go to sleep a while. It dreams of time; an interval in which what seems to happen never has occurred, the changes wrought are substanceless, and all events are nowhere. When the mind awakes, it but continues as it always was.

Let us today be children of the truth, and not deny our holy heritage. Our life is not as we imagine it. Who changes life because he shuts his eyes, or makes himself what he is not because he sleeps, and sees in dreams an opposite to what he is? We will not ask for death in any form today. Nor will we let imagined opposites to life abide even an instant where the Thought of life eternal has been set by God Himself.

His holy home we strive to keep today as He established it, and wills it be forever and forever. He is Lord of what we think today. And in His Thoughts, which have no opposite, we understand there is one life, and that we share with Him, with all creation, with their thoughts as well, whom He created in a unity of life that cannot separate in death and leave the Source of life from where it came.

We share one life because we have one Source, a Source from which perfection comes to us, remaining always in the holy minds which He created perfect. As we were, so are we now and will forever be. A sleeping mind must waken, as it sees its own perfection mirroring the Lord of life so perfectly it fades into what is reflected there. And now it is no more a mere reflection. It becomes the thing reflected, and the light which makes reflection possible. No vision now is needed. For the wakened mind is one that knows its Source, its Self, its Holiness.

Lesson 168

Your grace is given me. I claim it now.

God speaks to us. Shall we not speak to Him? He is not distant. He makes no attempt to hide from us. We try to hide from Him, and suffer from deception. He remains entirely accessible. He loves His Son. There is no certainty but this, yet this suffices. He will love His Son forever. When his mind remains asleep, He loves him still. And when his mind awakes, He loves him with a never-changing Love.

If you but knew the meaning of His Love, hope and despair would be impossible. For hope would be forever satisfied; despair of any kind unthinkable. His grace His answer is to all despair, for in it lies remembrance of His Love. Would He not gladly give the means by which His Will is recognized? His grace is yours by your acknowledgment. And memory of Him awakens in the mind that asks the means of Him whereby its sleep is done.

Today we ask of God the gift He has most carefully preserved within our hearts, waiting to be acknowledged. This the gift by which God leans to us and lifts us up, taking salvation's final step Himself. All steps but this we learn, instructed by His Voice. But finally He comes Himself, and takes us in His Arms and sweeps away the cobwebs of our sleep. His gift of grace is more than just an answer. It restores all memories the sleeping mind forgot; all certainty of what Love's meaning is.

God loves His Son. Request Him now to give the means by which this world will disappear, and vision first will come, with knowledge but an instant later. For in grace you see a light that covers all the world in love, and watch fear disappear from every face as hearts rise up and claim the light as theirs. What now remains that Heaven be delayed an instant longer? What is still undone when your forgiveness rests on everything?

It is a new and holy day today, for we receive what has been given us. Our faith lies in the Giver, not our own acceptance. We acknowledge our mistakes, but He to Whom all error is unknown is yet the One Who answers our mistakes by giving us the means to lay them down, and rise to Him in gratitude and love.

And He descends to meet us, as we come to Him. For what He has prepared for us He gives and we receive. Such is His Will, because He loves His Son. To Him we pray today, returning but the word He gave to us through His Own Voice, His Word, His Love:

Lesson 169

By grace I live. By grace I am released.

Grace is an aspect of the Love of God which is most like the state prevailing in the unity of truth. It is the world's most lofty aspiration, for it leads beyond the world entirely. It is past learning, yet the goal of learning, for grace cannot come until the mind prepares itself for true acceptance. Grace becomes inevitable instantly in those who have prepared a table where it can be gently laid and willingly received; an altar clean and holy for the gift.

Grace is acceptance of the Love of God within a world of seeming hate and fear. By grace alone the hate and fear are gone, for grace presents a state so opposite to everything the world contains, that those whose minds are lighted by the gift of grace can not believe the world of fear is real.

Grace is not learned. The final step must go beyond all learning. Grace is not the goal this course aspires to attain. Yet we prepare for grace in that an open mind can hear the Call to waken. It is not shut tight against God's Voice. It has become aware that there are things it does not know, and thus is ready to accept a state completely different from experience with which it is familiarly at home.

We have perhaps appeared to contradict our statement that the revelation of the Father and the Son as One has been already set. But we have also said the mind determines when that time will be, and has determined it. And yet we urge you to bear witness to the Word of God to hasten the experience of truth, and speed its advent into every mind that recognizes truth's effects on you.

Oneness is simply the idea God is. And in His Being, He encompasses all things. No mind holds anything but Him. We say "God is," and then we cease to speak, for in that knowledge words are meaningless. There are no lips to speak them, and no part of mind sufficiently distinct to feel that it is now aware of something not itself. It has united with its Source. And like its Source Itself, it merely is.

We cannot speak nor write nor even think of this at all. It comes to every mind when total recognition that its will is God's has been completely given and received completely. It returns the mind into the endless present, where the past and future cannot be conceived. It lies beyond salvation; past all thought of time, forgiveness and the holy face of Christ. The Son of God has merely disappeared into his Father, as his Father has in him. The world has never been at all. Eternity remains a constant state.

This is beyond experience we try to hasten. Yet forgiveness, taught and learned, brings with it the experiences which bear witness that the time the mind itself determined to abandon all but this is now at hand. We do not hasten it, in that what you will offer was concealed from Him Who teaches what forgiveness means.

All learning was already in His Mind, accomplished and complete. He recognized all that time holds, and gave it to all minds that each one might determine, from a point where time was ended, when it is released to revelation and eternity. We have repeated several times before that you but make a journey that is done.

For oneness must be here. Whatever time the mind has set for revelation is entirely irrelevant to what must be a constant state, forever as it always was; forever to remain as it is now. We merely take the part assigned long since, and fully recognized as perfectly fulfilled by Him Who wrote salvation's script in His Creator's Name, and in the Name of His Creator's Son.

There is no need to further clarify what no one in the world can understand. When revelation of your oneness comes, it will be known and fully understood. Now we have work to do, for those in time can speak of things beyond, and listen to words which explain what is to come is past already. Yet what meaning can the words convey to those who count the hours still, and rise and work and go to sleep by them?

Suffice it, then, that you have work to do to play your part. The ending must remain obscure to you until your part is done. It does not matter. For your part is still what all the rest depends on. As you take the role assigned to you, salvation comes a little nearer each uncertain heart that does not beat as yet in tune with God.

Forgiveness is the central theme that runs throughout salvation, holding all its parts in meaningful relationships, the course it runs directed and its outcome sure. And now we ask for grace, the final gift salvation can bestow. Experience that grace provides will end in time, for grace foreshadows Heaven, yet does not replace the thought of time but for a little while.

The interval suffices. It is here that miracles are laid; to be returned by you from holy instants you receive, through grace in your experience, to all who see the light that lingers in your face. What is the face of Christ but his who went a moment into timelessness, and brought a clear reflection of the unity he felt an instant back to bless the world? How could you finally attain to it forever, while a part of you remains outside, unknowing, unawakened, and in need of you as witness to the truth?

Be grateful to return, as you were glad to go an instant, and accept the gifts that grace provided you. You carry them back to yourself. And revelation stands not far behind. Its coming is ensured. We ask for grace, and for experience that comes from grace. We welcome the release it offers everyone. We do not ask for the unaskable. We do not look beyond what grace can give. For this we can give in the grace that has been given us.

Our learning goal today does not exceed this prayer. Yet in the world, what could be more than what we ask this day of Him Who gives the grace we ask, as it was given Him?

BY GRACE I LIVE. BY GRACE I AM RELEASED. BY GRACE I GIVE. BY GRACE I WILL RELEASE.

Lesson 170

There is no cruelty in God and none in me.

No one attacks without intent to hurt. This can have no exception. When you think that you attack in self-defense, you mean that to be cruel is protection; you are safe because of cruelty. You mean that you believe to hurt another brings you freedom. And you mean that to attack is to exchange the state in which you are for something better, safer, more secure from dangerous invasion and from fear.

How thoroughly insane is the idea that to defend from fear is to attack! For here is fear begot and fed with blood, to make it grow and swell and rage. And thus is fear protected, not escaped. Today we learn a lesson which can save you more delay and needless misery than you can possibly imagine. It is this:

YOU MAKE WHAT YOU DEFEND AGAINST, AND BY YOUR OWN
DEFENSE AGAINST IT IS IT REAL AND INESCAPABLE. LAY DOWN
YOUR ARMS, AND ONLY THEN DO YOU PERCEIVE IT FALSE.

It seems to be the enemy without that you attack. Yet your defense sets up an enemy within; an alien thought at war with you, depriving you of peace, splitting your mind into two camps which seem wholly irreconcilable. For love now has an "enemy," an opposite; and fear, the alien, now needs your defense against the threat of what you really are.

If you consider carefully the means by which your fancied self-defense proceeds on its imagined way, you will perceive the premises on which the idea stands. First, it is obvious ideas must leave their source, for it is you who make attack, and must have first conceived of it. Yet you attack outside yourself, and separate your mind from him who is to be attacked, with perfect faith the split you made is real.

Next, are the attributes of love bestowed upon its "enemy." For fear becomes your safety and protector of your peace, to which you turn for solace and escape from doubts about your strength, and hope of rest in dreamless quiet. And as love is shorn of what belongs to it and it alone, love is endowed with attributes of fear. For love would ask you lay down all defense as merely foolish. And your arms indeed would crumble into dust. For such they are.

With love as enemy, must cruelty become a god. And gods demand that those who worship them obey their dictates, and refuse to question them. Harsh punishment is meted out relentlessly to those who ask if the demands are sensible or even sane. It is their enemies who are unreasonable and insane, while they are always merciful and just.

Today we look upon this cruel god dispassionately. And we note that though his lips are smeared with blood, and fire seems to flame from him, he is but made of stone. He can do nothing. We need not defy his power. He has none. And those who see in him their safety have no guardian, no strength to call upon in danger, and no mighty warrior to fight for them.

This moment can be terrible. But it can also be the time of your release from abject slavery. You make a choice, standing before this idol, seeing him exactly as he is. Will you restore to love what you have sought to wrest from it and lay before this mindless piece of stone? Or will you make another idol to replace it? For the god of cruelty takes many forms. Another can be found.

Yet do not think that fear is the escape from fear. Let us remember what the text has stressed about the obstacles to peace. The final one, the hardest to believe is nothing, and a seeming obstacle with the appearance of a solid block, impenetrable, fearful and beyond surmounting, is the fear of God Himself. Here is the basic premise which enthrones the thought of fear as god. For fear is loved by those who worship it, and love appears to be invested now with cruelty.

Where does the totally insane belief in gods of vengeance come from? Love has not confused its attributes with those of fear. Yet must the worshippers of fear perceive their own confusion in fear's "enemy"; its cruelty as now a part of love. And what becomes more fearful than the Heart of Love Itself? The blood appears to be upon His Lips; the fire comes from Him. And He is terrible above all else, cruel beyond conception, striking down all who acknowledge Him to be their God.

The choice you make today is certain. For you look for the last time upon this bit of carven stone you made, and call it god no longer. You have reached this place before, but you have chosen that this cruel god remain with you in still another form. And so the fear of God returned with you. This time you leave it there. And you return to a new world, unburdened by its weight; beheld not in its sightless eyes, but in the vision that your choice restored to you.

Now do your eyes belong to Christ, and He looks through them. Now your voice belongs to God and echoes His. And now your heart remains at peace forever. You have chosen Him in place of idols, and your attributes, given by your Creator, are restored to you at last. The Call for God is heard and answered. Now has fear made way for love, as God Himself replaces cruelty.

FATHER, WE ARE LIKE YOU. NO CRUELTY ABIDES IN US, FOR THERE IS NONE IN YOU. YOUR PEACE IS OURS. AND WE BLESS THE WORLD WITH WHAT WE HAVE RECEIVED FROM YOU ALONE. WE CHOOSE AGAIN, AND MAKE OUR CHOICE FOR ALL OUR BROTHERS, KNOWING THEY ARE ONE WITH US. WE BRING THEM YOUR SALVATION AS WE HAVE RECEIVED IT NOW. AND WE GIVE THANKS FOR THEM WHO RENDER US COMPLETE. IN THEM WE SEE YOUR GLORY, AND IN THEM WE FIND OUR PEACE. HOLY ARE WE BECAUSE YOUR HOLINESS HAS SET US FREE. AND WE GIVE THANKS. AMEN.

Lesson 171

REVIEW V
Introduction

We now review again. This time we are ready to give more effort and more time to what we undertake. We recognize we are preparing for another phase of understanding. We would take this step completely, that we may go on again more certain, more sincere, with faith upheld more surely. Our footsteps have not been unwavering, and doubts have made us walk uncertainly and slowly on the road this course sets forth. But now we hasten on, for we approach a greater certainty, a firmer purpose and a surer goal.

STEADY OUR FEET, OUR FATHER. LET OUR DOUBTS BE QUIET AND OUR HOLY MINDS BE STILL, AND SPEAK TO US. WE HAVE NO WORDS TO GIVE TO YOU. WE WOULD BUT LISTEN TO YOUR WORD, AND MAKE IT OURS. LEAD OUR PRACTICING AS DOES A FATHER LEAD A LITTLE CHILD ALONG A WAY HE DOES NOT UNDERSTAND. YET DOES HE FOLLOW, SURE THAT HE IS SAFE BECAUSE HIS FATHER LEADS THE WAY FOR HIM.

SO DO WE BRING OUR PRACTICING TO YOU. AND IF WE STUMBLE, YOU WILL RAISE US UP. IF WE FORGET THE WAY, WE COUNT UPON YOUR SURE REMEMBERING. WE WANDER OFF, BUT YOU WILL NOT FORGET TO CALL US BACK. QUICKEN OUR FOOTSTEPS NOW, THAT WE MAY WALK MORE CERTAINLY AND QUICKLY UNTO YOU. AND WE ACCEPT THE WORD YOU OFFER US TO UNIFY OUR PRACTICING, AS WE REVIEW THE THOUGHTS THAT YOU HAVE GIVEN US.

This is the thought which should precede the thoughts that we review. Each one but clarifies some aspect of this thought, or helps it be more meaningful, more personal and true, and more descriptive of the holy Self we share and now prepare to know again:

GOD IS BUT LOVE, AND THEREFORE SO AM I.

This Self alone knows Love. This Self alone is perfectly consistent in Its Thoughts; knows Its Creator, understands Itself, is perfect in Its knowledge and Its Love, and never changes from Its constant state of union with Its Father and Itself.

And it is this that waits to meet us at the journey's ending. Every step we take brings us a little nearer. This review will shorten time immeasurably, if we keep in mind that this remains our goal, and as we practice it is this to which we are approaching. Let us raise our hearts from dust to life, as we remember this is promised us, and that this course was sent to open up the path of light to us, and teach us, step by step, how to return to the eternal Self we thought we lost.

I take the journey with you. For I share your doubts and fears a little while, that you may come to me who recognize the road by which all fears and doubts are overcome. We walk together. I must understand uncertainty and pain, although I know they have no meaning. Yet a savior must remain with those he teaches, seeing what they see, but still retaining in his mind the way that led him out, and now will lead you out with him. God's Son is crucified until you walk along the road with me.

My resurrection comes again each time I lead a brother safely to the place at which the journey ends and is forgot. I am renewed each time a brother learns there is a way from misery and pain. I am reborn each time a brother's mind turns to the light in him and looks for me. I have forgotten no one. Help me now to lead you back to where the journey was begun, to make another choice with me.

Release me as you practice once again the thoughts I brought to you from Him Who sees your bitter need, and knows the answer God has given Him. Together we review these thoughts. Together we devote our time and effort to them. And together we will teach them to our brothers. God would not have Heaven incomplete. It waits for you, as I do. I am incomplete without your part in me. And as I am made whole we go together to our ancient home, prepared for us before time was and kept unchanged by time, immaculate and safe, as it will be at last when time is done.

Let this review be then your gift to me. For this alone I need; that you will hear the words I speak, and give them to the world. You are my voice, my eyes, my feet, my hands through which I save the world. The Self from which I call to you is but your own. To Him we go together. Take your brother's hand, for this is not a way we walk alone. In him I walk with you, and you with me. Our Father wills His Son be one with Him. What lives but must not then be one with you?

Let this review become a time in which we share a new experience for you, yet one as old as time and older still. Hallowed your Name. Your glory undefiled forever. And your wholeness now complete, as God established it. You are His Son, completing His extension in your own. We practice but an ancient truth we knew before illusion seemed to claim the world. And we remind the world that it is free of all illusions every time we say:

With this we start each day of our review. With this we start and end each period of practice time. And with this thought we sleep, to waken once again with these same words upon our lips, to greet another day. No thought that we review but we surround with it, and use the thoughts to hold it up before our minds, and keep it clear in our rememberance throughout the day. And thus, when we have finished this review, we will have recognized the words we speak are true.

Yet are the words but aids, and to be used, except at the beginning and the end of practice periods, but to recall the mind, as needed, to its purpose. We place faith in the experience that comes from practice, not the means we use. We wait for the experience, and recognize that it is only here conviction lies. We use the words, and try and try again to go beyond them to their meaning, which is far beyond their sound. The sound grows dim and disappears, as we approach the Source of meaning. It is Here that we find rest.

Lesson 171

God is but Love, and therefore so am I.

(151) All things are echoes of the Voice for God.

God is but Love, and therefore so am I.

(152) The power of decision is my own.

God is but Love, and therefore so am I.

Lesson 172

God is but Love, and therefore so am I.

(153) In my defenselessness my safety lies.

God is but Love, and therefore so am I.

(154) I am among the ministers of God.

God is but Love, and therefore so am I.

Lesson 173

God is but Love, and therefore so am I.

(155) I will step back and let Him lead the way.

God is but Love, and therefore so am I.

(156) I walk with God in perfect holiness.

God is but Love, and therefore so am I.

Lesson 174

God is but Love, and therefore so am I.

(157) Into His Presence would I enter now.

God is but Love, and therefore so am I.

(158) Today I learn to give as I receive.

God is but Love, and therefore so am I.

Lesson 175

God is but Love, and therefore so am I.

(159) I give the miracles I have received.

God is but Love, and therefore so am I.

(160) I am at home. Fear is the stranger here.

God is but Love, and therefore so am I.

Lesson 176

God is but Love, and therefore so am I.

(161) Give me your blessing, holy Son of God.

God is but Love, and therefore so am I.

(162) I am as God created me.

God is but Love, and therefore so am I.

Lesson 177

God is but Love, and therefore so am I.

(163) There is no death. The Son of God is free.

God is but Love, and therefore so am I.

(164) Now are we one with Him Who is our Source.

God is but Love, and therefore so am I.

Lesson 178

God is but Love, and therefore so am I.

(165) Let not my mind deny the Thought of God.

God is but Love, and therefore so am I.

(166) I am entrusted with the gifts of God.

God is but Love, and therefore so am I.

Lesson 179

God is but Love, and therefore so am I.

(167) There is one life, and that I share with God.

God is but Love, and therefore so am I.

(168) Your grace is given me. I claim it now.

God is but Love, and therefore so am I.

Lesson 180

God is but Love, and therefore so am I.

(169) By grace I live. By grace I am released.

God is but Love, and therefore so am I.

(170) There is no cruelty in God and none in me.

God is but Love, and therefore so am I.

Lesson 181

Introduction to Lessons 181-200

Our next few lessons make a special point of firming up your willingness to make your weak commitment strong; your scattered goals blend into one intent. You are not asked for total dedication all the time as yet. But you are asked to practice now in order to attain the sense of peace such unified commitment will bestow, if only intermittently. It is experiencing this that makes it sure that you will give your total willingness to following the way the course sets forth.

Our lessons now are geared specifically to widening horizons, and direct approaches to the special blocks that keep your vision narrow, and too limited to let you see the value of our goal. We are attempting now to lift these blocks, however briefly. Words alone can not convey the sense of liberation which their lifting brings. But the experience of freedom and of peace that comes as you give up your tight control of what you see speaks for itself. Your motivation will be so intensified that words become of little consequence. You will be sure of what you want, and what is valueless.

And so we start our journey beyond words by concentrating first on what impedes your progress still. Experience of what exists beyond defensiveness remains beyond achievement while it is denied. It may be there, but you cannot accept its presence. So we now attempt to go past all defenses for a little while each day. No more than this is asked, because no more than this is needed. It will be enough to guarantee the rest will come.

Lesson 181

I trust my brothers, who are one with me.

Trusting your brothers is essential to establishing and holding up your faith in your ability to transcend doubt and lack of sure conviction in yourself. When you attack a brother, you proclaim that he is limited by what you have perceived in him. You do not look beyond his errors. Rather, they are magnified, becoming blocks to your awareness of the Self that lies beyond your own mistakes, and past his seeming sins as well as yours.

Perception has a focus. It is this that gives consistency to what you see. Change but this focus, and what you behold will change accordingly. Your vision now will shift, to give support to the intent which has replaced the one you held before. Remove your focus on your brother's sins, and you experience the peace that comes from faith in sinlessness. This faith receives its only sure support from what you see in others past their sins. For their mistakes, if focused on, are witnesses to sins in you. And you will not transcend their sight and see the sinlessness that lies beyond.

Therefore, in practicing today, we first let all such little focuses give way to our great need to let our sinlessness become apparent. We instruct our minds that it is this we seek, and only this, for just a little while. We do not care about our future goals. And what we saw an instant previous has no concern for us within this interval of time wherein we practice changing our intent. We seek for innocence and nothing else. We seek for it with no concern but now.

A major hazard to success has been involvement with your past and future goals. You have been quite preoccupied with how extremely different the goals this course is advocating are from those you held before. And you have also been dismayed by the depressing and restricting thought that, even if you should succeed, you will inevitably lose your way again.

How could this matter? For the past is gone; the future but imagined. These concerns are but defenses against present change of focus in perception. Nothing more. We lay these pointless limitations by a little while. We do not look to past beliefs, and what we will believe will not intrude upon us now. We enter in the time of practicing with one intent; to look upon the sinlessness within.

We recognize that we have lost this goal if anger blocks our way in any form. And if a brother's sins occur to us, our narrowed focus will restrict our sight, and turn our eyes upon our own mistakes, which we will magnify and call our "sins." So, for a little while, without regard to past or future, should such blocks arise we will transcend them with instructions to our minds to change their focus, as we say:

IT IS NOT THIS THAT I WOULD LOOK UPON.
I TRUST MY BROTHERS, WHO ARE ONE WITH ME.

And we will also use this thought to keep us safe throughout the day. We do not seek for long-range goals. As each obstruction seems to block the vision of our sinlessness, we seek but for surcease an instant from the misery the focus upon sin will bring, and uncorrected will remain.

Nor do we ask for fantasies. For what we seek to look upon is really there. And as our focus goes beyond mistakes, we will behold a wholly sinless world. When seeing this is all we want to see, when this is all we seek for in the name of true perception, are the eyes of Christ inevitably ours. And the Love He feels for us becomes our own as well. This will become the only thing we see reflected in the world and in ourselves.

The world which once proclaimed our sins becomes the proof that we are sinless. And our love for everyone we look upon attests to our remembrance of the holy Self which knows no sin, and never could conceive of anything without Its sinlessness. We seek for this remembrance as we turn our minds to practicing today. We look neither ahead nor backwards. We look straight into the present. And we give our trust to the experience we ask for now. Our sinlessness is but the Will of God. This instant is our willing one with His.

Lesson 182

I will be still an instant and go home.

This world you seem to live in is not home to you. And somewhere in your mind you know that this is true. A memory of home keeps haunting you, as if there were a place that called you to return, although you do not recognize the voice, nor what it is the voice reminds you of. Yet still you feel an alien here, from somewhere all unknown. Nothing so definite that you could say with certainty you are an exile here. Just a persistent feeling, sometimes not more than a tiny throb, at other times hardly remembered, actively dismissed, but surely to return to mind again.

No one but knows whereof we speak. Yet some try to put by their suffering in games they play to occupy their time, and keep their sadness from them. Others will deny that they are sad, and do not recognize their tears at all. Still others will maintain that what we speak of is illusion, not to be considered more than but a dream. Yet who, in simple honesty, without defensiveness and self-deception, would deny he understands the words we speak?

We speak today for everyone who walks this world, for he is not at home. He goes uncertainly about in endless search, seeking in darkness what he cannot find; not recognizing what it is he seeks. A thousand homes he makes, yet none contents his restless mind. He does not understand he builds in vain. The home he seeks can not be made by him. There is no substitute for Heaven. All he ever made was hell.

Perhaps you think it is your childhood home that you would find again. The childhood of your body, and its place of shelter, are a memory now so distorted that you merely hold a picture of a past that never happened. Yet there is a Child in you Who seeks His Father's house, and knows that He is alien here. This childhood is eternal, with an innocence that will endure forever. Where this Child shall go is holy ground. It is His Holiness that lights up Heaven, and that brings to earth the pure reflection of the light above, wherein are earth and Heaven joined as one.

It is this Child in you your Father knows as His Own Son. It is this Child Who knows His Father. He desires to go home so deeply, so unceasingly, His voice cries unto you to let Him rest a while. He does not ask for more than just a few instants of respite; just an interval in which He can return to breathe again the holy air that fills His Father's house. You are His home as well. He will return. But give Him just a little time to be Himself, within the peace that is His home, resting in silence and in peace and love.

This Child needs your protection. He is far from home. He is so little that He seems so easily shut out, His tiny voice so readily obscured, His call for help almost unheard amid the grating sounds and harsh and rasping noises of the world. Yet does He know that in you still abides His sure protection. You will fail Him not. He will go home, and you along with Him.

This Child is your defenselessness; your strength. He trusts in you. He came because He knew you would not fail. He whispers of His home unceasingly to you. For He would bring you back with Him, that He Himself might stay, and not return again where He does not belong, and where He lives an outcast in a world of alien thoughts. His patience has no limits. He will wait until you hear His gentle Voice within you, calling you to let Him go in peace, along with you, to where He is at home and you with Him.

When you are still an instant, when the world recedes from you, when valueless ideas cease to have value in your restless mind, then will you hear His Voice. So poignantly He calls to you that you will not resist Him longer. In that instant He will take you to His home, and you will stay with Him in perfect stillness, silent and at peace, beyond all words, untouched by fear and doubt, sublimely certain that you are at home.

Rest with Him frequently today. For He was willing to become a little Child that you might learn of Him how strong is he who comes without defenses, offering only love's messages to those who think he is their enemy. He holds the might of Heaven in His hand and calls them friend, and gives His strength to them, that they may see He would be Friend to them. He asks that they protect Him, for His home is far away, and He will not return to it alone.

Christ is reborn as but a little Child each time a wanderer would leave his home. For he must learn that what he would protect is but this Child, Who comes defenseless and Who is protected by defenselessness. Go home with Him from time to time today. You are as much an alien here as He.

Take time today to lay aside your shield which profits nothing, and lay down the spear and sword you raised against an enemy without existence. Christ has called you friend and brother. He has even come to ask your help in letting Him go home today, completed and completely. He has come as does a little child, who must beseech his father for protection and for love. He rules the universe, and yet He asks unceasingly that you return with Him, and take illusions as your gods no more.

You have not lost your innocence. It is for this you yearn. This is your heart's desire. This is the voice you hear, and this the call which cannot be denied. The holy Child remains with you. His home is yours. Today He gives you His defenselessness, and you accept it in exchange for all the toys of battle you have made. And now the way is open, and the journey has an end in sight at last. Be still an instant and go home with Him, and be at peace a while.

Lesson 183

I call upon God's Name and on my own.

God's Name is holy, but no holier than yours. To call upon His Name is but to call upon your own. A father gives his son his name, and thus identifies the son with him. His brothers share his name, and thus are they united in a bond to which they turn for their identity. Your Father's Name reminds you who you are, even within a world that does not know; even though you have not remembered it.

God's Name can not be heard without response, nor said without an echo in the mind that calls you to remember. Say His Name, and you invite the angels to surround the ground on which you stand, and sing to you as they spread out their wings to keep you safe, and shelter you from every worldly thought that would intrude upon your holiness.

Repeat God's Name, and all the world responds by laying down illusions. Every dream the world holds dear has suddenly gone by, and where it seemed to stand you find a star; a miracle of grace. The sick arise, healed of their sickly thoughts. The blind can see; the deaf can hear. The sorrowful cast off their mourning, and the tears of pain are dried as happy laughter comes to bless the world.

Repeat the Name of God, and little names have lost their meaning. No temptation but becomes a nameless and unwanted thing before God's Name. Repeat His Name, and see how easily you will forget the names of all the gods you valued. They have lost the name of god you gave them. They become anonymous and valueless to you, although before you let the Name of God replace their little names, you stood before them worshipfully, naming them as gods.

Repeat the Name of God, and call upon your Self, Whose Name is His. Repeat His Name, and all the tiny, nameless things on earth slip into right perspective. Those who call upon the Name of God can not mistake the nameless for the Name, nor sin for grace, nor bodies for the holy Son of God. And should you join a brother as you sit with him in silence, and repeat God's Name along with him within your quiet mind, you have established there an altar which reaches to God Himself and to His Son.

Practice but this today; repeat God's Name slowly again and still again. Become oblivious to every name but His. Hear nothing else. Let all your thoughts become anchored on this. No other word we use except at the beginning, when we say today's idea but once. And then God's Name becomes our only thought, our only word, the only thing that occupies our minds, the only wish we have, the only sound with any meaning, and the only Name of everything that we desire to see; of everything that we would call our own.

Thus do we give an invitation which can never be refused. And God will come, and answer it Himself. Think not He hears the little prayers of those who call on Him with names of idols cherished by the world. They cannot reach Him thus. He cannot hear requests that He be not Himself, or that His Son receive another name than His.

Repeat God's Name, and you acknowledge Him as sole Creator of reality. And you acknowledge also that His Son is part of Him, creating in His Name. Sit silently, and let His Name become the all-encompassing idea that holds your mind completely. Let all thoughts be still except this one. And to all other thoughts respond with this, and see God's Name replace the thousand little names you gave your thoughts, not realizing that there is one Name for all there is, and all that there will be.

Today you can achieve a state in which you will experience the gift of grace. You can escape all bondage of the world, and give the world the same release you found. You can remember what the world forgot, and offer it your own remembering. You can accept today the part you play in its salvation, and your own as well. And both can be accomplished perfectly.

Turn to the Name of God for your release, and it is given you. No prayer but this is necessary, for it holds them all within it. Words are insignificant, and all requests unneeded when God's Son calls on his Father's Name. His Father's Thoughts become his own. He makes his claim to all his Father gave, is giving still, and will forever give. He calls on Him to let all things he thought he made be nameless now, and in their place the holy Name of God becomes his judgment of their worthlessness.

All little things are silent. Little sounds are soundless now. The little things of earth have disappeared. The universe consists of nothing but the Son of God, who calls upon his Father. And his Father's Voice gives answer in his Father's holy Name. In this eternal, still relationship, in which communication far transcends all words, and yet exceeds in depth and height whatever words could possibly convey, is peace eternal. In our Father's Name, we would experience this peace today. And in His Name, it shall be given us.

Lesson 184

The Name of God is my inheritance.

You live by symbols. You have made up names for everything you see. Each one becomes a separate entity, identified by its own name. By this you carve it out of unity. By this you designate its special attributes, and set it off from other things by emphasizing space surrounding it. This space you lay between all things to which you give a different name; all happenings in terms of place and time; all bodies which are greeted by a name.

This space you see as setting off all things from one another is the means by which the world's perception is achieved. You see something where nothing is, and see as well nothing where there is unity; a space between all things, between all things and you. Thus do you think that you have given life in separation. By this split you think you are established as a unity which functions with an independent will.

What are these names by which the world becomes a series of discrete events, of things ununified, of bodies kept apart and holding bits of mind as separate awarenesses? You gave these names to them, establishing perception as you wished to have perception be. The nameless things were given names, and thus reality was given them as well. For what is named is given meaning and will then be seen as meaningful; a cause of true effect, with consequence inherent in itself.

This is the way reality is made by partial vision, purposefully set against the given truth. Its enemy is wholeness. It conceives of little things and looks upon them. And a lack of space, a sense of unity or vision that sees differently, become the threats which it must overcome, conflict with and deny.

Yet does this other vision still remain a natural direction for the mind to channel its perception. It is hard to teach the mind a thousand alien names, and thousands more. Yet you believe this is what learning means; its one essential goal by which communication is achieved, and concepts can be meaningfully shared.

This is the sum of the inheritance the world bestows. And everyone who learns to think that it is so accepts the signs and symbols that assert the world is real. It is for this they stand. They leave no doubt that what is named is there. It can be seen, as is anticipated. What denies that it is true is but illusion, for it is the ultimate reality. To question it is madness; to accept its presence is the proof of sanity.

Such is the teaching of the world. It is a phase of learning everyone who comes must go through. But the sooner he perceives on what it rests, how questionable are its premises, how doubtful its results, the sooner does he question its effects. Learning that stops with what the world would teach stops short of meaning. In its proper place, it serves but as a starting point from which another kind of learning can begin, a new perception can be gained, and all the arbitrary names the world bestows can be withdrawn as they are raised to doubt.

Think not you made the world. Illusions, yes! But what is true in earth and Heaven is beyond your naming. When you call upon a brother, it is to his body that you make appeal. His true Identity is hidden from you by what you believe he really is. His body makes response to what you call him, for his mind consents to take the name you give him as his own. And thus his unity is twice denied, for you perceive him separate from you, and he accepts this separate name as his.

It would indeed be strange if you were asked to go beyond all symbols of the world, forgetting them forever; yet were asked to take a teaching function. You have need to use the symbols of the world a while. But be you not deceived by them as well. They do not stand for anything at all, and in your practicing it is this thought that will release you from them. They become but means by which you can communicate in ways the world can understand, but which you recognize is not the unity where true communication can be found.

Thus what you need are intervals each day in which the learning of the world becomes a transitory phase; a prison house from which you go into the sunlight and forget the darkness. Here you understand the Word, the Name which God has given you; the one Identity which all things share; the one acknowledgment of what is true. And then step back to darkness, not because you think it real, but only to proclaim its unreality in terms which still have meaning in the world that darkness rules.

Use all the little names and symbols which delineate the world of darkness. Yet accept them not as your reality. The Holy Spirit uses all of them, but He does not forget creation has one Name, one meaning, and a single Source which unifies all things within Itself. Use all the names the world bestows on them but for convenience, yet do not forget they share the Name of God along with you.

God has no name. And yet His Name becomes the final lesson that all things are one, and at this lesson does all learning end. All names are unified; all space is filled with truth's reflection. Every gap is closed, and separation healed. The Name of God is the inheritance He gave to those who chose the teaching of the world to take the place of Heaven.

In our practicing, our purpose is to let our minds accept what God has given as the answer to the pitiful inheritance you made as fitting tribute to the Son He loves.

No one can fail who seeks the meaning of the Name of God. Experience must come to supplement the Word. But first you must accept the Name for all reality, and realize the many names you gave its aspects have distorted what you see, but have not interfered with truth at all. One Name we bring into our practicing. One Name we use to unify our sight.

And though we use a different name for each awareness of an aspect of God's Son, we understand that they have but one Name, which He has given them. It is this Name we use in practicing. And through Its use, all foolish separations disappear which kept us blind. And we are given strength to see beyond them. Now our sight is blessed with blessings we can give as we receive.

FATHER, OUR NAME IS YOURS. IN IT WE ARE UNITED WITH ALL LIVING THINGS, AND YOU WHO ARE THEIR ONE CREATOR. WHAT WE MADE AND CALL BY MANY DIFFERENT NAMES IS BUT A SHADOW WE HAVE TRIED TO CAST ACROSS YOUR OWN REALITY. AND WE ARE GLAD AND THANKFUL WE WERE WRONG. ALL OUR MISTAKES WE GIVE TO YOU, THAT WE MAY BE ABSOLVED FROM ALL EFFECTS OUR ERRORS SEEMED TO HAVE. AND WE ACCEPT THE TRUTH YOU GIVE, IN PLACE OF EVERY ONE OF THEM. YOUR NAME IS OUR SALVATION AND ESCAPE FROM WHAT WE MADE. YOUR NAME UNITES US IN THE ONENESS WHICH IS OUR INHERITANCE AND PEACE. AMEN.

Lesson 185

I want the peace of God.

To say these words is nothing. But to mean these words is everything. If you could but mean them for just an instant, there would be no further sorrow possible for you in any form; in any place or time. Heaven would be completely given back to full awareness, memory of God entirely restored, the resurrection of all creation fully recognized.

No one can mean these words and not be healed. He cannot play with dreams, nor think he is himself a dream. He cannot make a hell and think it real. He wants the peace of God, and it is given him. For that is all he wants, and that is all he will receive. Many have said these words. But few indeed have meant them. You have but to look upon the world you see around you to be sure how very few they are. The world would be completely changed, should any two agree these words express the only thing they want.

Two minds with one intent become so strong that what they will becomes the Will of God. For minds can only join in truth. In dreams, no two can share the same intent. To each, the hero of the dream is different; the outcome wanted not the same for both. Loser and gainer merely shift about in changing patterns, as the ratio of gain to loss and loss to gain takes on a different aspect or another form.

Yet compromise alone a dream can bring. Sometimes it takes the form of union, but only the form. The meaning must escape the dream, for compromising is the goal of dreaming. Minds cannot unite in dreams. They merely bargain. And what bargain can give them the peace of God? Illusions come to take His place. And what He means is lost to sleeping minds intent on compromise, each to his gain and to another's loss.

To mean you want the peace of God is to renounce all dreams. For no one means these words who wants illusions, and who therefore seeks the means which bring illusions. He has looked on them, and found them wanting. Now he seeks to go beyond them, recognizing that another dream would offer nothing more than all the others. Dreams are one to him. And he has learned their only difference is one of form, for one will bring the same despair and misery as do the rest.

The mind which means that all it wants is peace must join with other minds, for that is how peace is obtained. And when the wish for peace is genuine, the means for finding it is given, in a form each mind that seeks for it in honesty can understand. Whatever form the lesson takes is planned for him in such a way that he can not mistake it, if his asking is sincere. But if he asks without sincerity, there is no form in which the lesson will meet with acceptance and be truly learned.

Let us today devote our practicing to recognizing that we really mean the words we say. We want the peace of God. This is no idle wish. These words do not request another dream be given us. They do not ask for compromise, nor try to make another bargain in the hope that there may yet be one that can succeed where all the rest have failed. To mean these words acknowledges illusions are in vain, requesting the eternal in the place of shifting dreams which seem to change in what they offer, but are one in nothingness.

Today devote your practice periods to careful searching of your mind, to find the dreams you cherish still. What do you ask for in your heart? Forget the words you use in making your requests. Consider but what you believe will comfort you, and bring you happiness. But be you not dismayed by lingering illusions, for their form is not what matters now. Let not some dreams be more acceptable, reserving shame and secrecy for others. They are one. And being one, one question should be asked of all of them, "Is this what I would have, in place of Heaven and the peace of God?"

This is the choice you make. Be not deceived that it is otherwise. No compromise is possible in this. You choose God's peace, or you have asked for dreams. And dreams will come as you requested them. Yet will God's peace come just as certainly, and to remain with you forever. It will not be gone with every twist and turning of the road, to reappear, unrecognized, in forms which shift and change with every step you take.

You want the peace of God. And so do all who seem to seek for dreams. For them as well as for yourself, you ask but this when you make this request with deep sincerity. For thus you reach to what they really want, and join your own intent with what they seek above all things, perhaps unknown to them, but sure to you. You have been weak at times, uncertain in your purpose, and unsure of what you wanted, where to look for it, and where to turn for help in the attempt. Help has been given you. And would you not avail yourself of it by sharing it?

No one who truly seeks the peace of God can fail to find it. For he merely asks that he deceive himself no longer by denying to himself what is God's Will. Who can remain unsatisfied who asks for what he has already? Who could be unanswered who requests an answer which is his to give? The peace of God is yours.

For you was peace created, given you by its Creator, and established as His Own eternal gift. How can you fail, when you but ask for what He wills for you? And how could your request be limited to you alone? No gift of God can be unshared. It is this attribute that sets the gifts of God apart from every dream that ever seemed to take the place of truth.

No one can lose and everyone must gain whenever any gift of God has been requested and received by anyone. God gives but to unite. To take away is meaningless to Him. And when it is as meaningless to you, you can be sure you share one Will with Him, and He with you. And you will also know you share one Will with all your brothers, whose intent is yours.

It is this one intent we seek today, uniting our desires with the need of every heart, the call of every mind, the hope that lies beyond despair, the love attack would hide, the brotherhood that hate has sought to sever, but which still remains as God created it. With Help like this beside us, can we fail today as we request the peace of God be given us?

Lesson 186

Salvation of the world depends on me.

Here is the statement that will one day take all arrogance away from every mind. Here is the thought of true humility, which holds no function as your own but that which has been given you. It offers your acceptance of a part assigned to you, without insisting on another role. It does not judge your proper role. It but acknowledges the Will of God is done on earth as well as Heaven. It unites all wills on earth in Heaven's plan to save the world, restoring it to Heaven's peace.

Let us not fight our function. We did not establish it. It is not our idea. The means are given us by which it will be perfectly accomplished. All that we are asked to do is to accept our part in genuine humility, and not deny with self-deceiving arrogance that we are worthy. What is given us to do, we have the strength to do. Our minds are suited perfectly to take the part assigned to us by One Who knows us well.

Today's idea may seem quite sobering, until you see its meaning. All it says is that your Father still remembers you, and offers you the perfect trust He holds in you who are His Son. It does not ask that you be different in any way from what you are. What could humility request but this? And what could arrogance deny but this? Today we will not shrink from our assignment on the specious grounds that modesty is outraged. It is pride that would deny the Call for God Himself.

All false humility we lay aside today, that we may listen to God's Voice reveal to us what He would have us do. We do not doubt our adequacy for the function He will offer us. We will be certain only that He knows our strengths, our wisdom and our holiness. And if He deems us worthy, so we are. It is but arrogance that judges otherwise.

There is one way, and only one, to be released from the imprisonment your plan to prove the false is true has brought to you. Accept the plan you did not make instead. Judge not your value to it. If God's Voice assures you that salvation needs your part, and that the whole depends on you, be sure that it is so. The arrogant must cling to words, afraid to go beyond them to experience which might affront their stance. Yet are the humble free to hear the Voice which tells them what they are, and what to do.

Arrogance makes an image of yourself that is not real. It is this image which quails and retreats in terror, as the Voice for God assures you that you have the strength, the wisdom and the holiness to go beyond all images. You are not weak, as is the image of yourself. You are not ignorant and helpless. Sin can not tarnish the truth in you, and misery can come not near the holy home of God.

All this the Voice for God relates to you. And as He speaks, the image trembles and seeks to attack the threat it does not know, sensing its basis crumble. Let it go. Salvation of the world depends on you, and not upon this little pile of dust. What can it tell the holy Son of God? Why need he be concerned with it at all?

And so we find our peace. We will accept the function God has given us, for all illusions rest upon the weird belief that we can make another for ourselves. Our self-made roles are shifting, and they seem to change from mourner to ecstatic bliss of love and loving. We can laugh or weep, and greet the day with welcome or with tears. Our very being seems to change as we experience a thousand shifts in mood, and our emotions raise us high indeed, or dash us to the ground in hopelessness.

Is this the Son of God? Could He create such instability and call it Son? He Who is changeless shares His attributes with His creation. All the images His Son appears to make have no effect on what he is. They blow across his mind like wind-swept leaves that form a patterning an instant, break apart to group again, and scamper off. Or like mirages seen above a desert, rising from the dust.

These unsubstantial images will go, and leave your mind unclouded and serene, when you accept the function given you. The images you make give rise to but conflicting goals, impermanent and vague, uncertain and ambiguous. Who could be constant in his efforts, or direct his energies and concentrated drive toward goals like these? The functions which the world esteems are so uncertain that they change ten times an hour at their most secure. What hope of gain can rest on goals like this?

In lovely contrast, certain as the sun's return each morning to dispel the night, your truly given function stands out clear and wholly unambiguous. There is no doubt of its validity. It comes from One Who knows no error, and His Voice is certain of Its messages. They will not change, nor be in conflict. All of them point to one goal, and one you can attain. Your plan may be impossible, but God's can never fail because He is its Source.

Do as God's Voice directs. And if It asks a thing of you which seems impossible, remember Who it is that asks, and who would make denial. Then consider this; which is more likely to be right? The Voice that speaks for the Creator of all things, Who knows all things exactly as they are, or a distorted image of yourself, confused, bewildered, inconsistent and unsure of everything? Let not its voice direct you. Hear instead a certain Voice, which tells you of a function given you by your Creator Who remembers you, and urges that you now remember Him.

His gentle Voice is calling from the known to the unknowing. He would comfort you, although He knows no sorrow. He would make a restitution, though He is complete; a gift to you, although He knows that you have everything already. He has Thoughts which answer every need His Son perceives, although He sees them not. For Love must give, and what is given in His Name takes on the form most useful in a world of form.

These are the forms which never can deceive, because they come from Formlessness Itself. Forgiveness is an earthly form of love, which as it is in Heaven has no form. Yet what is needed here is given here as it is needed. In this form you can fulfill your function even here, although what love will mean to you when formlessness has been restored to you is greater still. Salvation of the world depends on you who can forgive. Such is your function here.

Lesson 187

I bless the world because I bless myself.

No one can give unless he has. In fact, giving is proof of having. We have made this point before. What seems to make it hard to credit is not this. No one can doubt that you must first possess what you would give. It is the second phase on which the world and true perception differ. Having had and given, then the world asserts that you have lost what you possessed. The truth maintains that giving will increase what you possess.

How is this possible? For it is sure that if you give a finite thing away, your body's eyes will not perceive it yours. Yet we have learned that things but represent the thoughts that make them. And you do not lack for proof that when you give ideas away, you strengthen them in your own mind. Perhaps the form in which the thought seems to appear is changed in giving. Yet it must return to him who gives. Nor can the form it takes be less acceptable. It must be more.

Ideas must first belong to you, before you give them. If you are to save the world, you first accept salvation for yourself. But you will not believe that this is done until you see the miracles it brings to everyone you look upon. Herein is the idea of giving clarified and given meaning. Now you can perceive that by your giving is your store increased.

Protect all things you value by the act of giving them away, and you are sure that you will never lose them. What you thought you did not have is thereby proven yours. Yet value not its form. For this will change and grow unrecognizable in time, however much you try to keep it safe. No form endures. It is the thought behind the form of things that lives unchangeable.

Give gladly. You can only gain thereby. The thought remains, and grows in strength as it is reinforced by giving. Thoughts extend as they are shared, for they can not be lost. There is no giver and receiver in the sense the world conceives of them. There is a giver who retains; another who will give as well. And both must gain in this exchange, for each will have the thought in form most helpful to him. What he seems to lose is always something he will value less than what will surely be returned to him.

Never forget you give but to yourself. Who understands what giving means must laugh at the idea of sacrifice. Nor can he fail to recognize the many forms which sacrifice may take. He laughs as well at pain and loss, at sickness and at grief, at poverty, starvation and at death. He recognizes sacrifice remains the one idea that stands behind them all, and in his gentle laughter are they healed.

Illusion recognized must disappear. Accept not suffering, and you remove the thought of suffering. Your blessing lies on everyone who suffers, when you choose to see all suffering as what it is. The thought of sacrifice gives rise to all the forms that suffering appears to take. And sacrifice is an idea so mad that sanity dismisses it at once.

Never believe that you can sacrifice. There is no place for sacrifice in what has any value. If the thought occurs, its very presence proves that error has arisen and correction must be made. Your blessing will correct it. Given first to you, it now is yours to give as well. No form of sacrifice and suffering can long endure before the face of one who has forgiven and has blessed himself.

The lilies that your brother offers you are laid upon your altar, with the ones you offer him beside them. Who could fear to look upon such lovely holiness? The great illusion of the fear of God diminishes to nothingness before the purity that you will look on here. Be not afraid to look. The blessedness you will behold will take away all thought of form, and leave instead the perfect gift forever there, forever to increase, forever yours, forever given away.

Now are we one in thought, for fear has gone. And here, before the altar to one God, one Father, one Creator and one Thought, we stand together as one Son of God. Not separate from Him Who is our Source; not distant from one brother who is part of our one Self Whose innocence has joined us all as one, we stand in blessedness, and give as we receive. The Name of God is on our lips. And as we look within, we see the purity of Heaven shine in our reflection of our Father's Love.

Now are we blessed, and now we bless the world. What we have looked upon we would extend, for we would see it everywhere. We would behold it shining with the grace of God in everyone. We would not have it be withheld from anything we look upon. And to ensure this holy sight is ours, we offer it to everything we see. For where we see it, it will be returned to us in form of lilies we can lay upon our altar, making it a home for Innocence Itself, Who dwells in us and offers us His Holiness as ours.

Lesson 188

The peace of God is shining in me now.

Why wait for Heaven? Those who seek the light are merely covering their eyes. The light is in them now. Enlightenment is but a recognition, not a change at all. Light is not of the world, yet you who bear the light in you are alien here as well. The light came with you from your native home, and stayed with you because it is your own. It is the only thing you bring with you from Him Who is your Source. It shines in you because it lights your home, and leads you back to where it came from and you are at home.

This light can not be lost. Why wait to find it in the future, or believe it has been lost already, or was never there? It can so easily be looked upon that arguments which prove it is not there become ridiculous. Who can deny the presence of what he beholds in him? It is not difficult to look within, for there all vision starts. There is no sight, be it of dreams or from a truer Source, that is not but the shadow of the seen through inward vision. There perception starts, and there it ends. It has no source but this.

The peace of God is shining in you now, and from your heart extends around the world. It pauses to caress each living thing, and leaves a blessing with it that remains forever and forever. What it gives must be eternal. It removes all thoughts of the ephemeral and valueless. It brings renewal to all tired hearts, and lights all vision as it passes by. All of its gifts are given everyone, and everyone unites in giving thanks to you who give, and you who have received.

The shining in your mind reminds the world of what it has forgotten, and the world restores the memory to you as well. From you salvation radiates with gifts beyond all measure, given and returned. To you, the giver of the gift, does God Himself give thanks. And in His blessing does the light in you shine brighter, adding to the gifts you have to offer to the world.

The peace of God can never be contained. Who recognizes it within himself must give it. And the means for giving it are in his understanding. He forgives because he recognized the truth in him. The peace of God is shining in you now, and in all living things. In quietness is it acknowledged universally. For what your inward vision looks upon is your perception of the universe.

Sit quietly and close your eyes. The light within you is sufficient. It alone has power to give the gift of sight to you. Exclude the outer world, and let your thoughts fly to the peace within. They know the way. For honest thoughts, untainted by the dream of worldly things outside yourself, become the holy messengers of God Himself.

These thoughts you think with Him. They recognize their home. And they point surely to their Source, Where God the Father and the Son are One. God's peace is shining on them, but they must remain with you as well, for they were born within your mind, as yours was born in God's. They lead you back to peace, from where they came but to remind you how you must return.

They heed your Father's Voice when you refuse to listen. And they urge you gently to accept His Word for what you are, instead of fantasies and shadows. They remind you that you are the co-creator of all things that live. For as the peace of God is shining in you, it must shine on them.

We practice coming nearer to the light in us today. We take our wandering thoughts, and gently bring them back to where they fall in line with all the thoughts we share with God. We will not let them stray. We let the light within our minds direct them to come home. We have betrayed them, ordering that they depart from us. But now we call them back, and wash them clean of strange desires and disordered wishes. We restore to them the holiness of their inheritance.

Thus are our minds restored with them, and we acknowledge that the peace of God still shines in us, and from us to all living things that share our life. We will forgive them all, absolving all the world from what we thought it did to us. For it is we who make the world as we would have it. Now we choose that it be innocent, devoid of sin and open to salvation. And we lay our saving blessing on it, as we say:

THE PEACE OF GOD IS SHINING IN ME NOW.
LET ALL THINGS SHINE UPON ME IN THAT PEACE,
AND LET ME BLESS THEM WITH THE LIGHT IN ME.

Lesson 189

I feel the Love of God within me now.

There is a light in you the world can not perceive. And with its eyes you will not see this light, for you are blinded by the world. Yet you have eyes to see it. It is there for you to look upon. It was not placed in you to be kept hidden from your sight. This light is a reflection of the thought we practice now. To feel the Love of God within you is to see the world anew, shining in innocence, alive with hope, and blessed with perfect charity and love.

Who could feel fear in such a world as this? It welcomes you, rejoices that you came, and sings your praises as it keeps you safe from every form of danger and of pain. It offers you a warm and gentle home in which to stay a while. It blesses you throughout the day, and watches through the night as silent guardian of your holy sleep. It sees salvation in you, and protects the light in you, in which it sees its own. It offers you its flowers and its snow, in thankfulness for your benevolence.

This is the world the Love of God reveals. It is so different from the world you see through darkened eyes of malice and of fear, that one belies the other. Only one can be perceived at all. The other one is wholly meaningless. A world in which forgiveness shines on everything, and peace offers its gentle light to everyone, is inconceivable to those who see a world of hatred rising from attack, poised to avenge, to murder and destroy.

Yet is the world of hatred equally unseen and inconceivable to those who feel God's Love in them. Their world reflects the quietness and peace that shines in them; the gentleness and innocence they see surrounding them; the joy with which they look out from the endless wells of joy within. What they have felt in them they look upon, and see its sure reflection everywhere.

What would you see? The choice is given you. But learn and do not let your mind forget this law of seeing: You will look upon that which you feel within. If hatred finds a place within your heart, you will perceive a fearful world, held cruelly in death's sharp-pointed, bony fingers. If you feel the Love of God within you, you will look out on a world of mercy and of love.

Today we pass illusions, as we seek to reach to what is true in us, and feel its all-embracing tenderness, its Love which knows us perfect as itself, its sight which is the gift its Love bestows on us. We learn the way today. It is as sure as Love itself, to which it carries us. For its simplicity avoids the snares the foolish convolutions of the world's apparent reasoning but serve to hide.

Simply do this: Be still, and lay aside all thoughts of what you are and what God is; all concepts you have learned about the world; all images you hold about yourself. Empty your mind of everything it thinks is either true or false, or good or bad, of every thought it judges worthy, and all the ideas of which it is ashamed. Hold onto nothing. Do not bring with you one thought the past has taught, nor one belief you ever learned before from anything. Forget this world, forget this course, and come with wholly empty hands unto your God.

Is it not He Who knows the way to you? You need not know the way to Him. Your part is simply to allow all obstacles that you have interposed between the Son and God the Father to be quietly removed forever. God will do His part in joyful and immediate response. Ask and receive. But do not make demands, nor point the road to God by which He should appear to you. The way to reach Him is merely to let Him be. For in that way is your reality proclaimed as well.

And so today we do not choose the way in which we go to Him. But we do choose to let Him come. And with this choice we rest. And in our quiet hearts and open minds, His Love will blaze its pathway of itself. What has not been denied is surely there, if it be true and can be surely reached. God knows His Son, and knows the way to him. He does not need His Son to show Him how to find His way. Through every opened door His Love shines outward from its home within, and lightens up the world in innocence.

Father, we do not know the way to You. But we have called, and You have answered us. We will not interfere. Salvation's ways are not our own, for they belong to You. And it is unto You we look for them. Our hands are open to receive Your gifts. We have no thoughts we think apart from You, and cherish no beliefs of what we are, or Who created us. Yours is the way that we would find and follow. And we ask but that Your Will, which is our own as well, be done in us and in the world, that it become a part of Heaven now. Amen.

Lesson 190

I choose the joy of God instead of pain.

Pain is a wrong perspective. When it is experienced in any form, it is a proof of self-deception. It is not a fact at all. There is no form it takes that will not disappear if seen aright. For pain proclaims God cruel. How could it be real in any form? It witnesses to God the Father's hatred of His Son, the sinfulness He sees in him, and His insane desire for revenge and death.

Can such projections be attested to? Can they be anything but wholly false? Pain is but witness to the Son's mistakes in what he thinks he is. It is a dream of fierce retaliation for a crime that could not be committed; for attack on what is wholly unassailable. It is a nightmare of abandonment by an Eternal Love, which could not leave the Son whom It created out of love.

Pain is a sign illusions reign in place of truth. It demonstrates God is denied, confused with fear, perceived as mad, and seen as traitor to Himself. If God is real, there is no pain. If pain is real, there is no God. For vengeance is not part of love. And fear, denying love and using pain to prove that God is dead, has shown that death is victor over life. The body is the Son of God, corruptible in death, as mortal as the Father he has slain.

Peace to such foolishness! The time has come to laugh at such insane ideas. There is no need to think of them as savage crimes, or secret sins with weighty consequence. Who but a madman could conceive of them as cause of anything? Their witness, pain, is mad as they, and no more to be feared than the insane illusions which it shields, and tries to demonstrate must still be true.

It is your thoughts alone that cause you pain. Nothing external to your mind can hurt or injure you in any way. There is no cause beyond yourself that can reach down and bring oppression. No one but yourself affects you. There is nothing in the world that has the power to make you ill or sad, or weak or frail. But it is you who have the power to dominate all things you see by merely recognizing what you are. As you perceive the harmlessness in them, they will accept your holy will as theirs. And what was seen as fearful now becomes a source of innocence and holiness.

My holy brother, think of this awhile: The world you see does nothing. It has no effects at all. It merely represents your thoughts. And it will change entirely as you elect to change your mind, and choose the joy of God as what you really want. Your Self is radiant in this holy joy, unchanged, unchanging and unchangeable, forever and forever. And would you deny a little corner of your mind its own inheritance, and keep it as a hospital for pain; a sickly place where living things must come at last to die?

The world may seem to cause you pain. And yet the world, as causeless, has no power to cause. As an effect, it cannot make effects. As an illusion, it is what you wish. Your idle wishes represent its pains. Your strange desires bring it evil dreams. Your thoughts of death envelop it in fear, while in your kind forgiveness does it live.

Pain is the thought of evil taking form, and working havoc in your holy mind. Pain is the ransom you have gladly paid not to be free. In pain is God denied the Son He loves. In pain does fear appear to triumph over love, and time replace eternity and Heaven. And the world becomes a cruel and a bitter place, where sorrow rules and little joys give way before the onslaught of the savage pain that waits to end all joy in misery.

Lay down your arms, and come without defense into the quiet place where Heaven's peace holds all things still at last. Lay down all thoughts of danger and of fear. Let no attack enter with you. Lay down the cruel sword of judgment that you hold against your throat, and put aside the withering assaults with which you seek to hide your holiness.

Here will you understand there is no pain. Here does the joy of God belong to you. This is the day when it is given you to realize the lesson that contains all of salvation's power. It is this: Pain is illusion; joy, reality. Pain is but sleep; joy is awakening. Pain is deception; joy alone is truth.

And so again we make the only choice that ever can be made; we choose between illusions and the truth, or pain and joy, or hell and Heaven. Let our gratitude unto our Teacher fill our hearts, as we are free to choose our joy instead of pain, our holiness in place of sin, the peace of God instead of conflict, and the light of Heaven for the darkness of the world.

Lesson 191

I am the holy Son of God Himself.

Here is your declaration of release from bondage of the world. And here as well is all the world released. You do not see what you have done by giving to the world the role of jailer to the Son of God. What could it be but vicious and afraid, fearful of shadows, punitive and wild, lacking all reason, blind, insane with hate?

What have you done that this should be your world? What have you done that this is what you see? Deny your own Identity, and this is what remains. You look on chaos and proclaim it is yourself. There is no sight that fails to witness this to you. There is no sound that does not speak of frailty within you and without; no breath you draw that does not seem to bring you nearer death; no hope you hold but will dissolve in tears.

Deny your own Identity, and you will not escape the madness which induced this weird, unnatural and ghostly thought that mocks creation and that laughs at God. Deny your own Identity, and you assail the universe alone, without a friend, a tiny particle of dust against the legions of your enemies. Deny your own Identity, and look on evil, sin and death, and watch despair snatch from your fingers every scrap of hope, leaving you nothing but the wish to die.

Yet what is it except a game you play in which Identity can be denied? You are as God created you. All else but this one thing is folly to believe. In this one thought is everyone set free. In this one truth are all illusions gone. In this one fact is sinlessness proclaimed to be forever part of everything, the central core of its existence and its guarantee of immortality.

But let today's idea find a place among your thoughts and you have risen far above the world, and all the worldly thoughts that hold it prisoner. And from this place of safety and escape you will return and set it free. For he who can accept his true Identity is truly saved. And his salvation is the gift he gives to everyone, in gratitude to Him Who pointed out the way to happiness that changed his whole perspective of the world.

One holy thought like this and you are free: You are the holy Son of God Himself. And with this holy thought you learn as well that you have freed the world. You have no need to use it cruelly, and then perceive this savage need in it. You set it free of your imprisonment. You will not see a devastating image of yourself walking the world in terror, with the world twisting in agony because your fears have laid the mark of death upon its heart.

Be glad today how very easily is hell undone. You need but tell yourself:

I AM THE HOLY SON OF GOD HIMSELF. I CANNOT SUFFER,
CANNOT BE IN PAIN; I CANNOT SUFFER LOSS, NOR FAIL TO DO
ALL THAT SALVATION ASKS.

And in that thought is everything you look on wholly changed.

A miracle has lighted up all dark and ancient caverns, where the rites of death echoed since time began. For time has lost its hold upon the world. The Son of God has come in glory to redeem the lost, to save the helpless, and to give the world the gift of his forgiveness. Who could see the world as dark and sinful, when God's Son has come again at last to set it free?

You who perceive yourself as weak and frail, with futile hopes and devastated dreams, born but to die, to weep and suffer pain, hear this: All power is given unto you in earth and Heaven. There is nothing that you cannot do. You play the game of death, of being helpless, pitifully tied to dissolution in a world which shows no mercy to you. Yet when you accord it mercy, will its mercy shine on you.

Then let the Son of God awaken from his sleep, and opening his holy eyes, return again to bless the world he made. In error it began, but it will end in the reflection of his holiness. And he will sleep no more and dream of death. Then join with me today. Your glory is the light that saves the world. Do not withhold salvation longer. Look about the world, and see the suffering there. Is not your heart willing to bring your weary brothers rest?

They must await your own release. They stay in chains till you are free. They cannot see the mercy of the world until you find it in yourself. They suffer pain until you have denied its hold on you. They die till you accept your own eternal life. You are the holy Son of God Himself. Remember this, and all the world is free. Remember this, and earth and Heaven are one.

Lesson 192

I have a function God would have me fill.

It is your Father's holy Will that you complete Himself, and that your Self shall be His sacred Son, forever pure as He, of love created and in love preserved, extending love, creating in its name, forever one with God and with your Self. Yet what can such a function mean within a world of envy, hatred and attack?

Therefore, you have a function in the world in its own terms. For who can understand a language far beyond his simple grasp? Forgiveness represents your function here. It is not God's creation, for it is the means by which untruth can be undone. And who would pardon Heaven? Yet on earth, you need the means to let illusions go. Creation merely waits for your return to be acknowledged, not to be complete.

Creation cannot even be conceived of in the world. It has no meaning here. Forgiveness is the closest it can come to earth. For being Heaven-born, it has no form at all. Yet God created One Who has the power to translate in form the wholly formless. What He makes are dreams, but of a kind so close to waking that the light of day already shines in them, and eyes already opening behold the joyful sights their offerings contain.

Forgiveness gently looks upon all things unknown in Heaven, sees them disappear, and leaves the world a clean and unmarked slate on which the Word of God can now replace the senseless symbols written there before. Forgiveness is the means by which the fear of death is overcome, because it holds no fierce attraction now and guilt is gone. Forgiveness lets the body be perceived as what it is; a simple teaching aid, to be laid by when learning is complete, but hardly changing him who learns at all.

The mind without the body cannot make mistakes. It cannot think that it will die, nor be the prey of merciless attack. Anger becomes impossible, and where is terror then? What fears could still assail those who have lost the source of all attack, the core of anguish and the seat of fear? Only forgiveness can relieve the mind of thinking that the body is its home. Only forgiveness can restore the peace that God intended for His holy Son. Only forgiveness can persuade the Son to look again upon his holiness.

With anger gone, you will indeed perceive that, for Christ's vision and the gift of sight, no sacrifice was asked, and only pain was lifted from a sick and tortured mind. Is this unwelcome? Is it to be feared? Or is it to be hoped for, met with thanks and joyously accepted? We are one, and therefore give up nothing. But we have indeed been given everything by God.

Yet do we need forgiveness to perceive that this is so. Without its kindly light we grope in darkness, using reason but to justify our rage and our attack. Our understanding is so limited that what we think we understand is but confusion born of error. We are lost in mists of shifting dreams and fearful thoughts, our eyes shut tight against the light; our minds engaged in worshipping what is not there.

Who can be born again in Christ but him who has forgiven everyone he sees or thinks of or imagines? Who could be set free while he imprisons anyone? A jailer is not free, for he is bound together with his prisoner. He must be sure that he does not escape, and so he spends his time in keeping watch on him. The bars that limit him become the world in which his jailer lives, along with him. And it is on his freedom that the way to liberty depends for both of them.

Therefore, hold no one prisoner. Release instead of bind, for thus are you made free. The way is simple. Every time you feel a stab of anger, realize you hold a sword above your head. And it will fall or be averted as you choose to be condemned or free. Thus does each one who seems to tempt you to be angry represent your savior from the prison house of death. And so you owe him thanks instead of pain.

Be merciful today. The Son of God deserves your mercy. It is he who asks that you accept the way to freedom now. Deny him not. His Father's Love for him belongs to you. Your function here on earth is only to forgive him, that you may accept him back as your Identity. He is as God created him. And you are what he is. Forgive him now his sins, and you will see that you are one with him.

Lesson 193

All things are lessons God would have me learn.

God does not know of learning. Yet His Will extends to what He does not understand, in that He wills the happiness His Son inherited of Him be undisturbed; eternal and forever gaining scope, eternally expanding in the joy of full creation, and eternally open and wholly limitless in Him. That is His Will. And thus His Will provides the means to guarantee that it is done.

God sees no contradictions. Yet His Son believes he sees them. Thus he has a need for One Who can correct his erring sight, and give him vision that will lead him back to where perception ceases. God does not perceive at all. Yet it is He Who gives the means by which perception is made true and beautiful enough to let the light of Heaven shine upon it. It is He Who answers what His Son would contradict, and keeps his sinlessness forever safe.

These are the lessons God would have you learn. His Will reflects them all, and they reflect His loving kindness to the Son He loves. Each lesson has a central thought, the same in all of them. The form alone is changed, with different circumstances and events; with different characters and different themes, apparent but not real. They are the same in fundamental content. It is this:

FORGIVE, AND YOU WILL SEE THIS DIFFERENTLY.

Certain it is that all distress does not appear to be but unforgiveness. Yet that is the content underneath the form. It is this sameness which makes learning sure, because the lesson is so simple that it cannot be rejected in the end. No one can hide forever from a truth so very obvious that it appears in countless forms, and yet is recognized as easily in all of them, if one but wants to see the simple lesson there.

FORGIVE, AND YOU WILL SEE THIS DIFFERENTLY.

These are the words the Holy Spirit speaks in all your tribulations, all your pain, all suffering regardless of its form. These are the words with which temptation ends, and guilt, abandoned, is revered no more. These are the words which end the dream of sin, and rid the mind of fear. These are the words by which salvation comes to all the world.

Shall we not learn to say these words when we are tempted to believe that pain is real, and death becomes our choice instead of life? Shall we not learn to say these words when we have understood their power to release all minds from bondage? These are words which give you power over all events that seem to have been given power over you. You see them rightly when you hold these words in full awareness, and do not forget these words apply to everything you see or any brother looks upon amiss.

How can you tell when you are seeing wrong, or someone else is failing to perceive the lesson he should learn? Does pain seem real in the perception? If it does, be sure the lesson is not learned. And there remains an unforgiveness hiding in the mind that sees the pain through eyes the mind directs.

God would not have you suffer thus. He would help you forgive yourself. His Son does not remember who he is. And God would have him not forget His Love, and all the gifts His Love brings with it. Would you now renounce your own salvation? Would you fail to learn the simple lessons Heaven's Teacher sets before you, that all pain may disappear and God may be remembered by His Son?

All things are lessons God would have you learn. He would not leave an unforgiving thought without correction, nor one thorn or nail to hurt His holy Son in any way. He would ensure his holy rest remain untroubled and serene, without a care, in an eternal home which cares for him. And He would have all tears be wiped away, with none remaining yet unshed, and none but waiting their appointed time to fall. For God has willed that laughter should replace each one, and that His Son be free again.

We will attempt today to overcome a thousand seeming obstacles to peace in just one day. Let mercy come to you more quickly. Do not try to hold it off another day, another minute or another instant. Time was made for this. Use it today for what its purpose is. Morning and night, devote what time you can to serve its proper aim, and do not let the time be less than meets your deepest need.

Give all you can, and give a little more. For now we would arise in haste and go unto our Father's house. We have been gone too long, and we would linger here no more. And as we practice, let us think about all things we saved to settle by ourselves, and kept apart from healing. Let us give them all to Him Who knows the way to look upon them so that they will disappear. Truth is His message; truth His teaching is. His are the lessons God would have us learn.

Each hour, spend a little time today, and in the days to come, in practicing the lesson in forgiveness in the form established for the day. And try to give it application to the happenings the hour brought, so that the next one is free of the one before. The chains of time are easily unloosened in this way. Let no one hour cast its shadow on the one that follows, and when that one goes, let everything that happened in its course go with it. Thus will you remain unbound, in peace eternal in the world of time.

This is the lesson God would have you learn: There is a way to look on everything that lets it be to you another step to Him, and to salvation of the world. To all that speaks of terror, answer thus:

I WILL FORGIVE, AND THIS WILL DISAPPEAR.

To every apprehension, every care and every form of suffering, repeat these selfsame words. And then you hold the key that opens Heaven's gate, and brings the Love of God the Father down to earth at last, to raise it up to Heaven. God will take this final step Himself. Do not deny the little steps He asks you take to Him.

Lesson 194

I place the future in the Hands of God.

Today's idea takes another step toward quick salvation, and a giant stride it is indeed! So great the distance is that it encompasses, it sets you down just short of Heaven, with the goal in sight and obstacles behind. Your foot has reached the lawns that welcome you to Heaven's gate; the quiet place of peace, where you await with certainty the final step of God. How far are we progressing now from earth! How close are we approaching to our goal! How short the journey still to be pursued!

Accept today's idea, and you have passed all anxiety, all pits of hell, all blackness of depression, thoughts of sin, and devastation brought about by guilt. Accept today's idea, and you have released the world from all imprisonment by loosening the heavy chains that locked the door to freedom on it. You are saved, and your salvation thus becomes the gift you give the world, because you have received.

In no one instant is depression felt, or pain experienced or loss perceived. In no one instant sorrow can be set upon a throne, and worshipped faithfully. In no one instant can one even die. And so each instant given unto God in passing, with the next one given Him already, is a time of your release from sadness, pain and even death itself.

God holds your future as He holds your past and present. They are one to Him, and so they should be one to you. Yet in this world, the temporal progression still seems real. And so you are not asked to understand the lack of sequence really found in time. You are but asked to let the future go, and place it in God's Hands. And you will see by your experience that you have laid the past and present in His Hands as well, because the past will punish you no more, and future dread will now be meaningless.

Release the future. For the past is gone, and what is present, freed from its bequest of grief and misery, of pain and loss, becomes the instant in which time escapes the bondage of illusions where it runs its pitiless, inevitable course. Then is each instant which was slave to time transformed into a holy instant, when the light that was kept hidden in God's Son is freed to bless the world. Now is he free, and all his glory shines upon a world made free with him, to share his holiness.

If you can see the lesson for today as the deliverance it really is, you will not hesitate to give as much consistent effort as you can, to make it be a part of you. As it becomes a thought that rules your mind, a habit in your problem-solving repertoire, a way of quick reaction to temptation, you extend your learning to the world. And as you learn to see salvation in all things, so will the world perceive that it is saved.

What worry can beset the one who gives his future to the loving Hands of God? What can he suffer? What can cause him pain, or bring experience of loss to him? What can he fear? And what can he regard except with love? For he who has escaped all fear of future pain has found his way to present peace, and certainty of care the world can never threaten. He is sure that his perception may be faulty, but will never lack correction. He is free to choose again when he has been deceived; to change his mind when he has made mistakes.

Place, then, your future in the Hands of God. For thus you call the memory of Him to come again, replacing all your thoughts of sin and evil with the truth of love. Think you the world could fail to gain thereby, and every living creature not respond with healed perception? Who entrusts himself to God has also placed the world within the Hands to which he has himself appealed for comfort and security. He lays aside the sick illusions of the world along with his, and offers peace to both.

Now are we saved indeed. For in God's Hands we rest untroubled, sure that only good can come to us. If we forget, we will be gently reassured. If we accept an unforgiving thought, it will be soon replaced by love's reflection. And if we are tempted to attack, we will appeal to Him Who guards our rest to make the choice for us that leaves temptation far behind. No longer is the world our enemy, for we have chosen that we be its friend.

Lesson 195

Love is the way I walk in gratitude.

Gratitude is a lesson hard to learn for those who look upon the world amiss. The most that they can do is see themselves as better off than others. And they try to be content because another seems to suffer more than they. How pitiful and deprecating are such thoughts! For who has cause for thanks while others have less cause? And who could suffer less because he sees another suffer more? Your gratitude is due to Him alone Who made all cause of sorrow disappear throughout the world.

It is insane to offer thanks because of suffering. But it is equally insane to fail in gratitude to One Who offers you the certain means whereby all pain is healed, and suffering replaced with laughter and with happiness. Nor could the even partly sane refuse to take the steps which He directs, and follow in the way He sets before them, to escape a prison that they thought contained no door to the deliverance they now perceive.

Your brother is your "enemy" because you see in him the rival for your peace; a plunderer who takes his joy from you, and leaves you nothing but a black despair so bitter and relentless that there is no hope remaining. Now is vengeance all there is to wish for. Now can you but try to bring him down to lie in death with you, as useless as yourself; as little left within his grasping fingers as in yours.

You do not offer God your gratitude because your brother is more slave than you, nor could you sanely be enraged if he seems freer. Love makes no comparisons. And gratitude can only be sincere if it be joined to love. We offer thanks to God our Father that in us all things will find their freedom. It will never be that some are loosed while others still are bound. For who can bargain in the name of love?

Therefore give thanks, but in sincerity. And let your gratitude make room for all who will escape with you; the sick, the weak, the needy and afraid, and those who mourn a seeming loss or feel apparent pain, who suffer cold or hunger, or who walk the way of hatred and the path of death. All these go with you. Let us not compare ourselves with them, for thus we split them off from our awareness of the unity we share with them, as they must share with us.

We thank our Father for one thing alone; that we are separate from no living thing, and therefore one with Him. And we rejoice that no exceptions ever can be made which would reduce our wholeness, nor impair or change our function to complete the One Who is Himself completion. We give thanks for every living thing, for otherwise we offer thanks for nothing, and we fail to recognize the gifts of God to us.

Then let our brothers lean their tired heads against our shoulders as they rest a while. We offer thanks for them. For if we can direct them to the peace that we would find, the way is opening at last to us. An ancient door is swinging free again; a long forgotten Word re-echoes in our memory, and gathers clarity as we are willing once again to hear.

Walk, then, in gratitude the way of love. For hatred is forgotten when we lay comparisons aside. What more remains as obstacles to peace? The fear of God is now undone at last, and we forgive without comparing. Thus we cannot choose to overlook some things, and yet retain some other things still locked away as "sins." When your forgiveness is complete you will have total gratitude, for you will see that everything has earned the right to love by being loving, even as your Self.

Today we learn to think of gratitude in place of anger, malice and revenge. We have been given everything. If we refuse to recognize it, we are not entitled therefore to our bitterness, and to a self-perception which regards us in a place of merciless pursuit, where we are badgered ceaselessly, and pushed about without a thought or care for us or for our future. Gratitude becomes the single thought we substitute for these insane perceptions. God has cared for us, and calls us Son. Can there be more than this?

Our gratitude will pave the way to Him, and shorten our learning time by more than you could ever dream of. Gratitude goes hand in hand with love, and where one is the other must be found. For gratitude is but an aspect of the Love which is the Source of all creation. God gives thanks to you, His Son, for being what you are; His Own completion and the Source of love, along with Him. Your gratitude to Him is one with His to you. For love can walk no road except the way of gratitude, and thus we go who walk the way to God.

Lesson 196

It can be but myself I crucify.

When this is firmly understood and kept in full awareness, you will not attempt to harm yourself, nor make your body slave to vengeance. You will not attack yourself, and you will realize that to attack another is but to attack yourself. You will be free of the insane belief that to attack a brother saves yourself. And you will understand his safety is your own, and in his healing you are healed.

Perhaps at first you will not understand how mercy, limitless and with all things held in its sure protection, can be found in the idea we practice for today. It may, in fact, appear to be a sign that punishment can never be escaped because the ego, under what it sees as threat, is quick to cite the truth to save its lies. Yet must it fail to understand the truth it uses thus. But you can learn to see these foolish applications, and deny the meaning they appear to have.

Thus do you also teach your mind that you are not an ego. For the ways in which the ego would distort the truth will not deceive you longer. You will not believe you are a body to be crucified. And you will see within today's idea the light of resurrection, looking past all thoughts of crucifixion and of death, to thoughts of liberation and of life.

Today's idea is one step we take in leading us from bondage to the state of perfect freedom. Let us take this step today, that we may quickly go the way salvation shows us, taking every step in its appointed sequence, as the mind relinquishes its burdens one by one. It is not time we need for this. It is but willingness. For what would seem to need a thousand years can easily be done in just one instant by the grace of God.

The dreary, hopeless thought that you can make attacks on others and escape yourself has nailed you to the cross. Perhaps it seemed to be salvation. Yet it merely stood for the belief the fear of God is real. And what is that but hell? Who could believe his Father is his deadly enemy, separate from him, and waiting to destroy his life and blot him from the universe, without the fear of hell upon his heart?

Such is the form of madness you believe, if you accept the fearful thought you can attack another and be free yourself. Until this form is changed, there is no hope. Until you see that this, at least, must be entirely impossible, how could there be escape? The fear of God is real to anyone who thinks this thought is true. And he will not perceive its foolishness, or even see that it is there, so that it would be possible to question it.

To question it at all, its form must first be changed at least as much as will permit fear of retaliation to abate, and the responsibility returned to some extent to you. From there you can at least consider if you want to go along this painful path. Until this shift has been accomplished, you can not perceive that it is but your thoughts that bring you fear, and your deliverance depends on you.

Our next steps will be easy, if you take this one today. From there we go ahead quite rapidly. For once you understand it is impossible that you be hurt except by your own thoughts, the fear of God must disappear. You cannot then believe that fear is caused without. And God, Whom you had thought to banish, can be welcomed back within the holy mind He never left.

Salvation's song can certainly be heard in the idea we practice for today. If it can but be you you crucify, you did not hurt the world, and need not fear its vengeance and pursuit. Nor need you hide in terror from the deadly fear of God projection hides behind. The thing you dread the most is your salvation. You are strong, and it is strength you want. And you are free, and glad of freedom. You have sought to be both weak and bound, because you feared your strength and freedom. Yet salvation lies in them.

There is an instant in which terror seems to grip your mind so wholly that escape appears quite hopeless. When you realize, once and for all, that it is you you fear, the mind perceives itself as split. And this had been concealed while you believed attack could be directed outward, and returned from outside to within. It seemed to be an enemy outside you had to fear. And thus a god outside yourself became your mortal enemy; the source of fear.

Now, for an instant, is a murderer perceived within you, eager for your death, intent on plotting punishment for you until the time when it can kill at last. Yet in this instant is the time as well in which salvation comes. For fear of God has disappeared. And you can call on Him to save you from illusions by His Love, calling Him Father and yourself His Son. Pray that the instant may be soon,–today. Step back from fear, and make advance to love.

There is no Thought of God that does not go with you to help you reach that instant, and to go beyond it quickly, surely and forever. When the fear of God is gone, there are no obstacles that still remain between you and the holy peace of God. How kind and merciful is the idea we practice! Give it welcome, as you should, for it is your release. It is indeed but you your mind can try to crucify. Yet your redemption, too, will come from you.

Lesson 197

It can be but my gratitude I earn.

Here is the second step we take to free your mind from the belief in outside force pitted against your own. You make attempts at kindness and forgiveness. Yet you turn them to attack again, unless you find external gratitude and lavish thanks. Your gifts must be received with honor, lest they be withdrawn. And so you think God's gifts are loans at best; at worst, deceptions which would cheat you of defenses, to ensure that when He strikes He will not fail to kill.

How easily are God and guilt confused by those who know not what their thoughts can do. Deny your strength, and weakness must become salvation to you. See yourself as bound, and bars become your home. Nor will you leave the prison house, or claim your strength, until guilt and salvation are not seen as one, and freedom and salvation are perceived as joined, with strength beside them, to be sought and claimed, and found and fully recognized.

The world must thank you when you offer it release from your illusions. Yet your thanks belong to you as well, for its release can only mirror yours. Your gratitude is all your gifts require, that they be a lasting offering of a thankful heart, released from hell forever. Is it this you would undo by taking back your gifts, because they were not honored? It is you who honor them and give them fitting thanks, for it is you who have received the gifts.

It does not matter if another thinks your gifts unworthy. In his mind there is a part that joins with yours in thanking you. It does not matter if your gifts seem lost and ineffectual. They are received where they are given. In your gratitude are they accepted universally, and thankfully acknowledged by the Heart of God Himself. And would you take them back, when He has gratefully accepted them?

God blesses every gift you give to Him, and every gift is given Him, because it can be given only to yourself. And what belongs to God must be His Own. Yet you will never realize His gifts are sure, eternal, changeless, limitless, forever giving out, extending love and adding to your never-ending joy while you forgive but to attack again.

Withdraw the gifts you give, and you will think that what is given you has been withdrawn. But learn to let forgiveness take away the sins you think you see outside yourself, and you can never think the gifts of God are lent but for a little while, before He snatches them away again in death. For death will have no meaning for you then.

And with the end of this belief is fear forever over. Thank your Self for this, for He is grateful only unto God, and He gives thanks for you unto Himself. To everyone who lives will Christ yet come, for everyone must live and move in Him. His Being in His Father is secure, because Their Will is One. Their gratitude to all They have created has no end, for gratitude remains a part of love.

Thanks be to you, the holy Son of God. For as you were created, you contain all things within your Self. And you are still as God created you. Nor can you dim the light of your perfection. In your heart the Heart of God is laid. He holds you dear, because you are Himself. All gratitude belongs to you, because of what you are.

Give thanks as you receive it. Be you free of all ingratitude to anyone who makes your Self complete. And from this Self is no one left outside. Give thanks for all the countless channels which extend this Self. All that you do is given unto Him. All that you think can only be His Thoughts, sharing with Him the holy Thoughts of God. Earn now the gratitude you have denied yourself when you forgot the function God has given you. But never think that He has ever ceased to offer thanks to you.

Lesson 198

Only my condemnation injures me.

Injury is impossible. And yet illusion makes illusion. If you can condemn, you can be injured. For you have believed that you can injure, and the right you have established for yourself can be now used against you, till you lay it down as valueless, unwanted and unreal. Then does illusion cease to have effects, and those it seemed to have will be undone. Then are you free, for freedom is your gift, and you can now receive the gift you gave.

Condemn and you are made a prisoner. Forgive and you are freed. Such is the law that rules perception. It is not a law that knowledge understands, for freedom is a part of knowledge. To condemn is thus impossible in truth. What seems to be its influence and its effects have not occurred at all. Yet must we deal with them a while as if they had. Illusion makes illusion. Except one. Forgiveness is illusion that is answer to the rest.

Forgiveness sweeps all other dreams away, and though it is itself a dream, it breeds no others. All illusions save this one must multiply a thousandfold. But this is where illusions end. Forgiveness is the end of dreams, because it is a dream of waking. It is not itself the truth. Yet does it point to where the truth must be, and gives direction with the certainty of God Himself. It is a dream in which the Son of God awakens to his Self and to his Father, knowing They are One.

Forgiveness is the only road that leads out of disaster, past all suffering, and finally away from death. How could there be another way, when this one is the plan of God Himself? And why would you oppose it, quarrel with it, seek to find a thousand ways in which it must be wrong; a thousand other possibilities?

Is it not wiser to be glad you hold the answer to your problems in your hand? Is it not more intelligent to thank the One Who gives salvation, and accept His gift with gratitude? And is it not a kindness to yourself to hear His Voice and learn the simple lessons He would teach, instead of trying to dismiss His words, and substitute your own in place of His?

His words will work. His words will save. His words contain all hope, all blessing and all joy that ever can be found upon this earth. His words are born in God, and come to you with Heaven's love upon them. Those who hear His words have heard the song of Heaven. For these are the words in which all merge as one at last. And as this one will fade away, the Word of God will come to take its place, for it will be remembered then and loved.

This world has many seeming separate haunts where mercy has no meaning, and attack appears as justified. Yet all are one; a place where death is offered to God's Son and to his Father. You may think They have accepted. But if you will look again upon the place where you beheld Their blood, you will perceive a miracle instead. How foolish to believe that They could die! How foolish to believe you can attack! How mad to think that you could be condemned, and that the holy Son of God can die!

The stillness of your Self remains unmoved, untouched by thoughts like these, and unaware of any condemnation which could need forgiveness. Dreams of any kind are strange and alien to the truth. And what but truth could have a Thought which builds a bridge to it that brings illusions to the other side?

Today we practice letting freedom come to make its home with you. The truth bestows these words upon your mind, that you may find the key to light and let the darkness end:

ONLY MY CONDEMNATION INJURES ME.
ONLY MY OWN FORGIVENESS SETS ME FREE.

Do not forget today that there can be no form of suffering that fails to hide an unforgiving thought. Nor can there be a form of pain forgiveness cannot heal.

Accept the one illusion which proclaims there is no condemnation in God's Son, and Heaven is remembered instantly; the world forgotten, all its weird beliefs forgotten with it, as the face of Christ appears unveiled at last in this one dream. This is the gift the Holy Spirit holds for you from God your Father. Let today be celebrated both on earth and in your holy home as well. Be kind to Both, as you forgive the trespasses you thought Them guilty of, and see your innocence shining upon you from the face of Christ.

Now is there silence all around the world. Now is there stillness where before there was a frantic rush of thoughts that made no sense. Now is there tranquil light across the face of earth, made quiet in a dreamless sleep. And now the Word of God alone remains upon it. Only that can be perceived an instant longer. Then are symbols done, and everything you ever thought you made completely vanished from the mind that God forever knows to be His only Son.

There is no condemnation in him. He is perfect in his holiness. He needs no thoughts of mercy. Who could give him gifts when everything is his? And who could dream of offering forgiveness to the Son of Sinlessness Itself, so like to Him Whose Son he is, that to behold the Son is to perceive no more, and only know the Father? In this vision of the

Son, so brief that not an instant stands between this single sight and timelessness itself, you see the vision of yourself, and then you disappear forever into God.

Today we come still nearer to the end of everything that yet would stand between this vision and our sight. And we are glad that we have come this far, and recognize that He Who brought us here will not forsake us now. For He would give to us the gift that God has given us through Him today. Now is the time for your deliverance. The time has come. The time has come today.

Lesson 199

I am not a body. I am free.

Freedom must be impossible as long as you perceive a body as yourself. The body is a limit. Who would seek for freedom in a body looks for it where it can not be found. The mind can be made free when it no longer sees itself as in a body, firmly tied to it and sheltered by its presence. If this were the truth, the mind were vulnerable indeed!

The mind that serves the Holy Spirit is unlimited forever, in all ways, beyond the laws of time and space, unbound by any preconceptions, and with strength and power to do whatever it is asked. Attack thoughts cannot enter such a mind, because it has been given to the Source of love, and fear can never enter in a mind that has attached itself to love. It rests in God. And who can be afraid who lives in Innocence, and only loves?

It is essential for your progress in this course that you accept today's idea, and hold it very dear. Be not concerned that to the ego it is quite insane. The ego holds the body dear because it dwells in it, and lives united with the home that it has made. It is a part of the illusion that has sheltered it from being found illusory itself.

Here does it hide, and here it can be seen as what it is. Declare your innocence and you are free. The body disappears, because you have no need of it except the need the Holy Spirit sees. For this, the body will appear as useful form for what the mind must do. It thus becomes a vehicle which helps forgiveness be extended to the all-inclusive goal that it must reach, according to God's plan.

Cherish today's idea, and practice it today and every day. Make it a part of every practice period you take. There is no thought that will not gain thereby in power to help the world, and none which will not gain in added gifts to you as well. We sound the call of freedom round the world with this idea. And would you be exempt from the acceptance of the gifts you give?

The Holy Spirit is the home of minds that seek for freedom. In Him they have found what they have sought. The body's purpose now is unambiguous. And it becomes perfect in the ability to serve an undivided goal. In conflict-free and unequivocal response to mind with but the thought of freedom as its goal, the body serves, and serves its purpose well. Without the power to enslave, it is a worthy servant of the freedom which the mind within the Holy Spirit seeks.

Be free today. And carry freedom as your gift to those who still believe they are enslaved within a body. Be you free, so that the Holy Spirit can make use of your escape from bondage, to set free the many who perceive themselves as bound and helpless and afraid. Let love replace their fears through you. Accept salvation now, and give your mind to Him Who calls to you to make this gift to Him. For He would give you perfect freedom, perfect joy, and hope that finds its full accomplishment in God.

You are God's Son. In immortality you live forever. Would you not return your mind to this? Then practice well the thought the Holy Spirit gives you for today. Your brothers stand released with you in it; the world is blessed along with you, God's Son will weep no more, and Heaven offers thanks for the increase of joy your practice brings even to it. And God Himself extends His Love and happiness each time you say:

I AM NOT A BODY. I AM FREE.
I HEAR THE VOICE THAT GOD HAS GIVEN ME,
AND IT IS ONLY THIS MY MIND OBEYS.

Lesson 200

There is no peace except the peace of God.

Seek you no further. You will not find peace except the peace of God. Accept this fact, and save yourself the agony of yet more bitter disappointments, bleak despair, and sense of icy hopelessness and doubt. Seek you no further. There is nothing else for you to find except the peace of God, unless you seek for misery and pain.

This is the final point to which each one must come at last, to lay aside all hope of finding happiness where there is none; of being saved by what can only hurt; of making peace of chaos, joy of pain, and Heaven out of hell. Attempt no more to win through losing, nor to die to live. You cannot but be asking for defeat.

Yet you can ask as easily for love, for happiness, and for eternal life in peace that has no ending. Ask for this, and you can only win. To ask for what you have already must succeed. To ask that what is false be true can only fail. Forgive yourself for vain imaginings, and seek no longer what you cannot find. For what could be more foolish than to seek and seek and seek again for hell, when you have but to look with open eyes to find that Heaven lies before you, through a door that opens easily to welcome you?

Come home. You have not found your happiness in foreign places and in alien forms that have no meaning to you, though you sought to make them meaningful. This world is not where you belong. You are a stranger here. But it is given you to find the means whereby the world no longer seems to be a prison house or jail for anyone.

Freedom is given you where you beheld but chains and iron doors. But you must change your mind about the purpose of the world, if you would find escape. You will be bound till all the world is seen by you as blessed, and everyone made free of your mistakes and honored as he is. You made him not; no more yourself. And as you free the one, the other is accepted as he is.

What does forgiveness do? In truth it has no function, and does nothing. For it is unknown in Heaven. It is only hell where it is needed, and where it must serve a mighty function. Is not the escape of God's beloved Son from evil dreams that he imagines, yet believes are true, a worthy purpose? Who could hope for more, while there appears to be a choice to make between success and failure; love and fear?

There is no peace except the peace of God, because He has one Son who cannot make a world in opposition to God's Will and to his own, which is the same as His. What could he hope to find in such a world? It cannot have reality, because it never was created. Is it here that he would seek for peace? Or must he see that, as he looks on it, the world can but deceive? Yet can he learn to look on it another way, and find the peace of God.

Peace is the bridge that everyone will cross, to leave this world behind. But peace begins within the world perceived as different, and leading from this fresh perception to the gate of Heaven and the way beyond. Peace is the answer to conflicting goals, to senseless journeys, frantic, vain pursuits, and meaningless endeavors. Now the way is easy, sloping gently toward the bridge where freedom lies within the peace of God.

Let us not lose our way again today. We go to Heaven, and the path is straight. Only if we attempt to wander can there be delay, and needless wasted time on thorny byways. God alone is sure, and He will guide our footsteps. He will not desert His Son in need, nor let him stray forever from his home. The Father calls; the Son will hear. And that is all there is to what appears to be a world apart from God, where bodies have reality.

Now is there silence. Seek no further. You have come to where the road is carpeted with leaves of false desires, fallen from the trees of hopelessness you sought before. Now are they underfoot. And you look up and on toward Heaven, with the body's eyes but serving for an instant longer now. Peace is already recognized at last, and you can feel its soft embrace surround your heart and mind with comfort and with love.

Today we seek no idols. Peace can not be found in them. The peace of God is ours, and only this will we accept and want. Peace be to us today. For we have found a simple, happy way to leave the world of ambiguity, and to replace our shifting goals and solitary dreams with single purpose and companionship. For peace is union, if it be of God. We seek no further. We are close to home, and draw still nearer every time we say:

THERE IS NO PEACE EXCEPT THE PEACE OF GOD,
AND I AM GLAD AND THANKFUL IT IS SO.

Lesson 201

REVIEW VI
Introduction

For this review we take but one idea each day, and practice it as often as is possible. Besides the time you give morning and evening, which should not be less than fifteen minutes, and the hourly remembrances you make throughout the day, use the idea as often as you can between them. Each of these ideas alone would be sufficient for salvation, if it were learned truly. Each would be enough to give release to you and to the world from every form of bondage, and invite the memory of God to come again.

With this in mind we start our practicing, in which we carefully review the thoughts the Holy Spirit has bestowed on us in our last twenty lessons. Each contains the whole curriculum if understood, practiced, accepted, and applied to all the seeming happenings throughout the day. One is enough. But from that one, there must be no exceptions made. And so we need to use them all and let them blend as one, as each contributes to the whole we learn.

These practice sessions, like our last review, are centered round a central theme with which we start and end each lesson. It is this:

I AM NOT A BODY. I AM FREE.
FOR I AM STILL AS GOD CREATED ME.

The day begins and ends with this. And we repeat it every time the hour strikes, or we remember, in between, we have a function that transcends the world we see. Beyond this, and a repetition of the special thought we practice for the day, no form of exercise is urged, except a deep relinquishment of everything that clutters up the mind, and makes it deaf to reason, sanity and simple truth.

We will attempt to get beyond all words and special forms of practicing for this review. For we attempt, this time, to reach a quickened pace along a shorter path to the serenity and peace of God. We merely close our eyes, and then forget all that we thought we knew and understood. For thus is freedom given us from all we did not know and failed to understand.

There is but one exception to this lack of structuring. Permit no idle thought to go unchallenged. If you notice one, deny its hold and hasten to assure your mind that this is not what it would have. Then gently let the thought which you denied be given up, in sure and quick exchange for the idea we practice for the day.

When you are tempted, hasten to proclaim your freedom from temptation, as you say:

THIS THOUGHT I DO NOT WANT. I CHOOSE INSTEAD _____.

And then repeat the idea for the day, and let it take the place of what you thought. Beyond such special applications of each day's idea, we will add but a few formal expressions or specific thoughts to aid in practicing. Instead, we give these times of quiet to the Teacher Who instructs in quiet, speaks of peace, and gives our thoughts whatever meaning they may have.

To Him I offer this review for you. I place you in His charge, and let Him teach you what to do and say and think, each time you turn to Him. He will not fail to be available to you, each time you call to Him to help you. Let us offer Him the whole review we now begin, and let us also not forget to Whom it has been given, as we practice day by day, advancing toward the goal He set for us; allowing Him to teach us how to go, and trusting Him completely for the way each practice period can best become a loving gift of freedom to the world.

I am not a body. I am free.
For I am still as God created me.

(181) I trust my brothers, who are one with me.

NO ONE BUT IS MY BROTHER. I AM BLESSED WITH ONENESS WITH
THE UNIVERSE AND GOD, MY FATHER, ONE CREATOR OF THE WHOLE
THAT IS MY SELF, FOREVER ONE WITH ME.

I am not a body. I am free.
For I am still as God created me.

Lesson 202

I am not a body. I am free.
For I am still as God created me.

(182) I will be still an instant and go home.

WHY WOULD I CHOOSE TO STAY AN INSTANT MORE WHERE I DO NOT
BELONG, WHEN GOD HIMSELF HAS GIVEN ME HIS VOICE TO CALL
ME HOME?

I am not a body. I am free.
For I am still as God created me.

Lesson 203

I am not a body. I am free.
For I am still as God created me.

(183) I call upon God's Name and on my own.

THE NAME OF GOD IS MY DELIVERANCE FROM EVERY THOUGHT OF
EVIL AND OF SIN, BECAUSE IT IS MY OWN AS WELL AS HIS.

I am not a body. I am free.
For I am still as God created me.

Lesson 204

I am not a body. I am free.
For I am still as God created me.

(184) The Name of God is my inheritance.

GOD'S NAME REMINDS ME THAT I AM HIS SON, NOT SLAVE TO
TIME, UNBOUND BY LAWS WHICH RULE THE WORLD OF SICK ILLUSIONS,
FREE IN GOD, FOREVER AND FOREVER ONE WITH HIM.

I am not a body. I am free.
For I am still as God created me.

Lesson 205

I am not a body. I am free.
For I am still as God created me.

(185) I want the peace of God.

THE PEACE OF GOD IS EVERYTHING I WANT. THE PEACE OF GOD IS
MY ONE GOAL; THE AIM OF ALL MY LIVING HERE, THE END I SEEK,
MY PURPOSE AND MY FUNCTION AND MY LIFE, WHILE I ABIDE
WHERE I AM NOT AT HOME.

I am not a body. I am free.
For I am still as God created me.

Lesson 206

I am not a body. I am free.
For I am still as God created me.

(186) Salvation of the world depends on me.

I AM ENTRUSTED WITH THE GIFTS OF GOD, BECAUSE I AM HIS SON.
AND I WOULD GIVE HIS GIFTS WHERE HE INTENDED THEM TO BE.

I am not a body. I am free.
For I am still as God created me.

Lesson 207

I am not a body. I am free.
For I am still as God created me.

(187) I bless the world because I bless myself.

GOD'S BLESSING SHINES UPON ME FROM WITHIN MY HEART,
WHERE HE ABIDES. I NEED BUT TURN TO HIM, AND EVERY SORROW
MELTS AWAY, AS I ACCEPT HIS BOUNDLESS LOVE FOR ME.

I am not a body. I am free.
For I am still as God created me.

Lesson 208

I am not a body. I am free.
For I am still as God created me.

(188) The peace of God is shining in me now.

I WILL BE STILL, AND LET THE EARTH BE STILL ALONG WITH ME. AND
IN THAT STILLNESS WE WILL FIND THE PEACE OF GOD. IT IS WITHIN
MY HEART, WHICH WITNESSES TO GOD HIMSELF.

I am not a body. I am free.
For I am still as God created me.

Lesson 209

I am not a body. I am free.
For I am still as God created me.

(189) I feel the Love of God within me now.

THE LOVE OF GOD IS WHAT CREATED ME. THE LOVE OF GOD IS
EVERYTHING I AM. THE LOVE OF GOD PROCLAIMED ME AS HIS
SON. THE LOVE OF GOD WITHIN ME SETS ME FREE.

I am not a body. I am free.
For I am still as God created me.

Lesson 210

I am not a body. I am free.
For I am still as God created me.

(190) I choose the joy of God instead of pain.

PAIN IS MY OWN IDEA. IT IS NOT A THOUGHT OF GOD, BUT ONE I
THOUGHT APART FROM HIM AND FROM HIS WILL. HIS WILL IS JOY,
AND ONLY JOY FOR HIS BELOVED SON. AND THAT I CHOOSE, INSTEAD
OF WHAT I MADE.

I am not a body. I am free.
For I am still as God created me.

Lesson 211

I am not a body. I am free.
For I am still as God created me.

(191) I am the holy Son of God Himself.

IN SILENCE AND IN TRUE HUMILITY I SEEK GOD'S GLORY, TO BEHOLD
IT IN THE SON WHOM HE CREATED AS MY SELF.

I am not a body. I am free.
For I am still as God created me.

Lesson 212

I am not a body. I am free.
For I am still as God created me.

(192) I have a function God would have me fill.

I SEEK THE FUNCTION THAT WOULD SET ME FREE FROM ALL THE VAIN
ILLUSIONS OF THE WORLD. ONLY THE FUNCTION GOD HAS GIVEN ME
CAN OFFER FREEDOM. ONLY THIS I SEEK, AND ONLY THIS WILL I
ACCEPT AS MINE.

I am not a body. I am free.
For I am still as God created me.

Lesson 213

I am not a body. I am free.
For I am still as God created me.

(193) All things are lessons God would have me learn.

A LESSON IS A MIRACLE WHICH GOD OFFERS TO ME, IN PLACE OF
THOUGHTS I MADE THAT HURT ME. WHAT I LEARN OF HIM BECOMES
THE WAY I AM SET FREE. AND SO I CHOOSE TO LEARN HIS LESSONS
AND FORGET MY OWN.

I am not a body. I am free.
For I am still as God created me.

Lesson 214

I am not a body. I am free.
For I am still as God created me.

(194) I place the future in the Hands of God.

THE PAST IS GONE; THE FUTURE IS NOT YET. NOW AM I FREED
FROM BOTH. FOR WHAT GOD GIVES CAN ONLY BE FOR GOOD. AND
I ACCEPT BUT WHAT HE GIVES AS WHAT BELONGS TO ME.

I am not a body. I am free.
For I am still as God created me.

Lesson 215

I am not a body. I am free.
For I am still as God created me.

(195) Love is the way I walk in gratitude.

THE HOLY SPIRIT IS MY ONLY GUIDE. HE WALKS WITH ME IN LOVE.
AND I GIVE THANKS TO HIM FOR SHOWING ME THE WAY TO GO.

I am not a body. I am free.
For I am still as God created me.

Lesson 216

I am not a body. I am free.
For I am still as God created me.

(196) It can be but myself I crucify.

ALL THAT I DO I DO UNTO MYSELF. IF I ATTACK, I SUFFER.
BUT IF I FORGIVE, SALVATION WILL BE GIVEN ME.

I am not a body. I am free.
For I am still as God created me.

Lesson 217

I am not a body. I am free.
For I am still as God created me.

(197) It can be but my gratitude I earn.

WHO SHOULD GIVE THANKS FOR MY SALVATION BUT MYSELF?
AND HOW BUT THROUGH SALVATION CAN I FIND THE SELF TO
WHOM MY THANKS ARE DUE?

I am not a body. I am free.
For I am still as God created me.

Lesson 218

I am not a body. I am free.
For I am still as God created me.

(198) Only my condemnation injures me.

MY CONDEMNATION KEEPS MY VISION DARK, AND THROUGH MY
SIGHTLESS EYES I CANNOT SEE THE VISION OF MY GLORY.
YET TODAY I CAN BEHOLD THIS GLORY AND BE GLAD.

I am not a body. I am free.
For I am still as God created me.

Lesson 219

I am not a body. I am free.
For I am still as God created me.

(199) I am not a body. I am free.

I AM GOD'S SON. BE STILL, MY MIND, AND THINK A MOMENT
UPON THIS. AND THEN RETURN TO EARTH, WITHOUT CONFUSION
AS TO WHAT MY FATHER LOVES FOREVER AS HIS SON.

I am not a body. I am free.
For I am still as God created me.

Lesson 220

I am not a body. I am free,
For I am still as God created me.

(200) There is no peace except the peace of God.

LET ME NOT WANDER FROM THE WAY OF PEACE, FOR I AM LOST ON
OTHER ROADS THAN THIS. BUT LET ME FOLLOW HIM WHO LEADS ME
HOME, AND PEACE IS CERTAIN AS THE LOVE OF GOD.

I am not a body. I am free.
For I am still as God created me.

Lesson 221

PART II

Introduction

Words will mean little now. We use them but as guides on which we do not now depend. For now we seek direct experience of truth alone. The lessons that remain are merely introductions to the times in which we leave the world of pain, and go to enter peace. Now we begin to reach the goal this course has set, and find the end toward which our practicing was always geared.

Now we attempt to let the exercise be merely a beginning. For we wait in quiet expectation for our God and Father. He has promised He will take the final step Himself. And we are sure His promises are kept. We have come far along the road, and now we wait for Him. We will continue spending time with Him each morning and at night, as long as makes us happy. We will not consider time a matter of duration now. We use as much as we will need for the result that we desire. Nor will we forget our hourly remembrance in between, calling to God when we have need of Him as we are tempted to forget our goal.

We will continue with a central thought for all the days to come, and we will use that thought to introduce our times of rest, and calm our minds at need. Yet we will not content ourselves with simple practicing in the remaining holy instants which conclude the year that we have given God. We say some simple words of welcome, and expect our Father to reveal Himself, as He has promised. We have called on Him, and He has promised that His Son will not remain unanswered when he calls His Name.

Now do we come to Him with but His Word upon our minds and hearts, and wait for Him to take the step to us that He has told us, through His Voice, He would not fail to take when we invited Him. He has not left His Son in all his madness, nor betrayed his trust in Him. Has not His faithfulness earned Him the invitation that He seeks to make us happy? We will offer it, and it will be accepted. So our times with Him will now be spent. We say the words of invitation that His Voice suggests, and then we wait for Him to come to us.

Now is the time of prophecy fulfilled. Now are all ancient promises upheld and fully kept. No step remains for time to separate from its accomplishment. For now we cannot fail. Sit silently and wait upon your Father. He has willed to come to you when you have recognized it is your will He do so. And you could have never come this far unless you saw, however dimly, that it is your will.

I am so close to you we cannot fail. Father, we give these holy times to You, in gratitude to Him Who taught us how to leave the world of sorrow in exchange for its replacement, given us by You. We look not backward now. We look ahead, and fix our eyes upon the journey's end. Accept these little gifts of thanks from us, as through Christ's vision we behold a world beyond the one we made, and take that world to be the full replacement of our own.

And now we wait in silence, unafraid and certain of Your coming. We have sought to find our way by following the Guide You sent to us. We did not know the way, but You did not forget us. And we know that You will not forget us now. We ask but that Your ancient promises be kept which are Your Will to keep. We will with You in asking this. The Father and the Son, Whose holy Will created all that is, can fail in nothing. In this certainty, we undertake these last few steps to You, and rest in confidence upon Your Love, which will not fail the Son who calls to You.

And so we start upon the final part of this one holy year, which we have spent together in the search for truth and God, Who is its one Creator. We have found the way He chose for us, and made the choice to follow it as He would have us go. His Hand has held us up. His Thoughts have lit the darkness of our minds. His Love has called to us unceasingly since time began.

We had a wish that God would fail to have the Son whom He created for Himself. We wanted God to change Himself, and be what we would make of Him. And we believed that our insane desires were the truth. Now we are glad that this is all undone, and we no longer think illusions true. The memory of God is shimmering across the wide horizons of our minds. A moment more, and it will rise again. A moment more, and we who are God's Sons are safely home, where He would have us be.

Now is the need for practice almost done. For in this final section, we will come to understand that we need only call to God, and all temptations disappear. Instead of words, we need but feel His Love. Instead of prayers, we need but call His Name. Instead of judging, we need but be still and let all things be healed. We will accept the way God's plan will end, as we received the way it started. Now it is complete. This year has brought us to eternity.

One further use for words we still retain. From time to time, instructions on a theme of special relevance will intersperse our daily lessons and the periods of wordless, deep experience which should come afterwards. These special thoughts should be reviewed each day, each one of them to be continued till the next is given you. They should be slowly read and thought about a little while, preceding one of the holy and blessed instants in the day. We give the first of these instructions now.

---

1. What is Forgiveness?

Forgiveness recognizes what you thought your brother did to you has not occurred. It does not pardon sins and make them real. It sees there was no sin. And in that view are all your sins forgiven. What is sin, except a false idea about God's Son? Forgiveness merely sees its falsity, and therefore lets it go. What then is free to take its place is now the Will of God.

An unforgiving thought is one which makes a judgment that it will not raise to doubt, although it is not true. The mind is closed, and will not be released. The thought protects projection, tightening its chains, so that distortions are more veiled and more obscure; less easily accessible to doubt, and further kept from reason. What can come between a fixed projection and the aim that it has chosen as its wanted goal?

An unforgiving thought does many things. In frantic action it pursues its goal, twisting and overturning what it sees as interfering with its chosen path. Distortion is its purpose, and the means by which it would accomplish it as well. It sets about its furious attempts to smash reality, without concern for anything that would appear to pose a contradiction to its point of view.

Forgiveness, on the other hand, is still, and quietly does nothing. It offends no aspect of reality, nor seeks to twist it to appearances it likes. It merely looks, and waits, and judges not. He who would not forgive must judge, for he must justify his failure to forgive. But he who would forgive himself must learn to welcome truth exactly as it is.

Do nothing, then, and let forgiveness show you what to do, through Him Who is your Guide, your Savior and Protector, strong in hope, and certain of your ultimate success. He has forgiven you already, for such is His function, given Him by God. Now must you share His function, and forgive whom He has saved, whose sinlessness He sees, and whom He honors as the Son of God.

Lesson 221

Peace to my mind. Let all my thoughts be still.

FATHER, I COME TO YOU TODAY TO SEEK THE PEACE THAT YOU ALONE CAN GIVE. I COME IN SILENCE. IN THE QUIET OF MY HEART, THE DEEP RECESSES OF MY MIND, I WAIT AND LISTEN FOR YOUR VOICE. MY FATHER, SPEAK TO ME TODAY. I COME TO HEAR YOUR VOICE IN SILENCE AND IN CERTAINTY AND LOVE, SURE YOU WILL HEAR MY CALL AND ANSWER ME.

Now do we wait in quiet. God is here, because we wait together. I am sure that He will speak to you, and you will hear. Accept my confidence, for it is yours. Our minds are joined. We wait with one intent; to hear our Father's answer to our call, to let our thoughts be still and find His peace, to hear Him speak to us of what we are, and to reveal Himself unto His Son.

Lesson 222

God is with me. I live and move in Him.

God is with me. He is my Source of life, the life within, the air I breathe, the food by which I am sustained, the water which renews and cleanses me. He is my home, wherein I live and move; the Spirit which directs my actions, offers me Its Thoughts, and guarantees my safety from all pain. He covers me with kindness and with care, and holds in love the Son He shines upon, who also shines on Him. How still is he who knows the truth of what He speaks today!

FATHER, WE HAVE NO WORDS EXCEPT YOUR NAME UPON OUR LIPS AND IN OUR MINDS, AS WE COME QUIETLY INTO YOUR PRESENCE NOW, AND ASK TO REST WITH YOU IN PEACE A WHILE.

Lesson 223

God is my life. I have no life but His.

I was mistaken when I thought I lived apart from God, a separate entity that moved in isolation, unattached, and housed within a body. Now I know my life is God's, I have no other home, and I do not exist apart from Him. He has no Thoughts that are not part of me, and I have none but those which are of Him.

OUR FATHER, LET US SEE THE FACE OF CHRIST INSTEAD OF OUR MISTAKES. FOR WE WHO ARE YOUR HOLY SON ARE SINLESS. WE WOULD LOOK UPON OUR SINLESSNESS, FOR GUILT PROCLAIMS THAT WE ARE NOT YOUR SON. AND WE WOULD NOT FORGET YOU LONGER. WE ARE LONELY HERE, AND LONG FOR HEAVEN, WHERE WE ARE AT HOME. TODAY WE WOULD RETURN. OUR NAME IS YOURS, AND WE ACKNOWLEDGE THAT WE ARE YOUR SON.

Lesson 224

God is my Father, and He loves His Son.

My true Identity is so secure, so lofty, sinless, glorious and great, wholly beneficent and free from guilt, that Heaven looks to It to give it light. It lights the world as well. It is the gift my Father gave to me; the one as well I give the world. There is no gift but this that can be either given or received. This is reality, and only this. This is illusion's end. It is the truth.

MY NAME, O FATHER, STILL IS KNOWN TO YOU. I HAVE FORGOTTEN IT, AND DO NOT KNOW WHERE I AM GOING, WHO I AM, OR WHAT IT IS I DO. REMIND ME, FATHER, NOW, FOR I AM WEARY OF THE WORLD I SEE. REVEAL WHAT YOU WOULD HAVE ME SEE INSTEAD.

Lesson 225

God is my Father, and His Son loves Him.

FATHER, I MUST RETURN YOUR LOVE FOR ME, FOR GIVING AND RECEIVING ARE THE SAME, AND YOU HAVE GIVEN ALL YOUR LOVE TO ME. I MUST RETURN IT, FOR I WANT IT MINE IN FULL AWARENESS, BLAZING IN MY MIND AND KEEPING IT WITHIN ITS KINDLY LIGHT, INVIOLATE, BELOVED, WITH FEAR BEHIND AND ONLY PEACE AHEAD. HOW STILL THE WAY YOUR LOVING SON IS LED ALONG TO YOU!

Brother, we find that stillness now. The way is open. Now we follow it in peace together. You have reached your hand to me, and I will never leave you. We are one, and it is but this oneness that we seek, as we accomplish these few final steps which end a journey that was not begun.

Lesson 226

My home awaits me. I will hasten there.

If I so choose, I can depart this world entirely. It is not death which makes this possible, but it is change of mind about the purpose of the world. If I believe it has a value as I see it now, so will it still remain for me. But if I see no value in the world as I behold it, nothing that I want to keep as mine or search for as a goal, it will depart from me. For I have not sought for illusions to replace the truth.

FATHER, MY HOME AWAITS MY GLAD RETURN. YOUR ARMS ARE OPEN AND I HEAR YOUR VOICE. WHAT NEED HAVE I TO LINGER IN A PLACE OF VAIN DESIRES AND OF SHATTERED DREAMS, WHEN HEAVEN CAN SO EASILY BE MINE?

Lesson 227

This is my holy instant of release.

FATHER, IT IS TODAY THAT I AM FREE, BECAUSE MY WILL IS YOURS. I THOUGHT TO MAKE ANOTHER WILL. YET NOTHING THAT I THOUGHT APART FROM YOU EXISTS. AND I AM FREE BECAUSE I WAS MISTAKEN, AND DID NOT AFFECT MY OWN REALITY AT ALL BY MY ILLUSIONS. NOW I GIVE THEM UP, AND LAY THEM DOWN BEFORE THE FEET OF TRUTH, TO BE REMOVED FOREVER FROM MY MIND. THIS IS MY HOLY INSTANT OF RELEASE. FATHER, I KNOW MY WILL IS ONE WITH YOURS.

And so today we find our glad return to Heaven, which we never really left. The Son of God this day lays down his dreams. The Son of God this day comes home again, released from sin and clad in holiness, with his right mind restored to him at last.

Lesson 228

God has condemned me not. No more do I.

My Father knows my holiness. Shall I deny His knowledge, and believe in what His knowledge makes impossible? Shall I accept as true what He proclaims as false? Or shall I take His Word for what I am, since He is my Creator, and the One Who knows the true condition of His Son?

FATHER, I WAS MISTAKEN IN MYSELF, BECAUSE I FAILED TO REALIZE THE SOURCE FROM WHICH I CAME. I HAVE NOT LEFT THAT SOURCE TO ENTER IN A BODY AND TO DIE. MY HOLINESS REMAINS A PART OF ME, AS I AM PART OF YOU. AND MY MISTAKES ABOUT MYSELF ARE DREAMS. I LET THEM GO TODAY. AND I STAND READY TO RECEIVE YOUR WORD ALONE FOR WHAT I REALLY AM.

Lesson 229

Love, which created me, is what I am.

I seek my own Identity, and find It in these words: "Love, which created me, is what I am." Now need I seek no more. Love has prevailed. So still It waited for my coming home, that I will turn away no longer from the holy face of Christ. And what I look upon attests the truth of the Identity I sought to lose, but which my Father has kept safe for me.

FATHER, MY THANKS TO YOU FOR WHAT I AM; FOR KEEPING MY IDENTITY UNTOUCHED AND SINLESS, IN THE MIDST OF ALL THE THOUGHTS OF SIN MY FOOLISH MIND MADE UP. AND THANKS TO YOU FOR SAVING ME FROM THEM. AMEN.

Lesson 230

Now will I seek and find the peace of God.

In peace I was created. And in peace do I remain. It is not given me to change my Self. How merciful is God my Father, that when He created me He gave me peace forever. Now I ask but to be what I am. And can this be denied me, when it is forever true?

Father, I seek the peace You gave as mine in my creation. What was given then must be here now, for my creation was apart from time, and still remains beyond all change. The peace in which Your Son was born into Your Mind is shining there unchanged. I am as You created me. I need but call on You to find the peace You gave. It is Your Will that gave it to Your Son.

Lesson 231

2. What is Salvation?

Salvation is a promise, made by God, that you would find your way to Him at last. It cannot but be kept. It guarantees that time will have an end, and all the thoughts that have been born in time will end as well. God's Word is given every mind which thinks that it has separate thoughts, and will replace these thoughts of conflict with the Thought of peace.

The Thought of peace was given to God's Son the instant that his mind had thought of war. There was no need for such a Thought before, for peace was given without opposite, and merely was. But when the mind is split there is a need of healing. So the Thought that has the power to heal the split became a part of every fragment of the mind that still was one, but failed to recognize its oneness. Now it did not know itself, and thought its own Identity was lost.

Salvation is undoing in the sense that it does nothing, failing to support the world of dreams and malice. Thus it lets illusions go. By not supporting them, it merely lets them quietly go down to dust. And what they hid is now revealed; an altar to the holy Name of God whereon His Word is written, with the gifts of your forgiveness laid before it, and the memory of God not far behind.

Let us come daily to this holy place, and spend a while together. Here we share our final dream. It is a dream in which there is no sorrow, for it holds a hint of all the glory given us by God. The grass is pushing through the soil, the trees are budding now, and birds have come to live within their branches. Earth is being born again in new perspective. Night has gone, and we have come together in the light.

From here we give salvation to the world, for it is here salvation was received. The song of our rejoicing is the call to all the world that freedom is returned, that time is almost over, and God's Son has but an instant more to wait until his Father is remembered, dreams are done, eternity has shined away the world, and only Heaven now exists at all.

Lesson 231

Father, I will but to remember You.

WHAT CAN I SEEK FOR, FATHER, BUT YOUR LOVE? PERHAPS I THINK I SEEK FOR SOMETHING ELSE; A SOMETHING I HAVE CALLED BY MANY NAMES. YET IS YOUR LOVE THE ONLY THING I SEEK, OR EVER SOUGHT. FOR THERE IS NOTHING ELSE THAT I COULD EVER REALLY WANT TO FIND. LET ME REMEMBER YOU. WHAT ELSE COULD I DESIRE BUT THE TRUTH ABOUT MYSELF?

This is your will, my brother. And you share this will with me, and with the One as well Who is our Father. To remember Him is Heaven. This we seek. And only this is what it will be given us to find.

Lesson 232

Be in my mind, my Father, through the day.

BE IN MY MIND, MY FATHER, WHEN I WAKE, AND SHINE ON ME THROUGHOUT THE DAY TODAY. LET EVERY MINUTE BE A TIME IN WHICH I DWELL WITH YOU. AND LET ME NOT FORGET MY HOURLY THANKSGIVING THAT YOU HAVE REMAINED WITH ME, AND ALWAYS WILL BE THERE TO HEAR MY CALL TO YOU AND ANSWER ME. AS EVENING COMES, LET ALL MY THOUGHTS BE STILL OF YOU AND OF YOUR LOVE. AND LET ME SLEEP SURE OF MY SAFETY, CERTAIN OF YOUR CARE, AND HAPPILY AWARE I AM YOUR SON.

This is as every day should be. Today, practice the end of fear. Have faith in Him Who is your Father. Trust all things to Him. Let Him reveal all things to you, and be you undismayed because you are His Son.

Lesson 233

I give my life to God to guide today.

FATHER, I GIVE YOU ALL MY THOUGHTS TODAY. I WOULD HAVE NONE OF MINE. IN PLACE OF THEM, GIVE ME YOUR OWN. I GIVE YOU ALL MY ACTS AS WELL, THAT I MAY DO YOUR WILL INSTEAD OF SEEKING GOALS WHICH CANNOT BE OBTAINED, AND WASTING TIME IN VAIN IMAGININGS. TODAY I COME TO YOU. I WILL STEP BACK AND MERELY FOLLOW YOU. BE YOU THE GUIDE, AND I THE FOLLOWER WHO QUESTIONS NOT THE WISDOM OF THE INFINITE, NOR LOVE WHOSE TENDERNESS I CANNOT COMPREHEND, BUT WHICH IS YET YOUR PERFECT GIFT TO ME.

Today we have one Guide to lead us on. And as we walk together, we will give this day to Him with no reserve at all. This is His day. And so it is a day of countless gifts and mercies unto us.

Lesson 234

Father, today I am Your Son again.

Today we will anticipate the time when dreams of sin and guilt are gone, and we have reached the holy peace we never left. Merely a tiny instant has elapsed between eternity and timelessness. So brief the interval there was no lapse in continuity, nor break in thoughts which are forever unified as one. Nothing has ever happened to disturb the peace of God the Father and the Son. This we accept as wholly true today.

WE THANK YOU, FATHER, THAT WE CANNOT LOSE THE MEMORY OF YOU AND OF YOUR LOVE. WE RECOGNIZE OUR SAFETY, AND GIVE THANKS FOR ALL THE GIFTS YOU HAVE BESTOWED ON US, FOR ALL THE LOVING HELP WE HAVE RECEIVED, FOR YOUR ETERNAL PATIENCE, AND THE WORD WHICH YOU HAVE GIVEN US THAT WE ARE SAVED.

Lesson 235

God in His mercy wills that I be saved.

I need but look upon all things that seem to hurt me, and with perfect certainty assure myself, "God wills that I be saved from this," and merely watch them disappear. I need but keep in mind my Father's Will for me is only happiness, to find that only happiness has come to me. And I need but remember that God's Love surrounds His Son and keeps his sinlessness forever perfect, to be sure that I am saved and safe forever in His Arms. I am the Son He loves. And I am saved because God in His mercy wills it so.

FATHER, YOUR HOLINESS IS MINE. YOUR LOVE CREATED ME, AND MADE MY SINLESSNESS FOREVER PART OF YOU. I HAVE NO GUILT NOR SIN IN ME, FOR THERE IS NONE IN YOU.

Lesson 236

I rule my mind, which I alone must rule.

I have a kingdom I must rule. At times, it does not seem I am its king at all. It seems to triumph over me, and tell me what to think, and what to do and feel. And yet it has been given me to serve whatever purpose I perceive in it. My mind can only serve. Today I give its service to the Holy Spirit to employ as He sees fit. I thus direct my mind, which I alone can rule. And thus I set it free to do the Will of God.

FATHER, MY MIND IS OPEN TO YOUR THOUGHTS, AND CLOSED TODAY TO EVERY THOUGHT BUT YOURS. I RULE MY MIND, AND OFFER IT TO YOU. ACCEPT MY GIFT, FOR IT IS YOURS TO ME.

Lesson 237

Now would I be as God created me.

Today I will accept the truth about myself. I will arise in glory, and allow the light in me to shine upon the world throughout the day. I bring the world the tidings of salvation which I hear as God my Father speaks to me. And I behold the world that Christ would have me see, aware it ends the bitter dream of death; aware it is my Father's Call to me.

CHRIST IS MY EYES TODAY, AND HE THE EARS THAT LISTEN TO THE VOICE FOR GOD TODAY. FATHER, I COME TO YOU THROUGH HIM WHO IS YOUR SON, AND MY TRUE SELF AS WELL. AMEN.

Lesson 238

On my decision all salvation rests.

FATHER, YOUR TRUST IN ME HAS BEEN SO GREAT, I MUST BE WORTHY. YOU CREATED ME, AND KNOW ME AS I AM. AND YET YOU PLACED YOUR SON'S SALVATION IN MY HANDS, AND LET IT REST ON MY DECISION. I MUST BE BELOVED OF YOU INDEED. AND I MUST BE STEADFAST IN HOLINESS AS WELL, THAT YOU WOULD GIVE YOUR SON TO ME IN CERTAINTY THAT HE IS SAFE WHO STILL IS PART OF YOU, AND YET IS MINE, BECAUSE HE IS MY SELF.

And so, again today, we pause to think how much our Father loves us. And how dear His Son, created by His Love, remains to Him Whose Love is made complete in him.

Lesson 239

The glory of my Father is my own.

Let not the truth about ourselves today be hidden by a false humility. Let us instead be thankful for the gifts our Father gave us. Can we see in those with whom He shares His glory any trace of sin and guilt? And can it be that we are not among them, when He loves His Son forever and with perfect constancy, knowing he is as He created him?

WE THANK YOU, FATHER, FOR THE LIGHT THAT SHINES FOREVER IN US. AND WE HONOR IT, BECAUSE YOU SHARE IT WITH US. WE ARE ONE, UNITED IN THIS LIGHT AND ONE WITH YOU, AT PEACE WITH ALL CREATION AND OURSELVES.

Lesson 240

Fear is not justified in any form.

Fear is deception. It attests that you have seen yourself as you could never be, and therefore look upon a world which is impossible. Not one thing in this world is true. It does not matter what the form in which it may appear. It witnesses but to your own illusions of yourself. Let us not be deceived today. We are the Sons of God. There is no fear in us, for we are each a part of Love Itself.

HOW FOOLISH ARE OUR FEARS! WOULD YOU ALLOW YOUR SON TO SUFFER? GIVE US FAITH TODAY TO RECOGNIZE YOUR SON, AND SET HIM FREE. LET US FORGIVE HIM IN YOUR NAME, THAT WE MAY UNDERSTAND HIS HOLINESS, AND FEEL THE LOVE FOR HIM WHICH IS YOUR OWN AS WELL.

Lesson 241

Section 3. What is the World?

The world is false perception. It is born of error, and it has not left its source. It will remain no longer than the thought that gave it birth is cherished. When the thought of separation has been changed to one of true forgiveness, will the world be seen in quite another light; and one which leads to truth, where all the world must disappear and all its errors vanish. Now its source has gone, and its effects are gone as well.

The world was made as an attack on God. It symbolizes fear. And what is fear except love's absence? Thus the world was meant to be a place where God could enter not, and where His Son could be apart from Him. Here was perception born, for knowledge could not cause such insane thoughts. But eyes deceive, and ears hear falsely. Now mistakes become quite possible, for certainty has gone.

The mechanisms of illusion have been born instead. And now they go to find what has been given them to seek. Their aim is to fulfill the purpose which the world was made to witness and make real. They see in its illusions but a solid base where truth exists, upheld apart from lies. Yet everything that they report is but illusion which is kept apart from truth.

As sight was made to lead away from truth, it can be redirected. Sounds become the call for God, and all perception can be given a new purpose by the One Whom God appointed Savior to the world. Follow His light, and see the world as He beholds it. Hear His Voice alone in all that speaks to you. And let Him give you peace and certainty, which you have thrown away, but Heaven has preserved for you in Him.

Let us not rest content until the world has joined our changed perception. Let us not be satisfied until forgiveness has been made complete. And let us not attempt to change our function. We must save the world. For we who made it must behold it through the eyes of Christ, that what was made to die can be restored to everlasting life.

Lesson 241

This holy instant is salvation come.

What joy there is today! It is a time of special celebration. For today holds out the instant to the darkened world where its release is set. The day has come when sorrows pass away and pain is gone. The glory of salvation dawns today upon a world set free. This is the time of hope for countless millions. They will be united now, as you forgive them all. For I will be forgiven by you today.

WE HAVE FORGIVEN ONE ANOTHER NOW, AND SO WE COME AT LAST TO YOU AGAIN. FATHER, YOUR SON, WHO NEVER LEFT, RETURNS TO HEAVEN AND HIS HOME. HOW GLAD ARE WE TO HAVE OUR SANITY RESTORED TO US, AND TO REMEMBER THAT WE ALL ARE ONE.

Lesson 242

This day is God's. It is my gift to Him.

I will not lead my life alone today. I do not understand the world, and so to try to lead my life alone must be but foolishness. But there is One Who knows all that is best for me. And He is glad to make no choices for me but the ones that lead to God. I give this day to Him, for I would not delay my coming home, and it is He Who knows the way to God.

And so we give today to You. We come with wholly open minds. We do not ask for anything that we may think we want. Give us what You would have received by us. You know all our desires and our wants. And You will give us everything we need in helping us to find the way to You.

Lesson 243

Today I will judge nothing that occurs.

I will be honest with myself today. I will not think that I already know what must remain beyond my present grasp. I will not think I understand the whole from bits of my perception, which are all that I can see. Today I recognize that this is so. And so I am relieved of judgments that I cannot make. Thus do I free myself and what I look upon, to be in peace as God created us.

FATHER, TODAY I LEAVE CREATION FREE TO BE ITSELF. I HONOR ALL ITS PARTS, IN WHICH I AM INCLUDED. WE ARE ONE BECAUSE EACH PART CONTAINS YOUR MEMORY, AND TRUTH MUST SHINE IN ALL OF US AS ONE.

Lesson 244

I am in danger nowhere in the world.

YOUR SON IS SAFE WHEREVER HE MAY BE, FOR YOU ARE THERE WITH HIM. HE NEED BUT CALL UPON YOUR NAME, AND HE WILL RECOLLECT HIS SAFETY AND YOUR LOVE, FOR THEY ARE ONE. HOW CAN HE FEAR OR DOUBT OR FAIL TO KNOW HE CANNOT SUFFER, BE ENDANGERED, OR EXPERIENCE UNHAPPINESS, WHEN HE BELONGS TO YOU, BELOVED AND LOVING, IN THE SAFETY OF YOUR FATHERLY EMBRACE?

And there we are in truth. No storms can come into the hallowed haven of our home. In God we are secure. For what can come to threaten God Himself, or make afraid what will forever be a part of Him?

Lesson 245

Your peace is with me, Father. I am safe.

YOUR PEACE SURROUNDS ME, FATHER. WHERE I GO, YOUR PEACE GOES THERE WITH ME. IT SHEDS ITS LIGHT ON EVERYONE I MEET. I BRING IT TO THE DESOLATE AND LONELY AND AFRAID. I GIVE YOUR PEACE TO THOSE WHO SUFFER PAIN, OR GRIEVE FOR LOSS, OR THINK THEY ARE BEREFT OF HOPE AND HAPPINESS. SEND THEM TO ME, MY FATHER. LET ME BRING YOUR PEACE WITH ME. FOR I WOULD SAVE YOUR SON, AS IS YOUR WILL, THAT I MAY COME TO RECOGNIZE MY SELF.

And so we go in peace. To all the world we give the message that we have received. And thus we come to hear the Voice for God, Who speaks to us as we relate His Word; Whose Love we recognize because we share the Word that He has given unto us.

Lesson 246

To love my Father is to love His Son.

Let me not think that I can find the way to God, if I have hatred in my heart. Let me not try to hurt God's Son, and think that I can know his Father or my Self. Let me not fail to recognize myself, and still believe that my awareness can contain my Father, or my mind conceive of all the love my Father has for me, and all the love which I return to Him.

I WILL ACCEPT THE WAY YOU CHOOSE FOR ME TO COME TO YOU, MY FATHER. FOR IN THAT WILL I SUCCEED, BECAUSE IT IS YOUR WILL. AND I WOULD RECOGNIZE THAT WHAT YOU WILL IS WHAT I WILL AS WELL, AND ONLY THAT. AND SO I CHOOSE TO LOVE YOUR SON. AMEN.

Lesson 247

Without forgiveness I will still be blind.

Sin is the symbol of attack. Behold it anywhere, and I will suffer. For forgiveness is the only means whereby Christ's vision comes to me. Let me accept what His sight shows me as the simple truth, and I am healed completely. Brother, come and let me look on you. Your loveliness reflects my own. Your sinlessness is mine. You stand forgiven, and I stand with you.

SO WOULD I LOOK ON EVERYONE TODAY. MY BROTHERS ARE YOUR SONS. YOUR FATHERHOOD CREATED THEM, AND GAVE THEM ALL TO ME AS PART OF YOU, AND MY OWN SELF AS WELL. TODAY I HONOR YOU THROUGH THEM, AND THUS I HOPE THIS DAY TO RECOGNIZE MY SELF.

Lesson 248

Whatever suffers is not part of me.

I have disowned the truth. Now let me be as faithful in disowning falsity. Whatever suffers is not part of me. What grieves is not myself. What is in pain is but illusion in my mind. What dies was never living in reality, and did but mock the truth about myself. Now I disown self-concepts and deceits and lies about the holy Son of God. Now am I ready to accept him back as God created him, and as he is.

FATHER, MY ANCIENT LOVE FOR YOU RETURNS, AND LETS ME LOVE YOUR SON AGAIN AS WELL. FATHER, I AM AS YOU CREATED ME. NOW IS YOUR LOVE REMEMBERED, AND MY OWN. NOW DO I UNDERSTAND THAT THEY ARE ONE.

Lesson 249

Forgiveness ends all suffering and loss.

Forgiveness paints a picture of a world where suffering is over, loss becomes impossible and anger makes no sense. Attack is gone, and madness has an end. What suffering is now conceivable? What loss can be sustained? The world becomes a place of joy, abundance, charity and endless giving. It is now so like to Heaven that it quickly is transformed into the light that it reflects. And so the journey which the Son of God began has ended in the light from which he came.

FATHER, WE WOULD RETURN OUR MINDS TO YOU. WE HAVE BETRAYED THEM, HELD THEM IN A VISE OF BITTERNESS, AND FRIGHTENED THEM WITH THOUGHTS OF VIOLENCE AND DEATH. NOW WOULD WE REST AGAIN IN YOU, AS YOU CREATED US.

Lesson 250

Let me not see myself as limited.

Let me behold the Son of God today, and witness to his glory. Let me not try to obscure the holy light in him, and see his strength diminished and reduced to frailty; nor perceive the lacks in him with which I would attack his sovereignty.

HE IS YOUR SON, MY FATHER. AND TODAY I WOULD BEHOLD HIS GENTLENESS INSTEAD OF MY ILLUSIONS. HE IS WHAT I AM, AND AS I SEE HIM SO I SEE MYSELF. TODAY I WOULD SEE TRULY, THAT THIS DAY I MAY AT LAST IDENTIFY WITH HIM.

Lesson 251

Section 4. What is Sin?

Sin is insanity. It is the means by which the mind is driven mad, and seeks to let illusions take the place of truth. And being mad, it sees illusions where the truth should be, and where it really is. Sin gave the body eyes, for what is there the sinless would behold? What need have they of sights or sounds or touch? What would they hear or reach to grasp? What would they sense at all? To sense is not to know. And truth can be but filled with knowledge, and with nothing else.

The body is the instrument the mind made in its efforts to deceive itself. Its purpose is to strive. Yet can the goal of striving change. And now the body serves a different aim for striving. What it seeks for now is chosen by the aim the mind has taken as replacement for the goal of self-deception. Truth can be its aim as well as lies. The senses then will seek instead for witnesses to what is true.

Sin is the home of all illusions, which but stand for things imagined, issuing from thoughts that are untrue. They are the "proof" that what has no reality is real. Sin "proves" God's Son is evil; timelessness must have an end; eternal life must die. And God Himself has lost the Son He loves, with but corruption to complete Himself, His Will forever overcome by death, love slain by hate, and peace to be no more.

A madman's dreams are frightening, and sin appears indeed to terrify. And yet what sin perceives is but a childish game. The Son of God may play he has become a body, prey to evil and to guilt, with but a little life that ends in death. But all the while his Father shines on him, and loves him with an everlasting Love which his pretenses cannot change at all.

How long, O Son of God, will you maintain the game of sin? Shall we not put away these sharp-edged children's toys? How soon will you be ready to come home? Perhaps today? There is no sin. Creation is unchanged. Would you still hold return to Heaven back? How long, O holy Son of God, how long?

Lesson 251

I am in need of nothing but the truth.

I sought for many things, and found despair. Now do I seek but one, for in that one is all I need, and only what I need. All that I sought before I needed not, and did not even want. My only need I did not recognize. But now I see that I need only truth. In that all needs are satisfied, all cravings end, all hopes are finally fulfilled and dreams are gone. Now have I everything that I could need. Now have I everything that I could want. And now at last I find myself at peace.

AND FOR THAT PEACE, OUR FATHER, WE GIVE THANKS. WHAT WE DENIED OURSELVES YOU HAVE RESTORED, AND ONLY THAT IS WHAT WE REALLY WANT.

Lesson 252

The Son of God is my Identity.

My Self is holy beyond all the thoughts of holiness of which I now conceive. Its shimmering and perfect purity is far more brilliant than is any light that I have ever looked upon. Its love is limitless, with an intensity that holds all things within it, in the calm of quiet certainty. Its strength comes not from burning impulses which move the world, but from the boundless Love of God Himself. How far beyond this world my Self must be, and yet how near to me and close to God!

FATHER, YOU KNOW MY TRUE IDENTITY. REVEAL IT NOW TO ME WHO AM YOUR SON, THAT I MAY WAKEN TO THE TRUTH IN YOU, AND KNOW THAT HEAVEN IS RESTORED TO ME.

Lesson 253

My Self is ruler of the universe.

It is impossible that anything should come to me unbidden by myself. Even in this world, it is I who rule my destiny. What happens is what I desire. What does not occur is what I do not want to happen. This must I accept. For thus am I led past this world to my creations, children of my will, in Heaven where my holy Self abides with them and Him Who has created me.

YOU ARE THE SELF WHOM YOU CREATED SON, CREATING LIKE YOURSELF AND ONE WITH YOU. MY SELF, WHICH RULES THE UNIVERSE, IS BUT YOUR WILL IN PERFECT UNION WITH MY OWN, WHICH CAN BUT OFFER GLAD ASSENT TO YOURS, THAT IT MAY BE EXTENDED TO ITSELF.

Lesson 254

Let every voice but God's be still in me.

FATHER, TODAY I WOULD BUT HEAR YOUR VOICE. IN DEEPEST SILENCE I WOULD COME TO YOU, TO HEAR YOUR VOICE AND TO RECEIVE YOUR WORD. I HAVE NO PRAYER BUT THIS: I COME TO YOU TO ASK YOU FOR THE TRUTH. AND TRUTH IS BUT YOUR WILL, WHICH I WOULD SHARE WITH YOU TODAY.

Today we let no ego thoughts direct our words or actions. When such thoughts occur, we quietly step back and look at them, and then we let them go. We do not want what they would bring with them. And so we do not choose to keep them. They are silent now. And in the stillness, hallowed by His Love, God speaks to us and tells us of our will, as we have chosen to remember Him.

Lesson 255

This day I choose to spend in perfect peace.

It does not seem to me that I can choose to have but peace today. And yet, my God assures me that His Son is like Himself. Let me this day have faith in Him Who says I am God's Son. And let the peace I choose be mine today bear witness to the truth of what He says. God's Son can have no cares, and must remain forever in the peace of Heaven. In His Name, I give today to finding what my Father wills for me, accepting it as mine, and giving it to all my Father's Sons, along with me.

AND SO, MY FATHER, WOULD I PASS THIS DAY WITH YOU. YOUR SON HAS NOT FORGOTTEN YOU. THE PEACE YOU GAVE HIM STILL IS IN HIS MIND, AND IT IS THERE I CHOOSE TO SPEND TODAY.

Lesson 256

God is the only goal I have today.

The way to God is through forgiveness here. There is no other way. If sin had not been cherished by the mind, what need would there have been to find the way to where you are? Who would still be uncertain? Who could be unsure of who he is? And who would yet remain asleep, in heavy clouds of doubt about the holiness of him whom God created sinless? Here we can but dream. But we can dream we have forgiven him in whom all sin remains impossible, and it is this we choose to dream today. God is our goal; forgiveness is the means by which our minds return to Him at last.

AND SO, OUR FATHER, WOULD WE COME TO YOU IN YOUR APPOINTED WAY. WE HAVE NO GOAL EXCEPT TO HEAR YOUR VOICE, AND FIND THE WAY YOUR SACRED WORD HAS POINTED OUT TO US.

Lesson 257

Let me remember what my purpose is.

If I forget my goal I can be but confused, unsure of what I am, and thus conflicted in my actions. No one can serve contradicting goals and serve them well. Nor can he function without deep distress and great depression. Let us therefore be determined to remember what we want today, that we may unify our thoughts and actions meaningfully, and achieve only what God would have us do this day.

Father, forgiveness is Your chosen means for our salvation. Let us not forget today that we can have no will but Yours. And thus our purpose must be Yours as well, if we would reach the peace You will for us.

Lesson 258

Let me remember that my goal is God.

All that is needful is to train our minds to overlook all little senseless aims, and to remember that our goal is God. His memory is hidden in our minds, obscured but by our pointless little goals which offer nothing, and do not exist. Shall we continue to allow God's grace to shine in unawareness, while the toys and trinkets of the world are sought instead? God is our only goal, our only Love. We have no aim but to remember Him.

Our goal is but to follow in the way that leads to You. We have no goal but this. What could we want but to remember You? What could we seek but our Identity?

Lesson 259

Let me remember that there is no sin.

Sin is the only thought that makes the goal of God seem unattainable. What else could blind us to the obvious, and make the strange and the distorted seem more clear? What else but sin engenders our attacks? What else but sin could be the source of guilt, demanding punishment and suffering? And what but sin could be the source of fear, obscuring God's creation; giving love the attributes of fear and of attack?

FATHER, I WOULD NOT BE INSANE TODAY. I WOULD NOT BE AFRAID OF LOVE, NOR SEEK FOR REFUGE IN ITS OPPOSITE. FOR LOVE CAN HAVE NO OPPOSITE. YOU ARE THE SOURCE OF EVERYTHING THERE IS. AND EVERYTHING THAT IS REMAINS WITH YOU, AND YOU WITH IT.

Lesson 260

Let me remember God created me.

FATHER, I DID NOT MAKE MYSELF, ALTHOUGH IN MY INSANITY I THOUGHT I DID. YET, AS YOUR THOUGHT, I HAVE NOT LEFT MY SOURCE, REMAINING PART OF WHO CREATED ME. YOUR SON, MY FATHER, CALLS ON YOU TODAY. LET ME REMEMBER YOU CREATED ME. LET ME REMEMBER MY IDENTITY. AND LET MY SINLESSNESS ARISE AGAIN BEFORE CHRIST'S VISION, THROUGH WHICH I WOULD LOOK UPON MY BROTHERS AND MYSELF TODAY.

Now is our Source remembered, and Therein we find our true Identity at last. Holy indeed are we, because our Source can know no sin. And we who are His Sons are like each other, and alike to Him.

Lesson 261

Section 5. What is the Body?

The body is a fence the Son of God imagines he has built, to separate parts of his Self from other parts. It is within this fence he thinks he lives, to die as it decays and crumbles. For within this fence he thinks that he is safe from love. Identifying with his safety, he regards himself as what his safety is. How else could he be certain he remains within the body, keeping love outside?

The body will not stay. Yet this he sees as double safety. For the Son of God's impermanence is "proof" his fences work, and do the task his mind assigns to them. For if his oneness still remained untouched, who could attack and who could be attacked? Who could be victor? Who could be his prey? Who could be victim? Who the murderer? And if he did not die, what "proof" is there that God's eternal Son can be destroyed?

The body is a dream. Like other dreams it sometimes seems to picture happiness, but can quite suddenly revert to fear, where every dream is born. For only love creates in truth, and truth can never fear. Made to be fearful, must the body serve the purpose given it. But we can change the purpose that the body will obey by changing what we think that it is for.

The body is the means by which God's Son returns to sanity. Though it was made to fence him into hell without escape, yet has the goal of Heaven been exchanged for the pursuit of hell. The Son of God extends his hand to reach his brother, and to help him walk along the road with him. Now is the body holy. Now it serves to heal the mind that it was made to kill.

You will identify with what you think will make you safe. Whatever it may be, you will believe that it is one with you. Your safety lies in truth, and not in lies. Love is your safety. Fear does not exist. Identify with love, and you are safe. Identify with love, and you are home. Identify with love, and find your Self.

Lesson 261

God is my refuge and security.

I will identify with what I think is refuge and security. I will behold myself where I perceive my strength, and think I live within the citadel where I am safe and cannot be attacked. Let me today seek not security in danger, nor attempt to find my peace in murderous attack. I live in God. In Him I find my refuge and my strength. In Him is my Identity. In Him is everlasting peace. And only there will I remember Who I really am.

LET ME NOT SEEK FOR IDOLS. I WOULD COME, MY FATHER, HOME TO YOU TODAY. I CHOOSE TO BE AS YOU CREATED ME, AND FIND THE SON WHOM YOU CREATED AS MY SELF.

Lesson 262

Let me perceive no differences today.

FATHER, YOU HAVE ONE SON. AND IT IS HE THAT I WOULD LOOK UPON TODAY. HE IS YOUR ONE CREATION. WHY SHOULD I PERCEIVE A THOUSAND FORMS IN WHAT REMAINS AS ONE? WHY SHOULD I GIVE THIS ONE A THOUSAND NAMES, WHEN ONLY ONE SUFFICES? FOR YOUR SON MUST BEAR YOUR NAME, FOR YOU CREATED HIM. LET ME NOT SEE HIM AS A STRANGER TO HIS FATHER, NOR AS STRANGER TO MYSELF. FOR HE IS PART OF ME AND I OF HIM, AND WE ARE PART OF YOU WHO ARE OUR SOURCE, ETERNALLY UNITED IN YOUR LOVE; ETERNALLY THE HOLY SON OF GOD.

We who are one would recognize this day the truth about ourselves. We would come home, and rest in unity. For there is peace, and nowhere else can peace be sought and found.

Lesson 263

My holy vision sees all things as pure.

FATHER, YOUR MIND CREATED ALL THAT IS, YOUR SPIRIT ENTERED INTO IT, YOUR LOVE GAVE LIFE TO IT. AND WOULD I LOOK UPON WHAT YOU CREATED AS IF IT COULD BE MADE SINFUL? I WOULD NOT PERCEIVE SUCH DARK AND FEARFUL IMAGES. A MADMAN'S DREAM IS HARDLY FIT TO BE MY CHOICE, INSTEAD OF ALL THE LOVELINESS WITH WHICH YOU BLESSED CREATION; ALL ITS PURITY, ITS JOY, AND ITS ETERNAL, QUIET HOME IN YOU.

And while we still remain outside the gate of Heaven, let us look on all we see through holy vision and the eyes of Christ. Let all appearances seem pure to us, that we may pass them by in innocence, and walk together to our Father's house as brothers and the holy Sons of God.

Lesson 264

I am surrounded by the Love of God.

FATHER, YOU STAND BEFORE ME AND BEHIND, BESIDE ME, IN THE PLACE I SEE MYSELF, AND EVERYWHERE I GO. YOU ARE IN ALL THE THINGS I LOOK UPON, THE SOUNDS I HEAR, AND EVERY HAND THAT REACHES FOR MY OWN. IN YOU TIME DISAPPEARS, AND PLACE BECOMES A MEANINGLESS BELIEF. FOR WHAT SURROUNDS YOUR SON AND KEEPS HIM SAFE IS LOVE ITSELF. THERE IS NO SOURCE BUT THIS, AND NOTHING IS THAT DOES NOT SHARE ITS HOLINESS; THAT STANDS BEYOND YOUR ONE CREATION, OR WITHOUT THE LOVE WHICH HOLDS ALL THINGS WITHIN ITSELF. FATHER, YOUR SON IS LIKE YOURSELF. WE COME TO YOU IN YOUR OWN NAME TODAY, TO BE AT PEACE WITHIN YOUR EVERLASTING LOVE.

My brothers, join with me in this today. This is salvation's prayer. Must we not join in what will save the world, along with us?

Lesson 265

Creation's gentleness is all I see.

I have indeed misunderstood the world, because I laid my sins on it and saw them looking back at me. How fierce they seemed! And how deceived was I to think that what I feared was in the world, instead of in my mind alone. Today I see the world in the celestial gentleness with which creation shines. There is no fear in it. Let no appearance of my sins obscure the light of Heaven shining on the world. What is reflected there is in God's Mind. The images I see reflect my thoughts. Yet is my mind at one with God's. And so I can perceive creation's gentleness.

IN QUIET WOULD I LOOK UPON THE WORLD, WHICH BUT REFLECTS YOUR THOUGHTS, AND MINE AS WELL. LET ME REMEMBER THAT THEY ARE THE SAME, AND I WILL SEE CREATION'S GENTLENESS.

Lesson 266

My holy Self abides in you, God's Son.

FATHER, YOU GAVE ME ALL YOUR SONS, TO BE MY SAVIORS AND MY COUNSELORS IN SIGHT; THE BEARERS OF YOUR HOLY VOICE TO ME. IN THEM ARE YOU REFLECTED, AND IN THEM DOES CHRIST LOOK BACK UPON ME FROM MY SELF. LET NOT YOUR SON FORGET YOUR HOLY NAME. LET NOT YOUR SON FORGET HIS HOLY SOURCE. LET NOT YOUR SON FORGET HIS NAME IS YOURS.

This day we enter into Paradise, calling upon God's Name and on our own, acknowledging our Self in each of us; united in the holy Love of God. How many saviors God has given us! How can we lose the way to Him, when He has filled the world with those who point to Him, and given us the sight to look on them?

Lesson 267

My heart is beating in the peace of God.

Surrounding me is all the life that God created in His Love. It calls to me in every heartbeat and in every breath; in every action and in every thought. Peace fills my heart, and floods my body with the purpose of forgiveness. Now my mind is healed, and all I need to save the world is given me. Each heartbeat brings me peace; each breath infuses me with strength. I am a messenger of God, directed by His Voice, sustained by Him in love, and held forever quiet and at peace within His loving Arms. Each heartbeat calls His Name, and every one is answered by His Voice, assuring me I am at home in Him.

LET ME ATTEND YOUR ANSWER, NOT MY OWN. FATHER, MY HEART IS BEATING IN THE PEACE THE HEART OF LOVE CREATED. IT IS THERE AND ONLY THERE THAT I CAN BE AT HOME.

Lesson 268

Let all things be exactly as they are.

LET ME NOT BE YOUR CRITIC, LORD, TODAY, AND JUDGE AGAINST YOU. LET ME NOT ATTEMPT TO INTERFERE WITH YOUR CREATION, AND DISTORT IT INTO SICKLY FORMS. LET ME BE WILLING TO WITHDRAW MY WISHES FROM ITS UNITY, AND THUS TO LET IT BE AS YOU CREATED IT. FOR THUS WILL I BE ABLE, TOO, TO RECOGNIZE MY SELF AS YOU CREATED ME. IN LOVE WAS I CREATED, AND IN LOVE WILL I REMAIN FOREVER. WHAT CAN FRIGHTEN ME, WHEN I LET ALL THINGS BE EXACTLY AS THEY ARE?

Let not our sight be blasphemous today, nor let our ears attend to lying tongues. Only reality is free of pain. Only reality is free of loss. Only reality is wholly safe. And it is only this we seek today.

Lesson 269

My sight goes forth to look upon Christ's face.

I ASK YOUR BLESSING ON MY SIGHT TODAY. IT IS THE MEANS WHICH YOU HAVE CHOSEN TO BECOME THE WAY TO SHOW ME MY MISTAKES, AND LOOK BEYOND THEM. IT IS GIVEN ME TO FIND A NEW PERCEPTION THROUGH THE GUIDE YOU GAVE TO ME, AND THROUGH HIS LESSONS TO SURPASS PERCEPTION AND RETURN TO TRUTH. I ASK FOR THE ILLUSION WHICH TRANSCENDS ALL THOSE I MADE. TODAY I CHOOSE TO SEE A WORLD FORGIVEN, IN WHICH EVERYONE SHOWS ME THE FACE OF CHRIST, AND TEACHES ME THAT WHAT I LOOK UPON BELONGS TO ME; THAT NOTHING IS, EXCEPT YOUR HOLY SON.

Today our sight is blessed indeed. We share one vision, as we look upon the face of Him Whose Self is ours. We are one because of Him Who is the Son of God; of Him Who is our own Identity.

Lesson 270

I will not use the body's eyes today.

FATHER, CHRIST'S VISION IS YOUR GIFT TO ME, AND IT HAS POWER TO TRANSLATE ALL THAT THE BODY'S EYES BEHOLD INTO THE SIGHT OF A FORGIVEN WORLD. HOW GLORIOUS AND GRACIOUS IS THIS WORLD! YET HOW MUCH MORE WILL I PERCEIVE IN IT THAN SIGHT CAN GIVE. THE WORLD FORGIVEN SIGNIFIES YOUR SON ACKNOWLEDGES HIS FATHER, LETS HIS DREAMS BE BROUGHT TO TRUTH, AND WAITS EXPECTANTLY THE ONE REMAINING INSTANT MORE OF TIME WHICH ENDS FOREVER, AS YOUR MEMORY RETURNS TO HIM. AND NOW HIS WILL IS ONE WITH YOURS. HIS FUNCTION NOW IS BUT YOUR OWN, AND EVERY THOUGHT EXCEPT YOUR OWN IS GONE.

The quiet of today will bless our hearts, and through them peace will come to everyone. Christ is our eyes today. And through His sight we offer healing to the world through Him, the holy Son whom God created whole; the holy Son whom God created One.

Lesson 271

Section 6. What is the Christ?

Christ is God's Son as He created Him. He is the Self we share, uniting us with one another, and with God as well. He is the Thought which still abides within the Mind that is His Source. He has not left His holy home, nor lost the innocence in which He was created. He abides unchanged forever in the Mind of God.

Christ is the link that keeps you one with God, and guarantees that separation is no more than an illusion of despair, for hope forever will abide in Him. Your mind is part of His, and His of yours. He is the part in which God's Answer lies; where all decisions are already made, and dreams are over. He remains untouched by anything the body's eyes perceive. For though in Him His Father placed the means for your salvation, yet does He remain the Self Who, like His Father, knows no sin.

Home of the Holy Spirit, and at home in God alone, does Christ remain at peace within the Heaven of your holy mind. This is the only part of you that has reality in truth. The rest is dreams. Yet will these dreams be given unto Christ, to fade before His glory and reveal your holy Self, the Christ, to you at last.

The Holy Spirit reaches from the Christ in you to all your dreams, and bids them come to Him, to be translated into truth. He will exchange them for the final dream which God appointed as the end of dreams. For when forgiveness rests upon the world and peace has come to every Son of God, what could there be to keep things separate, for what remains to see except Christ's face?

And how long will this holy face be seen, when it is but the symbol that the time for learning now is over, and the goal of the Atonement has been reached at last? So therefore let us seek to find Christ's face and look on nothing else. As we behold His glory, will we know we have no need of learning or perception or of time, or anything except the holy Self, the Christ Whom God created as His Son.

Lesson 271

Christ's is the vision I will use today.

Each day, each hour, every instant, I am choosing what I want to look upon, the sounds I want to hear, the witnesses to what I want to be the truth for me. Today I choose to look upon what Christ would have me see, to listen to God's Voice, and seek the witnesses to what is true in God's creation. In Christ's sight, the world and God's creation meet, and as they come together all perception disappears. His kindly sight redeems the world from death, for nothing that He looks on but must live, remembering the Father and the Son; Creator and creation unified.

FATHER, CHRIST'S VISION IS THE WAY TO YOU. WHAT HE BEHOLDS INVITES YOUR MEMORY TO BE RESTORED TO ME. AND THIS I CHOOSE, TO BE WHAT I WOULD LOOK UPON TODAY.

Lesson 272

How can illusions satisfy God's Son?

FATHER, THE TRUTH BELONGS TO ME. MY HOME IS SET IN HEAVEN BY YOUR WILL AND MINE. CAN DREAMS CONTENT ME? CAN ILLUSIONS BRING ME HAPPINESS? WHAT BUT YOUR MEMORY CAN SATISFY YOUR SON? I WILL ACCEPT NO LESS THAN YOU HAVE GIVEN ME. I AM SURROUNDED BY YOUR LOVE, FOREVER STILL, FOREVER GENTLE AND FOREVER SAFE. GOD'S SON MUST BE AS YOU CREATED HIM.

Today we pass illusions by. And if we hear temptation call to us to stay and linger in a dream, we turn aside and ask ourselves if we, the Sons of God, could be content with dreams, when Heaven can be chosen just as easily as hell, and love will happily replace all fear.

Lesson 273

The stillness of the peace of God is mine.

Perhaps we are now ready for a day of undisturbed tranquility. If this is not yet feasible, we are content and even more than satisfied to learn how such a day can be achieved. If we give way to a disturbance, let us learn how to dismiss it and return to peace. We need but tell our minds, with certainty, "The stillness of the peace of God is mine," and nothing can intrude upon the peace that God Himself has given to His Son.

FATHER, YOUR PEACE IS MINE. WHAT NEED HAVE I TO FEAR THAT ANYTHING CAN ROB ME OF WHAT YOU WOULD HAVE ME KEEP? I CANNOT LOSE YOUR GIFTS TO ME. AND SO THE PEACE YOU GAVE YOUR SON IS WITH ME STILL, IN QUIETNESS AND IN MY OWN ETERNAL LOVE FOR YOU.

Lesson 274

Today belongs to love. Let me not fear.

Father, today I would let all things be as You created them, and give Your Son the honor due his sinlessness; the love of brother to his brother and his Friend. Through this I am redeemed. Through this as well the truth will enter where illusions were, light will replace all darkness, and Your Son will know he is as You created him.

A special blessing comes to us today, from Him Who is our Father. Give this day to Him, and there will be no fear today, because the day is given unto love.

Lesson 275

God's healing Voice protects all things today.

Let us today attend the Voice for God, which speaks an ancient lesson, no more true today than any other day. Yet has this day been chosen as the time when we will seek and hear and learn and understand. Join me in hearing. For the Voice for God tells us of things we cannot understand alone, nor learn apart. It is in this that all things are protected. And in this the healing of the Voice for God is found.

YOUR HEALING VOICE PROTECTS ALL THINGS TODAY, AND SO I LEAVE ALL THINGS TO YOU. I NEED BE ANXIOUS OVER NOTHING. FOR YOUR VOICE WILL TELL ME WHAT TO DO AND WHERE TO GO; TO WHOM TO SPEAK AND WHAT TO SAY TO HIM, WHAT THOUGHTS TO THINK, WHAT WORDS TO GIVE THE WORLD. THE SAFETY THAT I BRING IS GIVEN ME. FATHER, YOUR VOICE PROTECTS ALL THINGS THROUGH ME.

Lesson 276

The Word of God is given me to speak.

What is the Word of God? "My Son is pure and holy as Myself." And thus did God become the Father of the Son He loves, for thus was he created. This the Word His Son did not create with Him, because in this His Son was born. Let us accept His Fatherhood, and all is given us. Deny we were created in His Love and we deny our Self, to be unsure of Who we are, of Who our Father is, and for what purpose we have come. And yet, we need but to acknowledge Him Who gave His Word to us in our creation, to remember Him and so recall our Self.

FATHER, YOUR WORD IS MINE. AND IT IS THIS THAT I WOULD SPEAK TO ALL MY BROTHERS, WHO ARE GIVEN ME TO CHERISH AS MY OWN, AS I AM LOVED AND BLESSED AND SAVED BY YOU.

Lesson 277

Let me not bind Your Son with laws I made.

YOUR SON IS FREE, MY FATHER. LET ME NOT IMAGINE I HAVE BOUND HIM WITH THE LAWS I MADE TO RULE THE BODY. HE IS NOT SUBJECT TO ANY LAWS I MADE BY WHICH I TRY TO MAKE THE BODY MORE SECURE. HE IS NOT CHANGED BY WHAT IS CHANGEABLE. HE IS NOT SLAVE TO ANY LAWS OF TIME. HE IS AS YOU CREATED HIM, BECAUSE HE KNOWS NO LAW EXCEPT THE LAW OF LOVE.

Let us not worship idols, nor believe in any law idolatry would make to hide the freedom of the Son of God. He is not bound except by his beliefs. Yet what he is, is far beyond his faith in slavery or freedom. He is free because he is his Father's Son. And he cannot be bound unless God's truth can lie, and God can will that He deceive Himself.

Lesson 278

If I am bound, my Father is not free.

If I accept that I am prisoner within a body, in a world in which all things that seem to live appear to die, then is my Father prisoner with me. And this do I believe, when I maintain the laws the world obeys must I obey; the frailties and the sins which I perceive are real, and cannot be escaped. If I am bound in any way, I do not know my Father nor my Self. And I am lost to all reality. For truth is free, and what is bound is not a part of truth.

FATHER, I ASK FOR NOTHING BUT THE TRUTH. I HAVE HAD MANY FOOLISH THOUGHTS ABOUT MYSELF AND MY CREATION, AND HAVE BROUGHT A DREAM OF FEAR INTO MY MIND. TODAY, I WOULD NOT DREAM. I CHOOSE THE WAY TO YOU INSTEAD OF MADNESS AND INSTEAD OF FEAR. FOR TRUTH IS SAFE, AND ONLY LOVE IS SURE.

Lesson 279

Creation's freedom promises my own.

The end of dreams is promised me, because God's Son is not abandoned by His Love. Only in dreams is there a time when he appears to be in prison, and awaits a future freedom, if it be at all. Yet in reality his dreams are gone, with truth established in their place. And now is freedom his already. Should I wait in chains which have been severed for release, when God is offering me freedom now?

I WILL ACCEPT YOUR PROMISES TODAY, AND GIVE MY FAITH TO THEM. MY FATHER LOVES THE SON WHOM HE CREATED AS HIS OWN. WOULD YOU WITHHOLD THE GIFTS YOU GAVE TO ME?

Lesson 280

What limits can I lay upon God's Son?

Whom God created limitless is free. I can invent imprisonment for him, but only in illusions, not in truth. No Thought of God has left its Father's Mind. No Thought of God is limited at all. No Thought of God but is forever pure. Can I lay limits on the Son of God, whose Father willed that he be limitless, and like Himself in freedom and in love?

TODAY LET ME GIVE HONOR TO YOUR SON, FOR THUS ALONE I FIND THE WAY TO YOU. FATHER, I LAY NO LIMITS ON THE SON YOU LOVE AND YOU CREATED LIMITLESS. THE HONOR THAT I GIVE TO HIM IS YOURS, AND WHAT IS YOURS BELONGS TO ME AS WELL.

Lesson 281

Section 7. What is the Holy Spirit?

The Holy Spirit mediates between illusions and the truth. Since He must bridge the gap between reality and dreams, perception leads to knowledge through the grace that God has given Him, to be His gift to everyone who turns to Him for truth. Across the bridge that He provides are dreams all carried to the truth, to be dispelled before the light of knowledge. There are sights and sounds forever laid aside. And where they were perceived before, forgiveness has made possible perception's tranquil end.

The goal the Holy Spirit's teaching sets is just this end of dreams. For sights and sounds must be translated from the witnesses of fear to those of love. And when this is entirely accomplished, learning has achieved the only goal it has in truth. For learning, as the Holy Spirit guides it to the outcome He perceives for it, becomes the means to go beyond itself, to be replaced by the eternal truth.

If you but knew how much your Father yearns to have you recognize your sinlessness, you would not let His Voice appeal in vain, nor turn away from His replacement for the fearful images and dreams you made. The Holy Spirit understands the means you made, by which you would attain what is forever unattainable. And if you offer them to Him, He will employ the means you made for exile to restore your mind to where it truly is at home.

From knowledge, where He has been placed by God, the Holy Spirit calls to you, to let forgiveness rest upon your dreams, and be restored to sanity and peace of mind. Without forgiveness will your dreams remain to terrify you. And the memory of all your Father's Love will not return to signify the end of dreams has come.

Accept your Father's gift. It is a Call from Love to Love, that It be but Itself. The Holy Spirit is His gift, by which the quietness of Heaven is restored to God's beloved Son. Would you refuse to take the function of completing God, when all He wills is that you be complete?

Lesson 281

I can be hurt by nothing but my thoughts.

FATHER, YOUR SON IS PERFECT. WHEN I THINK THAT I AM HURT IN ANY WAY, IT IS BECAUSE I HAVE FORGOTTEN WHO I AM, AND THAT I AM AS YOU CREATED ME. YOUR THOUGHTS CAN ONLY BRING ME HAPPINESS. IF EVER I AM SAD OR HURT OR ILL, I HAVE FORGOTTEN WHAT YOU THINK, AND PUT MY LITTLE MEANINGLESS IDEAS IN PLACE OF WHERE YOUR THOUGHTS BELONG, AND WHERE THEY ARE. I CAN BE HURT BY NOTHING BUT MY THOUGHTS. THE THOUGHTS I THINK WITH YOU CAN ONLY BLESS. THE THOUGHTS I THINK WITH YOU ALONE ARE TRUE.

I will not hurt myself today. For I am far beyond all pain. My Father placed me safe in Heaven, watching over me. And I would not attack the Son He loves, for what He loves is also mine to love.

Lesson 282

I will not be afraid of love today.

If I could realize but this today, salvation would be reached for all the world. This the decision not to be insane, and to accept myself as God Himself, my Father and my Source, created me. This the determination not to be asleep in dreams of death, while truth remains forever living in the joy of love. And this the choice to recognize the Self Whom God created as the Son He loves, and Who remains my one Identity.

FATHER, YOUR NAME IS LOVE AND SO IS MINE. SUCH IS THE TRUTH. AND CAN THE TRUTH BE CHANGED BY MERELY GIVING IT ANOTHER NAME? THE NAME OF FEAR IS SIMPLY A MISTAKE. LET ME NOT BE AFRAID OF TRUTH TODAY.

Lesson 283

My true Identity abides in You.

FATHER, I MADE AN IMAGE OF MYSELF, AND IT IS THIS I CALL THE SON OF GOD. YET IS CREATION AS IT ALWAYS WAS, FOR YOUR CREATION IS UNCHANGEABLE. LET ME NOT WORSHIP IDOLS. I AM HE MY FATHER LOVES. MY HOLINESS REMAINS THE LIGHT OF HEAVEN AND THE LOVE OF GOD. IS NOT WHAT IS BELOVED OF YOU SECURE? IS NOT THE LIGHT OF HEAVEN INFINITE? IS NOT YOUR SON MY TRUE IDENTITY, WHEN YOU CREATED EVERYTHING THAT IS?

Now are we One in shared Identity, with God our Father as our only Source, and everything created part of us. And so we offer blessing to all things, uniting lovingly with all the world, which our forgiveness has made one with us.

Lesson 284

I can elect to change all thoughts that hurt.

Loss is not loss when properly perceived. Pain is impossible. There is no grief with any cause at all. And suffering of any kind is nothing but a dream. This is the truth, at first to be but said and then repeated many times; and next to be accepted as but partly true, with many reservations. Then to be considered seriously more and more, and finally accepted as the truth. I can elect to change all thoughts that hurt. And I would go beyond these words today, and past all reservations, and arrive at full acceptance of the truth in them.

FATHER, WHAT YOU HAVE GIVEN CANNOT HURT, SO GRIEF AND PAIN MUST BE IMPOSSIBLE. LET ME NOT FAIL TO TRUST IN YOU TODAY, ACCEPTING BUT THE JOYOUS AS YOUR GIFTS; ACCEPTING BUT THE JOYOUS AS THE TRUTH.

Lesson 285

My holiness shines bright and clear today.

Today I wake with joy, expecting but the happy things of God to come to me. I ask but them to come, and realize my invitation will be answered by the thoughts to which it has been sent by me. And I will ask for only joyous things the instant I accept my holiness. For what would be the use of pain to me, what purpose would my suffering fulfill, and how would grief and loss avail me if insanity departs from me today, and I accept my holiness instead?

FATHER, MY HOLINESS IS YOURS. LET ME REJOICE IN IT, AND THROUGH FORGIVENESS BE RESTORED TO SANITY. YOUR SON IS STILL AS YOU CREATED HIM. MY HOLINESS IS PART OF ME, AND ALSO PART OF YOU. AND WHAT CAN ALTER HOLINESS ITSELF?

Lesson 286

The hush of Heaven holds my heart today.

FATHER, HOW STILL TODAY! HOW QUIETLY DO ALL THINGS FALL IN PLACE! THIS IS THE DAY THAT HAS BEEN CHOSEN AS THE TIME IN WHICH I COME TO UNDERSTAND THE LESSON THAT THERE IS NO NEED THAT I DO ANYTHING. IN YOU IS EVERY CHOICE ALREADY MADE. IN YOU HAS EVERY CONFLICT BEEN RESOLVED. IN YOU IS EVERYTHING I HOPE TO FIND ALREADY GIVEN ME. YOUR PEACE IS MINE. MY HEART IS QUIET, AND MY MIND AT REST. YOUR LOVE IS HEAVEN, AND YOUR LOVE IS MINE.

The stillness of today will give us hope that we have found the way, and travelled far along it to a wholly certain goal. Today we will not doubt the end which God Himself has promised us. We trust in Him, and in our Self, Who still is One with Him.

Lesson 287

You are my goal, my Father. Only You.

Where would I go but Heaven? What could be a substitute for happiness? What gift could I prefer before the peace of God? What treasure would I seek and find and keep that can compare with my Identity? And would I rather live with fear than love?

YOU ARE MY GOAL, MY FATHER. WHAT BUT YOU COULD I DESIRE TO HAVE? WHAT WAY BUT THAT WHICH LEADS TO YOU COULD I DESIRE TO WALK? AND WHAT EXCEPT THE MEMORY OF YOU COULD SIGNIFY TO ME THE END OF DREAMS AND FUTILE SUBSTITUTIONS FOR THE TRUTH? YOU ARE MY ONLY GOAL. YOUR SON WOULD BE AS YOU CREATED HIM. WHAT WAY BUT THIS COULD I EXPECT TO RECOGNIZE MY SELF, AND BE AT ONE WITH MY IDENTITY?

Lesson 288

Let me forget my brother's past today.

THIS IS THE THOUGHT THAT LEADS THE WAY TO YOU, AND BRINGS ME TO MY GOAL. I CANNOT COME TO YOU WITHOUT MY BROTHER. AND TO KNOW MY SOURCE, I FIRST MUST RECOGNIZE WHAT YOU CREATED ONE WITH ME. MY BROTHER'S IS THE HAND THAT LEADS ME ON THE WAY TO YOU. HIS SINS ARE IN THE PAST ALONG WITH MINE, AND I AM SAVED BECAUSE THE PAST IS GONE. LET ME NOT CHERISH IT WITHIN MY HEART, OR I WILL LOSE THE WAY TO WALK TO YOU. MY BROTHER IS MY SAVIOR. LET ME NOT ATTACK THE SAVIOR YOU HAVE GIVEN ME. BUT LET ME HONOR HIM WHO BEARS YOUR NAME, AND SO REMEMBER THAT IT IS MY OWN.

Forgive me, then, today. And you will know you have forgiven me if you behold your brother in the light of holiness. He cannot be less holy than can I, and you can not be holier than he.

Lesson 289

The past is over. It can touch me not.

Unless the past is over in my mind, the real world must escape my sight. For I am really looking nowhere; seeing but what is not there. How can I then perceive the world forgiveness offers? This the past was made to hide, for this the world that can be looked on only now. It has no past. For what can be forgiven but the past, and if it is forgiven it is gone.

FATHER, LET ME NOT LOOK UPON A PAST THAT IS NOT THERE. FOR YOU HAVE OFFERED ME YOUR OWN REPLACEMENT, IN A PRESENT WORLD THE PAST HAS LEFT UNTOUCHED AND FREE OF SIN. HERE IS THE END OF GUILT. AND HERE AM I MADE READY FOR YOUR FINAL STEP. SHALL I DEMAND THAT YOU WAIT LONGER FOR YOUR SON TO FIND THE LOVELINESS YOU PLANNED TO BE THE END OF ALL HIS DREAMS AND ALL HIS PAIN?

Lesson 290

My present happiness is all I see.

Unless I look upon what is not there, my present happiness is all I see. Eyes that begin to open see at last. And I would have Christ's vision come to me this very day. What I perceive without God's Own Correction for the sight I made is frightening and painful to behold. Yet I would not allow my mind to be deceived by the belief the dream I made is real an instant longer. This the day I seek my present happiness, and look on nothing else except the thing I seek.

WITH THIS RESOLVE I COME TO YOU, AND ASK YOUR STRENGTH TO HOLD ME UP TODAY, WHILE I BUT SEEK TO DO YOUR WILL. YOU CANNOT FAIL TO HEAR ME, FATHER. WHAT I ASK HAVE YOU ALREADY GIVEN ME. AND I AM SURE THAT I WILL SEE MY HAPPINESS TODAY.

Lesson 291

Section 8. What is the Real World?

The real world is a symbol, like the rest of what perception offers. Yet it stands for what is opposite to what you made. Your world is seen through eyes of fear, and brings the witnesses of terror to your mind. The real world cannot be perceived except through eyes forgiveness blesses, so they see a world where terror is impossible, and witnesses to fear can not be found.

The real world holds a counterpart for each unhappy thought reflected in your world; a sure correction for the sights of fear and sounds of battle which your world contains. The real world shows a world seen differently, through quiet eyes and with a mind at peace. Nothing but rest is there. There are no cries of pain and sorrow heard, for nothing there remains outside forgiveness. And the sights are gentle. Only happy sights and sounds can reach the mind that has forgiven itself.

What need has such a mind for thoughts of death, attack and murder? What can it perceive surrounding it but safety, love and joy? What is there it would choose to be condemned, and what is there that it would judge against? The world it sees arises from a mind at peace within itself. No danger lurks in anything it sees, for it is kind, and only kindness does it look upon.

The real world is the symbol that the dream of sin and guilt is over, and God's Son no longer sleeps. His waking eyes perceive the sure reflection of his Father's Love; the certain promise that he is redeemed. The real world signifies the end of time, for its perception makes time purposeless.

The Holy Spirit has no need of time when it has served His purpose. Now He waits but that one instant more for God to take His final step, and time has disappeared, taking perception with it as it goes, and leaving but the truth to be itself. That instant is our goal, for it contains the memory of God. And as we look upon a world forgiven, it is He Who calls to us and comes to take us home, reminding us of our Identity which our forgiveness has restored to us.

Lesson 291

This is a day of stillness and of peace.

Christ's vision looks through me today. His sight shows me all things forgiven and at peace, and offers this same vision to the world. And I accept this vision in its name, both for myself and for the world as well. What loveliness we look upon today! What holiness we see surrounding us! And it is given us to recognize it is a holiness in which we share; it is the Holiness of God Himself.

THIS DAY MY MIND IS QUIET, TO RECEIVE THE THOUGHTS YOU OFFER ME. AND I ACCEPT WHAT COMES FROM YOU, INSTEAD OF FROM MYSELF. I DO NOT KNOW THE WAY TO YOU. BUT YOU ARE WHOLLY CERTAIN. FATHER, GUIDE YOUR SON ALONG THE QUIET PATH THAT LEADS TO YOU. LET MY FORGIVENESS BE COMPLETE, AND LET THE MEMORY OF YOU RETURN TO ME.

Lesson 292

A happy outcome to all things is sure.

God's promises make no exceptions. And He guarantees that only joy can be the final outcome found for everything. Yet it is up to us when this is reached; how long we let an alien will appear to be opposing His. And while we think this will is real, we will not find the end He has appointed as the outcome of all problems we perceive, all trials we see, and every situation that we meet. Yet is the ending certain. For God's Will is done in earth and Heaven. We will seek and we will find according to His Will, which guarantees that our will is done.

WE THANK YOU, FATHER, FOR YOUR GUARANTEE OF ONLY HAPPY OUTCOMES IN THE END. HELP US NOT INTERFERE, AND SO DELAY THE HAPPY ENDINGS YOU HAVE PROMISED US FOR EVERY PROBLEM THAT WE CAN PERCEIVE; FOR EVERY TRIAL WE THINK WE STILL MUST MEET.

Lesson 293

All fear is past and only love is here.

All fear is past, because its source is gone, and all its thoughts gone with it. Love remains the only present state, whose Source is here forever and forever. Can the world seem bright and clear and safe and welcoming, with all my past mistakes oppressing it, and showing me distorted forms of fear? Yet in the present love is obvious, and its effects apparent. All the world shines in reflection of its holy light, and I perceive a world forgiven at last.

FATHER, LET NOT YOUR HOLY WORLD ESCAPE MY SIGHT TODAY. NOR LET MY EARS BE DEAF TO ALL THE HYMNS OF GRATITUDE THE WORLD IS SINGING UNDERNEATH THE SOUNDS OF FEAR. THERE IS A REAL WORLD WHICH THE PRESENT HOLDS SAFE FROM ALL PAST MISTAKES. AND I WOULD SEE ONLY THIS WORLD BEFORE MY EYES TODAY.

Lesson 294

My body is a wholly neutral thing.

I am a Son of God. And can I be another thing as well? Did God create the mortal and corruptible? What use has God's beloved Son for what must die? And yet a neutral thing does not see death, for thoughts of fear are not invested there, nor is a mockery of love bestowed upon it. Its neutrality protects it while it has a use. And afterwards, without a purpose, it is laid aside. It is not sick nor old nor hurt. It is but functionless, unneeded and cast off. Let me not see it more than this today; of service for a while and fit to serve, to keep its usefulness while it can serve, and then to be replaced for greater good.

MY BODY, FATHER, CANNOT BE YOUR SON. AND WHAT IS NOT CREATED CANNOT BE SINFUL NOR SINLESS; NEITHER GOOD NOR BAD. LET ME, THEN, USE THIS DREAM TO HELP YOUR PLAN THAT WE AWAKEN FROM ALL DREAMS WE MADE.

Lesson 295

The Holy Spirit looks through me today.

Christ asks that He may use my eyes today, and thus redeem the world. He asks this gift that He may offer peace of mind to me, and take away all terror and all pain. And as they are removed from me, the dreams that seemed to settle on the world are gone. Redemption must be one. As I am saved, the world is saved with me. For all of us must be redeemed together. Fear appears in many different forms, but love is one.

MY FATHER, CHRIST HAS ASKED A GIFT OF ME, AND ONE I GIVE THAT IT BE GIVEN ME. HELP ME TO USE THE EYES OF CHRIST TODAY, AND THUS ALLOW THE HOLY SPIRIT'S LOVE TO BLESS ALL THINGS WHICH I MAY LOOK UPON, THAT HIS FORGIVING LOVE MAY REST ON ME.

Lesson 296

The Holy Spirit speaks through me today.

THE HOLY SPIRIT NEEDS MY VOICE TODAY, THAT ALL THE WORLD MAY LISTEN TO YOUR VOICE, AND HEAR YOUR WORD THROUGH ME. I AM RESOLVED TO LET YOU SPEAK THROUGH ME, FOR I WOULD USE NO WORDS BUT YOURS, AND HAVE NO THOUGHTS WHICH ARE APART FROM YOURS, FOR ONLY YOURS ARE TRUE. I WOULD BE SAVIOR TO THE WORLD I MADE. FOR HAVING DAMNED IT I WOULD SET IT FREE, THAT I MAY FIND ESCAPE, AND HEAR THE WORD YOUR HOLY VOICE WILL SPEAK TO ME TODAY.

We teach today what we would learn, and that alone. And so our learning goal becomes an unconflicted one, and possible of easy reach and quick accomplishment. How gladly does the Holy Spirit come to rescue us from hell, when we allow His teaching to persuade the world, through us, to seek and find the easy path to God.

Lesson 297

Forgiveness is the only gift I give.

Forgiveness is the only gift I give, because it is the only gift I want. And everything I give I give myself. This is salvation's simple formula. And I, who would be saved, would make it mine, to be the way I live within a world that needs salvation, and that will be saved as I accept Atonement for myself.

FATHER, HOW CERTAIN ARE YOUR WAYS; HOW SURE THEIR FINAL OUTCOME, AND HOW FAITHFULLY IS EVERY STEP IN MY SALVATION SET ALREADY, AND ACCOMPLISHED BY YOUR GRACE. THANKS BE TO YOU FOR YOUR ETERNAL GIFTS, AND THANKS TO YOU FOR MY IDENTITY.

Lesson 298

I love You, Father, and I love Your Son.

My gratitude permits my love to be accepted without fear. And thus am I restored to my reality at last. All that intruded on my holy sight forgiveness takes away. And I draw near the end of senseless journeys, mad careers and artificial values. I accept instead what God establishes as mine, sure that in that alone I will be saved; sure that I go through fear to meet my Love.

FATHER, I COME TO YOU TODAY, BECAUSE I WOULD NOT FOLLOW ANY WAY BUT YOURS. YOU ARE BESIDE ME. CERTAIN IS YOUR WAY. AND I AM GRATEFUL FOR YOUR HOLY GIFTS OF CERTAIN SANCTUARY, AND ESCAPE FROM EVERYTHING THAT WOULD OBSCURE MY LOVE FOR GOD MY FATHER AND HIS HOLY SON.

Lesson 299

Eternal holiness abides in me.

My holiness is far beyond my own ability to understand or know. Yet God, my Father, Who created it, acknowledges my holiness as His. Our Will, together, understands it. And Our Will, together, knows that it is so.

FATHER, MY HOLINESS IS NOT OF ME. IT IS NOT MINE TO BE DESTROYED BY SIN. IT IS NOT MINE TO SUFFER FROM ATTACK. ILLUSIONS CAN OBSCURE IT, BUT CAN NOT PUT OUT ITS RADIANCE, NOR DIM ITS LIGHT. IT STANDS FOREVER PERFECT AND UNTOUCHED. IN IT ARE ALL THINGS HEALED, FOR THEY REMAIN AS YOU CREATED THEM. AND I CAN KNOW MY HOLINESS. FOR HOLINESS ITSELF CREATED ME, AND I CAN KNOW MY SOURCE BECAUSE IT IS YOUR WILL THAT YOU BE KNOWN.

Lesson 300

Only an instant does this world endure.

This is a thought which can be used to say that death and sorrow are the certain lot of all who come here, for their joys are gone before they are possessed, or even grasped. Yet this is also the idea that lets no false perception keep us in its hold, nor represent more than a passing cloud upon a sky eternally serene. And it is this serenity we seek, unclouded, obvious and sure, today.

WE SEEK YOUR HOLY WORLD TODAY. FOR WE, YOUR LOVING SONS, HAVE LOST OUR WAY A WHILE. BUT WE HAVE LISTENED TO YOUR VOICE, AND LEARNED EXACTLY WHAT TO DO TO BE RESTORED TO HEAVEN AND OUR TRUE IDENTITY. AND WE GIVE THANKS TODAY THE WORLD ENDURES BUT FOR AN INSTANT. WE WOULD GO BEYOND THAT TINY INSTANT TO ETERNITY.

Lesson 301

Section 9. What is the Second Coming?

Christ's Second Coming, which is sure as God, is merely the correction of mistakes, and the return of sanity. It is a part of the condition that restores the never lost, and re-establishes what is forever and forever true. It is the invitation to God's Word to take illusion's place; the willingness to let forgiveness rest upon all things without exception and without reserve.

It is the all-inclusive nature of Christ's Second Coming that permits it to embrace the world and hold you safe within its gentle advent, which encompasses all living things with you. There is no end to the release the Second Coming brings, as God's creation must be limitless. Forgiveness lights the Second Coming's way, because it shines on everything as one. And thus is oneness recognized at last.

The Second Coming ends the lessons that the Holy Spirit teaches, making way for the Last Judgment, in which learning ends in one last summary that will extend beyond itself, and reaches up to God. The Second Coming is the time in which all minds are given to the hands of Christ, to be returned to spirit in the name of true creation and the Will of God.

The Second Coming is the one event in time which time itself can not affect. For every one who ever came to die, or yet will come or who is present now, is equally released from what he made. In this equality is Christ restored as one Identity, in which the Sons of God acknowledge that they all are one. And God the Father smiles upon His Son, His one creation and His only joy.

Pray that the Second Coming will be soon, but do not rest with that. It needs your eyes and ears and hands and feet. It needs your voice. And most of all it needs your willingness. Let us rejoice that we can do God's Will, and join together in its holy light. Behold, the Son of God is one in us, and we can reach our Father's Love through Him.

Lesson 301

And God Himself shall wipe away all tears.

FATHER, UNLESS I JUDGE I CANNOT WEEP. NOR CAN I SUFFER PAIN, OR FEEL I AM ABANDONED OR UNNEEDED IN THE WORLD. THIS IS MY HOME BECAUSE I JUDGE IT NOT, AND THEREFORE IS IT ONLY WHAT YOU WILL. LET ME TODAY BEHOLD IT UNCONDEMNED, THROUGH HAPPY EYES FORGIVENESS HAS RELEASED FROM ALL DISTORTION. LET ME SEE YOUR WORLD INSTEAD OF MINE. AND ALL THE TEARS I SHED WILL BE FORGOTTEN, FOR THEIR SOURCE IS GONE. FATHER, I WILL NOT JUDGE YOUR WORLD TODAY.

God's world is happy. Those who look on it can only add their joy to it, and bless it as a cause of further joy in them. We wept because we did not understand. But we have learned the world we saw was false, and we will look upon God's world today.

Lesson 302

Where darkness was I look upon the light.

FATHER, OUR EYES ARE OPENING AT LAST. YOUR HOLY WORLD AWAITS US, AS OUR SIGHT IS FINALLY RESTORED AND WE CAN SEE. WE THOUGHT WE SUFFERED. BUT WE HAD FORGOT THE SON WHOM YOU CREATED. NOW WE SEE THAT DARKNESS IS OUR OWN IMAGINING, AND LIGHT IS THERE FOR US TO LOOK UPON. CHRIST'S VISION CHANGES DARKNESS INTO LIGHT, FOR FEAR MUST DISAPPEAR WHEN LOVE HAS COME. LET ME FORGIVE YOUR HOLY WORLD TODAY, THAT I MAY LOOK UPON ITS HOLINESS AND UNDERSTAND IT BUT REFLECTS MY OWN.

Our Love awaits us as we go to Him, and walks beside us showing us the way. He fails in nothing. He the End we seek, and He the Means by which we go to Him.

Lesson 303

The holy Christ is born in me today.

Watch with me, angels, watch with me today. Let all God's holy Thoughts surround me, and be still with me while Heaven's Son is born. Let earthly sounds be quiet, and the sights to which I am accustomed disappear. Let Christ be welcomed where He is at home. And let Him hear the sounds He understands, and see but sights that show His Father's Love. Let Him no longer be a stranger here, for He is born again in me today.

YOUR SON IS WELCOME, FATHER. HE HAS COME TO SAVE ME FROM THE EVIL SELF I MADE. HE IS THE SELF THAT YOU HAVE GIVEN ME. HE IS BUT WHAT I REALLY AM IN TRUTH. HE IS THE SON YOU LOVE ABOVE ALL THINGS. HE IS MY SELF AS YOU CREATED ME. IT IS NOT CHRIST THAT CAN BE CRUCIFIED. SAFE IN YOUR ARMS LET ME RECEIVE YOUR SON.

Lesson 304

Let not my world obscure the sight of Christ.

I can obscure my holy sight, if I intrude my world upon it. Nor can I behold the holy sights Christ looks upon, unless it is His vision that I use. Perception is a mirror, not a fact. And what I look on is my state of mind, reflected outward. I would bless the world by looking on it through the eyes of Christ. And I will look upon the certain signs that all my sins have been forgiven me.

YOU LEAD ME FROM THE DARKNESS TO THE LIGHT; FROM SIN TO HOLINESS. LET ME FORGIVE, AND THUS RECEIVE SALVATION FOR THE WORLD. IT IS YOUR GIFT, MY FATHER, GIVEN ME TO OFFER TO YOUR HOLY SON, THAT HE MAY FIND AGAIN THE MEMORY OF YOU, AND OF YOUR SON AS YOU CREATED HIM.

Lesson 305

There is a peace that Christ bestows on us.

Who uses but Christ's vision finds a peace so deep and quiet, undisturbable and wholly changeless, that the world contains no counterpart. Comparisons are still before this peace. And all the world departs in silence as this peace envelops it, and gently carries it to truth, no more to be the home of fear. For love has come, and healed the world by giving it Christ's peace.

FATHER, THE PEACE OF CHRIST IS GIVEN US, BECAUSE IT IS YOUR WILL THAT WE BE SAVED. HELP US TODAY BUT TO ACCEPT YOUR GIFT, AND JUDGE IT NOT. FOR IT HAS COME TO US TO SAVE US FROM OUR JUDGMENT ON OURSELVES.

Lesson 306

The gift of Christ is all I seek today.

What but Christ's vision would I use today, when it can offer me a day in which I see a world so like to Heaven that an ancient memory returns to me? Today I can forget the world I made. Today I can go past all fear, and be restored to love and holiness and peace. Today I am redeemed, and born anew into a world of mercy and of care; of loving kindness and the peace of God.

AND SO, OUR FATHER, WE RETURN TO YOU, REMEMBERING WE NEVER WENT AWAY; REMEMBERING YOUR HOLY GIFTS TO US. IN GRATITUDE AND THANKFULNESS WE COME, WITH EMPTY HANDS AND OPEN HEARTS AND MINDS, ASKING BUT WHAT YOU GIVE. WE CANNOT MAKE AN OFFERING SUFFICIENT FOR YOUR SON. BUT IN YOUR LOVE THE GIFT OF CHRIST IS HIS.

Lesson 307

Conflicting wishes cannot be my will.

FATHER, YOUR WILL IS MINE, AND ONLY THAT. THERE IS NO OTHER WILL FOR ME TO HAVE. LET ME NOT TRY TO MAKE ANOTHER WILL, FOR IT IS SENSELESS AND WILL CAUSE ME PAIN. YOUR WILL ALONE CAN BRING ME HAPPINESS, AND ONLY YOURS EXISTS. IF I WOULD HAVE WHAT ONLY YOU CAN GIVE, I MUST ACCEPT YOUR WILL FOR ME, AND ENTER INTO PEACE WHERE CONFLICT IS IMPOSSIBLE, YOUR SON IS ONE WITH YOU IN BEING AND IN WILL, AND NOTHING CONTRADICTS THE HOLY TRUTH THAT I REMAIN AS YOU CREATED ME.

And with this prayer we enter silently into a state where conflict cannot come, because we join our holy will with God's, in recognition that they are the same.

Lesson 308

This instant is the only time there is.

I have conceived of time in such a way that I defeat my aim. If I elect to reach past time to timelessness, I must change my perception of what time is for. Time's purpose cannot be to keep the past and future one. The only interval in which I can be saved from time is now. For in this instant has forgiveness come to set me free. The birth of Christ is now, without a past or future. He has come to give His present blessing to the world, restoring it to timelessness and love. And love is ever-present, here and now.

THANKS FOR THIS INSTANT, FATHER. IT IS NOW I AM REDEEMED. THIS INSTANT IS THE TIME YOU HAVE APPOINTED FOR YOUR SON'S RELEASE, AND FOR SALVATION OF THE WORLD IN HIM.

Lesson 309

I will not fear to look within today.

Within me is eternal innocence, because it is God's Will that it be there forever and forever. I, His Son, whose will is limitless as is His Own, can will no change in this. For to deny my Father's Will is to deny my own. To look within is but to find my will as God created it, and as it is. I fear to look within because I think I made another will that is not true, and made it real. Yet it has no effects. Within me is the Holiness of God. Within me is the memory of Him.

THE STEP I TAKE TODAY, MY FATHER, IS MY SURE RELEASE FROM IDLE DREAMS OF SIN. YOUR ALTAR STANDS SERENE AND UNDEFILED. IT IS THE HOLY ALTAR TO MY SELF, AND THERE I FIND MY TRUE IDENTITY.

Lesson 310

In fearlessness and love I spend today.

THIS DAY, MY FATHER, WOULD I SPEND WITH YOU, AS YOU HAVE CHOSEN ALL MY DAYS SHOULD BE. AND WHAT I WILL EXPERIENCE IS NOT OF TIME AT ALL. THE JOY THAT COMES TO ME IS NOT OF DAYS NOR HOURS, FOR IT COMES FROM HEAVEN TO YOUR SON. THIS DAY WILL BE YOUR SWEET REMINDER TO REMEMBER YOU, YOUR GRACIOUS CALLING TO YOUR HOLY SON, THE SIGN YOUR GRACE HAS COME TO ME, AND THAT IT IS YOUR WILL I BE SET FREE TODAY.

We spend this day together, you and I. And all the world joins with us in our song of thankfulness and joy to Him Who gave salvation to us, and Who set us free. We are restored to peace and holiness. There is no room in us for fear today, for we have welcomed love into our hearts.

Lesson 311

Section 10. What is the Last Judgment?

Christ's Second Coming gives the Son of God this gift: to hear the Voice for God proclaim that what is false is false, and what is true has never changed. And this the judgment is in which perception ends. At first you see a world that has accepted this as true, projected from a now corrected mind. And with this holy sight, perception gives a silent blessing and then disappears, its goal accomplished and its mission done.

The final judgment on the world contains no condemnation. For it sees the world as totally forgiven, without sin and wholly purposeless. Without a cause, and now without a function in Christ's sight, it merely slips away to nothingness. There it was born, and there it ends as well. And all the figures in the dream in which the world began go with it. Bodies now are useless, and will therefore fade away, because the Son of God is limitless.

You who believed that God's Last Judgment would condemn the world to hell along with you, accept this holy truth: God's Judgment is the gift of the Correction He bestowed on all your errors, freeing you from them, and all effects they ever seemed to have. To fear God's saving grace is but to fear complete release from suffering, return to peace, security and happiness, and union with your own Identity.

God's Final Judgment is as merciful as every step in His appointed plan to bless His Son, and call him to return to the eternal peace He shares with him. Be not afraid of love. For it alone can heal all sorrow, wipe away all tears, and gently waken from his dream of pain the Son whom God acknowledges as His. Be not afraid of this. Salvation asks you give it welcome. And the world awaits your glad acceptance, which will set it free.

This is God's Final Judgment: "You are still My holy Son, forever innocent, forever loving and forever loved, as limitless as your Creator, and completely changeless and forever pure. Therefore awaken and return to Me. I am your Father and you are My Son."

Lesson 311

I judge all things as I would have them be.

Judgment was made to be a weapon used against the truth. It separates what it is being used against, and sets it off as if it were a thing apart. And then it makes of it what you would have it be. It judges what it cannot understand, because it cannot see totality and therefore judges falsely. Let us not use it today, but make a gift of it to Him Who has a different use for it. He will relieve us of the agony of all the judgments we have made against ourselves, and re-establish peace of mind by giving us God's Judgment of His Son.

FATHER, WE WAIT WITH OPEN MIND TODAY, TO HEAR YOUR JUDGMENT OF THE SON YOU LOVE. WE DO NOT KNOW HIM, AND WE CANNOT JUDGE. AND SO WE LET YOUR LOVE DECIDE WHAT HE WHOM YOU CREATED AS YOUR SON MUST BE.

Lesson 312

I see all things as I would have them be.

Perception follows judgment. Having judged, we therefore see what we would look upon. For sight can merely serve to offer us what we would have. It is impossible to overlook what we would see, and fail to see what we have chosen to behold. How surely, therefore, must the real world come to greet the holy sight of anyone who takes the Holy Spirit's purpose as his goal for seeing. And he cannot fail to look upon what Christ would have him see, and share Christ's Love for what he looks upon.

I HAVE NO PURPOSE FOR TODAY EXCEPT TO LOOK UPON A LIBERATED WORLD, SET FREE FROM ALL THE JUDGMENTS I HAVE MADE. FATHER, THIS IS YOUR WILL FOR ME TODAY, AND THEREFORE IT MUST BE MY GOAL AS WELL.

Lesson 313

Now let a new perception come to me.

FATHER, THERE IS A VISION WHICH BEHOLDS ALL THINGS AS SINLESS, SO THAT FEAR HAS GONE, AND WHERE IT WAS IS LOVE INVITED IN. AND LOVE WILL COME WHEREVER IT IS ASKED. THIS VISION IS YOUR GIFT. THE EYES OF CHRIST LOOK ON A WORLD FORGIVEN. IN HIS SIGHT ARE ALL ITS SINS FORGIVEN, FOR HE SEES NO SIN IN ANYTHING HE LOOKS UPON. NOW LET HIS TRUE PERCEPTION COME TO ME, THAT I MAY WAKEN FROM THE DREAM OF SIN AND LOOK WITHIN UPON MY SINLESSNESS, WHICH YOU HAVE KEPT COMPLETELY UNDEFILED UPON THE ALTAR TO YOUR HOLY SON, THE SELF WITH WHICH I WOULD IDENTIFY.

Let us today behold each other in the sight of Christ. How beautiful we are! How holy and how loving! Brother, come and join with me today. We save the world when we have joined. For in our vision it becomes as holy as the light in us.

Lesson 314

I seek a future different from the past.

From new perception of the world there comes a future very different from the past. The future now is recognized as but extension of the present. Past mistakes can cast no shadows on it, so that fear has lost its idols and its images, and being formless, it has no effects. Death will not claim the future now, for life is now its goal, and all the needed means are happily provided. Who can grieve or suffer when the present has been freed, extending its security and peace into a quiet future filled with joy?

FATHER, WE WERE MISTAKEN IN THE PAST, AND CHOOSE TO USE THE PRESENT TO BE FREE. NOW DO WE LEAVE THE FUTURE IN YOUR HANDS, LEAVING BEHIND OUR PAST MISTAKES, AND SURE THAT YOU WILL KEEP YOUR PRESENT PROMISES, AND GUIDE THE FUTURE IN THEIR HOLY LIGHT.

Lesson 315

All gifts my brothers give belong to me.

Each day a thousand treasures come to me with every passing moment. I am blessed with gifts throughout the day, in value far beyond all things of which I can conceive. A brother smiles upon another, and my heart is gladdened. Someone speaks a word of gratitude or mercy, and my mind receives this gift and takes it as its own. And everyone who finds the way to God becomes my savior, pointing out the way to me, and giving me his certainty that what he learned is surely mine as well.

I THANK YOU, FATHER, FOR THE MANY GIFTS THAT COME TO ME TODAY AND EVERY DAY FROM EVERY SON OF GOD. MY BROTHERS ARE UNLIMITED IN ALL THEIR GIFTS TO ME. NOW MAY I OFFER THEM MY THANKFULNESS, THAT GRATITUDE TO THEM MAY LEAD ME ON TO MY CREATOR AND HIS MEMORY.

Lesson 316

All gifts I give my brothers are my own.

As every gift my brothers give is mine, so every gift I give belongs to me. Each one allows a past mistake to go, and leave no shadow on the holy mind my Father loves. His grace is given me in every gift a brother has received throughout all time, and past all time as well. My treasure house is full, and angels watch its open doors that not one gift is lost, and only more are added. Let me come to where my treasures are, and enter in where I am truly welcome and at home, among the gifts that God has given me.

FATHER, I WOULD ACCEPT YOUR GIFTS TODAY. I DO NOT RECOGNIZE THEM. YET I TRUST THAT YOU WHO GAVE THEM WILL PROVIDE THE MEANS BY WHICH I CAN BEHOLD THEM, SEE THEIR WORTH, AND CHERISH ONLY THEM AS WHAT I WANT.

Lesson 317

I follow in the way appointed me.

I have a special place to fill; a role for me alone. Salvation waits until I take this part as what I choose to do. Until I make this choice, I am the slave of time and human destiny. But when I willingly and gladly go the way my Father's plan appointed me to go, then will I recognize salvation is already here, already given all my brothers and already mine as well.

FATHER, YOUR WAY IS WHAT I CHOOSE TODAY. WHERE IT WOULD LEAD ME DO I CHOOSE TO GO; WHAT IT WOULD HAVE ME DO I CHOOSE TO DO. YOUR WAY IS CERTAIN, AND THE END SECURE. THE MEMORY OF YOU AWAITS ME THERE. AND ALL MY SORROWS END IN YOUR EMBRACE, WHICH YOU HAVE PROMISED TO YOUR SON, WHO THOUGHT MISTAKENLY THAT HE HAD WANDERED FROM THE SURE PROTECTION OF YOUR LOVING ARMS.

Lesson 318

In me salvation's means and end are one.

In me, God's holy Son, are reconciled all parts of Heaven's plan to save the world. What could conflict, when all the parts have but one purpose and one aim? How could there be a single part that stands alone, or one of more or less importance than the rest? I am the means by which God's Son is saved, because salvation's purpose is to find the sinlessness that God has placed in me. I was created as the thing I seek. I am the goal the world is searching for. I am God's Son, His one eternal Love. I am salvation's means and end as well.

LET ME TODAY, MY FATHER, TAKE THE ROLE YOU OFFER ME IN YOUR REQUEST THAT I ACCEPT ATONEMENT FOR MYSELF. FOR THUS DOES WHAT IS THEREBY RECONCILED IN ME BECOME AS SURELY RECONCILED TO YOU.

Lesson 319

I came for the salvation of the world.

Here is a thought from which all arrogance has been removed, and only truth remains. For arrogance opposes truth. But when there is no arrogance the truth will come immediately, and fill up the space the ego left unoccupied by lies. Only the ego can be limited, and therefore it must seek for aims which are curtailed and limiting. The ego thinks that what one gains, totality must lose. And yet it is the Will of God I learn that what one gains is given unto all.

FATHER, YOUR WILL IS TOTAL. AND THE GOAL WHICH STEMS FROM IT SHARES ITS TOTALITY. WHAT AIM BUT THE SALVATION OF THE WORLD COULD YOU HAVE GIVEN ME? AND WHAT BUT THIS COULD BE THE WILL MY SELF HAS SHARED WITH YOU?

Lesson 320

My Father gives all power unto me.

The Son of God is limitless. There are no limits on his strength, his peace, his joy, nor any attributes his Father gave in his creation. What he wills with his Creator and Redeemer must be done. His holy will can never be denied, because his Father shines upon his mind, and lays before it all the strength and love in earth and Heaven. I am he to whom all this is given. I am he in whom the power of my Father's Will abides.

YOUR WILL CAN DO ALL THINGS IN ME, AND THEN EXTEND TO ALL THE WORLD AS WELL THROUGH ME. THERE IS NO LIMIT ON YOUR WILL. AND SO ALL POWER HAS BEEN GIVEN TO YOUR SON.

Lesson 321

Section 11. What is Creation?

Creation is the sum of all God's Thoughts, in number infinite, and everywhere without all limit. Only love creates, and only like itself. There was no time when all that it created was not there. Nor will there be a time when anything that it created suffers any loss. Forever and forever are God's Thoughts exactly as they were and as they are, unchanged through time and after time is done.

God's Thoughts are given all the power that their own Creator has. For He would add to love by its extension. Thus His Son shares in creation, and must therefore share in power to create. What God has willed to be forever One will still be One when time is over; and will not be changed throughout the course of time, remaining as it was before the thought of time began.

Creation is the opposite of all illusions, for creation is the truth. Creation is the holy Son of God, for in creation is His Will complete in every aspect, making every part container of the whole. Its oneness is forever guaranteed inviolate; forever held within His holy Will, beyond all possibility of harm, of separation, imperfection and of any spot upon its sinlessness.

We are creation; we the Sons of God. We seem to be discrete, and unaware of our eternal unity with Him. Yet back of all our doubts, past all our fears, there still is certainty. For love remains with all its Thoughts, its sureness being theirs. God's memory is in our holy minds, which know their oneness and their unity with their Creator. Let our function be only to let this memory return, only to let God's Will be done on earth, only to be restored to sanity, and to be but as God created us.

Our Father calls to us. We hear His Voice, and we forgive creation in the Name of its Creator, Holiness Itself, Whose Holiness His Own creation shares; Whose Holiness is still a part of us.

Lesson 321

Father, my freedom is in You alone.

I DID NOT UNDERSTAND WHAT MADE ME FREE, NOR WHAT MY FREEDOM IS, NOR WHERE TO LOOK TO FIND IT. FATHER, I HAVE SEARCHED IN VAIN UNTIL I HEARD YOUR VOICE DIRECTING ME. NOW I WOULD GUIDE MYSELF NO MORE. FOR I HAVE NEITHER MADE NOR UNDERSTOOD THE WAY TO FIND MY FREEDOM. BUT I TRUST IN YOU. YOU WHO ENDOWED ME WITH MY FREEDOM AS YOUR HOLY SON WILL NOT BE LOST TO ME. YOUR VOICE DIRECTS ME, AND THE WAY TO YOU IS OPENING AND CLEAR TO ME AT LAST. FATHER, MY FREEDOM IS IN YOU ALONE. FATHER, IT IS MY WILL THAT I RETURN.

Today we answer for the world, which will be freed along with us. How glad are we to find our freedom through the certain way our Father has established. And how sure is all the world's salvation, when we learn our freedom can be found in God alone.

Lesson 322

I can give up but what was never real.

I sacrifice illusions; nothing more. And as illusions go I find the gifts illusions tried to hide, awaiting me in shining welcome, and in readiness to give God's ancient messages to me. His memory abides in every gift that I receive of Him. And every dream serves only to conceal the Self which is God's only Son, the likeness of Himself, the Holy One Who still abides in Him forever, as He still abides in me.

FATHER, TO YOU ALL SACRIFICE REMAINS FOREVER INCONCEIVABLE. AND SO I CANNOT SACRIFICE EXCEPT IN DREAMS. AS YOU CREATED ME, I CAN GIVE UP NOTHING YOU GAVE ME. WHAT YOU DID NOT GIVE HAS NO REALITY. WHAT LOSS CAN I ANTICIPATE EXCEPT THE LOSS OF FEAR, AND THE RETURN OF LOVE INTO MY MIND?

Lesson 323

I gladly make the "sacrifice" of fear.

HERE IS THE ONLY "SACRIFICE" YOU ASK OF YOUR BELOVED SON; YOU ASK HIM TO GIVE UP ALL SUFFERING, ALL SENSE OF LOSS AND SADNESS, ALL ANXIETY AND DOUBT, AND FREELY LET YOUR LOVE COME STREAMING IN TO HIS AWARENESS, HEALING HIM OF PAIN, AND GIVING HIM YOUR OWN ETERNAL JOY. SUCH IS THE "SACRIFICE" YOU ASK OF ME, AND ONE I GLADLY MAKE; THE ONLY "COST" OF RESTORATION OF YOUR MEMORY TO ME, FOR THE SALVATION OF THE WORLD.

And as we pay the debt we owe to truth,–a debt that merely is the letting go of self-deceptions and of images we worshipped falsely–truth returns to us in wholeness and in joy. We are deceived no longer. Love has now returned to our awareness. And we are at peace again, for fear has gone and only love remains.

Lesson 324

I merely follow, for I would not lead.

FATHER, YOU ARE THE ONE WHO GAVE THE PLAN FOR MY SALVATION TO ME. YOU HAVE SET THE WAY I AM TO GO, THE ROLE TO TAKE, AND EVERY STEP IN MY APPOINTED PATH. I CANNOT LOSE THE WAY. I CAN BUT CHOOSE TO WANDER OFF A WHILE, AND THEN RETURN. YOUR LOVING VOICE WILL ALWAYS CALL ME BACK, AND GUIDE MY FEET ARIGHT. MY BROTHERS ALL CAN FOLLOW IN THE WAY I LEAD THEM. YET I MERELY FOLLOW IN THE WAY TO YOU, AS YOU DIRECT ME AND WOULD HAVE ME GO.

So let us follow One Who knows the way. We need not tarry, and we cannot stray except an instant from His loving Hand. We walk together, for we follow Him. And it is He Who makes the ending sure, and guarantees a safe returning home.

Lesson 325

All things I think I see reflect ideas.

This is salvation's keynote: What I see reflects a process in my mind, which starts with my idea of what I want. From there, the mind makes up an image of the thing the mind desires, judges valuable, and therefore seeks to find. These images are then projected outward, looked upon, esteemed as real and guarded as one's own. From insane wishes comes an insane world. From judgment comes a world condemned. And from forgiving thoughts a gentle world comes forth, with mercy for the holy Son of God, to offer him a kindly home where he can rest a while before he journeys on, and help his brothers walk ahead with him, and find the way to Heaven and to God.

OUR FATHER, YOUR IDEAS REFLECT THE TRUTH, AND MINE APART FROM YOURS BUT MAKE UP DREAMS. LET ME BEHOLD WHAT ONLY YOURS REFLECT, FOR YOURS AND YOURS ALONE ESTABLISH TRUTH.

Lesson 326

I am forever an Effect of God.

FATHER, I WAS CREATED IN YOUR MIND, A HOLY THOUGHT THAT NEVER LEFT ITS HOME. I AM FOREVER YOUR EFFECT, AND YOU FOREVER AND FOREVER ARE MY CAUSE. AS YOU CREATED ME I HAVE REMAINED. WHERE YOU ESTABLISHED ME I STILL ABIDE. AND ALL YOUR ATTRIBUTES ABIDE IN ME, BECAUSE IT IS YOUR WILL TO HAVE A SON SO LIKE HIS CAUSE THAT CAUSE AND ITS EFFECT ARE INDISTINGUISHABLE. LET ME KNOW THAT I AM AN EFFECT OF GOD, AND SO I HAVE THE POWER TO CREATE LIKE YOU. AND AS IT IS IN HEAVEN, SO ON EARTH. YOUR PLAN I FOLLOW HERE, AND AT THE END I KNOW THAT YOU WILL GATHER YOUR EFFECTS INTO THE TRANQUIL HEAVEN OF YOUR LOVE, WHERE EARTH WILL VANISH, AND ALL SEPARATE THOUGHTS UNITE IN GLORY AS THE SON OF GOD.

Let us today behold earth disappear, at first transformed, and then, forgiven, fade entirely into God's holy Will.

Lesson 327

I need but call and You will answer me.

I am not asked to take salvation on the basis of an unsupported faith. For God has promised He will hear my call, and answer me Himself. Let me but learn from my experience that this is true, and faith in Him must surely come to me. This is the faith that will endure, and take me farther and still farther on the road that leads to Him. For thus I will be sure that He has not abandoned me and loves me still, awaiting but my call to give me all the help I need to come to Him.

FATHER, I THANK YOU THAT YOUR PROMISES WILL NEVER FAIL IN MY EXPERIENCE, IF I BUT TEST THEM OUT. LET ME ATTEMPT THEREFORE TO TRY THEM, AND TO JUDGE THEM NOT. YOUR WORD IS ONE WITH YOU. YOU GIVE THE MEANS WHEREBY CONVICTION COMES, AND SURETY OF YOUR ABIDING LOVE IS GAINED AT LAST.

Lesson 328

I choose the second place to gain the first.

What seems to be the second place is first, for all things we perceive are upside down until we listen to the Voice for God. It seems that we will gain autonomy but by our striving to be separate, and that our independence from the rest of God's creation is the way in which salvation is obtained. Yet all we find is sickness, suffering and loss and death. This is not what our Father wills for us, nor is there any second to His Will. To join with His is but to find our own. And since our will is His, it is to Him that we must go to recognize our will.

THERE IS NO WILL BUT YOURS. AND I AM GLAD THAT NOTHING I IMAGINE CONTRADICTS WHAT YOU WOULD HAVE ME BE. IT IS YOUR WILL THAT I BE WHOLLY SAFE, ETERNALLY AT PEACE. AND HAPPILY I SHARE THAT WILL WHICH YOU, MY FATHER, GAVE AS PART OF ME.

Lesson 329

I have already chosen what You will.

FATHER, I THOUGHT I WANDERED FROM YOUR WILL, DEFIED IT, BROKE ITS LAWS, AND INTERPOSED A SECOND WILL MORE POWERFUL THAN YOURS. YET WHAT I AM IN TRUTH IS BUT YOUR WILL, EXTENDED AND EXTENDING. THIS AM I, AND THIS WILL NEVER CHANGE. AS YOU ARE ONE, SO AM I ONE WITH YOU. AND THIS I CHOSE IN MY CREATION, WHERE MY WILL BECAME FOREVER ONE WITH YOURS. THAT CHOICE WAS MADE FOR ALL ETERNITY. IT CANNOT CHANGE, AND BE IN OPPOSITION TO ITSELF. FATHER, MY WILL IS YOURS. AND I AM SAFE, UNTROUBLED AND SERENE, IN ENDLESS JOY, BECAUSE IT IS YOUR WILL THAT IT BE SO.

Today we will accept our union with each other and our Source. We have no will apart from His, and all of us are one because His Will is shared by all of us. Through it we recognize that we are one. Through it we find our way at last to God.

Lesson 330

I will not hurt myself again today.

Let us this day accept forgiveness as our only function. Why should we attack our minds, and give them images of pain? Why should we teach them they are powerless, when God holds out His power and His Love, and bids them take what is already theirs? The mind that is made willing to accept God's gifts has been restored to spirit, and extends its freedom and its joy, as is the Will of God united with its own. The Self which God created cannot sin, and therefore cannot suffer. Let us choose today that He be our Identity, and thus escape forever from all things the dream of fear appears to offer us.

FATHER, YOUR SON CAN NOT BE HURT. AND IF WE THINK WE SUFFER, WE BUT FAIL TO KNOW OUR ONE IDENTITY WE SHARE WITH YOU. WE WOULD RETURN TO IT TODAY, TO BE MADE FREE FOREVER FROM ALL OUR MISTAKES, AND TO BE SAVED FROM WHAT WE THOUGHT WE WERE.

Lesson 331

Section 12. What is the Ego?

The ego is idolatry; the sign of limited and separated self, born in a body, doomed to suffer and to end its life in death. It is the "will" that sees the Will of God as enemy, and takes a form in which it is denied. The ego is the "proof" that strength is weak and love is fearful, life is really death, and what opposes God alone is true.

The ego is insane. In fear it stands beyond the Everywhere, apart from All, in separation from the Infinite. In its insanity it thinks it has become a victor over God Himself. And in its terrible autonomy it "sees" the Will of God has been destroyed. It dreams of punishment, and trembles at the figures in its dreams; its enemies, who seek to murder it before it can ensure its safety by attacking them.

The Son of God is egoless. What can he know of madness and the death of God, when he abides in Him? What can he know of sorrow and of suffering, when he lives in eternal joy? What can he know of fear and punishment, of sin and guilt, of hatred and attack, when all there is surrounding him is everlasting peace, forever conflict-free and undisturbed, in deepest silence and tranquility?

To know reality is not to see the ego and its thoughts, its works, its acts, its laws and its beliefs, its dreams, its hopes, its plans for its salvation, and the cost belief in it entails. In suffering, the price for faith in it is so immense that crucifixion of the Son of God is offered daily at its darkened shrine, and blood must flow before the altar where its sickly followers prepare to die.

Yet will one lily of forgiveness change the darkness into light; the altar to illusions to the shrine of Life Itself. And peace will be restored forever to the holy minds which God created as His Son, His dwelling place, His joy, His love, completely His, completely one with Him.

Lesson 331

There is no conflict, for my will is Yours.

HOW FOOLISH, FATHER, TO BELIEVE YOUR SON COULD CAUSE HIMSELF TO SUFFER! COULD HE MAKE A PLAN FOR HIS DAMNATION, AND BE LEFT WITHOUT A CERTAIN WAY TO HIS RELEASE? YOU LOVE ME, FATHER. YOU COULD NEVER LEAVE ME DESOLATE, TO DIE WITHIN A WORLD OF PAIN AND CRUELTY. HOW COULD I THINK THAT LOVE HAS LEFT ITSELF? THERE IS NO WILL EXCEPT THE WILL OF LOVE. FEAR IS A DREAM, AND HAS NO WILL THAT CAN CONFLICT WITH YOURS. CONFLICT IS SLEEP, AND PEACE

AWAKENING. DEATH IS ILLUSION; LIFE, ETERNAL TRUTH. THERE IS NO OPPOSITION TO YOUR WILL. THERE IS NO CONFLICT, FOR MY WILL IS YOURS.

Forgiveness shows us that God's Will is One, and that we share it. Let us look upon the holy sights forgiveness shows today, that we may find the peace of God. Amen.

Lesson 332

Fear binds the world. Forgiveness sets it free.

The ego makes illusions. Truth undoes its evil dreams by shining them away. Truth never makes attack. It merely is. And by its presence is the mind recalled from fantasies, awaking to the real. Forgiveness bids this presence enter in, and take its rightful place within the mind. Without forgiveness is the mind in chains, believing in its own futility. Yet with forgiveness does the light shine through the dream of darkness, offering it hope, and giving it the means to realize the freedom that is its inheritance.

WE WOULD NOT BIND THE WORLD AGAIN TODAY. FEAR HOLDS IT PRISONER. AND YET YOUR LOVE HAS GIVEN US THE MEANS TO SET IT FREE. FATHER, WE WOULD RELEASE IT NOW. FOR AS WE OFFER FREEDOM, IT IS GIVEN US. AND WE WOULD NOT REMAIN AS PRISONERS, WHILE YOU ARE HOLDING FREEDOM OUT TO US.

Lesson 333

Forgiveness ends the dream of conflict here.

Conflict must be resolved. It cannot be evaded, set aside, denied, disguised, seen somewhere else, called by another name, or hidden by deceit of any kind, if it would be escaped. It must be seen exactly as it is, where it is thought to be, in the reality which has been given it, and with the purpose that the mind accorded it. For only then are its defenses lifted, and the truth can shine upon it as it disappears.

FATHER, FORGIVENESS IS THE LIGHT YOU CHOSE TO SHINE AWAY ALL CONFLICT AND ALL DOUBT, AND LIGHT THE WAY FOR OUR RETURN TO YOU. NO LIGHT BUT THIS CAN END OUR EVIL DREAM. NO LIGHT BUT THIS CAN SAVE THE WORLD. FOR THIS ALONE WILL NEVER FAIL IN ANYTHING, BEING YOUR GIFT TO YOUR BELOVED SON.

Lesson 334

Today I claim the gifts forgiveness gives.

I will not wait another day to find the treasures that my Father offers me. Illusions are all vain, and dreams are gone even while they are woven out of thoughts that rest on false perceptions. Let me not accept such meager gifts again today. God's Voice is offering the peace of God to all who hear and choose to follow Him. This is my choice today. And so I go to find the treasures God has given me.

I SEEK BUT THE ETERNAL. FOR YOUR SON CAN BE CONTENT WITH NOTHING LESS THAN THIS. WHAT, THEN, CAN BE HIS SOLACE BUT WHAT YOU ARE OFFERING TO HIS BEWILDERED MIND AND FRIGHTENED

HEART, TO GIVE HIM CERTAINTY AND BRING HIM PEACE? TODAY I WOULD BEHOLD MY BROTHER SINLESS. THIS YOUR WILL FOR ME, FOR SO WILL I BEHOLD MY SINLESSNESS.

Lesson 335

I choose to see my brother's sinlessness.

Forgiveness is a choice. I never see my brother as he is, for that is far beyond perception. What I see in him is merely what I wish to see, because it stands for what I want to be the truth. It is to this alone that I respond, however much I seem to be impelled by outside happenings. I choose to see what I would look upon, and this I see, and only this. My brother's sinlessness shows me that I would look upon my own. And I will see it, having chosen to behold my brother in its holy light.

WHAT COULD RESTORE YOUR MEMORY TO ME, EXCEPT TO SEE MY BROTHER'S SINLESSNESS? HIS HOLINESS REMINDS ME THAT HE WAS CREATED ONE WITH ME, AND LIKE MYSELF. IN HIM I FIND MY SELF, AND IN YOUR SON I FIND THE MEMORY OF YOU AS WELL.

Lesson 336

Forgiveness lets me know that minds are joined.

Forgiveness is the means appointed for perception's ending. Knowledge is restored after perception first is changed, and then gives way entirely to what remains forever past its highest reach. For sights and sounds, at best, can serve but to recall the memory that lies beyond them all. Forgiveness sweeps away distortions, and opens the hidden altar to the truth. Its lilies shine into the mind, and call it to return and look within, to find what it has vainly sought without. For here, and only here, is peace of mind restored, for this the dwelling place of God Himself.

IN QUIET MAY FORGIVENESS WIPE AWAY MY DREAMS OF SEPARATION AND OF SIN. THEN LET ME, FATHER, LOOK WITHIN, AND FIND YOUR PROMISE OF MY SINLESSNESS IS KEPT; YOUR WORD REMAINS UNCHANGED WITHIN MY MIND, YOUR LOVE IS STILL ABIDING IN MY HEART.

Lesson 337

My sinlessness protects me from all harm.

My sinlessness ensures me perfect peace, eternal safety, everlasting love, freedom forever from all thought of loss; complete deliverance from suffering. And only happiness can be my state, for only happiness is given me. What must I do to know all this is mine? I must accept Atonement for myself, and nothing more. God has already done all things that need be done. And I must learn I need do nothing of myself, for I need but accept my Self, my sinlessness, created for me, now already mine, to feel God's Love protecting me from harm, to understand my Father loves His Son; to know I am the Son my Father loves.

YOU WHO CREATED ME IN SINLESSNESS ARE NOT MISTAKEN ABOUT WHAT I AM. I WAS MISTAKEN WHEN I THOUGHT I SINNED, BUT I ACCEPT ATONEMENT FOR MYSELF. FATHER, MY DREAM IS ENDED NOW. AMEN.

Lesson 338

I am affected only by my thoughts.

It needs but this to let salvation come to all the world. For in this single thought is everyone released at last from fear. Now has he learned that no one frightens him, and nothing can endanger him. He has no enemies, and he is safe from all external things. His thoughts can frighten him, but since these thoughts belong to him alone, he has the power to change them and exchange each fear thought for a happy thought of love. He crucified himself. Yet God has planned that His beloved Son will be redeemed.

YOUR PLAN IS SURE, MY FATHER,—ONLY YOURS. ALL OTHER PLANS WILL FAIL. AND I WILL HAVE THOUGHTS THAT WILL FRIGHTEN ME, UNTIL I LEARN THAT YOU HAVE GIVEN ME THE ONLY THOUGHT THAT LEADS ME TO SALVATION. MINE ALONE WILL FAIL, AND LEAD ME NOWHERE. BUT THE THOUGHT YOU GAVE ME PROMISES TO LEAD ME HOME, BECAUSE IT HOLDS YOUR PROMISE TO YOUR SON.

Lesson 339

I will receive whatever I request.

No one desires pain. But he can think that pain is pleasure. No one would avoid his happiness. But he can think that joy is painful, threatening and dangerous. Everyone will receive what he requests. But he can be confused indeed about the things he wants; the state he would attain. What can he then request that he would want when he receives it? He has asked for what will frighten him, and bring him suffering. Let us resolve today to ask for what we really want, and only this, that we may spend this day in fearlessness, without confusing pain with joy, or fear with love.

FATHER, THIS IS YOUR DAY. IT IS A DAY IN WHICH I WOULD DO NOTHING BY MYSELF, BUT HEAR YOUR VOICE IN EVERYTHING I DO; REQUESTING ONLY WHAT YOU OFFER ME, ACCEPTING ONLY THOUGHTS YOU SHARE WITH ME.

Lesson 340

I can be free of suffering today.

FATHER, I THANK YOU FOR TODAY, AND FOR THE FREEDOM I AM CERTAIN IT WILL BRING. THIS DAY IS HOLY, FOR TODAY YOUR SON WILL BE REDEEMED. HIS SUFFERING IS DONE. FOR HE WILL HEAR YOUR VOICE DIRECTING HIM TO FIND CHRIST'S VISION THROUGH FORGIVENESS, AND BE FREE FOREVER FROM ALL SUFFERING. THANKS FOR TODAY, MY FATHER. I WAS BORN INTO THIS WORLD BUT TO ACHIEVE THIS DAY, AND WHAT IT HOLDS IN JOY AND FREEDOM FOR YOUR HOLY SON AND FOR THE WORLD HE MADE, WHICH IS RELEASED ALONG WITH HIM TODAY.

Be glad today! Be glad! There is no room for anything but joy and thanks today. Our Father has redeemed His Son this day. Not one of us but will be saved today. Not one who will remain in fear, and none the Father will not gather to Himself, awake in Heaven in the Heart of Love.

Lesson 341

Section 13. What is a Miracle?

A miracle is a correction. It does not create, nor really change at all. It merely looks on devastation, and reminds the mind that what it sees is false. It undoes error, but does not attempt to go beyond perception, nor exceed the function of forgiveness. Thus it stays within time's limits. Yet it paves the way for the return of timelessness and love's awakening, for fear must slip away under the gentle remedy it brings.

A miracle contains the gift of grace, for it is given and received as one. And thus it illustrates the law of truth the world does not obey, because it fails entirely to understand its ways. A miracle inverts perception which was upside down before, and thus it ends the strange distortions that were manifest. Now is perception open to the truth. Now is forgiveness seen as justified.

Forgiveness is the home of miracles. The eyes of Christ deliver them to all they look upon in mercy and in love. Perception stands corrected in His sight, and what was meant to curse has come to bless. Each lily of forgiveness offers all the world the silent miracle of love. And each is laid before the Word of God, upon the universal altar to Creator and creation in the light of perfect purity and endless joy.

The miracle is taken first on faith, because to ask for it implies the mind has been made ready to conceive of what it cannot see and does not understand. Yet faith will bring its witnesses to show that what it rested on is really there. And thus the miracle will justify your faith in it, and show it rested on a world more real than what you saw before; a world redeemed from what you thought was there.

Miracles fall like drops of healing rain from Heaven on a dry and dusty world, where starved and thirsty creatures come to die. Now they have water. Now the world is green. And everywhere the signs of life spring up, to show that what is born can never die, for what has life has immortality.

Lesson 341

I can attack but my own sinlessness,
And it is only that which keeps me safe.

FATHER, YOUR SON IS HOLY. I AM HE ON WHOM YOU SMILE IN LOVE AND TENDERNESS SO DEAR AND DEEP AND STILL THE UNIVERSE SMILES BACK ON YOU, AND SHARES YOUR HOLINESS. HOW PURE, HOW SAFE, HOW HOLY, THEN, ARE WE, ABIDING IN YOUR SMILE, WITH ALL YOUR LOVE BESTOWED UPON US, LIVING ONE WITH YOU, IN BROTHERHOOD AND FATHERHOOD COMPLETE; IN SINLESSNESS SO PERFECT THAT THE LORD OF SINLESSNESS CONCEIVES US AS HIS SON, A UNIVERSE OF THOUGHT COMPLETING HIM.

Let us not, then, attack our sinlessness, for it contains the Word of God to us. And in its kind reflection we are saved.

Lesson 342

I let forgiveness rest upon all things,
For thus forgiveness will be given me.

I THANK YOU, FATHER, FOR YOUR PLAN TO SAVE ME FROM THE HELL I MADE. IT IS NOT REAL. AND YOU HAVE GIVEN ME THE MEANS TO PROVE ITS UNREALITY TO ME. THE KEY IS IN MY HAND, AND I HAVE REACHED THE DOOR BEYOND WHICH LIES THE END OF DREAMS. I STAND BEFORE THE GATE OF HEAVEN, WONDERING IF I SHOULD ENTER IN AND BE AT HOME. LET ME NOT WAIT AGAIN TODAY. LET ME FORGIVE ALL THINGS, AND LET CREATION BE AS YOU WOULD HAVE IT BE AND AS IT IS. LET ME REMEMBER THAT I

AM YOUR SON, AND OPENING THE DOOR AT LAST, FORGET ILLUSIONS IN THE BLAZING LIGHT OF TRUTH, AS MEMORY OF YOU RETURNS TO ME.

Brother, forgive me now. I come to you to take you home with me. And as we go, the world goes with us on our way to God.

Lesson 343

I am not asked to make a sacrifice
To find the mercy and the peace of God.

THE END OF SUFFERING CAN NOT BE LOSS. THE GIFT OF EVERYTHING CAN BE BUT GAIN. YOU ONLY GIVE. YOU NEVER TAKE AWAY. AND YOU CREATED ME TO BE LIKE YOU, SO SACRIFICE BECOMES IMPOSSIBLE FOR ME AS WELL AS YOU. I, TOO, MUST GIVE. AND SO ALL THINGS ARE GIVEN UNTO ME FOREVER AND FOREVER. AS I WAS CREATED I REMAIN. YOUR SON CAN MAKE NO SACRIFICE, FOR HE MUST BE COMPLETE, HAVING THE FUNCTION OF COMPLETING YOU. I AM COMPLETE BECAUSE I AM YOUR SON. I CANNOT LOSE, FOR I CAN ONLY GIVE, AND EVERYTHING IS MINE ETERNALLY.

The mercy and the peace of God are free. Salvation has no cost. It is a gift that must be freely given and received. And it is this that we would learn today.

Lesson 344

Today I learn the law of love; that what
I give my brother is my gift to me.

THIS IS YOUR LAW, MY FATHER, NOT MY OWN. I HAVE NOT UNDERSTOOD WHAT GIVING MEANS, AND THOUGHT TO SAVE WHAT I DESIRED FOR MYSELF ALONE. AND AS I LOOKED UPON THE TREASURE THAT I THOUGHT I HAD, I FOUND AN EMPTY PLACE WHERE NOTHING EVER WAS OR IS OR WILL BE. WHO CAN SHARE A DREAM? AND WHAT CAN AN ILLUSION OFFER ME? YET HE WHOM I FORGIVE WILL GIVE ME GIFTS BEYOND THE WORTH OF ANYTHING ON EARTH. LET MY FORGIVEN BROTHERS FILL MY STORE WITH HEAVEN'S TREASURES, WHICH ALONE ARE REAL. THUS IS THE LAW OF LOVE FULFILLED. AND THUS YOUR SON ARISES AND RETURNS TO YOU.

How near we are to one another, as we go to God. How near is He to us. How close the ending of the dream of sin, and the redemption of the Son of God.

Lesson 345

I offer only miracles today,
For I would have them be returned to me.

FATHER, A MIRACLE REFLECTS YOUR GIFTS TO ME, YOUR SON. AND EVERY ONE I GIVE RETURNS TO ME, REMINDING ME THE LAW OF LOVE IS UNIVERSAL. EVEN HERE, IT TAKES A FORM WHICH CAN BE RECOGNIZED AND SEEN TO WORK. THE MIRACLES I GIVE ARE GIVEN BACK IN JUST THE FORM I NEED TO HELP ME WITH THE PROBLEMS I PERCEIVE. FATHER, IN HEAVEN IT IS DIFFERENT, FOR THERE, THERE ARE

NO NEEDS. BUT HERE ON EARTH, THE MIRACLE IS CLOSER TO YOUR GIFTS THAN ANY OTHER GIFT THAT I CAN GIVE. THEN LET ME GIVE THIS GIFT ALONE TODAY, WHICH, BORN OF TRUE FORGIVENESS, LIGHTS THE WAY THAT I MUST TRAVEL TO REMEMBER YOU.

Peace to all seeking hearts today. The light has come to offer miracles to bless the tired world. It will find rest today, for we will offer what we have received.

Lesson 346

**Today the peace of God envelops me,
And I forget all things except His Love.**

FATHER, I WAKE TODAY WITH MIRACLES CORRECTING MY PERCEPTION OF ALL THINGS. AND SO BEGINS THE DAY I SHARE WITH YOU AS I WILL SHARE ETERNITY, FOR TIME HAS STEPPED ASIDE TODAY. I DO NOT SEEK THE THINGS OF TIME, AND SO I WILL NOT LOOK UPON THEM. WHAT I SEEK TODAY TRANSCENDS ALL LAWS OF TIME AND THINGS PERCEIVED IN TIME. I WOULD FORGET ALL THINGS EXCEPT YOUR LOVE. I WOULD ABIDE IN YOU, AND KNOW NO LAWS EXCEPT YOUR LAW OF LOVE. AND I WOULD FIND THE PEACE WHICH YOU CREATED FOR YOUR SON, FORGETTING ALL THE FOOLISH TOYS I MADE AS I BEHOLD YOUR GLORY AND MY OWN.

And when the evening comes today, we will remember nothing but the peace of God. For we will learn today what peace is ours, when we forget all things except God's Love.

Lesson 347

**Anger must come from judgment. Judgment is
The weapon I would use against myself,
To keep the miracle away from me.**

Father, I want what goes against my will, and do not want what is my will to have. Straighten my mind, my Father. It is sick. But You have offered freedom, and I choose to claim Your gift today. And so I give all judgment to the One You gave to me to judge for me. He sees what I behold, and yet He knows the truth. He looks on pain, and yet He understands it is not real, and in His understanding it is healed. He gives the miracles my dreams would hide from my awareness. Let Him judge today. I do not know my will, but He is sure it is Your Own. And He will speak for me, and call Your miracles to come to me.

Listen today. Be very still, and hear the gentle Voice for God assuring you that He has judged you as the Son He loves.

Lesson 348

**I have no cause for anger or for fear,
For You surround me. And in every need
That I perceive, Your grace suffices me.**

FATHER, LET ME REMEMBER YOU ARE HERE, AND I AM NOT ALONE. SURROUNDING ME IS EVERLASTING LOVE. I HAVE NO CAUSE FOR ANYTHING EXCEPT THE PERFECT PEACE AND JOY I SHARE WITH YOU. WHAT NEED HAVE I FOR ANGER OR FOR FEAR? SURROUNDING ME IS PERFECT SAFETY. CAN I BE AFRAID, WHEN YOUR ETERNAL PROMISE GOES WITH ME? SURROUNDING ME IS PERFECT SINLESSNESS. WHAT CAN I FEAR, WHEN YOU CREATED ME IN HOLINESS AS PERFECT AS YOUR OWN?

God's grace suffices us in everything that He would have us do. And only that we choose to be our will as well as His.

Lesson 349

**Today I let Christ's vision look upon
All things for me and judge them not, but give
Each one a miracle of love instead.**

SO WOULD I LIBERATE ALL THINGS I SEE, AND GIVE TO THEM THE FREEDOM THAT I SEEK. FOR THUS DO I OBEY THE LAW OF LOVE, AND GIVE WHAT I WOULD FIND AND MAKE MY OWN. IT WILL BE GIVEN ME, BECAUSE I HAVE CHOSEN IT AS THE GIFT I WANT TO GIVE. FATHER, YOUR GIFTS ARE MINE. EACH ONE THAT I ACCEPT GIVES ME A MIRACLE TO GIVE. AND GIVING AS I WOULD RECEIVE, I LEARN YOUR HEALING MIRACLES BELONG TO ME.

Our Father knows our needs. He gives us grace to meet them all. And so we trust in Him to send us miracles to bless the world, and heal our minds as we return to Him.

Lesson 350

**Miracles mirror God's eternal Love.
To offer them is to remember Him,
And through His memory to save the world.**

WHAT WE FORGIVE BECOMES A PART OF US, AS WE PERCEIVE OURSELVES. THE SON OF GOD INCORPORATES ALL THINGS WITHIN HIMSELF AS YOU CREATED HIM. YOUR MEMORY DEPENDS ON HIS FORGIVENESS. WHAT HE IS, IS UNAFFECTED BY HIS THOUGHTS. BUT WHAT HE LOOKS UPON IS THEIR DIRECT RESULT. THEREFORE, MY FATHER, I WOULD TURN TO YOU. ONLY YOUR MEMORY WILL SET ME FREE. AND ONLY MY FORGIVENESS TEACHES ME TO LET YOUR MEMORY RETURN TO ME, AND GIVE IT TO THE WORLD IN THANKFULNESS.

And as we gather miracles from Him, we will indeed be grateful. For as we remember Him, His Son will be restored to us in the reality of Love.

Lesson 351

Section 14. What Am I?

I am God's Son, complete and healed and whole, shining in the reflection of His Love. In me is His creation sanctified and guaranteed eternal life. In me is love perfected, fear impossible, and joy established without opposite. I am the holy home of God Himself. I am the Heaven where His Love resides. I am His holy Sinlessness Itself, for in my purity abides His Own.

Our use for words is almost over now. Yet in the final days of this one year we gave to God together, you and I, we found a single purpose that we shared. And thus you joined with me, so what I am are you as well. The truth of what we are is not for words to speak of nor describe. Yet we can realize our function here, and words can speak of this and teach it, too, if we exemplify the words in us.

We are the bringers of salvation. We accept our part as saviors of the world, which through our joint forgiveness is redeemed. And this, our gift, is therefore given us. We look on everyone as brother, and perceive all things as kindly and as good. We do not seek a function that is past the gate of Heaven. Knowledge will return when we have done our part. We are concerned only with giving welcome to the truth.

Ours are the eyes through which Christ's vision sees a world redeemed from every thought of sin. Ours are the ears that hear the Voice for God proclaim the world as sinless. Ours the minds that join together as we bless the world. And from the oneness that we have attained we call to all our brothers, asking them to share our peace and consummate our joy.

We are the holy messengers of God who speak for Him, and carrying His Word to everyone whom He has sent to us, we learn that it is written on our hearts. And thus our minds are changed about the aim for which we came, and which we seek to serve. We bring glad tidings to the Son of God, who thought he suffered. Now is he redeemed. And as he sees the gate of Heaven stand open before him, he will enter in and disappear into the Heart of God.

Lesson 351

My sinless brother is my guide to peace.
My sinful brother is my guide to pain.
And which I choose to see I will behold.

WHO IS MY BROTHER BUT YOUR HOLY SON? AND IF I SEE HIM SINFUL I PROCLAIM MYSELF A SINNER, NOT A SON OF GOD; ALONE AND FRIENDLESS IN A FEARFUL WORLD. YET THIS PERCEPTION IS A CHOICE I MAKE, AND CAN RELINQUISH. I CAN ALSO SEE MY BROTHER SINLESS, AS YOUR HOLY SON. AND WITH THIS CHOICE I SEE MY SINLESSNESS, MY EVERLASTING COMFORTER AND FRIEND BESIDE ME, AND MY WAY SECURE AND CLEAR. CHOOSE, THEN, FOR ME, MY FATHER, THROUGH YOUR VOICE. FOR HE ALONE GIVES JUDGMENT IN YOUR NAME.

Lesson 352

Judgment and love are opposites. From one
Come all the sorrows of the world. But from
The other comes the peace of God Himself.

FORGIVENESS LOOKS ON SINLESSNESS ALONE, AND JUDGES NOT. THROUGH THIS I COME TO YOU. JUDGMENT WILL BIND MY EYES AND MAKE ME BLIND. YET LOVE, REFLECTED IN FORGIVENESS HERE, REMINDS ME YOU HAVE GIVEN ME A WAY TO FIND YOUR PEACE AGAIN. I AM REDEEMED WHEN I ELECT TO FOLLOW IN THIS WAY. YOU HAVE NOT LEFT ME COMFORTLESS. I HAVE WITHIN ME BOTH THE MEMORY OF YOU, AND ONE WHO LEADS ME TO IT. FATHER, I WOULD HEAR YOUR VOICE AND FIND YOUR PEACE TODAY. FOR I WOULD LOVE MY OWN IDENTITY, AND FIND IN IT THE MEMORY OF YOU.

Lesson 353

My eyes, my tongue, my hands, my feet today
Have but one purpose; to be given Christ
To use to bless the world with miracles.

FATHER, I GIVE ALL THAT IS MINE TODAY TO CHRIST, TO USE IN ANY WAY THAT BEST WILL SERVE THE PURPOSE THAT I SHARE WITH HIM. NOTHING IS MINE ALONE, FOR HE AND I HAVE JOINED IN PURPOSE. THUS HAS LEARNING COME ALMOST TO ITS APPOINTED END. A WHILE I WORK WITH HIM TO SERVE HIS PURPOSE. THEN I LOSE MYSELF IN MY IDENTITY, AND RECOGNIZE THAT CHRIST IS BUT MY SELF.

Lesson 354

We stand together, Christ and I, in peace
And certainty of purpose. And in Him
Is His Creator, as He is in me.

MY ONENESS WITH THE CHRIST ESTABLISHES ME AS YOUR SON, BEYOND THE REACH OF TIME, AND WHOLLY FREE OF EVERY LAW BUT YOURS. I HAVE NO SELF EXCEPT THE CHRIST IN ME. I HAVE NO PURPOSE BUT HIS OWN. AND HE IS LIKE HIS FATHER. THUS MUST I BE ONE WITH YOU AS WELL AS HIM. FOR WHO IS CHRIST EXCEPT YOUR SON AS YOU CREATED HIM? AND WHAT AM I EXCEPT THE CHRIST IN ME?

Lesson 355

There is no end to all the peace and joy,
And all the miracles that I will give,
When I accept God's Word. Why not today?

WHY SHOULD I WAIT, MY FATHER, FOR THE JOY YOU PROMISED ME? FOR YOU WILL KEEP YOUR WORD YOU GAVE YOUR SON IN EXILE. I AM SURE MY TREASURE WAITS FOR ME, AND I NEED BUT REACH OUT MY HAND TO FIND IT. EVEN NOW MY FINGERS TOUCH IT. IT IS VERY CLOSE. I NEED NOT WAIT AN INSTANT MORE TO BE AT PEACE FOREVER. IT IS YOU I CHOOSE, AND MY IDENTITY ALONG WITH YOU. YOUR SON WOULD BE HIMSELF, AND KNOW YOU AS HIS FATHER AND CREATOR, AND HIS LOVE.

Lesson 356

Sickness is but another name for sin.
Healing is but another name for God.
The miracle is thus a call to Him.

FATHER, YOU PROMISED YOU WOULD NEVER FAIL TO ANSWER ANY CALL YOUR SON MIGHT MAKE TO YOU. IT DOES NOT MATTER WHERE HE IS, WHAT SEEMS TO BE HIS PROBLEM, NOR WHAT HE BELIEVES HE HAS

BECOME. HE IS YOUR SON, AND YOU WILL ANSWER HIM. THE MIRACLE REFLECTS YOUR LOVE, AND THUS IT ANSWERS HIM. YOUR NAME REPLACES EVERY THOUGHT OF SIN, AND WHO IS SINLESS CANNOT SUFFER PAIN. YOUR NAME GIVES ANSWER TO YOUR SON, BECAUSE TO CALL YOUR NAME IS BUT TO CALL HIS OWN.

Lesson 357

Truth answers every call we make to God,
Responding first with miracles, and then
Returning unto us to be itself.

Forgiveness, truth's reflection, tells me how to offer miracles, and thus escape the prison house in which I think I live. Your holy Son is pointed out to me, first in my brother; then in me. Your Voice instructs me patiently to hear Your Word, and give as I receive. And as I look upon Your Son today, I hear Your Voice instructing me to find the way to You, as You appointed that the way shall be:

"BEHOLD HIS SINLESSNESS, AND BE YOU HEALED."

Lesson 358

No call to God can be unheard nor left
Unanswered. And of this I can be sure;
His answer is the one I really want.

YOU WHO REMEMBER WHAT I REALLY AM ALONE REMEMBER WHAT I REALLY WANT. YOU SPEAK FOR GOD, AND SO YOU SPEAK FOR ME. AND WHAT YOU GIVE ME COMES FROM GOD HIMSELF. YOUR VOICE, MY FATHER, THEN IS MINE AS WELL, AND ALL I WANT IS WHAT YOU OFFER ME, IN JUST THE FORM YOU CHOOSE THAT IT BE MINE. LET ME REMEMBER ALL I DO NOT KNOW, AND LET MY VOICE BE STILL, REMEMBERING. BUT LET ME NOT FORGET YOUR LOVE AND CARE, KEEPING YOUR PROMISE TO YOUR SON IN MY AWARENESS ALWAYS. LET ME NOT FORGET MYSELF IS NOTHING, BUT MY SELF IS ALL.

Lesson 359

God's answer is some form of peace. All pain
Is healed; all misery replaced with joy.
All prison doors are opened. And all sin
Is understood as merely a mistake.

FATHER, TODAY WE WILL FORGIVE YOUR WORLD, AND LET CREATION BE YOUR OWN. WE HAVE MISUNDERSTOOD ALL THINGS. BUT WE HAVE NOT MADE SINNERS OF THE HOLY SONS OF GOD. WHAT YOU CREATED SINLESS SO ABIDES FOREVER AND FOREVER. SUCH ARE WE. AND WE REJOICE TO LEARN THAT WE HAVE MADE MISTAKES WHICH HAVE NO REAL EFFECTS ON US. SIN IS IMPOSSIBLE, AND ON THIS FACT FORGIVENESS RESTS UPON A CERTAIN BASE MORE SOLID THAN THE SHADOW WORLD WE SEE. HELP US FORGIVE, FOR WE WOULD BE REDEEMED. HELP US FORGIVE, FOR WE WOULD BE AT PEACE

. Lesson 360

Peace be to me, the holy Son of God.
Peace to my brother, who is one with me.
Let all the world be blessed with peace through us.

FATHER, IT IS YOUR PEACE THAT I WOULD GIVE, RECEIVING IT OF YOU. I AM YOUR SON, FOREVER JUST AS YOU CREATED ME, FOR THE GREAT RAYS REMAIN FOREVER STILL AND UNDISTURBED WITHIN ME. I WOULD REACH TO THEM IN SILENCE AND IN CERTAINTY, FOR NOWHERE ELSE CAN CERTAINTY BE FOUND. PEACE BE TO ME, AND PEACE TO ALL THE WORLD. IN HOLINESS WERE WE CREATED, AND IN HOLINESS DO WE REMAIN. YOUR SON IS LIKE TO YOU IN PERFECT SINLESSNESS. AND WITH THIS THOUGHT WE GLADLY SAY "AMEN."

Lesson 361

FINAL LESSONS

Introduction

Our final lessons will be left as free of words as possible. We use them but at the beginning of our practicing, and only to remind us that we seek to go beyond them. Let us turn to Him Who leads the way and makes our footsteps sure. To Him we leave these lessons, as to Him we give our lives henceforth. For we would not return again to the belief in sin that made the world seem ugly and unsafe, attacking and destroying, dangerous in all its ways, and treacherous beyond the hope of trust and the escape from pain.

His is the only way to find the peace that God has given us. It is His way that everyone must travel in the end, because it is this ending God Himself appointed. In the dream of time it seems to be far off. And yet, in truth, it is already here; already serving us as gracious guidance in the way to go. Let us together follow in the way that truth points out to us. And let us be the leaders of our many brothers who are seeking for the way, but find it not.

And to this purpose let us dedicate our minds, directing all our thoughts to serve the function of salvation. Unto us the aim is given to forgive the world. It is the goal that God has given us. It is His ending to the dream we seek, and not our own. For all that we forgive we will not fail to recognize as part of God Himself. And thus His memory is given back, completely and complete.

It is our function to remember Him on earth, as it is given us to be His Own completion in reality. So let us not forget our goal is shared, for it is that remembrance which contains the memory of God, and points the way to Him and to the Heaven of His peace. And shall we not forgive our brother, who can offer this to us? He is the way, the truth and life that shows the way to us. In him resides salvation, offered us through our forgiveness, given unto him.

We will not end this year without the gift our Father promised to His holy Son. We are forgiven now. And we are saved from all the wrath we thought belonged to God, and found it was a dream. We are restored to sanity, in which we understand that anger is insane, attack is mad, and vengeance merely foolish fantasy. We have been saved from wrath because we learned we were mistaken. Nothing more than that. And is a father angry at his son because he failed to understand the truth?

We come in honesty to God and say we did not understand, and ask Him to help us to learn His lessons, through the Voice of His Own Teacher. Would He hurt His Son? Or would He rush to answer him, and say, "This is My Son, and all I have is his"? Be certain He will answer thus, for these are His Own words to you. And more than that can no one ever have, for in these words is all there is, and all that there will be throughout all time and in eternity.

Lessons 361 to 365

> This holy instant would I give to You.
> Be You in charge. For I would follow You,
> Certain that Your direction gives me peace.

And if I need a word to help me, He will give it to me. If I need a thought, that will He also give. And if I need but stillness and a tranquil, open mind, these are the gifts I will receive of Him. He is in charge by my request. And He will hear and answer me, because He speaks for God my Father and His holy Son.

Lesson 362

> This holy instant would I give to You.
> Be You in charge. For I would follow You,
> Certain that Your direction gives me peace.

And if I need a word to help me, He will give it to me. If I need a thought, that will He also give. And if I need but stillness and a tranquil, open mind, these are the gifts I will receive of Him. He is in charge by my request. And He will hear and answer me, because He speaks for God my Father and His holy Son.

Lesson 363

> This holy instant would I give to You.
> Be You in charge. For I would follow You,
> Certain that Your direction gives me peace.

And if I need a word to help me, He will give it to me. If I need a thought, that will He also give. And if I need but stillness and a tranquil, open mind, these are the gifts I will receive of Him. He is in charge by my request. And He will hear and answer me, because He speaks for God my Father and His holy Son.

Lesson 364

> This holy instant would I give to You.
> Be You in charge. For I would follow You,
> Certain that Your direction gives me peace.

And if I need a word to help me, He will give it to me. If I need a thought, that will He also give. And if I need but stillness and a tranquil, open mind, these are the gifts I will receive of Him. He is in charge by my request. And He will hear and answer me, because He speaks for God my Father and His holy Son.

Lesson 365

This holy instant would I give to You.
Be You in charge. For I would follow You,
Certain that Your direction gives me peace.

And if I need a word to help me, He will give it to me. If I need a thought, that will He also give. And if I need but stillness and a tranquil, open mind, these are the gifts I will receive of Him. He is in charge by my request. And He will hear and answer me, because He speaks for God my Father and His holy Son.

EPILOGUE

This course is a beginning, not an end. Your Friend goes with you. You are not alone. No one who calls on Him can call in vain. Whatever troubles you, be certain that He has the answer, and will gladly give it to you, if you simply turn to Him and ask it of Him. He will not withhold all answers that you need for anything that seems to trouble you. He knows the way to solve all problems, and resolve all doubts. His certainty is yours. You need but ask it of Him, and it will be given you.

You are as certain of arriving home as is the pathway of the sun laid down before it rises, after it has set, and in the half-lit hours in between. Indeed, your pathway is more certain still. For it can not be possible to change the course of those whom God has called to Him. Therefore obey your will, and follow Him Whom you accepted as your voice, to speak of what you really want and really need. His is the Voice for God and also yours. And thus He speaks of freedom and of truth.

No more specific lessons are assigned, for there is no more need of them. Henceforth, hear but the Voice for God and for your Self when you retire from the world, to seek reality instead. He will direct your efforts, telling you exactly what to do, how to direct your mind, and when to come to Him in silence, asking for His sure direction and His certain Word. His is the Word that God has given you. His is the Word you chose to be your own.

And now I place you in His hands, to be His faithful follower, with Him as Guide through every difficulty and all pain that you may think is real. Nor will He give you pleasures that will pass away, for He gives only the eternal and the good. Let Him prepare you further. He has earned your trust by speaking daily to you of your Father and your brother and your Self. He will continue. Now you walk with Him, as certain as is He of where you go; as sure as He of how you should proceed; as confident as He is of the goal, and of your safe arrival in the end.

The end is certain, and the means as well. To this we say "Amen." You will be told exactly what God wills for you each time there is a choice to make. And He will speak for God and for your Self, thus making sure that hell will claim you not, and that each choice you make brings Heaven nearer to your reach. And so we walk with Him from this time on, and turn to Him for guidance and for peace and sure direction. Joy attends our way. For we go homeward to an open door which God has held unclosed to welcome us.

We trust our ways to Him and say "Amen." In peace we will continue in His way, and trust all things to Him. In confidence we wait His answers, as we ask His Will in everything we do. He loves God's Son as we would love him. And He teaches us how to behold him through His eyes, and love him as He does. You do not walk alone. God's angels hover near and all about. His Love surrounds you, and of this be sure; that I will never leave you comfortless.

Love, Light and the Peace of God,

Jesus

Made in the USA
Charleston, SC
26 September 2012